THE OXFORD BOOK OF
TRAVEL VERSE

THE
OXFORD BOOK
OF
TRAVEL VERSE

Chosen and edited by
KEVIN CROSSLEY-HOLLAND

Oxford   New York
OXFORD UNIVERSITY PRESS
1986

Oxford University Press, Walton Street, Oxford OX2 6DP

Oxford New York Toronto
Delhi Bombay Calcutta Madras Karachi
Petaling Jaya Singapore Hong Kong Tokyo
Nairobi Dar es Salaam Cape Town
Melbourne Auckland

and associated companies in
Beirut Berlin Ibadan Nicosia

Oxford is a trade mark of Oxford University Press

British Library Cataloguing in Publication Data
The Oxford book of travel verse.
1. Travel—Poetry 2. English poetry
I. Crossley-Holland, Kevin
821'.008'032 PR1195.T/
ISBN 0–19–214156–2

Library of Congress Cataloging in Publication Data
The Oxford book of travel verse.
Includes index.
1. English poetry. 2. Voyages and travels—Poetry.
3. Travel—Poetry. 4. Poetry of places.
I. Crossley-Holland, Kevin.
PR1195.V68095 1986 821'.008'355 86–2419
ISBN 0–19–214156–2

Set by Wyvern Typesetting Ltd.
Printed in Great Britain by
Richard Clay (The Chaucer Press) Ltd.
Bungay, Suffolk

for
Keith Harrison

CONTENTS

EUROPE OF THE SOUTH

FRANCE

IBERIA

ITALY

EUROPE OF THE NORTH
THE LOW COUNTRIES

GERMANY AND AUSTRIA

SWITZERLAND

BEYOND THE IRON CURTAIN

SCANDINAVIA WITH ICELAND

AFRICA

ASIA

THE INDIAN SUBCONTINENT

THE FAR EAST

OCEANIA

THE AMERICAS

SOUTH AMERICA AND THE CARIBBEAN

HOME THOUGHTS

CONTENTS

INTRODUCTION

THE British have long prided themselves on being a nation of enthusiastic and resourceful travellers. As pilgrims and missionaries and explorers, in the armed services and as mercenaries, as diplomats and teachers and merchants, as Grand Tourists and package tourists, they have quartered this shining planet.

It is perfectly possible to describe this penchant for travel in terms of geographical situation, and historical challenge and necessity. But deeper than specific reason and local condition lies common impulse, so it may not be out of place to begin by saying something about how writers have described or reflected those basic states of heart and mind that have always prompted, or even driven, humankind to travel—restlessness, curiosity, boredom, escapism, a sense of adventure, even a predilection for fear, and a longing for the experience travel can offer of simplicity and wholeness and the old-made-new.

More than one thousand years ago, an Englishman cried

> the solitary bird screams,
> irresistible, urges the heart to the whale's way
> over the stretch of the seas . . .[1]

And in our own century, with his haunting words 'I must down to the seas again, to the lonely sea and the sky', John Masefield (11)[2] echoed the Anglo-Saxon poet. Both of them, it seems to me, are identifying the travel-impulse or wanderlust as a kind of generic restlessness. Theirs is a pure longing entirely divorced from reason, or intention.

Not dissimilar (but not quite the same!) is the mainspring romantically ascribed by Kipling to his tramp, who sees himself as one of a breed who

> cannot use one bed too long,
> But must get 'ence, the same as I 'ave done,
> An' go observin' matters till they die.[3]

Here already motive has crept in. The tramp's restlessness is coupled with burning curiosity. Likewise, Robert Browning seems to attribute to 'Waring' (his friend Alfred Domett who absented himself from London for twenty-nine years) not only travel-fever but also boredom:

> What's become of Waring
> Since he gave us all the slip,
> Chose land-travel or seafaring,
> Boots and chest or staff and scrip,
> Rather than pace up and down
> Any longer London-town?

---

[1] 'The Seafarer', trans. by the editor.
[2] Numbers in parentheses refer to poems in this anthology.
[3] 'Sestina of the Tramp-Royal'.

It is not very far from here to the argument advanced by Robert Burton in
The Anatomy of Melancholy. Why should people travel? On the one hand, says
Burton, 'peregrination charms our senses with such unspeakable and sweet
variety'; on the other, the person who never travels is 'a kind of prisoner . . .
that from his cradle to his old age beholds the same still; still, still the same,
the same!'

A longing to escape Burton's treadmill of the same has, in our own time,
with its huge growth of tourism, certainly become the most widespread
travel-impulse of all. Escapism *per se* has not occasioned much good writing
about the experience of travel, but of course, it also lies behind much
armchair travel writing, or what is sometimes rather grandly called travel in
the mind. Samuel Taylor Coleridge in Xanadu and Edward Lear at sea with
the Jumblies and W. B. Yeats on Innisfree have much in common with
Robert Louis Stevenson when he says:

> I should like to rise and go
> Where the golden apples grow:
> Where below another sky
> Parrot islands anchored lie.[4]

They are all writing of imaginary otherworlds; they find consolation in the
marvellous.

To experience the kind of 'sweet variety' Burton speaks of means to lay
oneself open to the vicissitudes of travel. One cannot stay packaged in a
cocoon and hope to experience the germ of Italy or Greece or, indeed,
experience anything distinctive and singular at all. The traveller must learn
to expect discomforts, delays, disappointments such as those weathered by
Miss Emily Brittle on her way to India (5), James Boswell in Mannheim
(119), and David Constantine watching for dolphins (102); and then, won
incidentally or waiting at the end of the road, there occurs some sight or
meeting or experience that is worth all the effort and, one knows, achieved
only because of it. This is why a relish for the unexpected, adaptability, and a
sense of humour have regularly been seen as desirable qualifications for the
good traveller.

Albert Camus took this line of thought one step further. 'What gives value
to travel', he wrote, 'is fear.'

It is the fact that, at a certain moment, when we are so far from our own country (a
French newspaper acquires incalculable value. And those evenings when in cafés
you try to get close to other men just to touch them with your elbow), we are seized by
a vague fear, and an instinctive desire to go back to the protection of old habits. This
is the most obvious benefit of travel. At that moment we are febrile but also porous.[5]

But the emotion of fear is not only a traveller's companion; it can also be his
incentive. I am not thinking of the tens of thousands who follow relatively
tame and trodden paths, but of the hundreds who are trail-blazers. These
are the travellers who actually court hardship, in whom a sense of adventure
has hardened into a readiness regularly to face danger as an explorer or

---

[4] *A Child's Garden of Verses.*   [5] *Selected Essays and Notebooks.*

mountaineer or round-the-world sailor. It is not difficult to sense the relief of Thomas Perry (233), one of Captain Cook's seamen, as he at last turns his back on the Antipodes and heads for home, while the mountaineer Wilfred Noyce's 'Breathless' (228), written at Camp IV on Mount Everest, is a poem torn from the teeth.

There is one more theory (at least) about the travel-impulse, and it is attractively argued by Samuel Rogers. In adulthood, he says, ambition and worry and fatigue and sickness of spirit replace the taste for natural and simple pleasures and golden hours of childhood:

Now travel, and foreign travel more particularly, restores to us in a great degree what we have lost ... at every step, as we proceed, the slightest circumstance amuses and interests. All is new and strange. We surrender ourselves, and feel once again as children.[6]

This sense of wonder, like fear, both arises from the experience of travel and leads to it. The prospect of rejuvenation! Butler's words are corroborated time and again in poems in which the everyday is seen as unfamiliar. The drawing of water from a well or the sight of a man ploughing or a restaurant scene in Cairo or Shanghai seem wildly exotic. David Holbrook, indeed, comments on just this while taking a day trip to France (42) and noting the marvellous otherness of lives and sights and sounds 'hardly a stone's throw away':

> Nothing: I want nothing but to look at the bread,
> The big sticks, *les baguettes*, *les ficelles*,
> *Les croissants*. I just want to stand here
> And smell the smell of France, and study
> The culture of *le boulanger*.

This is where the traveller's viewpoint and poet's purpose draw close. One sees the slightest circumstance as new and strange; the other wishes to make it seem so. First, however, the poet has to make that circumstance new to himself. And to travel, with perceptions heightened, is one helpful and attractive means of doing so.

*   *   *

The idea of making a journey to a sacred place as an act of devotion was certainly not unknown to the Anglo-Saxons, but it was, of course, in medieval Europe that pilgrimages became really popular. A new interest in the idea of travel as adventure, partly generated and partly reflected by a wave of guidebooks and pilgrims' diaries, and further fuelled by the highly successful *Mandeville's Travels* (1357), attracted a steady stream of visitors to Compostela and Rome and Jerusalem and many other venerated places. In his itinerary *Jerusalem History*, Jacques de Vitry tartly commented that

Some light-minded and inquisitive persons go on pilgrimages not out of devotion, but out of mere curiosity and love of novelty. All they want to do is travel through

---

[6] *Italy.*

unknown lands to investigate the absurd, exaggerated stories they have heard about the east.

Chaucer's Wife of Bath, no doubt, was one such:

> And thryse had she been at Ierusalem.
> She hadde passed many a straunge streem.
> At Rome she hadde been and at Boloigne,
> In Galice, at seint Iame and at Coloigne.
> She coude much of wandring by the weye.
> Gat tothed was she, soothly for to seye.

The medieval itineraries that were written in verse, such as 'The Stacions of Rome', on the whole make flat-footed and wearisome reading. But something of the medieval enthusiasm for these long journeys and the physical hardship they entailed is evident in 'The Pilgrims' Sea Voyage and Seasickness' (45) and 'The Way to Jerusalem' (44).

The anthology's interest in Christian experience and churchmen does not cease with the end of the Middle Ages. On the contrary, administrators such as William Strachey (254), first Secretary of the Colony of Virginia, speak in the name of Church as well as State; to the voices of pilgrims like John Henry Newman (69) and G. K. Chesterton (183), author of one of the inexplicably few good travellers' poems about Jerusalem, are added those of churchmen resident abroad, such as Reginald Heber, Bishop of Calcutta (206); while Thomas Pringle, a Scot who took his family to South Africa in 1820, comes upon evidence (194) of thwarted missionary endeavour in the mountain-wilderness:

> A roofless ruin, scathed by flame and smoke,
> Tells where the decent Mission-chapel stood;
> While the baboon with jabbering cry doth mock
> The pilgrim, pausing in his pensive mood
> To ask—'Why is it thus? Shall Evil baffle Good?'

Finally, the medieval passion for relics and modern curiosity—the proper curiosity that keeps its eyes and mind open—come nicely together in Geoffrey Grigson's 'Discoveries of Bones and Stones' (40), a poem that also touches on something the traveller is constantly aware of, 'the casualness of discovery'.

There was nothing casual, however, about the daring and determined gentlemen who discovered and colonized the New World. Edmund Spenser lauded their enterprise in laying open new regions, 'Indian Peru' and the 'Amazon huge river' and 'fruitfullest Virginia'; in *Tamburlaine*, Christopher Marlowe thrillingly celebrated the growing awareness of geography and new colonial ambition; while George Chapman emphasized the travellers' sense of patriotism and the recurring quest for gold:

> Guiana, whose rich feet are mines of gold,
> Whose forehead knocks against the roof of stars,
> Stands on her tip-toes at fair England looking,
> Kissing her hand, bowing her mighty breast,

> And every sign of all submission making
> To be her sister, and the daughter both
> Of our most sacred maid.[7]

These explorations find their greatest direct expression in the pages of
Richard Hakluyt's *Voyages*, a work just as germane to the understanding of
the Age of Elizabeth as the plays of Shakespeare. And here, the same spirit
is at work in Sir Richard Grenville's superbly confident 'In Praise of
Seafaring Men' (1), in Thomas Deloney's 'The Winning of Cales' (46), in
an epigram about Sir Francis Drake (2), and in poems from the New World
by William Strachey (254) and Robert Hayman (255) whose verses were a
deliberate attempt to woo colonists to join him in Newfoundland. What a
pity it is that Sir Walter Ralegh, the greatest of all poet-travellers, never
chose to write directly about his voyages.

The more sober successors to these Elizabethan and early seventeenth-
century travellers are the eighteenth- and nineteenth-century diplomats,
local government officials, soldiery, landowners, and teachers who
(sometimes philanthropic and sympathetic, often ruthless) consolidated
England's dominion over her newly established colonies—India and
Canada and Australia and all places pink! One catches something of the
optimism with which they habitually travelled in George Berkeley's 'Verses
on the Prospect of Planting Arts and Learning in America' (257), while Sir
Edwin Arnold (181, 210, 223) and Thomas Skinner (207) and Alfred
Domett (236) seem to speak for the total fascinated immersion in 'abroad',
everything from humdrum minutiae to whole philosophies, so characteristic
of the welter of contemporary diaries, memoirs, travel books, and poetry.

Some of these travellers wrote observantly about the relationship
between occupier and occupied, and not always in terms flattering to the
British. Sir Alfred Lyall, for example, paints a far from unsympathetic
portrait of a Rajpoot rebel (212), hounded by the English in his own
homeland; and in 'Studies at Delhi' (211) he turns from the English playing
badminton next to the site of a recent Indian Mutiny battle to scrutinize one
spectator:

> Near me a Musulmán, civil and mild,
>   Watched as the shuttlecocks rose and fell;
> And he said, as he counted his beads and smiled,
>   'God smite their souls to the depths of hell.'

The lines of a man who is accustomed to watching and listening, to noting
discrepancy between word and thought and seeing both sides of a question.

The diplomat-poet and politician-poet are, of course, familiar figures in
the history of English verse and Lyall, Foreign Secretary to the Government
of India, was working in a long and distinguished tradition: Chaucer left no
direct impressions of his sojourn in Italy, but Sir Thomas Wyatt in Spain
(272) and Sir George Etheredge in Regensburg (117), Matthew Prior at
The Hague (105), Ambrose Philips in Copenhagen (152), and Lady Mary
Wortley Montagu, accompanying her husband to Constantinople (174), all

---

[7] George Chapman, 'De Guiana carmen Epicum' (1596).

wrote delectable poems arising from their travels, while George Turberville, secretary to Queen Elizabeth I's Ambassador to Moscow, penned
marvellously detailed and scathing verse letters about Russian character
and landscape (141 and 142) to his friends in England.

* * *

During the second part of the eighteenth century, educated English
travellers began to visit southern Europe in greater numbers than ever
before. In the name of education, parents sent their sons abroad, usually
accompanied by a guardian-cum-tutor, to learn French and Italian, marvel
at the awesome landscape of the Alps, and see the glories of classical Rome
and Renaissance Florence and Venice for themselves. In short, they
conceived the idea of a Grand Tour, a journey by carriage or on foot
through France, the Rhineland, Switzerland, and Italy lasting for anything
up to two years.

In 'The Progress of Error' (4), William Cowper derides the whole
process of the Grand Tour as superficial, and Samuel Taylor Coleridge in
'The Delinquent Travellers' (6) pokes fun at the new passion for travel:

> Keep moving! Steam, or Gas, or Stage,
> Hold, cabin, steerage, hencoop's cage—
> Tour, Journey, Voyage, Lounge, Ride, Walk,
> Skim, Sketch, Excursion, Travel-talk—
> For move you must! 'Tis now the rage,
> The law and fashion of the Age.

Travel may broaden the mind but it does not necessarily deepen it. Many
Grand Tourists did, of course, respond superficially to what was, literally, a
chance in a lifetime. But many others would have agreed with Lord Byron in
Italy (67) that, although 'States fall, arts fade', and they were confronted by
little more than a series of ruined shells and deserted scapes, the power of
Imagination could so play over them that 'For us repeopled were the solitary
shore'.

These travellers tended to look down their noses at contemporary Italy.
Joseph Addison (61), for example, deplored the lack of individual liberty
('Thee, Goddess, thee, Britannia's Isle adores', wrote Addison) and found
the Italians paltry and altogether unworthy inheritors of their great Classical
and Renaissance legacy. While in France, in the name of the same liberty,
William Wordsworth (24) passionately subscribed to the ideals of the
Revolution, with its famous cry of 'Liberté! Égalité! Fraternité!'; and in
Greece, Lord Byron gave money and formed the 'Byron Brigade' and
fought for Greek independence:

> The mountains look on Marathon—
> And Marathon looks on the sea;
> And musing there an hour alone,
> I dreamed that Greece might still be free.   (93)

For the Romantics, a journey was scarcely worth the candle if, at its end, they had not endorsed some cause or witnessed 'types and symbols of eternity'. But they were not the only poets writing at the end of the eighteenth and beginning of the nineteenth centuries to be inspired by travel. Other writers, more old-fashioned maybe, inheritors of the light tread and wit of Pope and Dryden, and little concerned with the eternal verities, took as their theme the hazards of travel. Thomas Hood (26) warns 'how a little English girl will perhaps be served in France' while for Thomas Moore, moving from the high to low style in just four lines (7), it is the ubiquity of the English themselves that is travel's worst hazard:

> And is there then no earthly place
> Where we can rest, in dream Elysian,
> Without some cursed, round English face,
> Popping up near, to break the vision?

William Parsons, a regularly entertaining epigrammatic poet, cleverly exposes in just six lines (64) both the duplicity of the Italians and the *naïveté* (at least when away from home) of the English. And Sir George Dallas, in his *The India Guide* (5), most amusingly illustrates the alarm, or at least the sense of exposure, that so many travellers experienced after leaving the shelter of their own homes and, for the first time in their lives, rubbing shoulders with all sorts and conditions of men.

From the middle of the nineteenth century, travel verse becomes more voluminous and more various. The Victorian poet-travellers did not have the preconceived notions of classical grandeur of their eighteenth-century forebears or the lofty ideals of the Romantics. In Europe, we find them off the beaten track, able to take advantage of improved (though not necessarily more enjoyable) travelling conditions, and the advent of the railway system:

> Breakfast at 6, and train 6.30,
> Tickets to Königswinter (mem.
> The seats unutterably dirty).   (8)

And we find them often ruminative, prompted by the experience of travel to compare past and present: Matthew Arnold brooding on the 'giant stones' at Carnac and thinking of his dead brother (29), William Makepeace Thackeray tucking into a bowl of *bouillabaisse* (28) and gently reminiscing, George Eliot brooding on Spain's Moorish inheritance (54)...

Outside Europe, the Victorians not only continued to man the colonies but extended the Grand Tour itinerary to include Egypt and the Holy Land—the first English to travel in appreciable numbers to the far end of the Mediterranean since the crusaders and pilgrims of the Middle Ages. The poems by William Lisle Bowles (176) and J. W. Burgon (180) stand at the head of a tradition of verses about trips up the Nile and visits to Pharaonic archaeological sites that has continued from that day to this, while the abuse of monuments described by Richard Hengist Horne (177) surfaces again in the form of an anonymous graffito-poem scrawled on the Taj Mahal (204). Alas, there seems to be no Arabist poets to stand alongside such prose-writers as Doughty and T. E. Lawrence and Wilfred Thesiger; the long-standing English attraction to a hot dry climate and desert is, however, intimated in Wilfred Scawen Blunt's 'The Oasis of Sidi Khaled' (182) and more recent poems by Dorothy Wellesley (184) and Rex Warner (185).

*   *   *

At first pegged back by the turmoil of the First World War and the ensuing economic doldrums, foreign travel for professional (and peaceable) purposes has during the last two generations increased from year to year, while travel for pleasure, above all as escapism, has become overwhelmingly popular. When we meet an aborigine in the company of Hugo Williams and with Lawrence Durrell—perhaps the finest travel poet of our times—watch half-castes drinking coconut milk in Rio de Janeiro, when we pad across an archaeological site in Greenland with Francis Berry, sit with D. J. Enright dreaming in the Shanghai Restaurant, and then go on with James Kirkup to watch a steamy bout of Sumo wrestling, we very soon get an idea of the immense range of thematic and geographical possibilities available to the enterprising modern poet-traveller.

For a few contemporary poets, travel and the experiences occasioned by travel have become a central preoccupation—and they take their place alongside prose-writers such as Eric Newby and Patrick Leigh-Fermor and Jan Morris in what is generally regarded as a golden age of travel writing. To read the work of such writers as Alan Ross (243) and D. J. Enright (189 and 229) and, above all, Lawrence Durrell (98–9, 186, 251, 265) is to enter a world that is at its best governed, in Durrell's own phrase, by 'a science of intuitions': the poet so identifies with some landscape and its people and their interrelationship that, without necessarily being particularly knowledgeable about them, he can interpret them convincingly, even profoundly.

Many good travel poems work in the same kind of way. Their first attraction is exotic surface colour and vigour; their second is a demonstration of difference, genuine difference of custom or behaviour or appearance, between the world of the poem and the poet's own experience; the third is their revelation of the correspondences, the shared humanity that enables us to empathize with the apparently disparate. In 'Anthropology: Cricket at Kano' (203), in which a Tuareg tribesman sees meaning in the game's rituals, Stewart Brown takes things one stage further, acknowledging the correspondence but concluding:

> So, at stumps, nomad and exile
> pursue their disparate paths,
> amicably separate, rooted in certainties
>
> centuries old, our rootlessness
> a fragile bond that will not bear embrace.

With this allusion to identity and rootlessness, travel poetry engages with one of the main concerns of twentieth-century literature. Such talk of belonging is not confined to Stewart Brown's poem. On the contrary, the idea that through travel people learn not only about other people and places but about themselves is a leitmotif of modern travel verse. George Barker gives this theme of self-discovery a wider meaning in 'The Oak and the Olive' (282), writing not only as individual but as Englishman and north-west European.

As often as not, it is the moment when the traveller pauses and looks over his shoulder that he finds himself looking into a mirror. Sudden longing for home, or the act of returning home, also leads him on an inward journey:

> Red after years of failure or bright with fame,
> The eyes of homecomers thank these historical cliffs:
> 'The mirror can no longer lie nor the clock reproach;
> In the shadow under the yew, at the children's party,
> Everything must be explained.'[8]

*   *   *

I have understood travel to mean travel abroad and taken travel verse to mean both verse about the nature of travel and verse occasioned by it. Readers who want an anthology of poetry about the British Isles can do no better than *The Faber Book of Poetry and Place*, edited by Geoffrey Grigson (Faber & Faber, 1980).

Although it would have been perfectly possible to compile a different selection of travel verse written in English, making use of work by Americans and poets from many other countries, I decided against doing so on the grounds that I did not wish to lose or at least dilute two fascinating elements in the present anthology: one is the way in which a group of poems pertaining to a specific country reflects and reveals something of Britain's changing association with it; the other has to do with recurring patterns of response. (So, for example, the pattern discernible in the group of poems about North America comprises admiration and envy of American idealism, excitement at such material wealth and breathtaking cityscapes, scorn at such philistinism.) It is to draw attention to these elements, and for the sake of sheer convenience, that the poems are arranged geographically.

I have, however, drawn the lines loosely so as to include work by Scottish and Welsh poets and those Irish writers not averse to union with their English peers in an anthology of this kind. I have also reprinted poems by a number of English-speaking writers from overseas who came or have come to live in this country, including Christina Rossetti, Roy Campbell, Sylvia Plath, Peter Porter, Gerda Mayer, and Fleur Adcock. Their presence, indeed, adds a further dimension to the matter of belonging touched on above:

> Home, as I explained to a weeping niece,
> home is London; and England, Ireland, Europe.[9]

---

[8] W. H. Auden, 'Dover'.   [9] Fleur Adcock, 'Instead of an Interview' (244).

Almost all the poets represented here were writing from direct experience. The exceptions are Thomas Deloney, Andrew Marvell (on the Bermudas), John Milton, Mark Akenside (on Greece), Thomas Warton (on South America), Erasmus Darwin, Daniel Defoe, Thomas Beddoes (on Egypt), and Martin Farquhar Tupper (on North Africa). They have been included either because they have something authoritative to say about a country and England's association with it, or because they touch on some ingredient that seems well-nigh essential. What would the Nile be without a crocodile?

This is essentially an anthology in which, where people and places are not presented impersonally, the poet himself speaks to camera. I have to the last remained in two minds about whether it is also proper to include dramatic monologues. In what sense, for instance, is Robert Browning's 'Up at a Villa—Down in the City' a travel poem? The result is that a few monologues are present, and do perhaps vary the anthology's texture, but only a few.

This has been a delightful book to edit, not least because so many friends have helped with suggestions. I am particularly indebted for advice and assistance to Fleur Adcock, Richard Barber, Jonathan Barker, Julia Boffey, Sue Bradbury, Edward Chaney, Andrew Cocks, Peter and Nicole Crossley-Holland, Barry Cunliffe, Kenneth East, Rod Farmer, Ian Gardhouse, Richard Garnett, Karl-Heinz Göller, David Handforth, Caroline Hobhouse, Matthew Huntley, Jenny Insull, Anke Janssen, Gwyn Jones, Roger Lonsdale, Judith Luna (my kind and keen editor), Derek Pearsall, Peter Porter, Richard Poulton, Alec Reid, Jane Robinson, Patrick Sims-Williams, Anthony Thwaite, George Tulloch, M. Van Wyck Smith, Philip Ward, and, for her indefatigable and good-humoured typing, Lynda Willson. Nicolette Zeeman at short notice kindly made the prose translations of poems 44 and 45.

Further, Francis Berry, Stewart Brown, Michael Dennis Browne, Gavin Ewart, David Holbrook, Patrick Leigh-Fermor, Gerda Mayer, Norman Nicholson, and Wynford Vaughan-Thomas (in addition to the several poets listed above) were kind enough to answer specific questions I put to them about their own poems.

As has always been my experience, the staff of the British Library have been courteous and helpful, while without the existence of the London Library it would have been impossible for me, living now in Suffolk, to compile this anthology; I am indebted to its solicitous Librarian and staff. I would also like to record my gratitude to Peter Davis and his tireless staff at Church End Library, Finchley, and to the Central Library, Bury St Edmunds.

Sandy Farmer, my research assistant, has worked on this anthology at almost every stage—planning, reading, assembling, sifting, and excavating for the Notes and References. I could scarcely have compiled it without her assistance and we must share responsibility for its form and content. For all her hard work and good company, I sincerely thank her.

Finally, to my wife Gillian, far more than conventional thanks. Her warm encouragement, discernment, and patience have been a true support, my point of departure and return.

EN ROUTE

SIR RICHARD GRENVILLE

c. 1541–1591

I *In Praise of Seafaring Men, in Hopes of Good Fortune*

Who seeks the way to win renown,
Or flies with wings of high desire,
Who seeks to wear the laurel crown,
Or hath the mind that would aspire,
Let him his native soil eschew,
Let him go range, and seek a new.

Each haughty heart is well content,
With every chance that shall betide;
No hag can hinder his intent;
He steadfast stands, though fortune slide.
The sun, quoth he, doth shine as well
Abroad, as erst where I did dwell.

In change of streams each fish can live,
Each fowl content with every air,
Each haughty heart remaineth still,
And not be drowned in deep despair:
Wherefore I judge all lands alike,
To haughty hearts who fortune seek.

To pass the seas some think a toil,
Some think it strange abroad to roam;
Some think it a grief to leave their soil,
Their parents, kinfolk, and their home.
Think so who list, I like it not;
I must abroad to try my lot.

Who list at home at cart to drudge,
And cark and care for worldly trash,
With buckled shoes let him go trudge,
Instead of lance or whip to slash;
A mind that base his kind will show
Is carrion meet to feed a crow.

cark] labour anxiously

If Jason of that mind had been,
The Grecians when they came to Troy,
Had never so the Trojans foiled
Nor put them all to such annoy:
Wherefore who lust may live at home,
To purchase fame I will go roam.

ANONYMOUS

late 16th–early 17th century

2   *Epigram: On Sir Francis Drake*

Sir Drake, whom well the world's end knew,
    Which thou didst compass round,
And whom both poles of heaven once saw,
    Which north and south do bound,
The stars above would make thee known,
    If men here silent were;
The Sun himself cannot forget
    His fellow traveller.

THOMAS PRYS

c.1564–1634

3   *A Poem to show the Trouble that befell him when he was at Sea*

I followed, o splendid season,
the water over the world to Spain,
thinking that, taking to the sea,
I should come by all treasure.
Wandering, sieving the waters
needily, is the seaman's fate.
I bought a ship, stripped the land
for money for the venture;
victualled it fitly and fair,
victualled where butlers abounded.
I gathered men, a gloomy task,
for utterly vain sea-faring,
some vicious dark-hued Jews,

hell-bellied and abusive.
I took ship to train the men,
then came the need for cursing.
There was a roaring on board,
the master calling muster.
'*Turn the capstan*,' he howled an order,
'*Weigh anchor, all you younkers!*'
A question, '*Where is Meyrick?*'
Then the words, '*Coil the cable quick!*'
Deubott the carpenter's diligent,
'*Assay the pump, you see the pit.*'
'Turn you to fire and be damned!'
'*Trim the ship, whip* to it, yare!
Make haste there, haste, you waster!
Bring in the bowline, you boor!
Bear hard up to throw off plague;
bear aloof if it rains toads!
You, Bunny, fast the bonnet,
sound fine with the line and lead.
Veer the sheet, impotent booby;
about again, if a hundred times!'
Farewell England and dry sand
and Scilly, lovely island.
Roll away with royal wings
to parley off the Burlings.

'*Here's Atkins. Where is Woodcock?*
Bear all night right to the Rock.
Beware of any mishap;
our course is the southern cape.
Take height in all good sense.
Thou Poyns, yonder is the Pole.'

Today we hold in dark tides,
we'll veer away tomorrow.
'You, *Hulling, loose the halliard!*
Off you go along the yard!
Bring near the timber, tomboy!
What cheer? A can of beer, boy!
Munson, hoist up the mainsail.
Be merry, I see a sail.
Give chase, for all I've got!
Out topsail, you lout tipsy!
Give Way!' In the winter storm
we mustered and mastered the wind,

younkers] youngsters

starboard and larboard labouring.
'*Clear abaft*, keep clear of trouble!
Port hard the helm, bastard one!
Steady thus, man! Do you hear?
Keep the prize (*look out wisely,*
hear thou, lad) *under thy lee.*
Now fire a piece in order.'
Instead, he shot three into her.
'*Shoot again a broadside, gunner!*
We'll be brave if we have her.
Fight for store and leave sorrow,
fear not, shoot the wild fire now!
Lay her aboard!' In all the din,
'*Now enter*, venture over!'
Whilst fighting, open discredit,
we lost our men on the vessel in smoke.
'*Give back, lest all be taken!*
Is there a means *to save some men?*'
We took an unfortunate day,
we find we mind this Monday,
loudly bewailing fortune's blow,
'*O Lord, here is too hard luck!*'
Foulk Harry, awkward booby,
is drowned in the battle's din;
Brown Robin Austin withal
is dead, and so is Duddal,
Wenford, Rowland and Winfield,
William and Cobham are killed.
Tom, Meyrick, Dick, each one
is hurt, and so is Horton.
Our ship in grappling so
is *weak and full of leak below,*
and if a storm now takes us
we'll be in too hard a state.
'Go to, pain; let's get to port!
Barris, the beer is sour.'

Thus I got a sleep of care
in payment for this venture.
I doubt if Thomas from here
will get home safe from the green sea.
Before I will pillage or part
buy a ship, I'll be a shepherd.

Translated from the Welsh by Gwyn Williams

WILLIAM COWPER
1731–1800

4

from *The Progress of Error*

From school to Cam or Isis, and thence home;
And thence with all convenient speed to Rome,
With reverend tutor clad in habit lay,
To tease for cash and quarrel with all day;
With memorandum-book for every town,
And every post, and where the chaise broke down;
His stock, a few French phrases got by heart,
With much to learn, but nothing to impart
The youth, obedient to his sire's commands,
Sets off a wanderer into foreign lands.
Surprised at all they meet, the gosling pair
With awkward gait, stretched neck, and silly stare,
Discover huge cathedrals built with stone,
And steeples towering high, much like our own;
But show peculiar light by many a grin
At popish practices observed within.
    Ere long some bowing, smirking, smart Abbé
Remarks two loiterers that have lost their way;
And always being primed with *politesse*
For men or their appearance and address,
With much compassion undertakes the task
To tell them more than they have wit to ask;
Points to inscriptions wheresoe'er they tread,
Such as, when legible, were never read,
But being cankered now and half worn out,
Craze antiquarian brains with endless doubt;
Some headless hero, or some Caesar shows—
Defective only in his Roman nose;
Exhibits elevations, drawings, plans,
Models of Herculanean pots and pans;
And sells them medals, which, if neither rare
Nor ancient, will be so, preserved with care.
    Strange the recital! from whatever cause
His great improvement and new light he draws,
The squire, once bashful, is shamefaced no more,
But teems with powers he never felt before:
Whether increased momentum, and the force,
With which from clime to clime he sped his course
(As axles sometimes kindle as they go),
Chafed him, and brought dull nature to a glow;

Or whether clearer skies and softer air,
That made Italian flowers so sweet and fair,
Freshening his lazy spirits as he ran;
Unfolded genially and spread the man;
Returning he proclaims by many a grace,
By shrugs and strange contortions of his face,
How much a dunce that has been sent to roam
Excels a dunce that has been kept at home.

SIR GEORGE DALLAS
1758–1833

5   from *The India Guide; or, Journal of a Voyage to
       the East Indies in the Year MDCCLXXX*

If you, my dear mother, had e'er been at sea,
On a trip to the Indies you ne'er had sent me;
If half what I suffered I e'er had supposed,
The voyage in itself I'd have flatly opposed.
What though 'tis too late to repent I left home,
'Tis not so to grieve that I ventured to roam;
Nor would I yield up my consent e'er again,
To plough distant seas in pursuit of a swain!
With tossing and tumbling my bones were so sore,
Such an up and down motion I ne'er felt before;
Many days had elapsed e'er I first got a notion
That to keep on my legs I must humour the motion.
For the space of six weeks not an eye could I close,
As mountains on mountains alternately rose;
Each roll with fresh tremors my bosom impressed,
As a prelude alas! to the mansions of rest;
Ah! fondest of parents! ah! could you but peep
At your frolicsome Brittle thus tossed on the deep!
In terms of affection you'd Heaven implore
To waft her again to her dear native shore.

.   .   .   .

O! how shall I picture, in *delicate* strain,
The scene which ensued when I first crossed the main;
Or, how shall my muse in *clean* numbers bewail,
My early hard lot, when, reclined o'er a pail,

5 Brittle] Miss Emily Brittle, the purported author of this 'Poetical Epistle'

I was racked by seasickness and pains in my head,
Which gave me such torture I wished myself dead!
Forgive the chaste nymph should she wish to conceal
All the risings and swimmings too often I feel;
For whenever it happens the weather's not mild,
I'm as sick and as squeamish as Jenny with child.
You have seen bales of goods and mercantile wares
Raised by pulleys to windows up two pair of stairs;
So stuck in a chair, made on purpose for this,
Sailors hoist upon deck every India-bound miss:
When poised in the air, I happened to show
Too much of my legs to the boat's crew below,
Who, laughing, occasioned the blush of distress.
Indeed, dear Mama, I am obliged to confess,
That indecency so much on shipboard prevailed,
I scarce heard aught else from the moment I sailed.
　　The noise in the ship, from every quarter,
Almost split the brain of your poor little daughter:
Twice a week 'twas the custom the drums loud to rattle,
As a signal below to prepare for a battle.
The sailors on deck were forever a-brawling,
The ladies below in piano were squalling;
The bulkheads of cabins were constantly creaking,
In concert with pigs, who as often were squeaking;
Such a clatter above from the chick to the goose,
I thought the livestock on the poop had broke lose;
Dogs, puppies and monkeys of ev'ry degree,
Howled peals of loud discord in harsh symphony,
Whilst near to my cabin a sad noisy brute
Most cruelly tortured a poor German flute.
Another, a sprightly amusement to find,
A broken bad fiddle with three strings would grind;
And to add to discordance, our third mate Tarpawl
Some vulgar low tune would be certain to bawl.
But to picture the whole I am really unable,
'Twas worse than the noise at the building of Babel;
I declare my poor ears were so sadly distressed
That for many a week I ne'er got any rest.
Had Signor Corelli but witnessed the scene,
The musical soul would have died of the spleen!
Ah! Stanley protect me! hadst thou been but near,
Though blind, thou'dst have prayed to be deaf in each ear:
In short my weak nerves were so deeply affected,
The tone of my mind was at times so dejected,
That Doctor Pomposus was forced to heap up
An opiate each night, my spirits to keep up.

It was often the case on a rough squally day,
At dinner our ship on her beam-ends would lay;
Then tables and chairs on the floor all would jumble,
Knives, dishes and bottles upon us would tumble:
As late, when a roll brought us all to the floor,
Whilst the ladies were screaming, the gentlemen swore,
Our Purser, as big as a bullock at least,
Lay on poor little me, like an overfed beast.
Not many weeks since, I had only to scoop
From my lap the contents of a tureen of soup;
And when with clean clothes I again had sat down,
A vile leg of mutton fell right on my gown.
Sometimes I was soiled from my head to my toe
With nasty pork chops, or a greasy pilau.
Full many a glass of good wine, I may say,
By a violent toss was thrown down the wrong way;
And, as on board ship we have no one to scrub,
As for three months at least there's no thumping the tub,
So I think it but proper that *delicate* women
Should lay in a plentiful stock of clean linen.
    Whenever I walk on the deck, I am sure
To be shocked by such language as none can endure:
Such scolding! such roaring! such blasting of eyes!
You'd think that the crew in rebellion would rise!

·   ·   ·   ·   ·   ·   ·   ·

    Scarce the cloth is removed but the gentlemen go
To discuss a few bottles of Stainforth and Co.
And from dinner sometimes to the hour of nine,
They get drunk and roar catches to pass away time.
And often, in order to show their politeness,
With vile shocking songs will be certain to fright'n us;
Such songs! as to you I can never explain,
For the lowest of women would blush at their strain:
The rude Bachanalians 'twould greatly amuse
My virgin young innocence oft to confuse;
For whenever to tipple below they thought fit,
Loud obscenity passed round their table for wit.
At first with fine cotton I stopped up each ear
That I might not their impudent ribaldry hear;
But I found 'twas in vain, as the words would get in
Through those parts where the cotton would chance to be thin:
And as in the cabin which lay next to mine,
In the passage they drank out twelve chests of red wine,
So of that kind of knowledge I've got a great store,
Of which I had scarce any notion before.

Another diversion the young men would prize,
'Twas in seeing us all from our pigeon-holes rise;
With them 'tis a proof of politeness, they think,
The ladies' perfections in bumpers to drink;
For often they boast they have had a full view
Of Prim and Flirtetta, myself and Miss Prue.
But what man of good breeding will offer to peep
At a group of fine girls as they lay all asleep?
Since deeming her charms are from all eyes debarred,
The most delicate maid is at times off her guard;
And they who presume this advantage to take
All pretension to manners must surely forsake.
In our ship 'twas one scene, on my word, I may say,
Of boring and stopping on both sides all day:
If we filled up one hole, 'twas the same as before,
With their gimlets another they'd presently bore.
The ship's carpenter swore he was worn of his legs
By constantly running to fill them with pegs:
And when to repel them we found 'twas in vain,
We politely entreated they'd ne'er peep again;
But the vandals still forced us at night to lie down
With a petticoat on, and a morning bed-gown;
If we failed to wear these, they were sure to look through
To see if our shapes they uncovered could view.
Such, such are the scenes which arise to torment her,
Who ploughs foaming billows in search of adventure,
That had you, dear mother, e'er been in a ship
You ne'er would have sent me on such a vile trip,
And surely, myself, I'd the voyage have declined
If half what I suffered I e'er had opined!

SAMUEL TAYLOR COLERIDGE

1772–1834

6   *The Delinquent Travellers*

Some are home-sick—some two or three,
Their third year on the Arctic Sea—
Brave Captain Lyon tells us so[1]—
Spite of those charming Esquimaux.
But O, what scores are sick of Home,
Agog for Paris or for Rome!

[1] *The Private Journal of Captain G. F. Lyon of the Mt. Hecla, during the recent voyage of discovery under Captain Parry* (1824).

Nay! tho' contented to abide,
You should prefer your own fireside;
Yet since grim War has ceased its madding,
And Peace has set John Bull agadding,
'Twould such a vulgar taste betray,
For very shame you must away!
'What? not yet seen the coast of France!
The folks will swear, for lack of bail,
You've spent your last five years in jail!'

Keep moving! Steam, or Gas, or Stage,
Hold, cabin, steerage, hencoop's cage—
Tour, Journey, Voyage, Lounge, Ride, Walk,
Skim, Sketch, Excursion, Travel-talk—
For move you must! 'Tis now the rage,
The law and fashion of the Age.
If you but perch, where Dover tallies,
So strangely with the coast of Calais,
With a good glass and knowing look,
You'll soon get matter for a book!
Or else, in Gas-car, take your chance
Like that adventurous king of France,
Who, once, with twenty thousand men
Went up—and then came down again;
At least, he moved if nothing more:
And if there's nought left to explore,
Yet while your well-greased wheels keep spinning,
The traveller's honoured name you're winning,
And, snug as Jonas in the Whale,
You may loll back and dream a tale.
Move, or be moved—there's no protection,
Our Mother Earth has ta'en the infection—
(That rogue Copernicus, 'tis said
First put the whirring in her head),
A planet She, and can't endure
T'exist without her annual Tour:
The *name* were else a mere misnomer,
Since Planet is but Greek for *Roamer*.
The atmosphere, too, can do no less
Than ventilate her emptiness,
Bilks turn-pike gates, for no one cares,
And gives herself a thousand airs—
While streams and shopkeepers, we see,
Will have their run toward the sea—
And if, meantime, like old King Log,
Or ass with tether and a clog,

Must graze at home! to yawn and bray
'I guess we shall have rain to-day!'
Nor clog nor tether can be worse
Than the dead palsy of the purse.
Money, I've heard a wise man say,
Makes herself wings and flies away:
Ah! would She take it in her head
To make a pair for me instead!
At all events, the Fancy's free,
No traveller so bold as she.
From Fear and Poverty released
I'll saddle Pegasus, at least,
And when she's seated to her mind,
I within I can mount behind:
And since this outward I, you know,
Must stay because he cannot go,
My fellow-travellers shall be they
Who go because they cannot stay—
Rogues, rascals, sharpers, blanks and prizes,
Delinquents of all sorts and sizes,
Fraudulent bankrupts, Knights burglarious,
And demireps of means precarious—
All whom Law thwarted, Arms or Arts,
Compel to visit foreign parts,
All hail! No compliments, I pray,
I'll follow where you lead the way!
But ere we cross the main once more,
Methinks, along my native shore,
Dismounting from my steed I'll stray
Beneath the cliffs of Dumpton Bay,
Where, Ramsgate and Broadstairs between,
Rude caves and grated doors are seen:
And here I'll watch till break of day,
(For Fancy in her magic might
Can turn broad noon to starless night!)
When lo! methinks a sudden band
Of smock-clad smugglers round me stand.
Denials, oaths, in vain I try,
At once they gag me for a spy,
And stow me in the boat hard by.
Suppose us fairly now afloat,
Till Boulogne mouth receives our Boat.
But, bless us! what a numerous band
Of cockneys anglicize the strand!
Delinquent bankrupts, leg-bailed debtors,
Some for the news, and some for letters—

With hungry look and tarnished dress,
French shrugs and British surliness.
Sick of the country for their sake
Of them and France *French leave* I take—
And lo! a transport comes in view
I hear the merry motley crew,
Well skilled in pocket to make entry,
Of Dieman's Land the elected Gentry,
And founders of Australian Races.—
The Rogues! I see it in their faces!
Receive me, Lads! I'll go with you,
Hunt the black swan and kangaroo,
And that New Holland we'll presume
Old England with some elbow-room.
Across the mountains we will roam,
And each man make himself a home:
Or, if old habits ne'er forsaking,
Like clock-work of the Devil's making,
Ourselves inveterate rogues should be,
We'll have a virtuous progeny;
And on the dunghill of our vices
Raise human pine-apples and spices.
Of all the children of John Bull
With empty heads and bellies full,
Who ramble East, West, North and South,
With leaky purse and open mouth,
In search of varieties exotic
The usefullest and most patriotic,
And merriest, too, believe me, Sirs!
Are your Delinquent Travellers!

THOMAS MOORE
1779–1852

7   from *Rhymes on the Road*

And is there then no earthly place
   Where we can rest, in dream Elysian,
Without some cursed, round English face,
   Popping up near, to break the vision?

6 Dieman's Land] Tasmania

'Mid northern lakes, 'mid southern vines,
    Unholy cits we're doomed to meet;
Nor highest Alps nor Apennines
    Are sacred from Threadneedle-street!

If up the Simplon's path we wind,
Fancying we leave this world behind,
Such pleasant sounds salute one's ear
As—'Baddish news from 'Change, my dear—
The Funds—(phew, curse this ugly hill!)
Are lowering fast—(what! higher still?)—
And—(zooks, we're mounting up to Heaven!)—
Will soon be down to sixty-seven.'

Go where we may—rest where we will,
Eternal London haunts us still.
The trash of Almack's or Fleet-Ditch—
And scarce a pin's head difference *which*—
Mixes, though even to Greece we run,
With every rill from Helicon!
And, if this rage for travelling lasts,
If Cockneys, of all sects and castes,
Old maidens, aldermen, and squires,
Will leave their puddings and coal fires,
To gape at things in foreign lands
No soul among them understands—
If Blues desert their coteries,
To show off 'mong the Wahabees—
If neither sex nor age controls,
    Nor fear of Mamelukes forbids
Young ladies, with pink parasols,
    To glide among the Pyramids—
Why, then, farewell all hope to find
A spot that's free from London-kind!
Who knows, if to the West we roam,
But we may find some *Blue* 'at home'
    Among the *Blacks* of Carolina—
Or, flying to the Eastward, see
Some Mrs Hopkins, taking tea
    And toast upon the Wall of China!

CHARLES STUART CALVERLEY
1831–1884

8   *Dover to Munich*

Farewell, farewell! Before our prow
  Leaps in white foam the noisy channel;
A tourist's cap is on my brow,
  My legs are cased in tourist's flannel:

Around me gasp the invalids—
  The quantity to-night is fearful—
I take a brace or so of weeds,
  And feel (as yet) extremely cheerful.

The night wears on:—my thirst I quench
  With one imperial pint of porter;
Then drop upon a casual bench—
  (The bench is short, but I am shorter)—

Place 'neath my head the *havre-sac*
  Which I have stowed my little all in,
And sleep, though moist about the back,
  Serenely in an old tarpaulin.

*

Bed at Ostend at 5 a.m.
  Breakfast at 6, and train 6.30,
Tickets to Königswinter (mem.
  The seats unutterably dirty).

And onward thro' those dreary flats
  We move, and scanty space to sit on,
Flanked by stout girls with steeple hats,
  And waists that paralyse a Briton;—

By many a tidy little town,
  Where tidy little Fraus sit knitting;
(The men's pursuits are, lying down,
  Smoking perennial pipes, and spitting);

And doze, and execrate the heat,
  And wonder how far off Cologne is,
And if we shall get aught to eat,
  Till we get there, save raw polonies:

polonies] sausages made of partly cooked pork

Until at last the 'gray old pile'
  Is seen, is past, and three hours later
We're ordering steaks, and talking vile
  Mock-German to an Austrian waiter.

            *

Königswinter, hateful Königswinter!
  Burying-place of all I loved so well!
Never did the most extensive printer
  Print a tale so dark as thou couldst tell!

In the sapphire West the eve yet lingered,
  Bathed in kindly light those hill-tops cold;
Fringed each cloud, and, stooping rosy-fingered,
  Changed Rhine's waters into molten gold;—

While still nearer did his light waves splinter
  Into silvery shafts the streaming light;
And I said I loved thee, Königswinter,
  For the glory that was thine that night.

And we gazed, till slowly disappearing,
  Like a day-dream, passed the pageant by,
And I saw but those lone hills, uprearing
  Dull dark shapes against a hueless sky.

Then I turned, and on those bright hopes pondered
  Whereof yon gay fancies were the type;
And my hand mechanically wandered
  Towards my left-hand pocket for a pipe.

Ah! why starts each eyeball from its socket,
  As, in Hamlet, start the guilty Queen's?
There, deep-hid in its accustomed pocket,
  Lay my sole pipe, smashed to smithereens!

            *

      On, on the vessel steals;
      Round go the paddle-wheels,
      And now the tourist feels
         As he should;
      For king-like rolls the Rhine,
      And the scenery's divine,
      And the victuals and the wine
         Rather good.

From every crag we pass'll
Rise up some hoar old castle;
The hanging fir-groves tassel
        Every slope;
And the vine her lithe arm stretches
Over peasants singing catches—
And you'll make no end of sketches,
        I should hope.

We've a nun here (called Thérèse),
Two couriers out of place,
One Yankee with a face
        Like a ferret's:
And three youths in scarlet caps
Drinking chocolate and schnapps—
A diet which perhaps
        Has its merits.

And day again declines:
In shadow sleep the vines,
And the last ray thro' the pines
        Feebly glows,
Then sinks behind yon ridge;
And the usual evening midge
Is settling on the bridge
        Of my nose.

And keen's the air and cold,
And the sheep are in the fold,
And Night walks sable-stoled
        Thro' the trees;
And on the silent river
The floating starbeams quiver;—
And now, the saints deliver
        Us from fleas.

*

Avenues of broad white houses,
    Basking in the noontide glare;—
Streets, which foot of traveller shrinks from,
    As on hot plates shrinks the bear;—

Elsewhere lawns, and vista'd gardens,
    Statues white, and cool arcades,
Where at eve the German warrior
    Winks upon the German maids;—

Such is Munich:—broad and stately,
    Rich of hue, and fair of form;
But, towards the end of August,
    Unequivocally *warm*.

There, the long dim galleries threading,
    May the artist's eye behold
Breathing from the 'deathless canvas'
    Records of the years of old:

Pallas there, and Jove, and Juno,
    'Take' once more their 'walks abroad',
Under Titian's fiery woodlands
    And the saffron skies of Claude:

There the Amazons of Rubens
    Lift the failing arm to strike,
And the pale light falls in masses
    On the horsemen of Vandyke;

And in Berghem's pools reflected
    Hang the cattle's graceful shapes,
And Murillo's soft boy-faces
    Laugh amid the Seville grapes;

And all purest, loveliest fancies
    That in poets' souls may dwell
Started into shape and substance
    At the touch of Raphael.

Lo! her wan arms folded meekly,
    And the glory of her hair
Falling as a robe around her,
    Kneels the Magdalen in prayer;

And the white-robed Virgin-mother
    Smiles, as centuries back she smiled,
Half in gladness, half in wonder,
    On the calm face of her Child:—

And that mighty Judgment-vision
    Tells how man essayed to climb
Up the ladder of the ages,
    Past the frontier-walls of Time;

Heard the trumpet-echoes rolling
　Thro' the phantom-peopled sky,
And the still voice bid this mortal
　Put on immortality.

*

Thence we turned, what time the blackbird
　Pipes to vespers from his perch,
And from out the clattering city
　Passed into the silent church;

Marked the shower of sunlight breaking
　Thro' the crimson panes o'erhead,
And on pictured wall and window
Read the histories of the dead:

Till the kneelers round us, rising,
　Crossed their foreheads and were gone;
And o'er aisle and arch and cornice,
　Layer on layer, the night came on.

ROBERT LOUIS STEVENSON
1850–1894

9 *Christmas at Sea*

The sheets were frozen hard, and they cut the naked hand;
The decks were like a slide, where a seaman scarce could stand;
The wind was a nor'wester, blowing squally off the sea;
And cliffs and spouting breakers were the only things a-lee.

They heard the surf a-roaring before the break of day;
But 'twas only with the peep of light we saw how ill we lay.
We tumbled every hand on deck instanter, with a shout.
And we gave her the maintops'l, and stood by to go about.

All day we tacked and tacked between the South Head and the North;
All day we hauled the frozen sheets, and got no further forth;
All day as cold as charity, in bitter pain and dread,
For very life and nature we tacked from head to head.

We gave the South a wider berth, for there the tide-race roared;
But every tack we made we brought the North Head close aboard:
So's we saw the cliffs and houses, and the breakers running high,
And the coastguard in his garden, with his glass against his eye.

The frost was on the village roofs as white as ocean foam;
The good red fires were burning bright in every 'longshore home;
The windows sparkled clear, and the chimneys volleyed out;
And I vow we sniffed the victuals as the vessel went about.

The bells upon the church were rung with a mighty jovial cheer;
For it's just that I should tell you how (of all days in the year)
This day of our adversity was blessèd Christmas morn,
And the house above the coastguard's was the house where I was born.

O well I saw the pleasant room, the pleasant faces there,
My mother's silver spectacles, my father's silver hair;
And well I saw the firelight, like a flight of homely elves,
Go dancing round the china-plates that stand upon the shelves.

And well I knew the talk they had, the talk that was of me,
Of the shadow on the household and the son that went to sea;
And O the wicked fool I seemed, in every kind of way,
To be here and hauling frozen ropes on blessèd Christmas Day.

They lit the high sea-light, and the dark began to fall.
'All hands to loose topgallant sails,' I heard the captain call.
'By the Lord, she'll never stand it,' our first mate, Jackson, cried.
... 'It's the one way or the other, Mr Jackson,' he replied.

She staggered to her bearings, but the sails were new and good,
And the ship smelt up to windward just as though she understood.
As the winter's day was ending, in the entry of the night,
We cleared the weary headland, and passed below the light.

And they heaved a mighty breath, every soul on board but me,
As they saw her nose again pointing handsome out to sea;
But all that I could think of, in the darkness and the cold,
Was just that I was leaving home and my folks were growing old.

RUDYARD KIPLING
1865–1936

10   *Jobson's Amen*

'Blessèd be the English and all their ways and works.
Cursèd be the Infidels, Hereticks, and Turks!'
'Amen,' quo' Jobson, 'but where I used to lie
Was neither Candle, Bell nor Book to curse my brethren by:

'But a palm-tree in full bearing, bowing down, bowing down,
To a surf that drove unsparing at the brown, walled town—
Conches in a temple, oil-lamps in a dome—
And a low moon out of Africa said: "This way home!"'

'Blessed be the English and all that they profess.
Cursed be the Savages that prance in nakedness!'
'Amen,' quo' Jobson, 'but where I used to lie
Was neither shirt nor pantaloons to catch my brethren by:

'But a well-wheel slowly creaking, going round, going round,
By a water-channel leaking over drowned, warm ground—
Parrots very busy in the trellised pepper-vine—
And a high sun over Asia shouting: "Rise and shine!"'

'Blessèd be the English and everything they own.
Cursèd be the Infidels that bow to wood and stone!'
'Amen,' quo' Jobson, 'but where I used to lie
Was neither pew nor Gospelleer to save my brethren by:

'But a desert stretched and stricken, left and right, left and right,
Where the piled mirages thicken under white-hot light—
A skull beneath a sand-hill and a viper coiled inside—
And a red wind out of Libya roaring: "Run and hide!"'

'Blessèd be the English and all they make or do.
Cursèd be the Hereticks who doubt that this is true!'
'Amen,' quo' Jobson, 'but where I mean to die
Is neither rule nor calliper to judge the matter by:

'But Himalaya heavenward-heading, sheer and vast, sheer and vast,
In a million summits bedding on the last world's past—
A certain sacred mountain where the scented cedars climb,
And—the feet of my Beloved hurrying back through Time!'

JOHN MASEFIELD
1878–1967

11   *Sea-Fever*

I must down to the seas again, to the lonely sea and the sky,
And all I ask is a tall ship and a star to steer her by,
And the wheel's kick and the wind's song and the white sails shaking,
And a grey mist on the sea's face and a grey dawn breaking.

I must down to the seas again, for the call of the running tide
Is a wild call and a clear call that may not be denied;
And all I ask is a windy day with the white clouds flying,
And the flung spray and the blown spume, and the sea-gulls crying.

I must down to the seas again, to the vagrant gypsy life,
To the gull's way and the whale's way where the wind's like a whetted
    knife;
And all I ask is a merry yarn from a laughing fellow-rover,
And quiet sleep and a sweet dream when the long trick's over.

DOROTHY WELLESLEY,
DUCHESS OF WELLINGTON
1889–1956

12   *First Flight*

Here is the perfect vision: in the dawn,
In smudgy dusk I rise above the plain
Of the Persian desert, daubed with shadow still,
And instantly below me lies the hill,
That rubbish heap once called the City of Rhey,
Where Caliph Harun Al-Rashid was born.

Behind me Zoroaster's mountain rises:
White Demavend turns fire to unseen day.
Like an unravelling tape streams back the way
That leads into the kernel of all Asia.

12 City of Rhey] lost city in the desert near Teheran   Harun Al-Rashid] (766–809), of
Arabian Nights, was the fifth and greatest of the dynasty of thirty-seven Abassid caliphs
Zoroaster's] Zoroaster was an Iranian religious reformer and founder of Zoroastrianism or
Parsisism, as it is known in India

The desert skims below.
Like caterpillar trails the camels go
Marked broadly by their stacks of camel thorn.
Those fretful eruptions are the hills of Persia;
Those striped brocades her bright precarious corn.
Now is the world, the planet where I was born,
Dwindled, reduced in this light blue of morn
To detail seen upon a gigantic scale.

Beyond the Bears the dark begins to fail,
Now comes the light weltering through Carls' Wain,
Now between stars the dawn begins to flow,
Washing around their points in spate of green.

Beside my hand the stars hang close, go out,
Spent candles. Now the moon most surely dies,
So haggard hangs she on the Persian peaks,
Who whitens misty on an English lawn.

Now in great spirals going
I drop to the Caspian Sea.

Onward to Colchis!
                  Now is a peccant world
Seen at the purest angle of the vision:
In perfect, in poetic state she lies.

NOEL COWARD
1899–1973

13   *Mad Dogs and Englishmen*

In tropical climes there are certain times of day,
When all the citizens retire
To tear their clothes off and perspire.
It's one of those rules that the greatest fools obey,
Because the sun is much too sultry
And one must avoid its ultry-violet ray ...
The natives grieve when the white men leave their huts,
Because they're obviously definitely nuts!

12 Colchis] district of Asia Minor at the eastern extremity of the Black Sea; in Greek
mythology the destination of the Argonauts

Mad dogs and Englishmen
Go out in the midday sun.
The Japanese don't care to,
The Chinese wouldn't dare to,
Hindoos and Argentines sleep firmly from twelve to one,
But Englishmen detest a
Siesta.
In the Philippines there are lovely screens
To protect you from the glare.
In the Malay States there are hats like plates
Which the Britishers won't wear.
At twelve noon
The natives swoon
And no further work is done,
But mad dogs and Englishmen
Go out in the midday sun.

It's such a surprise for the Eastern eyes to see,
That though the English are effete
They're quite impervious to heat.
When the white man rides every native hides in glee,
Because the simple creatures hope he
Will impale his solar topee on a tree ...
It seems such a shame when the English claim the earth
That they give rise to such hilarity and mirth.

Mad dogs and Englishmen
Go out in the midday sun.
The toughest Burmese bandit
Can never understand it.
In Rangoon the heat of noon
Is just what the natives shun.
They put their Scotch or rye down
And lie down.
In a jungle town
Where the sun beats down
To the rage of man and beast,
The English garb
Of the English sahib
Merely gets a bit more creased.
In Bangkok
At twelve o'clock
They foam at the mouth and run,
But mad dogs and Englishmen
Go out in the midday sun.

Mad dogs and Englishmen
Go out in the midday sun.
The smallest Malay rabbit
Deplores this foolish habit.
In Hong Kong
They strike a gong
And fire off a noonday gun,
To reprimand each inmate
Who's in late.
In the mangrove swamps
Where the python romps
There is peace from twelve to two.
Even caribous
Lie around and snooze,
For there's nothing else to do.
In Bengal
To move at all
Is seldom, if ever done,
But mad dogs and Englishmen
Go out in the midday sun.

A. S. J. TESSIMOND

1902–1962

14   *Where?*

You are in love with a country
Where people laugh in the sun
And the people are warm as the sunshine and live and move easily
And women with honeycoloured skins and men with no frowns on
    their faces
Sit on white terraces drinking red wine
While the sea spreads peacock feathers on cinnamon sands
And palms weave sunlight into sheaves of gold
And at night the shadows are indigo velvet
And there is dancing to soft, soft, soft guitars
Played by copper fingers under a froth of stars.

Perhaps your country is where you think you will find it.
Or perhaps it has not yet come or perhaps it has gone.
Perhaps it is east of the sun and west of the moon.
Perhaps it is a country called the Hesperides
And Avalon and Atlantis and Eldorado:

A country which Gauguin looked for in Tahiti and Lawrence in
  Mexico,
And whether they found it only they can say, and they not now.
Perhaps you will find it where you alone can see it,
But if you can see it, though no one else can, it will be there,
It will be yours.

CECIL DAY-LEWIS

1904–1972

15 *The Tourists*

Arriving was their passion.
Into the new place out of the blue
Flying, sailing, driving—
How well these veteran tourists knew
Each fashion of arriving.

Leaving a place behind them,
There was no sense of loss: they fed
Upon the act of leaving—
So hot their hearts for the land ahead—
As a kind of pre-conceiving.

Arrival has stern laws, though,
Condemning men to lose their eyes
If they have treated travel
As a brief necessary disease,
A pause before arrival.

And merciless the fate is
Of him who leaves nothing behind,
No hostage, no reversion:
He travels on, not only blind
But a stateless person.

Fleeing from love and hate,
Pursuing change, consumed by motion,
Such arrivistes, unseeing,
Forfeit through endless self-evasion
The estate of simple being.

LOUIS MacNEICE
1907–1963

16   *Solitary Travel*

Breakfasting alone in Karachi, Delhi, Calcutta,
Dacca, Singapore, Kuala Lumpur, Colombo, Cape Town,
But always under water or glass, I find
Such a beginning makes the day seem blind.

The hotels are all the same, it might be pawpaw
Instead of grapefruit, different flowers on the table,
But the waiters, coffee-coloured or yellow or black,
All smile, but, should you smile, give nothing back.

And taking coffee alone in the indistinguishable airports,
Though the land outside be empty or man-crammed, oven or icebox,
I feel the futility of moving on
To what, though not a conclusion, stays foregone.

But the Customs clamour, the stamp is raised, the passport
Like a chess game played by mail records the latest
Move of just one square. Which is surely seen
By the black bishop and the unsleeping queen.

And so to the next hotel to the selfsame breakfast,
Same faces of manager, waiter, fellow-traveller,
Same lounge or bar whose test-tube walls enfold
The self-indulgent disenchanted old.

Time and the will lie sidestepped. If I could only
Escape into icebox or oven, escape among people
Before tomorrow from this neutral zone
Where all tomorrows must be faced alone. . . .

SIR CHARLES JOHNSTON
1912–

17   *Air Travel in Arabia*

Then Petra flashed by in a wink.
It looked like Eaton Square—but pink.

G. S. FRASER
1915–1980

18   *The Traveller Has Regrets*

The traveller has regrets
For the receding shore
That with its many nets
Has caught, not to restore,
The white lights in the bay,
The blue lights on the hill,
Though night with many stars
May travel with him still,
But night has nought to say,
Only a colour and shape
Changing like cloth shaking,
A dancer with a cape
Whose dance is heart-breaking,
Night with its many stars
Can warn travellers
There's only time to kill
And nothing much to say:
But the blue lights on the hill,
The white lights in the bay
Told us the meal was laid
And that the bed was made
And that we could not stay.

EUROPE OF THE SOUTH

FRANCE

ANONYMOUS
c. 1623

19

The Journey into France

I came from England into France
Neither to learn to cringe, nor dance,
   Nor yet to ride, nor fence;
Nor for to do such things as those
Who have returned without a nose,
   They carried out from hence.

But I to Paris rode along,
Much like John Dory in the song,
   Upon a holy tide:
I on an ambling nag did get,
I hope it is not paid for yet,
   I spurred him on each side.

And to St Denis first we came
To see the sights at Notre-Dame,
   The man that shows them snuffles:
Where who is apt for to believe,
May see our Lady's right-hand sleeve,
   And her old pantofles.

Her hair, her milk, her very gown,
Which she did wear in Bethleem town,
   When in the inn she lay:
Yet all the world knows that's a fable,
For so good clothes ne'er lay in stable
   Upon a lock of hay.

No carpenter could by his trade,
Gain so much wealth as to have made
   A gown of so rich stuff:
Yet they (poor fools) think for her credit,
They must believe old Joseph did it,
   'Cause she deserved enough.

There is the lanthorn, which the Jews
(When Judas led them forth) did use,
    It weighs my weight down right:
But to believe it you must think,
The Jews did put a candle in't,
    And then 'twas wondrous light.

There is one of the Cross's nails,
Which who so sees his bonnet veils,
    And if he list may kneel:
Some say it's false, 'twas never so,
Yet feeling it thus much I know,
    It is as true as steel.

There's one saint there hath lost his toes,
Another his head, but not his nose,
    A finger and a thumb:
Now when we had seen these holy rags,
We went to th' inn and took our nags,
    And so away did come.

We came to Paris on the Seine,
It's wondrous fair, but nothing clean,
    'Tis Europe's greatest town:
How strong it is I need not tell it,
For all the world may easily smell it,
    That walk it up and down.

There's many strange things for to see,
The Hospital, the Gallery,
    The Place Royal doth excel:
The New Bridge and the statues there,
At Notre-Dame St Christopher,
    The steeple bears the bell.

For learning the University,
And for old clothes the Frippery,
    The house the queen did build:
St Innocent's, whose earth devours,
Dead corpse in four and twenty hours,
    And there the king was killed.

The Bastille, and St Denis' street,
The Shateele much like London Fleet,

Shateele] the enormous towers of the Grand Châtelet, built in 870 to defend the Great Bridge
(Grand Pont) on the right bank of the Seine

The Arsenal, no toy:
But if you'll see the prettiest thing,
Go to the court and see the King,
    It is a hopeful boy.

He is by all his dukes and peers,
Reverenced as much for wit as years,
    Nor must you think it much:
For he with little switch doth play,
And can make fine dirt pies of clay,
    Oh never king made such.

A bird that can but catch a fly,
Or prate, doth please His Majesty,
    'Tis known to every one:
The Duke de Guise gave him a parrot,
And he had twenty cannons for it,
    For his new galleon.

Oh that I e'er might have the hap,
To get the bird which in the map
    We call the Indian Ruck:
I'd give it him, and look to be
As great and wise as Luinee,
    Or else I had ill luck.

Birds round about his chamber stand,
And he them feeds with his own hand,
    'Tis his humility:
And if they do lack anything,
They may but whistle for the King,
    And he comes presently.

Now for these virtuous parts he must
Entitled be Lewis the Just,
    Great Henry's rightful heir:
When to his style to add more words,
You may better call him King of Birds,
    Instead of lost Navarre.

He hath beside a pretty firk,
Taught him by nature for to work

Luinee] Charles d'Albert de Luynes (1578–1621), favourite of Louis XIII and Marshal of France   Lewis the Just] Louis XIII (1601–43), son of Henri IV (Henri de Navarre). He became king at the age of 9   firk] gift or skill

In iron with great ease:
Sometimes unto his forge he goes,
And there he puffs and there he blows,
And makes both locks and keys.

Which puts a doubt in every one,
Whether he were Mars' or Vulcan's son,
Some few suspect his mother:
Yet let them all say what they will,
I am resolved and will think still,
As much the t'one as t'other.

His queen's a pretty little wench,
But born in Spain, speaks little French,
She's ne'er like to be mother:
For her incestuous house could not
Have any children but begot
By uncle or by brother.

Now why should Lewis being so Just
Content himself to take his lust,
On his Luina's mate:
And suffer his pretty little queen,
From all her race that yet hath been,
So to degenerate.

'Twere charity for to be known,
To love others' children as his own,
And keep them: 'Tis no shame;
Unless that he would greater be,
Then was his father King Henry,
Who (men thought) did the same.

JOHN GAY
1685–1732

20 *Epistle to the Right Honourable William Pulteney,*
Esq.

Pult'ney, methinks you blame my breach of word;
What, cannot Paris one poor page afford?
Yes, I can sagely, when the times are past,
Laugh at those follies which I strove to taste,

And each amusement, which we shared, review,
Pleased with mere talking, since I talk to you.
But how shall I describe in humble prose,
Their balls, assemblies, operas, and beaus?
In prose! you cry: Oh no, the Muse must aid,
And leave Parnassus for the Tuileries' shade;
Shall he (who late Britannia's city trod,
And led the draggled Muse, with pattens shod,
Through dirty lanes, and alley's doubtful ways)
Refuse to write, when Paris asks his lays?

Well then, I'll try. Descend, ye beauteous Nine,
In all the colours of the rainbow shine,
Let sparkling stars your neck and ear adorn,
Lay on the blushes of the crimson morn,
So may ye balls and gay assemblies grace,
And at the Opera claim the foremost place.

Trav'llers should ever fit expression choose,
Nor with low phrase the lofty theme abuse.
When they describe the state of eastern lords,
Pomp and magnificence should swell their words;
And when they paint the serpent's scaly pride,
Their lines should hiss, their numbers smoothly slide:
But they, unmindful of poetic rules,
Describe alike macaws, and Great-Moguls.
Dampier would thus, without ill-meaning satire,
Dress forth in simple style the *petit-maître*.

In Paris, there's a race of animals
(I've seen them at their operas and balls).
They stand erect, they dance whene'er they walk,
Monkeys in action, perroquets in talk;
They're crowned with feathers, like the cockatoo,
And, like chameleons, daily change their hue;
From patches justly placed they borrow graces,
And with vermilion lacquer o'er their faces;
This custom, as we visibly discern,
They, by frequenting ladies' toilettes, learn.
Thus might the trav'ller easy truth impart.
Into the subject let me nobly start!

How happy lives the man, how sure to charm,
Whose knot embroidered flutters down his arm!
On him the ladies cast the yielding glance,
Sigh in his songs, and languish in his dance;

Dampier] William Dampier (1652–1715), navigator, explorer, and author of extremely popular
travel literature

While wretched is the wit, contemned, forlorn,
Whose gummy hat no scarlet plumes adorn;
No broidered flowers his worsted ankle grace,
Nor cane embossed with gold directs his pace;
No lady's favour on his sword is hung.
What, though Apollo dictate from his tongue,
His wit is spiritless and void of grace,
Who wants th' assurance of brocade and lace.
While the gay fop genteelly talks of weather,
The fair in raptures dote upon his feather;
Like a court lady though he write and spell,
His minuet step was fashioned by Marcell;
He dresses, fences. What avails to know?
For women choose their men, like silks, for show.
Is this the thing, you cry, that Paris boasts?
Is this the thing renowned among our toasts?
For such a flutt'ring sight we need not roam;
Our own assemblies shine with these at home.

Let us into the field of beauty start;
Beauty's a theme that ever warmed my heart.
Think not, ye fair, that I the sex accuse:
How shall I spare you, prompted by the Muse?
(The muses are all prudes) she rails, she frets,
Amidst this sprightly nation of coquettes;
Yet let not us their loose coquetry blame;
Women of ev'ry nation are the same.

You ask me, if Parisian dames, like ours,
With rattling dice profane the Sunday's hours;
If they the gamester's pale-eyed vigils keep,
And stake their honour while their husbands sleep.
Yes, sir; like English toasts, the dames of France
Will risk their income on a single chance.
Nannette last night at tricking pharaon played,
The cards the tailleur's sliding hand obeyed;
Today her neck no brilliant circle wears,
Nor the ray-darting pendant loads her ears.
Why does old Chloris an assembly hold?
Chloris each night divides the sharper's gold.
Corinna's cheek with frequent losses burns,
And no bold 'Trente le va' her fortune turns.
Ah, too rash virgin! where's thy virtue flown?
She pawns her person for the sharper's loan.

Marcell] a famous dancing master

Yet who with justice can the fair upbraid,
Whose debts of honour are so duly paid?

But let me not forget the toilette's cares,
Where art each morn the languid cheek repairs:
This red's too pale, nor gives a distant grace;
Madame today puts on her Opera face;
From this we scarce extract the milkmaid's bloom;
Bring the deep dye that warms across the room!
Now flames her cheek, so strong her charms prevail,
That on her gown the silken rose looks pale!
Not but that France some native beauty boasts,
Clermont and Charleroi might grace our toasts.

When the sweet-breathing spring unfolds the buds,
Love flies the dusty town for shady woods.
Then Tottenham fields with roving beauty swarm,
And Hampstead balls the city virgin warm;
Then Chelsea's meads o'erhear perfidious vows,
And the pressed grass defrauds the grazing cows.
'Tis here the same; but in a higher sphere,
For ev'n court ladies sin in open air.
What cit with a gallant would trust his spouse
Beneath the tempting shade of Greenwich boughs?
What peer of France would let his duchess rove,
Where Boulogne's closest woods invite to love?
But here no wife can blast her husband's fame,
Cuckold is grown an honourable name.
Stretched on the grass the shepherd sighs his pain,
And on the grass what shepherd sighs in vain?
On Chloe's lap here Damon laid along,
Melts with the languish of her am'rous song;
There Iris flies Palaemon through the glade,
Nor trips by chance—'til in the thickest shade;
Here Celimene defends her lips and breast,
For kisses are by struggling closer pressed;
Alexis there with eager flame grows bold,
Nor can the nymph his wanton fingers hold;
Be wise, Alexis; what, so near the road!
Hark, a coach rolls, and husbands are abroad!
Such were our pleasures in the days of yore,
When am'rous Charles Britannia's sceptre bore;
The nightly scene of joy the Park was made,
And love in couples peopled ev'ry shade.
But since at Court the rural taste is lost,
What mighty sums have velvet couches cost!

Sometimes the Tuileries' gaudy walk I love,
Where I through crowds of rustling manteaus rove;
As here from side to side my eyes I cast,
And gazed on all the glitt'ring train that passed,
Sudden a fop steps forth before the rest;
I knew the bold embroidery of his vest.
He thus accosts me with familiar air,
Parbleu! on a fait cet habit en Angleterre!
Quelle manche! ce galon est grossièrement rangé;
Voilà quelque chose de fort beau et dégagé!
This said, on his red heel he turns, and then
Hums a soft minuet, and proceeds again:
Well; now you've Paris seen, you'll frankly own
Your boasted London seems a country town;
Has Christianity yet reached your nation?
Are churches built? Are masquerades in fashion?
Do daily soups your dinners introduce?
Are music, snuff, and coaches yet in use?
Pardon me, sir; we know the Paris mode,
And gather politesse from Courts abroad.
Like you, our courtiers keep a num'rous train
To load their coach; and tradesmen dun in vain.
Nor has religion left us in the lurch,
And, as in France, our vulgar crowd the church;
Our ladies too support the masquerade,
The sex by nature love th' intriguing trade.
Straight the vain fop in ign'rant rapture cries,
Paris the barb'rous world will civilize!
Pray, Sir, point out among the passing band
The present Beauties who the town command.
See yonder dame; strict virtue chills her breast,
Mark in her eye demure the prude professed;
That frozen bosom native fire must want,
Which boasts of constancy to one gallant!
This next the spoils of fifty lovers wears,
Rich Dandin's brilliant favours grace her ears;
The necklace Florio's gen'rous flame bestowed,
Clitander's sparkling gems her finger load;
But now, her charms grown cheap by constant use,
She sins for scarves, clocked stockings, knots and shoes.
This next, with sober gait and serious leer,
Wearies her knees with morn and ev'ning prayer;
She scorns th' ignoble love of feeble pages,
But with three Abbots in one night engages.
This with the Cardinal her nights employs,
Where holy sinews consecrate her joys.

Why have I promised things beyond my power!
Five assignations wait me at this hour;
The sprightly Countess first my visit claims,
Tomorrow shall indulge inferior dames.
Pardon me, Sir, that thus I take my leave,
Gay Florimella slyly twitched my sleeve.

   Adieu, Monsieur—the Opera hours draws near.
Not see the Opera! all the world is there;
Where on the stage th' embroidered youth of France
In bright array attract the female glance:
This languishes, this struts to show his mien,
And not a gold-clocked stocking moves unseen.

   But hark! the full orchestra strike the strings;
The hero struts, and the whole audience sings.

   My jarring ear harsh grating murmurs wound,
Hoarse and confused, like Babel's mingled sound.
Hard chance had placed me near a noisy throat,
That in rough quavers bellowed ev'ry note.
Pray, Sir, says I, suspend awhile your song,
The Opera's drowned; your lungs are wondrous strong;
I wish to hear your Roland's ranting strain,
While he with rooted forests strows the plain.
Sudden he shrugs surprise, and answers quick,
Monsieur apparemment n'aime pas la musique.
Then turning round, he joined th' ungrateful noise;
And the loud chorus thundered with his voice.

   O soothe me with some soft Italian air,
Let harmony compose my tortured ear!
When Anastasia's voice commands the strain,
The melting warble thrills through ev'ry vein;
Thought stands suspense, and silence pleased attends,
While in her notes the heav'nly choir descends.

   But you'll imagine I'm a Frenchman grown,
Pleased and content with nothing but my own,
So strongly with this prejudice possessed,
He thinks French music and French painting best.
Mention the force of learn'd Corelli's notes,
Some scraping fiddler of their ball he quotes;
Talk of the spirit Raphael's pencil gives,
Yet warm with life whose speaking picture lives;
Yes, Sir, says he, in colour and design,
Rigaud and Raphael are extremely fine!

'Tis true, his country's love transports his breast
With warmer zeal than your old Greeks professed.
Ulysses loved his Ithaca of yore,
Yet that sage trav'ller left his native shore;
What stronger virtue in the Frenchman shines!
He to dear Paris all his life confines.
I'm not so fond. There are, I must confess,
Things which might make me love my country less.
I should not think my Britain had such charms,
If lost to learning, if enslaved by arms;
France has her Richelieus and her Colberts known,
And then, I grant it, France in science shone;
We too, I own, without such aids may chance
In ignorance and pride to rival France.

But let me not forget Corneille, Racine,
Boileau's strong sense, and Molière's hum'rous scene.
Let Cambray's name be sung above the rest,
Whose maxims, Pult'ney, warm thy patriot breast;
In Mentor's precepts wisdom strong and clear
Dictates sublime, and distant nations hear.
Hear all ye princes, who the world control,
What cares, what terrors haunt the tyrant's soul;
His constant train are anger, fear, distrust.
To be a king, is to be good and just;
His people he protects, their rights he saves,
And scorns to rule a wretched race of slaves.

Happy, thrice happy shall the monarch reign,
Where guardian laws despotic power restrain!
There shall the ploughshare break the stubborn land,
And bending harvest tire the peasant's hand:
There liberty her settled mansion boasts,
There commerce plenty brings from foreign coasts.
O Britain, guard thy laws, thy rights defend,
So shall these blessings to thy sons descend!

You'll think 'tis time some other theme to choose,
And not with beaus and fops fatigue the Muse!
Should I let satire loose on English ground,
There fools of various character abound;
But here my verse is to one race confined,
All Frenchmen are of *petit-maître* kind.

JOSEPH WARTON

1722–1800

21   *Verses Written at Montauban in France, 1750*

Tarn, how delightful wind thy willowed waves,
But ah! they fructify a land of slaves!
In vain thy barefoot, sunburnt peasants hide
With luscious grapes yon hill's romantic side;
No cups nectareous shall their toil repay,
The priest's, the soldier's, and the fermier's prey;
Vain glows this sun, in cloudless glory dressed,
That strikes fresh vigour through the pining breast;
Give me, beneath a colder, changeful sky,
My soul's best, only pleasure, Liberty!
What millions perished near thy mournful flood
When the red papal tyrant cried out—'Blood!'
Less fierce the Saracen, and quivered Moor,
That dashed thy infants 'gainst the stones of yore.
Be warned, ye nations round; and trembling see
Dire superstition quench humanity!
By all the chiefs in freedom's battles lost,
By wise and virtuous Alfred's awful ghost;
By old Galgacus' scythed, iron car,
That, swiftly whirling through the walks of war,
Dashed Roman blood, and crushed the foreign throngs;
By holy Druids' courage-breathing songs;
By fierce Bonduca's shield and foaming steeds;
By the bold Peers that met on Thames's meads;
By the fifth Henry's helm and lightning spear;
O Liberty, my warm petition hear;
Be Albion still thy joy! with her remain,
Long as the surge shall lash her oak-crowned plain!

red papal tyrant] in 1621 Montauban (defended by Huguenot forces) was unsuccessfully
besieged by the Catholic forces of Louis XIII and de Luynes (the 'red papal tyrant')

WILLIAM BECKFORD
1759–1844

22   *Ode*

To orisons, the midnight bell
Had tolled each silent inmate from his cell;
    The hour was come to muse, or pray,
Or work mysterious rites that shun the day:
    My steps some whisp'ring influence led,
Up to yon pine-clad mountain's gloomy head:
    Hollow and deep the gust did blow,
And torrents dashed into the vales below:
    At length, the toilsome height attained,
Quick fled the moon, and sudden stillness reigned.
    As fearful turned my searching eye,
Glanced near a shadowy form, and fleeted by;
    Anon, before me full it stood;
A saintly figure, pale, in pensive mood.
    Damp horror thrilled me till he spoke,
And accents faint the charm-bound silence broke:
    'Long, trav'ller! ere this region near,
Say did not whisp'rings strange arrest thine ear?
    My summons 'twas to bid thee come,
Where sole the friend of nature loves to roam.
    Ages long past, this drear abode
To solitude I sanctified, and God:
    'Twas here, by love of wisdom brought,
Her truest lore, self-knowledge, first I sought;
    Devoted here my worldly wealth,
To win my chosen sons immortal health.
    Midst these dun woods and mountains steep,
Midst the wild horrors of yon desert deep,
    Midst yawning caverns, wat'ry dells,
Midst long, sequestered aisles, and peaceful cells,
    No passions fell distract the mind,
To nature, silence, and herself consigned.
    In these still mansions who shall bide,
'Tis mine, with Heaven's appointment, to decide;
    But, hither, I invite not all:
Some want the will to come, and more the call;
    But all, mark well my parting voice!
Led, or by chance, necessity, or choice
    (Ah! with our genius dread to sport),
Sage lessons here may learn of high import.

Know! Silence is the nurse of Truth:
Know! Temperance long retards the flight of youth:
Learn here, how penitence and prayer
Man's fallen race for happier worlds prepare:
Learn mild demeanor, void of art,
And bear, amidst the world, the hermit's heart.
Fix, trav'ller! deep this heaven-taught lore:
Know, Bruno brings it, and returns no more.'
(Half sighed, half smiled his long farewell)
He turned, and vanished in the bright'ning dell.

WILLIAM WORDSWORTH
1770–1850

23

It is a beauteous Evening, calm and free;
The holy time is quiet as a Nun
Breathless with adoration; the broad sun
Is sinking down in its tranquillity;
The gentleness of heaven is on the Sea:
Listen! the mighty Being is awake
And doth with his eternal motion make
A sound like thunder—everlastingly.
Dear Child![1] dear Girl! that walkest with me here,
If thou appear'st untouched by solemn thought,
Thy nature is not therefore less divine:
Thou liest in Abraham's bosom[2] all the year;
And worshipp'st at the Temple's inner shrine,
God being with thee when we know it not.

24

from *The Prelude*

Residence in France and French Revolution

It was a beautiful and silent day
That overspread the countenance of earth,
Then fading, with unusual quietness,
When from the Loire I parted, and through scenes
Of vineyard, orchard, meadow-ground and tilth,
Calm waters, gleams of sun, and breathless trees,

[1] Caroline, Wordsworth's daughter by Annette Vallon.
[2] Where the souls bound for heaven rest after death (cf. Luke 16: 22).

Towards the fierce Metropolis turned my steps
Their homeward way to England. From his Throne
The King had fallen; the congregated Host,
Dire cloud upon the front of which was written
The tender mercies of the dismal wind
That bore it, on the Plains of Liberty
Had burst innocuously, say more, the swarm
That came elate and jocund, like a Band
Of Eastern Hunters, to enfold in ring
Narrowing itself by moments and reduce
To the last punctual spot of their despair
A race of victims, so they seemed, *themselves*
Had shrunk from sight of their own task, and fled
In terror. Desolation and dismay
Remained for them whose fancies had grown rank
With evil expectations, confidence
And perfect triumph to the better cause.
The State, as if to stamp the final seal
On her security, and to the world
Shew what she was, a high and fearless soul,
Or rather in a spirit of thanks to those
Who had stirred up her slackening faculties
To a new transition, had assumed with joy
The body and the venerable name
Of a Republic. Lamentable crimes,
'Tis true, had gone before this hour, the work
Of massacre, in which the senseless sword
Was prayed to as a judge; but these were past,
Earth free from them for ever, as was thought,
Ephemeral monsters, to be seen but once;
Things that could only shew themselves and die.

    This was the time in which enflamed with hope,
To Paris I returned. Again I ranged,
More eagerly than I had done before,
Through the wide City, and in progress passed
The Prison where the unhappy Monarch lay,
Associate with his Children and his Wife
In bondage, and the Palace lately stormed
With roar of cannon, and a numerous Host.
I crossed (a blank and empty area then)
The Square of the Carousel, few weeks back
Heaped up with dead and dying, upon these
And other sights looking as doth a man
Upon a volume whose contents he knows
Are memorable, but from him locked up,
Being written in a tongue he cannot read,

So that he questions the mute leaves with pain
And half upbraids their silence. But that night
When on my bed I lay, I was most moved
And felt most deeply in what world I was;
My room was high and lonely, near the roof
Of a large Mansion or Hotel, a spot
That would have pleased me in more quiet times,
Nor was it wholly without pleasure then.
With unextinguished taper I kept watch,
Reading at intervals. The fear gone by
Pressed on me almost like a fear to come.
I thought of those September Massacres,
Divided from me by a little month,
And felt and touched them, a substantial dread;
The rest was conjured up from tragic fictions,
And mournful Calendars of true history,
Remembrances and dim admonishments.
'The horse is taught his manage, and the wind
Of heaven wheels round and treads in his own steps,
Year follows year, the tide returns again,
Day follows day, all things have second birth;
The earthquake is not satisfied at once.'
And in such way I wrought upon myself,
Until I seemed to hear a voice that cried,
To the whole City, 'Sleep no more.' To this
Add comments of a calmer mind, from which
I could not gather full security,
But at the best it seemed a place of fear,
Unfit for the repose of night,
Defenceless as a wood where tigers roam.

    Betimes next morning to the Palace Walk
Of Orleans I repaired and entering there
Was greeted, among divers other notes,
By voices of the Hawkers in the crowd
Bawling, *Denunciation of the crimes
Of Maximilian Robespierre.* The speech
Which in their hands they carried was the same
Which had been recently pronounced, the day
When Robespierre, well knowing for what mark
Some words of indirect reproof had been
Intended, rose in hardihood, and dared
The Man who had an ill surmise of him
To bring his charge in openness; whereat
When a dead pause ensued, and no one stirred,
In silence of all present, from his seat
Louvet walked singly through the avenue

And took his station in the Tribune, saying,
'I, Robespierre, accuse thee!' 'Tis well known
What was the issue of that charge, and how
Louvet was left alone without support
Of his irresolute Friends; but these are things
Of which I speak, only as they were storm
Or sunshine to my individual mind,
No further. Let me then relate that now,
In some sort seeing with my proper eyes
That Liberty, and Life, and Death, would soon
To the remotest corners of the land
Lie in the arbitrement of those who ruled
The capital City, what was struggled for,
And by what combatants victory must be won;
The indecision on their part whose aim
Seemed best, and the straightforward path of those
Who in attack or in defence alike
Were strong through their impiety, greatly I
Was agitated; yea I could almost
Have prayed that throughout earth upon all souls
Worthy of liberty, upon every soul
Matured to live in plainness and in truth,
The gift of tongues might fall, and men arrive
From the four quarters of the winds to do
For France what without help she could not do,
A work of honour; think not that to this
I added, work of safety; from such thought
And the least fear about the end of things,
I was as far as Angels are from guilt.

SIR WALTER SCOTT

1771–1832

25   *Saint Cloud*

Soft spread the southern summer night
    Her veil of darksome blue;
Ten thousand stars combined to light
    The terrace of Saint Cloud.

Saint Cloud] deserted palace on the Seine; built by Louis XIV, used by Napoleon, and scene
of many great events in French history

The evening breezes gently sighed,
   Like breath of lover true,
Bewailing the deserted pride
   And wreck of sweet Saint Cloud.

The drum's deep roll was heard afar,
   The bugle wildly blew
Good-night to Hulan and Hussar,
   That garrison Saint Cloud.

The startled Naiads from the shade
   With broken urns withdrew,
And silenced was that proud cascade,
   The glory of Saint Cloud.

We sat upon its steps of stone,
   Nor could its silence rue,
When waked, to music of our own,
   The echoes of Saint Cloud.

Slow Seine might hear each lovely note
   Fall light as summer dew,
While through the moonless air they float,
   Prolonged from fair Saint Cloud.

And sure a melody more sweet
   His waters never knew,
Though music's self was wont to meet
   With princes at Saint Cloud.

Nor then, with more delighted ear,
   The circle round her drew,
Than ours, when gathered round to hear
   Our songstress at Saint Cloud.

Few happy hours poor mortals pass,—
   Then give those hours their due,
And rank among the foremost class
   Our evenings at Saint Cloud.

THOMAS HOOD
1799–1845

26   *To Henrietta, on her Departure for Calais*

When little people go abroad, wherever they may roam,
They will not just be treated as they used to be at home;
So take a few promiscuous hints, to warn you in advance,
Of how a little English girl will perhaps be served in France.

Of course you will be Frenchified; and first, it's my belief,
They'll dress you in their foreign style as à-la-mode as beef,
With a little row of bee-hives, as a border to your frock,
And a pair of frilly trousers, like a little bantam cock.

But first they'll seize your bundle (if you have one) in a crack,
And tie it, with a tape, by way of bustle on your back;
And make your waist so high or low, your shape will be a riddle,
For anyhow you'll never have your middle in the middle.

Your little English sandals for a while will hold together,
But woe betide you when the stones have worn away the leather;
For they'll poke your little pettitoes (and there will be a hobble!)
In such a pair of shoes as none but carpenters can cobble!

You'll have to learn a *chou* is quite another sort of thing
To that you put your foot in; that a *belle* is not to ring;
That a *corne* is not the knubble that brings trouble to your toes,
Nor *peut-être* a potato, as some Irish folks suppose.

But pray, at meals, remember this, the French are so polite,
No matter what you eat and drink, 'whatever is, is right'!
So when you're told at dinner time that some delicious stew
Is cat instead of rabbit, you must answer, '*Tant mi-eux*'!

ELIZABETH BARRETT BROWNING
1806–1861

27   from *Aurora Leigh*

                              I mused
Up and down, up and down, the terraced streets,
The glittering boulevards, the white colonnades
Of fair fantastic Paris who wears trees
Like plumes, as if man made them, spire and tower
As if they had grown by nature, tossing up
Her fountains in the sunshine of the squares,
As if in beauty's game she tossed the dice,
Of blew the silver down-balls of her dreams
To sow futurity with seeds of thought
And count the passage of her festive hours.

The city swims in verdure, beautiful
As Venice on the waters, the sea-swan.
What bosky gardens dropped in close-walled courts
Like plums in ladies' laps who start and laugh:
What miles of streets that run on after trees,
Still carrying all the necessary shops,
Those open caskets with the jewels seen!
And trade is art, and art's philosophy,
In Paris. There's a silk for instance, there,
As worth an artist's study for the folds
As that bronze opposite! nay, the bronze has faults,
Art's here too artful,—conscious as a maid
Who leans to mark her shadow on the wall
Until she lose a vantage in her step.
Yet Art walks forward, and knows where to walk;
The artists also are idealists,
Too absolute for nature, logical
To austerity in the application of
The special theory,—not a soul content
To paint a crooked pollard and an ass,
As the English will because they find it so
And like it somehow.—There the old Tuileries
Is pulling its high cap down on its eyes,
Confounded, conscience-stricken, and amazed
By the apparition of a new fair face
In those devouring mirrors. Through the grate

Within the gardens, what a heap of babes,
Swept up like leaves beneath the chestnut-trees
From every street and alley of the town,
By ghosts perhaps that blow too bleak this way
A-looking for their heads! dear pretty babes,
I wish them luck to have their ball-play out
Before the next change. Here the air is thronged
With statues poised upon their columns fine,
As if to stand a moment were a feat,
Against that blue! What squares,—what breathing-room
For a nation that runs fast,—ay, runs against
The dentist's teeth at the corner in pale rows,
Which grin at progress, in an epigram.

I walked the day out, listening to the chink
Of the first Napoleon's bones in his second grave,
By victories guarded 'neath the golden dome
That caps all Paris like a bubble. 'Shall
These dry bones live?' thought Louis Philippe once,
And lived to know. Herein is argument
For kings and politicians, but still more
For poets, who bear buckets to the well
Of ampler draught.
                            These crowds are very good
For meditation (when we are very strong)
Though love of beauty makes us timorous,
And draws us backward from the coarse town-sights
To count the daisies upon dappled fields
And hear the streams bleat on among the hills
In innocent and indolent repose,
While still with silken elegiac thoughts
We wind out from us the distracting world
And die into the chrysalis of a man,
And leave the best that may, to come of us,
In some brown moth. I would be bold and bear
To look into the swarthiest face of things,
For God's sake who has made them.

WILLIAM MAKEPEACE THACKERAY
1811–1863

28   *The Ballad of Bouillabaisse*

A street there is in Paris famous,
   For which no rhyme our language yields,
Rue Neuve des Petits Champs its name is—
   The New Street of the Little Fields;
And here's an inn, not rich and splendid,
   But still in comfortable case;
The which in youth I often attended,
   To eat a bowl of Bouillabaisse.

This Bouillabaisse a noble dish is—
   A sort of soup or broth, or brew,
Or hotchpotch, of all sorts of fishes,
   That Greenwich never could outdo;
Green herbs, red peppers, mussels, saffern,
   Soles, onions, garlic, roach, and dace;
All these you eat at Terré's tavern,
   In that one dish of Bouillabaisse.

Indeed, a rich and savoury stew 'tis;
   And true philosophers, methinks,
Who love all sorts of natural beauties,
   Should love good victuals and good drinks.
And Cordelier or Benedictine
   Might gladly, sure, his lot embrace,
Nor find a fast-day too afflicting
   Which served him up a Bouillabaisse.

I wonder if the house still there is?
   Yes, here the lamp is, as before;
The smiling red-cheeked écaillère is
   Still opening oysters at the door.
Is Terré still alive and able?
   I recollect his droll grimace;
He'd come and smile before your table,
   And hope you liked your Bouillabaisse.

We enter—nothing's changed or older.
   'How's Monsieur Terré, waiter, pray?'
The waiter stares and shrugs his shoulder—
   'Monsieur is dead this many a day.'

'It is the lot of saint and sinner,
  So honest Terré's run his race!'
'What will Monsieur require for dinner?'
  'Say, do you still cook Bouillabaisse?'

'Oh, oui, Monsieur,' 's the waiter's answer;
  'Quel vin Monsieur désire-t-il?'
'Tell me a good one.'—'That I can, Sir:
  The Chambertin with yellow seal.'
'So Terré's gone,' I say, and sink in
  My old accustomed corner-place;
'He's done with feasting and with drinking,
  With Burgundy and Bouillabaisse.'

My old accustomed corner here is,
  The table still is in the nook;
Ah! vanished many a busy year is,
  This well-known chair since last I took.
When first I saw ye, *cari luoghi*,
  I'd scarce a beard upon my face,
And now a grizzled, grim old fogy,
  I sit and wait for Bouillabaisse.

Where are you, old companions trusty,
  Of early days, here met to dine?
Come, waiter! quick, a flagon crusty—
  I'll pledge them in the good old wine.
The kind old voices and old faces
  My memory can quick retrace;
Around the board they take their places,
  And share the wine and Bouillabaisse.

There's Jack has made a wondrous marriage;
  There's laughing Tom is laughing yet;
There's brave Augustus drives his carriage;
  There's poor old Fred in the Gazette;
On James's head the grass is growing:
  Good Lord! the world has wagged apace
Since here we set the Claret flowing,
  And drank, and ate the Bouillabaisse.

Ah me! how quick the days are flitting!
  I mind me of a time that's gone,
When here I'd sit, as now I'm sitting,
  In this same place—but not alone.

A fair young form was nestled near me,
　A dear, dear face looked fondly up,
And sweetly spoke and smiled to cheer me
　—There's no one now to share my cup.

*

I drink it as the Fates ordain it.
　Come, fill it, and have done with rhymes:
Fill up the lonely glass, and drain it
　In memory of dear old times.
Welcome the wine, whate'er the seal is;
　And sit you down and say your grace
With thankful heart, whate'er the meal is.
　—Here comes the smoking Bouillabaisse!

MATTHEW ARNOLD
1822–1888

29　　　　*Scenes from Carnac*

Far on its rocky knoll descried
Saint Michael's chapel cuts the sky.
I climbed; beneath me, bright and wide,
Lay the lone coast of Brittany.

Bright in the sunset, weird and still,
It lay beside the Atlantic wave,
As though the wizard Merlin's will
Yet charmed it from his forest-grave.

Behind me on their grassy sweep,
Bearded with lichen, scrawled and grey,
The giant stones of Carnac sleep,
In the mild evening of the May.

No priestly stern procession now
Moves through their rows of pillars old;
No victims bleed, no Druids bow—
Sheep make the daisied aisles their fold.

From bush to bush the cuckoo flies,
The orchis red gleams everywhere;
Gold furze with broom in blossom vies,
The blue-bells perfume all the air.

And o'er the glistening, lonely land,
Rise up, all round, the Christian spires;
The church of Carnac, by the strand,
Catches the westering sun's last fires.

And there, across the watery way,
See, low above the tide at flood,
The sickle-sweep of Quiberon Bay,
Whose beach once ran with loyal blood!

And beyond that, the Atlantic wide!
All round, no soul, no boat, no hail;
But, on the horizon's verge descried,
Hangs, touched with light, one snowy sail!

Ah! where is he, who should have come
Where that far sail is passing now,
Past the Loire's mouth, and by the foam
Of Finistère's unquiet brow,

Home, round into the English wave?
—He tarries where the Rock of Spain
Mediterranean waters lave;
He enters not the Atlantic main.

Oh, could he once have reached this air
Freshened by plunging tides, by showers!
Have felt this breath he loved, of fair
Cool northern fields, and grass, and flowers!

He longed for it—pressed on. In vain!
At the Straits failed that spirit brave.
The south was parent of his pain,
The south is mistress of his grave.

A. C. SWINBURNE

1837–1909

30   *'Insularum Ocelle'*

Sark, fairer than aught in the world that the lit skies cover,
Laughs inly behind her cliffs, and the seafarers mark
As a shrine where the sunlight serves, though the blown clouds hover,
    Sark.

We mourn, for love of a song that outsang the lark,
That nought so lovely beholden of Sirmio's lover
Made glad in Propontis the flight of his Pontic bark.

Here earth lies lordly, triumphal as heaven is above her,
And splendid and strange as the sea that upbears as an ark,
As a sign for the rapture of storm-spent eyes to discover,
    Sark.

AGNES MARY ROBINSON

1857–1944

31   *An Orchard at Avignon*

The hills are white, but not with snow:
    They are as pale in summer time,
For herb or grass may never grow
    Upon their slopes of lime.

Within the circle of the hills
    A ring, all flowering in a round,
An orchard-ring of almond fills
    The plot of stony ground.

More fair than happier trees, I think
    Grown in well-watered pasture land
These parched and stunted branches, pink
    Above the stones and sand.

O white, austere, ideal place,
    Where very few will care to come,
Where spring hath lost the waving grace
    She wears for us at home!

Fain would I sit and watch for hours
    The holy whiteness of thy hills,
Their wreath of pale auroral flowers,
    Their peace the silence fills.

A place of secret peace thou art,
    Such peace as in an hour of pain
One moment fills the amazèd heart,
    And never comes again.

30 Sirmio's lover] Catullus   Propontis] Sea of Marmara

SIR OWEN SEAMAN
1861–1936

32   *The Englishman on the French Stage*

When I'm in France, for Frenchmen's sake
   It it my rule to wear
What in their innocence they take
   To be a British air.

I like to feel, when our Allies
   My dress and manners scan,
That they can readily surmise,
   'There goes an Englishman.'

But, since they never cross the wave
   To get the facts correct—
How Englishmen this side behave,
   What suitings we affect—

I have to imitate the type
   Dear to the Paris stage,
Hallowed by humorous mimes and ripe
   With immemorial age.

In chequered tweeds I go all day,
   Loud stockings on my legs;
And for my early *déjeuner*
   I order ham and eggs.

On cheeks habitually nude
   Red whiskers I emplace,
And make my frontal teeth protrude
   Some way outside my face.

A kodak and a bright-red guide
   In either arm I hug,
As down the boulevard's length I stride,
   Emitting blasts of plug.

My hobnails on the pavement ring;
   My brogues are caked with loam;
I read *The Daily Tale*—a thing
   I rarely do at home.

Strange slang and unfamiliar oaths
    My conversation spice;
I ask for what my body loathes—
    A morning tub of ice.

When *gardiens* lift their voices high
    Some trespass to condemn,
To their gesticulations I
    Oppose a perfect phlegm.

Enfin (in fine), when I'm in France
    I try my best to do
In every sort of circumstance
    What they expect me to.

It keeps the Entente fresh and hot
    To recognize in me
Its unimpaired ideal of what
    An Englishman should be.

ARTHUR SYMONS
1865–1945

33   from *Scènes de la Vie de Bohème*
                  Episode of a Night of May

The coloured lanterns lit the trees, the grass,
The little tables underneath the trees,
And the rays dappled like a delicate breeze
    Each wine-illumined glass.

The pink light flickered, and a shadow ran
Along the ground as couples came and went;
The waltzing fiddles sounded from the tent,
    And *Giroflée* began.

They sauntered arm in arm, these two; the smiles
Grew chilly, as the best spring evenings do.
The words were warmer, but the words came few,
    And pauses fell at whiles.

33 *Giroflée*] refrain of a nursery song (Que t'as de belles filles / Giroflé, Girofla... Elles sont belles et gentilles / Giroflé, Girofla) also used as a dance tune

But she yawned prettily. 'Come then,' said he.
He found a chair, Veuve Clicquot, some cigars.
They emptied glasses and admired the stars,
    The lanterns, night, the sea,

Nature, the newest opera, the dog
(So clever) who could shoulder arms and dance;
He mentioned Alphonse Daudet's last romance,
    Last Sunday's river-fog,

Love, Immortality; the talk ran down
To these mere lees: they wearied each of each,
And tortured ennui into hollow speech,
    And yawned, to hide a frown.

She jarred his nerves; he bored her—and so soon.
Both were polite, and neither cared to say
The word that mars a perfect night of May.
    They watched the waning moon.

CHARLOTTE MEW
1869–1928

34   *Le Sacré-Cœur*

(Montmartre)

It is dark up here on the heights,
    Between the dome and the stars it is quiet too,
While down there under the crowded lights
    Flares the importunate face of you,
Dear Paris of the hot white hands, the scarlet lips, the scented hair,
    Une jolie fille à vendre, très cher;
    A thing of gaiety, a thing of sorrow,
    Bought to-night, possessed, and tossed
    Back to the mart again to-morrow,
        Worth and over, what you cost;
While half your charm is that you are
Withal, like some unpurchasable star,
    So old, so young and infinite and lost.

It is dark on the dome-capped hill,
    Serenely dark, divinely still,

Yet here is the Man who bought you first
    Dying of his immortal smart,
Your Lover, the King with the broken heart,
    Who while you, feasting, drink your fill,
        Pass round the cup
        Not looking up,
Calls down to you, 'I thirst.'

'A king with a broken heart! *Mon Dieu!*
    One breaks so many, *cela peut se croire*,
To remember all *c'est la mer à boire*,
    And the first, *mais comme c'est vieux.*
Perhaps there is still some keepsake—or
    One has possibly sold it for a song:
On ne peut pas toujours pleurer les morts,
    And this One—He has been dead so long!'

AUBREY BEARDSLEY
1872–1898

35   *The Three Musicians*

Along the path that skirts the wood,
    The three musicians wend their way,
Pleased with their thoughts, each other's mood,
    Franz Himmel's latest roundelay,
The morning's work, a new-found theme, their breakfast and the
    summer day.

One's a soprano, lightly frocked
    In cool white muslin that just shows
Her brown silk stockings gaily clocked,
    Plump arms and elbows tipped with rose,
And frills of petticoats and things, and outlines as the warm wind
    blows.

Beside her a slim, gracious boy
    Hastens to mend her tresses' fall,
And dies her favour to enjoy,
    And dies for *réclame* and recall
At Paris and St Petersburgh, Vienna and St James's Hall.

---

35 soprano] Beardsley's 'heroine', as he called her, is modelled on the German pianist
Sophie Menter, 1846–1918

The third's a Polish Pianist
　　With big engagements everywhere,
A light heart and an iron wrist.
　　And shocks and shoals of yellow hair,
And fingers that can trill on sixths and fill beginners with despair.

The three musicians stroll along
　　And pluck the ears of ripened corn,
Break into odds and ends of song,
　　And mock the woods with Siegfried's horn,
And fill the air with Gluck, and fill the tweeded tourist's soul with
　　　scorn.

The Polish genius lags behind,
　　And, with some poppies in his hand,
Picks out the strings and wood and wind
　　Of an imaginary band,
Enchanted that for once his men obey his beat and understand.

The charming cantatrice reclines
　　And rests a moment where she sees
Her château's roof that hotly shines
　　Amid the dusky summer trees,
And fans herself, half shuts her eyes, and smoothes the frock about her
　　　knees.

The gracious boy is at her feet,
　　And weighs his courage with his chance;
His fears soon melt in noonday heat.
　　The tourist gives a furious glance,
Red as his guide-book grows, moves on, and offers up a prayer for
　　　France.

JAMES ELROY FLECKER

1884–1915

36　　　　　　　*Rioupéroux*

　　High and solemn mountains guard Rioupéroux
　　—Small untidy village where the river drives a mill—
　　Frail as wood anemones, white and frail were you,
　　And drooping a little, like the slender daffodil.

36 Rioupéroux] south-east of Grenoble in the department of Isère

O I will go to France again, and tramp the valley through,
And I will change these gentle clothes for clog and corduroy,
And work with the mill-hands of black Rioupéroux,
And walk with you, and talk with you, like any other boy.

IVOR GURNEY
1890–1937

37   *Tobacco Plant*

We wondered at the tobacco plants there in France
And hung on the rafters brown where our bacon hangs
Sunny in the clear light autumn wind a-dance;
Or to be looked at upwards in its dry ranks,
But the wonder more when in cold nights fumes arose
From the hidden bags, and the frost a moment grew less.

'What! you love smoking, indeed?' he said, and I
Spoke with love of Virginia and Egypt, but not a
Good word for tobacco issue wherever given
And the talk passed to my love of the dear French heaven,
Her people, her soldiers, her books, music and lovely land.
Speaking broken French he could hardly easily understand,
Until I spoke of Daudet, whose book I loved
And of Ronsard, Molière, others, the *Journals* that proved
Friendly enough in that news-lacking and forlorn land.
Talking of all my love, all, in forlorn exile.

Till, looking up in the comfort of that fire-warm room
I saw the tobacco plants—brown leaves on the beams
Reminding gratitude of tobacco's never-ending boon,
Happy to see the leaf, after the smoked thing in gleams
Whirling white puffs contented to the ceiling's gloom.
And thank the gods for one thing in these damned extremes,
And his man's friendliness so good to have, and lost so soon.

WILFRED OWEN
1893—1918

38   *Hospital Barge at Cérisy*

Budging the sluggard ripples of the Somme,
A barge round old Cérisy slowly slewed.
Softly her engines down the current screwed
And chuckled in her, with contented hum.

Till fairy tinklings struck their croonings dumb.
The waters rumpling at the stern subdued.
The lock-gate took her bulging amplitude.
Gently from out the gurgling lock she swum.

One reading by that sunset raised his eyes
To watch her lessening westward quietly,
Till, as she neared the bend, her funnel screamed.

And that long lamentation made him wise
How unto Avalon, in agony,
Kings passed in the dark barge, which Merlin dreamed.

ROY CAMPBELL
1901–1957

39   *Horses on the Camargue*

To A. F. Tschiffely

In the grey wastes of dread,
The haunt of shattered gulls where nothing moves
But in a shroud of silence like the dead,
I heard a sudden harmony of hooves,
And, turning, saw afar
A hundred snowy horses unconfined,
The silver runaways of Neptune's car
Racing, spray-curled, like waves before the wind.

---

38 Cérisy] Cerisy-la-Forêt, situated between Bayeux and Saint-Lô in north-west France

Sons of the Mistral, fleet
As him with whose strong gusts they love to flee,
Who shod the flying thunders on their feet
And plumed them with the snortings of the sea;
Theirs is no earthly breed
Who only haunt the verges of the earth
And only on the sea's salt herbage feed—
Surely the great white breakers gave them birth.
For when for years a slave,
A horse of the Camargue, in alien lands,
Should catch some far-off fragrance of the wave
Carried far inland from his native sands,
Many have told the tale
Of how in fury, foaming at the rein,
He hurls his rider; and with lifted tail,
With coal-red eyes and cataracting mane,
Heading his course for home,
Though sixty foreign leagues before him sweep,
Will never rest until he breathes the foam
And hears the native thunder of the deep.
But when the great gusts rise
And lash their anger on these arid coasts,
When the scared gulls career with mournful cries
And whirl across the waste like driven ghosts:
When hail and fire converge,
The only souls to which they strike no pain
Are the white-crested fillies of the surge
And the white horses of the windy plain.
Then in their strength and pride
The stallions of the wilderness rejoice;
They feel their Master's trident in their side,
And high and shrill they answer to his voice.
With white tails smoking free,
Long streaming manes, and arching necks, they show
Their kinship to their sisters of the sea—
And forward hurl their thunderbolts of snow.
Still out of hardship bred,
Spirits of power and beauty and delight
Have ever on such frugal pastures fed
And loved to course with tempests through the night.

Camargue] a great plain at the mouth of the Rhône used for grazing by wild horses and cattle
trident] Neptune's trident and the trident used by the stewards of the Camargue

GEOFFREY GRIGSON
1905–1985

40 *Discoveries of Bones and Stones*

I

Certain bones are from other bones distinguished
as not being common bones,
such as plesiosaurus bones, or the skull
in this plain deal cupboard
(plug inserted, as a notice directs,
so that I see this skull's brown regularity) of
my name-saint—supposing my parents had
thought that way—of at any rate Geoffroi
Abbot of Savigny,[1] founder or may be promoter
of Fountains in our country and Furness.[2]

This uncommon cranium (with a piece of the shirt
of Thomas of Canterbury) I find—how it pours—
in a modern church, having stopped to ring
the ferry over the Manche, which he crossed more slowly,
in case there's a strike.

Such is the casualness of discovery.

II

On this same journey, inspired by that gentle
regularity of the cranium of my more or less
name-saint, I have, on the other hand, since tried to see
the uncommon skull of St Aubert;
a peculiarity more celebrated into which
Michael Archangel, Provost of Heaven,
stuck his annoyed finger leaving a hole, to remind
Aubert to build on that hoar rock in the waters
which Victor Hugo has named Cheops of the West.

But the sacristan was on holiday. No one
had the key.

---

[1] Elected Abbot in 1122.
[2] Both Cistercian foundations from Savigny.

---

that hoar rock] Mont-Saint-Michel

III

Also at Gruchy where dung among granite
persists, where sea, down, far down a pack animal's lane
between hills, between nettles
is a palpable vee of his blue, I find
the site of the natal home, as announced
by a rusty notice, of
Angelus Millet.

   Having just been pulled down, grey granite
stones lie around, which enclosed you, Master of
blue unexpected in squalor of sabots.

IV

Do not expect about these discoveries
conclusions or comments; on texts such as, pieties wear out,
Mister Order of Merit,
be the stones or the bones of the matter
never so uncommon; such as, works—Furness,
Mont-Saint-Michel, or the Angelus even—are better
than bones or a scatter of stones. Or, bones in
live flesh are better than scattered dry bones. Or
of course, all bones are bones.

W. R. RODGERS
1909–1969

41   *Summer Journey*

Now it's July, hot and sleepy and still;
The noontide hanging motionless over the hill
Like a pike in a pool. And the glossy flies
Are flashing like great sun-whips across the eyes.
Summer is at its height,
The hastening season halted in its flight,
Its fans fixed.
And here we are in the Pays-Basque, travelling through Soule,
Labourd, and Basse-Navarre—names more musical to me
Than musk or kumiss or mangosteen.
Guéthary where the Atlantic curled in and cauliflowered up,
And the lightning jagged the sky like icicles:
Bidarry in the evening, the vines veining the hillside,

And the hills drawn up over our heads like shawls.
And us talking all night of war and Resistance.
Remember the Pyrenees, with their hundred double-chins,
Remember Soure, the sheep bells on the road,
And the panniered donkeys; the smuggler's path to Spain,
And the lovely inns; the meal at Mauléon;
The mayor's home-made liquor at Ustaritz
That Sunday afternoon. O
Remember the people so kind: remember the night you got blind
On Pernod?
And remember those great sleepy houses with their wide and wavy
    roofs
That cover cattle and people and wine and copper pans:
Houses eyelashed and shuttered against the summer heat,
Blindly white outside but with nests of darkness in them
As reticent and withdrawn as the Basques with their thin-pursed lips.
Slow country, rooted in resistance, not in rest.
Slow over the wall the fat peaches fall.
Slowly across the all-absorbing fields
Collusive move the peasant and his plough.
And slowly down the street the ox comes now
With winking bell. How it gives one the feel
Of the creaking cart and the ever-turning wheel.
Slow country, but quick people. What's so gay
As the little Basque drum tipping and tapping away
To the agile pipe that wriggles about like an eel.
Remember the group who sang in the café that day?
And the village fête on Sunday where we saw
The circle of life complete, saw the day
Turn from morning to night, from light to grey,
And the people counterwise from grave to gay,
From church to dance and then from dance to play.
Sunday morning, seven by the clock,
And the village silent except for the cock
Ricochetting far away: and over the roof
Are the dark Pyrenees, overweening and aloof
As ever. A boy comes into the square
And a pigeon rises and flashes the rosy air.
Never was morning so clear. And one by one
A rope of bees bubbles up into the sun.
A bell is calling the people to early Mass,
The doors open, I watch the church-goers pass
To where within the ancient womb
A blaze of incense and a bloom
Of candles ring the bridegroom-priest
Who bodies forth the Mystery
That has been all men's history:

Two thousand years behind him say
This is as it was in our day.
O how the grounded women sing
To galleried men all answering
As heaven answers earth.
Voice marries voice as if by choice;
And so the ancient circle's closed, the service done. See, there,
The man with the basket of plants outside the church,
Selling them to the farmers. But they leave him in the lurch;
They are eager to follow the band across the churchyard green
To the yellow Presbytery house, shaded by chestnuts and limes
And dappled by light, where numberless times
They have come about birth and death. But today they are free
To celebrate in a dance the curé's jubilee.
And now the red-sashed dancers, looking so cool and so clean,
Form themselves into a figure. The drummer wipes
His brow and begins to tap, and a young priest pipes.
And the curé comes out on the steps and smiles to see them so keen.
Yes. This morning the world went into the church.
Now the church comes into the world. So,
In life we oppose and appease each other.
And under the gentle trees the crowd gathers thicker and faster,
And a red setter dog looks everywhere for the curé, his master.
Now bright before our glance
Comes forth each white-clad mummer
To figure forth in a dance
The rise and fall of summer,
Needle-pipe and thimble-drum
Leading the way to kingdom-come.
Still oozes the old wound
The summer Prince is slain,
His blood's the poppy seed
That will rise up again
To fill the winter fields with newly-springing grain.
Afternoon, late afternoon, and the sun still hot,
As we cross the square. And all the houses have
A hat of plane-tree leaves pulled over their eyes
Against the light. But what a buzz and a fuzz
Of people are gathered to watch the *pelota*.
We can hear the *pock* of the ball against the great curved wall
Behind the church. And now we can see the players
With the basket-claws on their hands, scooping
And pawing the ball. A priest is swooping
Among them in magpie flight. He plays
In his long black robe; the others in white,
Sweeping like swallows across the court in the evening light.
Tiers on tiers of people are 'oh-ing!' and 'ah-ing!',

Watching and greeting with cries the well-placed shot.
How they mouth-in each move and stop of the ball!
And the cobbler is singing the score. The people cheer
The winning ball, and the band blares out 'all clear'.
And now the bubbling crowd boils over on to the court
To dance the evening through, until their throats are dry,
Dancing to the pipe and the little titupping drum.
And in the dusky cafés the lads and girls may be talking,
But as soon as the little drum blinks, all the talk goes blank;
A curly catching tune, and their trigger-feet are off
In a flash from the shadowy gloom,
Lads with billowing shirts, and girls with willowy skirts
Slanting along the street, linking hands as they go
In a fine kite-tail procession; or twirling toe to toe,
Weaving a wicker-work figure round all who won't give room.
And the listening moon comes up and looks down on the dizzy scene,
On the dancers flitting like moths round the group at the café table
Where two old dignified men are battling over a bottle
Twisting in wordy wedlock like eels all ready to throttle.
Outlay and intake of breath, rise and fall
Of a season, ins and outs of a dance.
Happy people. No greed for tomorrow
Greys your face like frost. O
May all your valleys be fat
With wine, and full be every vat.

DAVID HOLBROOK

1923–

42   *A Day in France*

' *'Sieurs et dames!'* and the door slams:
I stand gawping. *'Qu'est ce que monsieur désire?'*
Nothing: I want nothing but to look at the bread,
The big sticks, *les baguettes, les ficelles,*
Les croissants. I just want to stand here
And smell the smell of France, and study
The culture of *le boulanger*: when I get my breath
I buy a loaf and three strawberry boats.

I am enraptured, because I understand every word.

We sit and drink two coffees: a ton of ice
Hisses slowly from a lorry into a fishing boat.

Between us and the quay, the Paris train
Trundles along the dock, suddenly crushes
The motor scooter of a wretched schoolboy
Who has left it too near the track: drama!
His mother, waitress in a waterfront café,
Threatens to ding him: everyone shakes their heads.
We are in distress for the boy who, ruefully,
Examines his buckled wheels; *tout le monde*
Gives him advice. End of act one, scene three.

Now we are on Dieppe beach: on the pebbles,
A bottle of Muscadet, a portion of *frites*,
Pâté de campagne, bread, goat cheese and cherries.
I do not want to do anything else in life
Except to sit on these grey stones, madly in love,
And eat this picnic, and stare at the slack grey sea.

At one point on the crossing we could see both coasts,
Boulogne and Dover: hardly a stone's throw away
This other world, of the cheap bowls of *moules*,
Mackerel really rainbowed, and crabs still alive
Stirring grotesquely as the housewives handle them:
Escargots de mer, *bulots*, and a huge turbot:
Endless street markets of live crated chickens,
Hundreds of snails crawling over the basket
And garlic as big as your fist.

                    At noon
As I am painting a cemetery on the cliffs
A bell with a dreadful resonance sounds the Angelus,
The sound of French continuity humming out over the sea.
The great hum embraces me and I hear the angels: it tells me
I must die, and I weep respectfully among the graves.

As I pack up, a girl is waiting for her lover:
As the afternoon declines he arrives, handsome, on a bicycle.

At last, after a struggle with the wobbly *bidet*,
In *le cabinet de toilette*, we lay our heads on the long bolster
Listening to the thin vowel sounds of the lighthouse foghorn.

GILLIAN CLARKE

1937–

43

from *A Journal from France*

Seamstress at St. Léon

As we eat crushed strawberry ice
under a bee-heavy vine
we watch for the seamstress to come.
Through the open doorway we hear
her chatter, see her Singers
glint with gold roses in the dark room.

Embroidery cloths abandoned
at the roadside table; a weir
of lace falls from her chair; silks
spill blossoming from a basket.
Under its turning ribbon of gauze
her tea cools in a white cup.

She sings in the dark interior.
From the sills of the gardenless house
fuchsia and geranium blaze.
Her windows are framed with French knots,
the cracks seeded with lazy daisy.
Her rubber plant reaches the eaves.

Nothing troubles the afternoon dust
or breaks the tenor of bees
but her counterpoint. Out of sight
in their web of scaffolding
under the bridge, workmen whistle
and a hammer rings over water.

A fan of shadow slowly includes us.
Her tea is cold. Imperceptibly
the thicket of roses grows closer.
We make out the sinuous gilding
of sewing machines, vine leaves, stems
and iron tendrils of their treadles.

St. Léon] a small town on the river Vézère south of Périgueux

Lace glimmerings at dusk. A foam
of linen, flowers, silences.
Sunlight has flowed from her sills
of yellow stone. Bats are shuttling
their delicate black silks to mesh
that dark doorway on her absence.

IBERIA

ANONYMOUS

*c.*1425

44   *The Way to Jerusalem*

By younde the Brugge on thi right hand,
To Sent Salvator the waie is liggand,
Where ii. pottez may thou se,
In the wiche water turnet to vyn at Architriclyne.
And mony other reliquez ben there,
But the mountez ben wonder he, & fere.
Wymmen in that land use no vullen,
But alle in lether be thei wounden:
And her hevedez wonderly ben trust,
Standing in her forhemed as a crest,
In rowld clouthez lappet alle be forn
Like to the prikke of a n'unicorn.
And men have doubelettez full schert,
Bare legget and light to stert.
A knight, a boie wit out hose,
A sqwyer also thei schull not lose.
A knave bere iii. dartez in his hand,
And so thei schull go walkand:
Here wyn is thecke as any blode,
And that wull make men wode.
Bedding ther is nothing faire,
Mony pilgrimez hit doth apaire:
Tabelez use thei non of to ete,
But on the bare flore they make her sete:
And so they sitte alle infere,
As in Irlande the same manere.
Then from the citee of Lyonz so fre,
On thi lyft hand the waie schalt thou see,

At that Brugge that I of have saide,
Over an heethe to Astergo is layde.
That is a cite and faire is sette,
There the gret mountaines togeder be mette:
And so forthe to Villa Frank schalt thou go,
A faire contraye, and vinez also.
The raspis groeth ther in thi waie.
Yf thee lust thou maie asaie.
From thennez a deepe dale schalt thou have,
Up unto the Mount of Fave.
He hullez, and of the Spanyse see a(s)cry:
That noyse is full grevose pardy.
And so forth even to Sent Jamez,
Alle waie pylgrimez suche havez,
And then to Mount nostre Dame,
The prior ther hath muche schame.
And then so forthe to Luaon,
Other villagez ther be mony oon.
And then to Sent Jamez that holy place;
There maie thou fynde full faire grace.
On this side the toune milez too,
By a chappell schalt thou go:
Upon a hull hit stondez on hee,
Where Sent Jamez ferst schalt thou see.

[At León] the way to Salvatierra lies over the bridge on your right hand. In Salvatierra you can see two jars in which the water turned to wine at Architriclyne, as well as many other relics. The mountains are amazingly high and remote. In that place women don't wear wool, but are completely swathed in leather: and their heads are strangely trussed with a rolled cloth all coiled up in front, which sticks out in a crest from their foreheads like the horn of a unicorn. Men have very short doublets and are bare-legged, lightly attired for running: (?) a knight is just a fellow without stockings, (??) and they don't honour a squire any better either. Lads will go around carrying three darts in their hand. Their wine is as thick as blood and makes men wild. The beds there are foul and discomfort many pilgrims. The people do not eat at tables, but settle themselves on the bare ground, all sitting together in the same way as they do in Ireland.

Coming from the noble city of León, at the bridge I have already mentioned you will see on your left hand the way that runs over the heath to Astorga; this city is beautifully set at the spot where great mountains meet. And then you will go on to Villafranca del Bierzo, a lovely area with vines and sweet wine grapes growing along the road: you can try them if you want to. From there you must follow a deep valley up to the Mount of Fave, high hills (?) from where you will catch sight of the Spanish Sea, whose reputation, God knows, is so terrible. And it will be like this as far as Santiago de Compostela—(?) pilgrims will have such terrain all the way. Next you go to the convent of Mount Notre Dame, whose prior is quite disgraced; and then on to Lugo, and many other villages; finally to Santiago de Compostela, that holy place of St James: may you there be blessed with the grace of God. Go to a chapel standing up high on a hill two miles this side of town, from which you will first see Santiago . . .

trans. by Nicolette Zeeman

ANONYMOUS
mid 15th century

45   *The Pilgrims' Sea Voyage and Seasickness*

Men may leue alle gamys,
That saylen to seynt Jamys!
Ffor many a man hit gramys,
    When they begyn to sayle.
Ffor when they hauve take the see,
At Sandwyche, or at Wynchylsee.
At Brystow, or where that hit bee.
    Theyr hertes begyn to fayle.

Anone the mastyr commaundeth fast
To hys shyp-men in alle the hast,
To dresse hem sone about the mast,
    Theyr takelyng to make.
With 'howe! hissa!' then they cry,
'What, howe, mate! thow stondyst to ny,
Thy felow may nat hale the by';
    Thus they begyn to crake.

A boy or tweyn anone up styen,
And ouerthwart the sayle-yerde lyen;—
'Y how! taylia!' the remenaunt cryen,
    And pulle with alle theyr myght.
'Bestowe the boote, bote-swayne, anon,
That our pylgryms may pley theron;
For som ar lyke to cowgh and grone
    Or hit be full mydnyght.

'Hale the bowelyne! now, vere the shete!—
Cooke, make redy anoon our mete,
Our pylgryms haue no lust to ete,
    I pray god yeue hem rest!'
'Go to the helm! what, howe! no nere?
Steward, felow! A pot of bere!'
'Ye shalle have, sir, with good chere,
    Anon alle of the best.'

'Y howe! trussa! hale in the brayles!
Thow halyst nat, be god, thow fayles!
O se howe welle owre good shyp sayles!'
    And thus they say among.
'Hale in the wartake!' 'Hit shal be done.'
'Steward! couer the boorde anone,
And set bred and salt thereone,
    And tary nat to long.'

Then cometh oone and seyth, 'be mery;
Ye shall haue a storme or a pery.'
'Holde thow thy pese! thow canst no whery,
    Thow medlyst wondyr sore.'
Thys mene whyle the pylgryms ly,
And haue theyr bowlys fast theym by,
And cry aftyr hote maluesy,
    'Thow helpe for to restore.'

And som wold haue a saltyd tost,
Ffor they myght ete neyther sode ne rost;
A man myght sone pay for theyr cost,
    As for oo day or twayne.
Some layde theyr bookys on theyr kne,
And rad so long they myght nat se;—
'Allas! myne hede wolle cleue on thre!'
    Thus seyth another certayne.

Then commeth owre owner lyke a lorde.
And speketh many a royall worde,
And dresseth hym to the hygh borde,
    To see alle thyng be welle.
Anone he calleth a carpentere,
And byddyth hym bryng with hym hys gere,
To make the cabans here and there,
    With many a febylle celle;

A sak of strawe were there ryght good,
Ffor som must lyg theym in theyr hood;
I had as lefe be in the wood,
    Without mete or drynk;
For when that we shall go to bedde,
The pumpe was nygh oure beddes hede,
A man were as good to be dede
    As smell thereof the stynk!

There are not many laughs for those that sail to Santiago de Compostela! For when they set sail a good number of them are sorry; once on board at Sandwich, Winchelsea, Bristol or wherever it is, their spirits begin to fail them.

Then the captain firmly orders his sailors to hurry and get ready at the mast so that they can raise the rigging right away. 'Heave ho,' they shout then; 'Look out, friend, you're standing too close, your mate hasn't room to pull,' they bawl.

One or two lads climb up and lie across the sailyard—'Heave! Pull up the lee-ropes!' the rest shout and haul with all their strength. 'Now, boatswain, get the boat ready so that the pilgrims can have a bit of fun, for some look set to be throwing up and groaning before even midnight's here.

Pull in the bowline! Now let out the skeat-ropes!'—'Cook, get our food ready for us: our pilgrims here have no desire to eat, God rest them!' See to the tiller! Hold on! No closer to the wind? Steward, mate, a pint!' 'Sir, you'll have the best right away, with pleasure.'

'Heave ho! furl in the sail! Haul up the brail-ropes! You're not pulling, by God, you're not doing your bit! Ah, see how she blows!'—and they go on like this all the time. 'Pull in the clews!' 'Right away.' 'Steward, spread the table at once, put out bread and salt, and don't be too long about it.'

Then somebody comes along and says 'Look cheerful—there's going to be a storm or a squall.' 'Shut your mouth! You don't know anything—this is interference all right.' In the meanwhile the pilgrims are lying with their bowls close beside them and shouting for hot Malmsey—'Oh that you would make us better.'

And one wants a piece of salted toast, since they can't eat meat, whether boiled or roasted; you might easily pay the costs for them for a day or two. Some set books on their knees and read until they can't see any more; 'It's dreadful! My head's going to split in three!' says another.

Then in a lordly manner the ship owner appears, talking like royalty, and he goes to the top deck to see that everything is well. Calling a carpenter, he tells him to bring his tools and build berths and a lot of flimsy cabins at regular intervals.

A sack of straw there would be a real blessing, for some have to lie in no more than their hoods; I would rather be in the wilds without food or drink;

for when we have to go to bed it turns out that the bilge-pump is just by our
bedhead—and you might as well be dead as smell that stink!

trans. by Nicolette Zeeman

THOMAS DELONEY
?1560–1600

46   *The Winning of Cales*

Long had the proud Spaniard advanced to conquer us,
    Threatening our country with fire and sword;
Often preparing their navy most sumptuous
    With all the provision Spain could afford.
        Dub a dub, dub a dub, thus strikes the drums:
        Tantara, tantara, Englishmen comes.

To the seas presently went our lord admiral,
    With knights courageous and captains full good;
The Earl of Essex, a prosperous general,
    With him prepared to pass the salt flood.
        Dub a dub, etc.

At Plymouth speedily, took they ship valiantly,
    Braver ships never were seen under sail,
With their fair colours spread, and streamers o'er their head
    Now bragging Spaniards, take heed of your tale.
        Dub a dub, etc.

Unto Cales cunningly, came we most happily,
    Where the king's navy did secretly ride;
Being upon their backs, piercing their butts of sack,
    Ere that the Spaniard our coming described.
        Tantara-rara, Englishmen comes,
        bounce-abounce, bounce-abounce, off went the guns.

Great was the crying, the running and riding,
    Which at that season was made in that place;
The beacons were fired, as need was required;
    To hide their great treasure they had little space.
        Dub a dub, dub a dub, thus strikes the drums:
        Alas they cried, Englishmen comes.

46 Cales] Cadiz   lord admiral] Lord Howard

There you might see their ships, how they were fired fast,
   And how their men drowned themselves in the sea;
There might you hear them cry, wail and weep piteously,
   When they saw no shift to 'scape thence away.
     Dub a dub, etc.

The great *St Philip*, the pride of the Spaniards,
   Was burnt to the bottom, and sunk in the sea;
But the *St Andrew*, and eke the *St Matthew*,
   We took in fight manly and brought them away.
     Dub a dub, etc.

The Earl of Essex, most valiant and hardy,
   With horsemen and footmen marched towards the town;
The enemies which saw them, full greatly affrighted,
   Did fly for their saveguard, and durst not come down.
     Dub a dub, etc.

'Now,' quoth the noble Earl, 'courage my soldiers all,
   Fight and be valiant, the spoil you shall have;
And be well rewarded all from the great to the small;
   But look that the women and children you save.'
     Dub a dub, etc.

The Spaniards at that sight, saw 'twas in vain to fight,
   Hung up their flags of truce, yielding the town;
We marched in presently, decking the walls on high,
   With our English colours which purchase renown.
     Dub a dub, etc.

Entering the houses then, of the most richest men,
   For gold and treasure we searched each day;
In some places we did find, pies baking in the oven,
   Meat at the fire roasting, and men run away.
     Dub a dub, etc.

Full of rich merchandise, every shop we did see:
   Damasks and satins and velvet full fair;
Which soldiers measured out by the length of their swords;
   Of all commodities each had a share.
     Dub a dub, etc.

Thus Cales was taken, and our brave general
   Marched to the market-place, there he did stand:
There many prisoners of good account were took:
   Many craved mercy, and mercy they found.
     Dub a dub, etc.

When as our brave General saw they delayed time,
And would not ransom the town as they said,
With their fair wainscots, their presses and bedsteads,
Their joint-stools and tables a fire we made;
And when the town burnt in a flame,
With tara, tantara, from thence we came.

WILLIAM MICKLE
1735–1788

47   *Sonnet on Passing the Bridge of Alcantra, near Lisbon,*

where Camoens is reported to have chosen his Station, when Age and Necessity compelled him to beg his daily Sustenance

Oft as at pensive eve I pass the brook
Where Lisboa's Maro, old and suppliant, stood,
Fancy, his injured eld and sorrows rude
Brought to my view. 'Twas night: with cheerless look
Methought he bowed the head in languid mood,
As pale with penury in darkling nook
Forlorn he watched. Sudden the skies partook
A mantling blaze, and warlike forms intrude.
Here Gama's semblance braves the boiling main,
And Lusitania's warriors hurl the spear;
But whence that flood of light that bids them rear
Their lofty brows! From thy neglected strain,
Camoens, unseen by vulgar eye it flows;
That glorious blaze, to thee, thy thankless country owes.

48   from *Almada Hill: An Epistle from Lisbon*

While you, my friend, from louring wintry plains
Now pale with snows, now black with drizzling rains,
From leafless woodlands, and dishonoured bowers
Mantled by gloomy mists, or lashed by showers
Of hollow moan, while not a struggling beam
Steals from the sun to play on Isis' stream;

---

47 Camoens] Luis de Camões (c. 1524–1580)   Maro] Virgil (Publius Vergilius Maro)
Gama] The great explorer Vasco da Gama is the hero of Camões's epic *Os Lusíadas*

While from these scenes by England's winter spread
Swift to the cheerful hearth your steps are led,
Pleased from the threatening tempest to retire
And join the circle round the social fire;
In other clime through sun-basked scenes I stray,
As the fair landscape leads my thoughtful way,
As upland path, oft winding, bids me rove
Where orange bowers invite, or olive grove,
No sullen phantoms brooding o'er my breast,
The genial influence of the clime I taste;
Yet still regardful of my native shore,
In every scene, my roaming eyes explore,
Whate'er its aspect, still, by memory brought,
My fading country rushes on my thought.

While now perhaps the classic page you turn,
And warmed with honest indignation burn,
'Til hopeless, sicklied by the climate's gloom,
Your generous fears call forth Britannia's doom,
What hostile spears her sacred lawns invade,
By friends deserted, by her chiefs betrayed,
Low fall'n and vanquished!—I, with mind serene
As Lisboa's sky, yet pensive as the scene
Around, and pensive seems the scene to me,
From other ills my country's fate foresee.

Not from the hands that wield Iberia's spear,
Not from the hands that Gaul's proud thunders bear,
Nor those that turn on Albion's breast the sword
Beat down of late by Albion when it gored
Their own, who impious doom their parent's fall
Beneath the world's great foe th' insidious Gaul;
Yes, not from these the immedicable wound
Of Albion—other is the bane profound
Destined alone to touch her mortal part;
Herself is sick and poisoned at the heart.

O'er Tago's banks where'er I roll mine eyes
The gallant deeds of ancient days arise;
The scenes the Lusian Muses fond displayed
Before me oft, as oft at eve I strayed
By Isis' hallowed stream. Oft now the strand
Where Gama marched his death-devoted[1] band,
While Lisboa awed with horror saw him spread
The daring sails that first to India led;

---

[1] 'The expedition of Vasco de Gama, the discoverer of the East-Indies, was extremely unpopular, as it was esteemed impracticable' (W.M.).

And oft Almada's castled steep inspires
The pensive Muse's visionary fires;
Almada Hill to English memory dear,
While shades of English heroes wander here!

   To ancient English valour sacred still
Remains, and ever shall, Almada Hill;
The hill and lawns to English valour given
What time the Arab Moors from Spain were driven,
Before the banners of the Cross subdued,
When Lisboa's towers were bathed in Moorish blood
By Gloster's lance.[2]—Romantic days that yield
Of gallant deeds a wide luxuriant field
Dear to the Muse that loves the fairy plains
Where ancient honour wild and ardent reigns.

   Where high o'er Tago's flood Almada lours,
Amid the solemn pomp of mouldering towers
Supinely seated, wide and far around
My eye delighted wanders.—Here the bound
Of fair Europa o'er the ocean rears
Its western edge; where dimly disappears
The Atlantic wave, the slow descending day
Mild beaming pours serene the gentle ray
Of Lusitania's winter, silvering o'er
The tower-like summits of the mountain shore;
Dappling the lofty cliffs that coldly throw
Their sable horrors o'er the vales below.
Far round the stately-shouldered river bends
Its giant arms, and sea-like wide extends
Its midland bays, with fertile islands crowned,
And lawns for English valour still renowned:
Given to Cornwallia's gallant sons of yore,
Cornwallia's name the smiling pastures bore;
And still their Lord his English lineage boasts
From Roland famous in the Croisade hosts.
Where seaward narrower rolls the shining tide
Through hills by hills embosomed on each side,
Monastic walls in every glen arise
In coldest white fair glistening to the skies
Amid the brown-browed rocks; and, far as sight,
Proud domes and villages arrayed in white
Climb o'er the steeps, and through the dusky green
Of olive groves, and orange bowers between,

---

[2] In 1147 Robert, Duke of Gloucester, on his way with English and Flemish crusaders to
Syria, helped Alphonso I lay siege to Moorish Lisbon; Alphonso gave him the castle of Almada
and the adjoining lands in gratitude.

Speckled with glowing red, unnumbered gleam—
And Lisboa towering o'er the lordly stream
Her marble palaces and temples spreads
Wildly magnific o'er the loaded heads
Of bending hills, along whose high-piled base
The port capacious, in a mooned embrace,
Throws her mast-forest, waving on the gale
The vanes of every shore that hoists the sail.

Here while the sun from Europe's breast retires.
Let fancy, roaming as the scene inspires,
Pursue the present and the past restore,
And Nature's purpose in her steps explore.

ROBERT SOUTHEY
1774–1843

49   *Recollections of a Day's Journey in Spain*[1]

Not less delighted do I call to mind,
Land of romance! thy wild and lovely scenes,
Than I beheld them first. Pleased I retrace
With memory's eye the placid Minho's course,
And catch its winding waters gleaming bright
Amid the broken distance. I review
Leon's wide wastes, and heights precipitous,
Seen with a pleasure not unmixed with dread,
As the sagacious mules along the brink
Wound patiently and show their way secure;
And rude Galicia's hovels, and huge rocks
And mountains, where, when all beside was dim,
Dark and broad-headed the tall pines erect
Rose on the farthest eminence distinct,
Cresting the evening sky.
                              Rain now falls thick,
And damp and heavy is the unwholesome air;
I by this friendly hearth remember Spain,
And tread in fancy once again the road,
Where twelve months since I held my way, and thought
Of England, and of all my heart held dear,
And wished this day were come.

[1] The first paragraph is a general recollection of León and Galicia. The third and fourth paragraphs focus on a day's walk from Venta to Navalmoral in the provinces of Toledo and Cáceres.

                                      The morning mist,
Well I remember, hovered o'er the heath,
When with the earliest dawn of day we left
The solitary Venta. Soon the sun
Rose in his glory; scattered by the breeze,
The thin fog rolled away, and now emerged
We saw where Oropesa's castled hill
Towered dark, and dimly seen; and now we passed
Torvalva's quiet huts, and on our way
Paused frequently, looked back, and gazed around,
Then journeyed on, yet turned and gazed again,
So lovely was the scene. That ducal pile
Of the Toledos now with all its towers
Shone in the sunlight. Half-way up the hill,
Embowered in olives, like the abode of Peace,
Lay Lagartina; and the cool, fresh gale,
Bending the young corn on the gradual slope,
Played o'er its varying verdure. I beheld
A convent near, and could almost have thought
The dwellers there must needs be holy men;
For, as they looked around them, all they saw
Was good.
              But, when the purple eve came on,
How did the lovely landscape fill my heart!
Trees, scattered among peering rocks, adorned
The near ascent; the vale was overspread
With ilex in its wintry foliage gay,
Old cork-trees through their soft and swelling bark
Bursting, and glaucous olives, underneath
Whose fertilizing influence the green herb
Grows greener, and, with heavier ears enriched,
The healthful harvest bends. Pellucid streams
Through many a vocal channel from the hills
Wound through the valley their melodious way,
And, o'er the intermediate woods descried,
Naval-Moral's church-tower announced to us
Our resting-place that night,—a welcome mark;
Though willingly we loitered to behold
In long expanse Plasencia's fertile plain,
And the high mountain-range which bounded it,
Now losing fast the roseate hue that eve
Shed o'er its summit and its snowy breast;
For eve was closing now. Faint and more faint
The murmurs of the goatherd's scattered flock
Were borne upon the air; and, sailing slow,
The broad-winged stork sought on the church-tower top
His consecrated nest. O lovely scenes!

I gazed upon you with intense delight,
And yet with thoughts that weigh the spirit down.
I was a stranger in a foreign land;
And, knowing that these eyes should nevermore
Behold that glorious prospect, Earth itself
Appeared the place of pilgrimage it is.

GEORGE GORDON, LORD BYRON
1788–1824

50   from *Childe Harold's Pilgrimage*

XIV

On, on the vessel flies, the land is gone,
And winds are rude in Biscay's sleepless bay.
Four days are sped, but with the fifth, anon,
New shores descried make every bosom gay;
And Cintra's mountain greets them on their way,
And Tagus dashing onward to the deep,
His fabled golden tribute bent to pay;
And soon on board the Lusian pilots leap,
And steer 'twixt fertile shores where yet few rustics reap.

XV

Oh, Christ! it is a goodly sight to see
What Heaven hath done for this delicious land:
What fruits of fragrance blush on every tree!
What goodly prospects o'er the hills expand!
But man would mar them with an impious hand:
And when the Almighty lifts his fiercest scourge
'Gainst those who most transgress his high command,
With treble vengeance will his hot shafts urge
Gaul's locust host, and earth from fellest foemen purge.

XVI

What beauties doth Lisboa first unfold!
Her image floating on that noble tide,
Which poets vainly pave with sands of gold,
But now whereon a thousand keels did ride

Of mighty strength, since Albion was allied,
And to the Lusians did her aid afford:
A nation swoln with ignorance and pride,
Who lick yet loathe the hand that waves the sword
To save them from the wrath of Gaul's unsparing lord.

XVII

But whoso entereth within this town,
That, sheening far, celestial seems to be,
Disconsolate will wander up and down,
'Mid many things unsightly to strange ee;
For hut and palace show like filthily:
The dingy denizens are reared in dirt;
Ne personage of high or mean degree
Doth care for cleanness of surtout or shirt;
Though shent with Egypt's plague, unkempt, unwashed, unhurt.

XVIII

Poor, paltry slaves! yet born 'midst noblest scenes—
Why, Nature, waste thy wonders on such men?
Lo! Cintra's glorious Eden intervenes
In variegated maze of mount and glen.
Ah me! what hand can pencil guide, or pen,
To follow half on which the eye dilates
Through views more dazzling unto mortal ken
Than those whereof such things the bard relates,
Who to the awe-struck world unlocked Elysium's gates!

XIX

The horrid crags, by toppling convent crowned,
The cork-trees hoar that clothe the shaggy steep,
The mountain-moss by scorching skies imbrowned,
The sunken glen, whose sunless shrubs must weep,
The tender azure of the unruffled deep,
The orange tints that gild the greenest bough,
The torrents that from cliff to valley leap,
The vine on high, the willow branch below,
Mixed in one mighty scene, with varied beauty glow.

RICHARD CHENEVIX TRENCH
1807–1886

51   *A Legend of Alhambra*

O hymned in many a poet's strain,
    Alhambra, by enchanter's hand
Exalted on this throne of Spain,
    A marvel of the land;

The last of thy imperial race,
    Alhambra, when he overstept
Thy portal's threshold, turned his face,
    He turned his face and wept.

In sooth it was a thing to weep,
    If then, as now, the level plain
Beneath was spreading like the deep,
    The broad unruffled main:

If, like a watch-tower of the sun,
    Above the Alpujarras rose,
Streaked, when the dying day was done,
    With evening's roseate snows.

Thy founts yet make a pleasant sound,
    And the twelve lions, couchant yet,
Sustain their ponderous burden, round
    The marble basin set.

But never, when the moon is bright
    O'er hill and golden-sanded stream,
And thy square turrets in the light
    And taper columns gleam,

Will village maiden dare to fill
    Her pitcher from that basin wide,
But rather seeks a niggard rill
    Far down the steep hill-side!

It was an Andalusian maid,
    With rose and pink-enwoven hair,
Who told me what the fear that stayed
    Their footsteps from that stair:

Alhambra] citadel and palace (thirteenth century) built by the Moorish kings at Granada

How, rising from that watery floor,
   A Moorish maiden, in the gleam
Of the wan moonlight, stands before
   The stirrer of the stream:

And mournfully she begs the grace,
   That they would speak the words divine,
And, sprinkling water in her face,
   Would make the sacred sign.

And whosoe'er will grant this boon,
   Returning with the morrow's light,
Shall find the fountain-pavement strewn
   With gold and jewels bright:

A regal gift! for once, they say,
   Her father ruled this broad domain,
The last who kept beneath his sway
   This pleasant place of Spain.

It surely is a fearful doom,
   That one so beautiful should have
No present quiet in her tomb,
   No hope beyond the grave.

It must be that some amulet
   Doth make all human pity vain,
Or that upon her brow is set
   The silent seal of pain,

Which none can meet—else long ago,
   Since many gentle hearts are there,
Some spirit, touched by joy or woe,
   Had answered to her prayer.

But so it is, that till this hour
   That mournful child beneath the moon
Still rises from her watery bower,
   To urge this simple boon—

To beg, as all have need of grace,
   That they would speak the words divine,
And, sprinkling water in her face,
   Would make the sacred sign.

52   *Gibraltar*

England, we love thee better than we know.—
   And this I learned when, after wand'rings long
   'Mid people of another stock and tongue,
I heard again thy martial music blow,
And saw thy gallant children to and fro
   Pace, keeping ward at one of those huge gates,
   Twin giants watching the Herculean Straits.
When first I came in sight of that brave show,
   It made the very heart within me dance,
   To think that thou thy proud foot shouldst advance
   Forward so far into the mighty sea.
Joy was it and exultation to behold
   Thine ancient standard's rich emblazonry,
A glorious picture by the wind unrolled.

GEORGE ELIOT
1819–1880

53   from *The Spanish Gypsy*

The Plaça Santiago

'Tis daylight still, but now the golden cross
Uplifted by the angel on the dome
Stands rayless in calm colour clear-defined
Against the northern blue; from turrets high
The flitting splendour sinks with folded wing
Dark-hid till morning, and the battlements
Wear soft relenting whiteness mellowed o'er
By summers generous and winters bland.
Now in the east the distance casts its veil
And gazes with a deepening earnestness.
The old rain-fretted mountains in their robes
Of shadow-broken grey; the rounded hills
Reddened with blood of Titans, whose huge limbs,
Entombed within, feed full the hardy flesh
Of cactus green and blue broad-sworded aloes;
The cypress soaring black above the lines
Of white court-walls; the jointed sugar-canes
Pale-golden with their feathers motionless
In the warm quiet:—all thought-teaching form

Utters itself in firm unshimmering hues.
For the great rock has screened the westering sun
That still on plains beyond streams vaporous gold
Among the branches; and within Bedmár
Has come the time of sweet serenity
When colour glows unglittering, and the soul
Of visible things shows silent happiness,
As that of lovers trusting though apart.
The ripe-cheeked fruits, the crimson-petalled flowers;
The wingèd life that pausing seems a gem
Cunningly carven on the dark green leaf;
The face of man with hues supremely blent
To difference fine as of a voice 'mid sounds:—
Each lovely light-dipped thing seems to emerge
Flushed gravely from baptismal sacrament.
All beauteous existence rests, yet wakes,
Lies still, yet conscious, with clear open eyes
And gentle breath and mild suffusèd joy.
'Tis day, but day that falls like melody
Repeated on a string with graver tones—
Tones such as linger in a long farewell.

The Plaça widens in the passive air—
The Plaça Santiago, where the church,
A mosque converted, shows an eyeless face
Red-checkered, faded, doing penance still—
Bearing with Moorish arch the imaged saint,
Apostle, baron, Spanish warrior,
Whose charger's hoofs trample the turbaned dead,
Whose banner with the Cross, the bloody sword,
Flashes athwart the Moslem's glazing eye,
And mocks his trust in Allah who forsakes.
Up to the church the Plaça gently slopes,
In shape most like the pious palmer's shell,
Girdled with low white houses; high above
Tower the strong fortress and sharp-angled wall
And well-flanked castle gate. From o'er the roofs,
And from the shadowed pátios cool, there spreads
The breath of flowers and aromatic leaves
Soothing the sense with bliss indefinite—
A baseless hope, a glad presentiment,
That curves the lip more softly, fills the eye
With more indulgent beam. And so it soothes,
So gently sways the pulses of the crowd
Who make a zone about the central spot

Bedmár] 21 miles east-north-east of Jaén in the south of Spain

Chosen by Roldan for his theatre.
Maids with arched eyebrows, delicate-pencilled, dark,
Fold their round arms below the kerchief full;
Men shoulder little girls; and grandames grey,
But muscular still, hold babies on their arms;
While mothers keep the stout-legged boys in front
Against their skirts, as old Greek pictures show
The Glorious Mother with the Boy divine.
Youths keep the places for themselves, and roll
Large lazy eyes, and call recumbent dogs
(For reasons deep below the reach of thought).
The old men cough with purpose, wish to hint
Wisdom within that cheapens jugglery,
Maintain a neutral air, and knit their brows
In observation. None are quarrelsome,
Noisy, or very merry; for their blood
Moves slowly into fervour—they rejoice
Like those dark birds that sweep with heavy wing,
Cheering their mates with melancholy cries.

But now the gilded balls begin to play
In rhythmic numbers, ruled by practice fine
Of eye and muscle: all the juggler's form
Consents harmonious in swift-gliding change,
Easily forward stretched or backward bent
With lightest step and movement circular
Round a fixed point: 'tis not the old Roldan now,
The dull, hard, weary, miserable man,
The soul all parched to languid appetite
And memory of desire: 'tis wondrous force
That moves in combination multiform
Towards conscious ends: 'tis Roldan glorious,
Holding all eyes like any meteor,
King of the moment save when Annibal
Divides the scene and plays the comic part,
Gazing with blinking glances up and down
Dancing and throwing nought and catching it,
With mimicry as merry as the tasks
Of penance-working shades in Tartarus.

54   from *The Spanish Gypsy*

Quit now the town, and with a journeying dream
Swift as the wings of sound yet seeming slow
Through multitudinous compression of stored sense

Roldan] a juggler

And spiritual space, see walls and towers
Lie in the silent whiteness of a trance,
Giving no sign of that warm life within
That moves and murmurs through their hidden heart.
Pass o'er the mountain, wind in sombre shade,
Then wind into the light and see the town
Shrunk to white crust upon the darker rock.
Turn east and south, descend, then rise anew
'Mid smaller mountains ebbing towards the plain:
Scent the fresh breath of the height-loving herbs
That, trodden by the pretty parted hoofs
Of nimble goats, sigh at the innocent bruise,
And with a mingled difference exquisite
Pour a sweet burthen on the buoyant air.
Pause now and be all ear. Far from the south,
Seeking the listening silence of the heights,
Comes a slow-dying sound—the Moslems' call
To prayer in afternoon. Bright in the sun
Like tall white sails on a green shadowy sea
Stand Moorish watch-towers: 'neath that eastern sky
Couches unseen the strength of Moorish Baza;
Where the meridian bends lies Guadix, hold
Of brave El Zagal. This is Moorish land,
Where Allah lives unconquered in dark breasts
And blesses still the many-nourishing earth
With dark-armed industry. See from the steep
The scattered olives hurry in grey throngs
Down towards the valley, where the little stream
Parts a green hollow 'twixt the gentler slopes;
And in that hollow, dwellings: not white homes
Of building Moors, but little swarthy tents
Such as of old perhaps on Asian plains,
Or wending westward past the Caucasus,
Our fathers raised to rest in. Close they swarm
About two taller tents, and viewed afar
Might seem a dark-robed crowd in penitence
That silent kneel; but come now in their midst
And watch a busy, bright-eyed, sportive life!
Tall maidens bend to feed the tethered goat,
The ragged kirtle fringing at the knee
Above the living curves, the shoulder's smoothness
Parting the torrent strong of ebon hair.
Women with babes, the wild and neutral glance
Swayed now to sweet desire of mothers' eyes,

Baza, Guadix] two towns north-east of Granada   El Zagal] El Zagal, the Valiant, was
one of the great Moorish heroes of the Reconquest in the fifteenth century; he became Sultan of
Granada

Rock their strong cradling arms and chant low strains
Taught by monotonous and soothing winds
That fall at night-time on the dozing ear.
The crones plait reeds, or shred the vivid herbs
Into the cauldron: tiny urchins crawl
Or sit and gurgle forth their infant joy.
Lads lying sphynx-like with uplifted breast
Propped on their elbows, their black manes tossed back,
Fling up the coin and watch its fatal fall,
Dispute and scramble, run and wrestle fierce,
Then fall to play and fellowship again;
Or in a thieving swarm they run to plague
The grandsires, who return with rabbits slung,
And with the mules fruit-laden from the fields.
Some striplings choose the smooth stones from the brook
To serve the slingers, cut the twigs for snares,
Or trim the hazel-wands, or at the bark
Of some exploring dog they dart away
With swift precision towards a moving speck.
These are the brood of Zarca's Gypsy tribe;
Most like an earth-born race bred by the Sun
On some rich tropic soil, the father's light
Flashing in coal-black eyes, the mother's blood
With bounteous elements feeding their young limbs.
The stalwart men and youths are at the wars
Following their chief, all save a trusty band
Who keep strict watch along the northern heights.

WILLIAM CORY
1823–1892

55   *The Bride's Song*

Oh, the white house, the bride's house;
    How quaint it looked to me,
With brown rocks, and vine-slope
    And round camelia tree.

Now kind house, and vine-slope
    We're fain to leave below,
We'll climb high to sweet briar
    And hear the northwind blow.

54 Zarca] Chieftain of the Zincali (gypsy tribe)

Oh, a month gone, a name gone
    And flowers of summer shed,
Oh, the rose-rain that fell on me
    The day that we were wed.

Oh, midnight, with starlight
    And freedom strange to me
For this, this, 'twas worth my while
    To flit across the sea.

ARTHUR SYMONS
1865–1945

56   *Spain*
                To Josefa

Josefa, when you sing,
With clapping hands, the sorrows of your Spain,
And all the bright-shawled ring
Laugh and clap hands again,
I think how all the sorrows were in vain.

The footlights flicker and spire
In tongues of flame before your tiny feet,
My warm-eyed gipsy, higher,
And in your eyes they meet
More than their light, more than their golden heat.

You sing of Spain, and all
Clap hands for Spain and you, and for the song;
One dances, and the hall
Rings like a beaten gong
With louder-handed clamours of the throng.

Spain, that with dancing mirth
Tripped lightly to the precipice, and fell
Until she felt the earth,
Suddenly, and knew well
That to have fallen through dreams is to touch hell;

Spain, brilliantly arrayed,
Decked for disaster, on disaster hurled,
Here, as in masquerade,
Mimes, to amuse the world,
Her ruin, a dancer rouged and draped and curled.

Mother of chivalry,
Mother of many sorrows borne for God,
Spain of the saints, is she
A slave beneath the rod,
A merry slave, and in her own abode?

She, who once found, has lost
A world beyond the waters, and she stands
Paying the priceless cost,
Lightly, with lives for lands,
Flowers in her hair, castanets in her hands.

ROBERT GRAVES
1895–1985

57
The Oleaster

Each night for seven nights beyond the gulf
A storm raged, out of hearing, and crooked flashes
Of lightning animated us. Before day-break
Rain fell munificently for the earth's need . . .

No, here they never plant the sweet olive
As some do (bedding slips in a prepared trench),
But graft it on the club of Hercules
The savage, inexpugnable oleaster
Whose roots and bole bunching from limestone crannies
Sprout impudent shoots born only to be lopped
Spring after Spring. Theirs is a loveless berry . . .

By mid-day we walk out, with naked feet,
Through pools on the road, gazing at waterfalls
Or a line of surf, but mostly at the trees
Whose elegant branches rain has duly blackened
And pressed their crowns to a sparkling silver.

Innumerable, plump with promise of oil,
The olives hang grass-green, in thankfulness
For a bitter sap and bitter New Year snows
That cleansed their bark . . .
                              Forgive me, dearest love,
If nothing I can say be strange or new.
I am no child of the hot South like you,
Though in rock rooted like an oleaster.

STEPHEN SPENDER
1909–

58   *Port Bou*

As a child holds a pet
Arms clutching but with hands that do not join
And the coiled animal looks through the gap
To outer freedom animal air,
So the earth-and-rock arms of this small harbour
Embrace but do not encircle the sea
Which, through a gap, vibrates into the ocean,
Where dolphins swim and liners throb.
In the bright winter sunlight I sit on the parapet
Of a bridge; my circling arms rest on a newspaper
And my mind is empty as the glittering stone
While I search for an image
(The one written above) and the words (written above)
To set down the childish headlands of Port Bou.
A lorry halts beside me with creaking brakes
And I look up at warm downwards-looking faces
Of militia men staring at my (French) newspaper.
'How do they write of our struggle over the frontier?'
I hold out the paper, but they cannot read it,
They want speech and to offer cigarettes.
In their waving flag-like faces the war finds peace. The famished
      mouths
Of rusted carbines lean against their knees,
Like leaning, rust-coloured, fragile reeds.
Wrapped in cloth—old granny in a shawl—
The stuttering machine-gun rests.
They shout—salute back as the truck jerks forward
Over the vigorous hill, beyond the headland.
An old man passes, his mouth dribbling,
From three rusted teeth, he shoots out: 'pom-pom-pom'.
The children run after; and, more slowly, the women;
Clutching their skirts, trail over the horizon.
Now Port Bou is empty, for the firing practice.
I am left alone on the parapet at the exact centre
Above the river trickling through the gulley, like that old man's saliva.
The exact centre, solitary as the bull's eye in a target.
Nothing moves against the background of stage-scenery houses
Save the skirring mongrels. The firing now begins

Port Bou] town just south of the French–Spanish border on the Costa Brava

Across the harbour mouth, from headland to headland,
White flecks of foam whipped by lead from the sea.
An echo spreads its cat-o'-nine tails
Thrashing the flanks of neighbour hills.
My circling arms rest on the newspaper,
My mind is paper on which dust and words sift,
I assure myself the shooting is only for practice
But I am the coward of cowards. The machine-gun stitches
My intestines with a needle, back and forth;
The solitary, spasmodic, white puffs from the carbines
Draw fear in white threads back and forth through my body.

TED HUGHES

1930–

59   *You Hated Spain*

                    Spain frightened you. Spain
Where I felt at home. The blood-raw light,
The oiled anchovy faces, the African
Black edges to everything, frightened you.
Your schooling had somehow neglected Spain.
The wrought-iron grille, death and the Arab drum.
You did not know the language, your soul was empty
Of the signs, and the welding light
Made your blood shrivel. Bosch
Held out a spidery hand and you took it
Timidly, a bobby-sox American.
You saw right down to the Goya funeral grin
And recognised it, and recoiled
As your poems winced into chill, as your panic
Clutched back towards college America.
So we sat as tourists at the bullfight
Watching bewildered bulls awkwardly butchered,
Seeing the grey-faced matador, at the barrier
Just below us, straightening his bent sword
And vomiting with fear. And the horn
That hid itself inside the blowfly belly
Of the toppled picador punctured
What was waiting for you. Spain
Was the land of your dreams: the dust-red cadaver
You dared not wake with, the puckering amputations
No literature course had glamorized.
The juju land behind your African lips.

Spain was what you tried to wake up from
And could not. I see you, in moonlight,
Walking the empty wharf at Alicante
Like a soul waiting for the ferry,
A new soul, still not understanding,
Thinking it is still your honeymoon
In the happy world, with your whole life waiting,
Happy, and all your poems still to be found.

SYLVIA PLATH

1932–1963

60   *The Goring*

Arena dust rusted by four bulls' blood to a dull redness,
The afternoon at a bad end under the crowd's truculence,
The ritual death each time botched among dropped capes, ill-judged
    stabs,
The strongest will seemed a will toward ceremony. Obese, dark-
Faced in his rich yellows, tassels, pompons, braid, the picador

Rode out against the fifth bull to brace his pike and slowly bear
Down deep into the bent bull-neck. Cumbrous routine, not artwork.
Instinct for art began with the bull's horn lofting in the mob's
Hush a lumped man-shape. The whole act formal, fluent as a dance.
Blood faultlessly broached redeemed the sullied air, the earth's
    grossness.

ITALY

JOSEPH ADDISON

1672–1719

61   from *A Letter from Italy*

Immortal glories in my mind revive,
And in my soul a thousand passions strive,
When Rome's exalted beauties I descry
Magnificent in piles of ruin lie.

An amphitheatre's amazing height
Here fills my eye with terror and delight,
That on its public shows unpeopled Rome,
And held uncrowded nations in its womb:
Here pillars rough with sculpture pierce the skies:
And here the proud triumphal arches rise,
Where the old Romans deathless acts displayed,
Their base degenerate progeny upbraid:
Whole rivers here forsake the fields below,
And wond'ring at their height through airy channels flow.
 Still to new scenes my wand'ring Muse retires,
And the dumb show of breathing rocks admires;
Where the smooth chisel all its force has shown,
And softened into flesh the rugged stone.
In solemn silence, a majestic band,
Heroes, and Gods, and Roman Consuls stand,
Stern tyrants, whom their cruelties renown,
And emperors in Parian marble frown;
While the bright dames, to whom they humbly sued,
Still show the charms that their proud hearts subdued.
 Fain would I Raphael's godlike art rehearse,
And show th' immortal labours in my verse,
Where from the mingled strength of shade and light
A new creation rises to my sight,
Such heav'nly figures from his pencil flow,
So warm with life his blended colours glow.
From theme to theme with secret pleasure tossed,
Amidst the soft variety I'm lost:
Here pleasing airs my ravished soul confound
With circling notes and labyrinths of sound;
Here domes and temples rise in distant views,
And opening palaces invite my Muse.
 How has kind heav'n adorned the happy land,
And scattered blessings with a wasteful hand!
But what avail her unexhausted stores,
Her blooming mountains, and her sunny shores,
With all the gifts that heav'n and earth impart,
The smiles of nature, and the charms of art,
While proud Oppression in her valleys reigns,
And Tyranny usurps her happy plains?
The poor inhabitant beholds in vain
The red'ning orange and the swelling grain:
Joyless he sees the growing oils and wines,
And in the myrtle's fragrant shade repines:
Starves, in the midst of nature's bounty cursed,
And in the loaden vineyard dies for thirst.

Oh Liberty, thou Goddess heavenly bright,
Profuse of bliss, and pregnant with delight!
Eternal pleasures in thy presence reign,
And smiling Plenty leads thy wanton train;
Eased of her load Subjection grows more light,
And Poverty looks cheerful in thy sight;
Thou mak'st the gloomy face of Nature gay,
Giv'st beauty to the Sun, and pleasure to the Day.
  Thee, Goddess, thee, Britannia's Isle adores;
How has she oft exhausted all her stores,
How oft in fields of death thy presence sought,
Nor thinks the mighty prize too dearly bought!
On foreign mountains may the sun refine
The grape's soft juice, and mellow it to wine,
With citron groves adorn a distant soil,
And the fat olive swell with floods of oil:
We envy not the warmer clime, that lies
In ten degrees of more indulgent skies,
Nor at the coarseness of our heaven repine,
Though o'er our heads the frozen Pleiads shine:
'Tis Liberty that crowns Britannia's Isle,
And makes her barren rocks and her bleak mountains smile.

GEORGE KEATE

1729–1797

62   from *Ancient and Modern Rome*

What, though oblivion in her sable shroud
Hath wrapped thy former splendour, yet ev'n now,
Some mould'ring fragments, ivy-crested tow'rs,
And arches, tott'ring to their fall, remain,
And in their antiquated liv'ry, speak
Their better fortune.—Pillars, that amidst
The solemn scene, by many an insult scarred,
Stand up historic; rifted vaults of fanes,
And palaces, whose wide disparted roofs
Threaten each visitant: and frequent seen
Some shattered urn that hath betrayed its charge,
To mix with vulgar dust.—Or should the charms
Of sculpture wake attention, here the eye
Finds rapturous delight, while it beholds,

The mimic stone so cunningly assume
The property of being, that it seems
As art could rival nature. Thus our sense
Is often fooled, when we before us view
Gigantic Hercules, on his huge club
Recline his weight enormous: or the limbs
Of matchless Flora, through her flowing robes,
Press decent on the sight: the graceful step,
And divine portance of the Delphic God:
Laocoon's anguish; and the beauteous form,
Too beauteous form, of fair Antinous!
Nor, shall the gladiators pass unmarked,
Greatly expressive; nor the manly force
Of Meleager; nor dejected air,
Of pensive Agrippina.—With new joy
The mind reflecting o'er th' enlivened bust
Shall pause, supremely pleased, as face to face,
Amidst the bright assembly we appear
Of chiefs, and sages, whose heroic deeds,
Beyond the storms of fate, superior shine
On fame's eternal record.—In their looks
We seem to read their story, ev'ry trace
Remark inquisitive, and oft return,
As some fresh action of their life revives,
To gaze, contemplate, and admire, again.
    Oh ever-wond'rous art, that from the schools
Of Greece, cam'st hither, to this favoured clime,
Yet rarely hast vouchsafed to pass the cliffs
Of the proud Apennine, or cheer the cold,
And genius-chilling regions of the North!
    As when a man descries the wished for port
Whither he's bound, and where before, his thoughts
Were long arrived, feels rising in his soul
A sudden transport; not unlike, perchance,
Is that sensation which the stranger's breast,
With expectation's fire already warmed,
Is conscious of, when standing on some height
His greedy eye takes in the nodding piles
Of old magnificence, or rapid darts
O'er the wide barren plain, where broken forms
Of turrets, and sepulchral monuments,
Skirt all the blue horizon.—Let's away
And wander midst the dank, and shadowy gloom
Of antique baths, or the Pantheon's round,
Well harmonized; where dignity, and grace,
And just proportion reign. The Circus too
Invites our steps, and the Tarpeian rock:

How much unlike, what poor Evander showed
Anchises' son, as through his humble state,
On Tiber's banks, the hospitable king
His princely guest conducted!—Mark e'en still,
Spite of the Gothic sword, the spiry tops
Of obelisks, whose sculptured sides confess
The mystic labours of Egyptian hands!
And those tall columns, that preserve your names,
Illustrious pair, who to th' exalted state
Of Emp'ror, joined the titles more august,
Of wise and good.—But, let us bend our course,
To where the Amphitheatre's old walls
Mantled in green, with many a winding, turn
In circuit vast; while, fancy paints to view
All Rome assembled on some festive day,
Rank above rank, with ev'ry face, intent
To see the death-doomed man, and nature yield
To force superior. The pursuit of arms
Had checked each softer impulse, and forbade
To call compassion virtue; nor was known
As in our times, the stage's wiser aim,
To steal instruction through the poet's song,
To melt the stubborn heart, and teach the eye
To shed the gen'rous tear for other's woe.

WILLIAM PARSONS
?1758–1828

63   *On Descending the River Po*

As down the rapid Po I chanced to glide,
And viewed its fertile banks on either side,
To both of which did formerly belong
A mighty master[1] in the art of song:
That, who in times long past, with daring aim,
For great Aeneas swelled the trump of fame;
And this, of later date, whose various page
Blends numerous subjects with Orlando's rage.
Eager to imitate each bard sublime,
How did I wish to build some lofty rhyme,
That, thus enshrined, my name with theirs might last
Through distant years, till time's long reign be past!

---

[1] Virgil was born near Mantua on one side of the Po, and Ariosto at Ferrara on the other.

—When sudden, from between the parted tide,
A pallid spectre rose, and thundering cried,
'Rash youth! who dar'st such haughty hopes avow,
I who was less presumptuous far than thou,
Who only asked to guide a single day
My father's steeds along th' etherial way,
Hurled from on high here met a wat'ry tomb,
Beware, nor tempt a still more dreadful doom!'
He said—and sunk beneath the circling wave;
Trembling I heard the stern advice he gave,
Felt my own littleness, and want of strength,
And thought no more to aim at works of length.

64   *The Man of Taste*[1]

                            An Epigram

While the coarse picture charms his eyes
In taste's proud transport Cymon cries,
        'How well Correggio there is known!'
The cicerone pulls the string,
Bids the daubed canvas upward spring;
        The true Correggio then is shown.

SAMUEL ROGERS
1763–1855

65   *Naples*

This region, surely, is not of the earth.[2]
Was it not dropped from heaven? Not a grove,
Citron or pine or cedar, not a grot
Sea-worn and mantled with the gadding vine,
But breathes enchantment. Not a cliff but flings
On the clear wave some image of delight,
Some cabin-roof glowing with crimson flowers,

---

[1] 'In the Church of St. Sepulchre at Parma, there is a very fine picture of Correggio, generally visited by Travellers, and the affected Connoisseur is often discover'd by his admiration of another which is only a cover to it' (W.P.).
[2] 'Un pezzo di cielo caduto in terra' (Sannazzaro).

---

63 pallid spectre] Phaeton, the son of Phoebus (the Sun)

Some ruined temple or fallen monument,
To muse on as the bark is gliding by.
And be it mine to muse there, mine to glide,
From day-break, when the mountain pales his fire
Yet more and more, and from the mountain-top,
Till then invisible, a smoke ascends,
Solemn and slow, as erst from Ararat,
When he, the Patriarch, who escaped the Flood,
Was with his house-hold sacrificing there—
From day-break to that hour, the last and best,
When, one by one, the fishing-boats come forth,
Each with its glimmering lantern at the prow,
And, when the nets are thrown, the evening-hymn
Steals o'er the trembling waters.
                              Everywhere
Fable and Truth have shed, in rivalry,
Each her peculiar influence. Fable came
And laughed and sung, arraying Truth in flowers,
Like a young child her grandam. Fable came;
Earth, sea and sky reflecting, as she flew,
A thousand, thousand colours not their own:
And at her bidding, lo! a dark descent
To Tartarus, and those thrice happy fields,
Those fields with ether pure and purple light
Ever invested, scenes by Him portrayed,
Who here was wont to wander, here invoke
The sacred Muses, here receive, record
What they revealed, and on the western shore
Sleeps in a silent grove, o'erlooking thee,
Beloved Parthenope.
                        Yet here, methinks,
Truth wants no ornament, in her own shape
Filling the mind by turns with awe and love,
By turns inclining to wild ecstasy,
And soberest meditation. Here the vines
Wed, each her elm, and o'er the golden grain
Hang their luxuriant clusters, chequering
The sunshine; where, when cooler shadows fall,
And the mild moon her fairy net-work weaves,
The lute, or mandoline, accompanied
By many a voice yet sweeter than their own,
Kindles, nor slowly; and the dance displays
The gentle arts and witcheries of love,
Its hopes and fears and feignings, till the youth
Drops on his knee as vanquished, and the maid,

by Him portrayed] Virgil   the dance] the tarantella

Her tambourine uplifting with a grace,
Nature's and Nature's only, bids him rise.

   But here the mighty Monarch underneath,
He in his palace of fire, diffuses round
A dazzling splendour. Here, unseen, unheard,
Opening another Eden in the wild,
His gifts he scatters; save, when issuing forth
In thunder, he blots out the sun, the sky,
And, mingling all things earthly as in scorn,
Exalts the valley, lays the mountain low,
Pours many a torrent from his burning lake,
And in an hour of universal mirth,
What time the trump proclaims the festival,
Buries some capital city, there to sleep
The sleep of ages—till a plough, a spade
Disclose the secret, and the eye of day
Glares coldly on the streets, the skeletons;
Each in his place, each in his gay attire,
And eager to enjoy.
                Let us go round;
And let the sail be slack, the course be slow,
That at our leisure, as we coast along,
We may contemplate, and from every scene
Receive its influence. The Cumaean towers,
There did they rise, sun-gilt; and here thy groves,
Delicious Baiae. Here (what would they not?)
The masters of the earth, unsatisfied,
Built in the sea; and now the boatman steers
O'er many a crypt and vault yet glimmering,
O'er many a broad and indestructible arch,
The deep foundations of their palaces;
Nothing now heard ashore, so great the change,
Save when the sea-mew clamours, or the owl
Hoots in the temple.
               What the mountainous isle,
Seen in the south? 'Tis where a monster dwelt,
Hurling his victims from the topmost cliff;
Then and then only merciful, so slow,
So subtle were the tortures they endured.
Fearing and feared he lived, cursing and cursed;
And still the dungeons in the rock breathe out
Darkness, distemper. Strange, that one so vile
Should from his den strike terror thro' the world;
Should, where withdrawn in his decrepitude,

---

mountainous isle] Capri   monster] Tiberius

Say to the noblest, be they where they might,
'Go from the earth!' and from the earth they went.
Yet such things were—and will be, when mankind
Losing all virtue, lose all energy;
And for the loss incur the penalty,
Trodden down and trampled.
                       Let us turn the prow
And, in the track of him who went to die,
Traverse this valley of waters, landing where
A waking dream awaits us. At a step
Two thousand years roll backward, and we stand,
Like those so long within that awful place,
Immovable, nor asking, Can it be?

   Once did I linger there alone, till day
Closed, and at length the calm of twilight came,
So grateful, yet so solemn! At the fount,
Just where the three ways meet, I stood and looked,
('Twas near a noble house, the house of Pansa)
And all was still as in the long, long night
That followed, when the shower of ashes fell,
When they that sought Pompeii, sought in vain;
It was not to be found. But now a ray,
Bright and yet brighter, on the pavement glanced,
And on the wheel-track worn for centuries,
And on the stepping-stones from side to side,
O'er which the maidens, with their water-urns,
Were wont to trip so lightly. Full and clear,
The moon was rising, and at once revealed
The name of every dweller, and his craft;
Shining throughout with an unusual lustre,
And lighting up this City of the Dead.

   Mark, where within, as though the embers lived,
The ample chimney-vault is dun with smoke.
There dwelt a miller; silent and at rest
His mill-stones now. In old companionship
Still do they stand as on the day he went,
Each ready for its office—but he comes not.
And there, hard by (where one in idleness
Has stopped to scrawl a ship, an armed man;
And in a tablet on the wall we read
Of shews ere long to be) a sculptor wrought,
Nor meanly; blocks, half-chiselled into life,
Waiting his call. Here long, as yet attests
The trodden floor, an olive-merchant drew
From many an earthen jar, no more supplied;

him who went to die] the Elder Pliny   that awful place] Pompeii

And here from his a vintner served his guests
Largely, the stain of his o'erflowing cups
Fresh on the marble. On the bench, beneath,
They sate and quaffed and looked on them that passed,
Gravely discussing the last news from Rome.
    But lo, engraven on a threshold-stone,
That word of courtesy, so sacred once,
Hail! At a master's greeting we may enter.
And lo, a fairy-palace! everywhere,
As through the courts and chambers we advance,
Floors of mosaic, walls of arabesque,
And columns clustering in patrician splendour.
But hark, a footstep! May we not intrude?
And now, methinks, I hear a gentle laugh,
And gentle voices mingling as in converse!
—And now a harp-string as struck carelessly,
And now—along the corridor it comes—
I cannot err, a filling as of baths!
—Ah, no, 'tis but a mockery of the sense,
Idle and vain! We are but where we were;
Still wandering in a City of the Dead!

WILLIAM WORDSWORTH
1770–1850

66   from *The Prelude*

Far different dejection once was mine,
A deep and genuine sadness then I felt;
The circumstances I will here relate
Even as they were. Upturning with a Band
Of Travellers, from the Valais we had clomb
Along the road that leads to Italy;
A length of hours, making of these our Guides,
Did we advance, and having reached an Inn
Among the mountains, we together ate
Our noon's repast, from which the Travellers rose,
Leaving us at the Board. Ere long we followed,
Descending by the beaten road that led
Right to a rivulet's edge, and there broke off.
The only track now visible was one
Upon the further side, right opposite,
And up a lofty Mountain. This we took

After a little scruple, and short pause,
And climbed with eagerness, though not, at length,
Without surprise and some anxiety
On finding that we did not overtake
Our Comrades gone before. By fortunate chance,
While every moment now encreased our doubts,
A Peasant met us, and from him we learned
That to the place which had perplexed us first
We must descend, and there should find the road
Which in the stony channel of the Stream
Lay a few steps, and then along its Banks:
And further, that thenceforward all our course
Was downwards, with the current of that Stream.
Hard of belief, we questioned him again,
And all the answers which the Man returned
To our inquiries, in their sense and substance,
Translated by the feelings which we had,
Ended in this; *that we had crossed the Alps.*

   Imagination! lifting up itself
Before the eye and progress of my Song
Like an unfathered vapour; here that Power,
In all the might of its endowments, came
Athwart me; I was lost as in a cloud,
Halted, without a struggle to break through.
And now recovering, to my Soul I say
'I recognise thy glory'. In such strength
Of usurpation, in such visitings
Of awful promise, when the light of sense
Goes out in flashes that have shewn to us
The invisible world, doth Greatness make abode,
There harbours whether we be young or old.
Our destiny, our nature, and our home,
Is with infinitude, and only there;
With hope it is, hope that can never die,
Effort, and expectation, and desire,
And something evermore about to be.
The mind beneath such banners militant
Thinks not of spoils or trophies, nor of aught
That may attest its prowess, blest in thoughts
That are their own perfection and reward,
Strong in itself, and in the access of joy
Which hides it like the overflowing Nile.

   The dull and heavy slackening that ensued
Upon those tidings by the Peasant given
Was soon dislodged; downwards we hurried fast,

And entered with the road which we had missed
Into a narrow chasm. The brook and road
Were fellow-travellers in this gloomy Pass,
And with them did we journey several hours
At a slow step. The immeasurable height
Of woods decaying, never to be decayed,
The stationary blasts of water-falls,
And every where along the hollow rent
Winds thwarting winds, bewildered and forlorn,
The torrents shooting from the clear blue sky,
The rocks that muttered close upon our ears,
Black drizzling crags that spake by the way-side
As if a voice were in them, the sick sight
And giddy prospect of the raving stream,
The unfettered clouds and region of the heavens,
Tumult and peace, the darkness and the light
Were all like workings of one mind, the features
Of the same face, blossoms upon one tree,
Characters of the great Apocalypse,
The types and symbols of Eternity,
Of first and last, and midst, and without end.

That night our lodging was an Alpine House,
An Inn, or Hospital, as they are named,
Standing in that same valley by itself,
And close upon the confluence of two Streams;
A dreary Mansion, large beyond all need,
With high and spacious rooms, deafened and stunned
By noise of waters, making innocent Sleep
Lie melancholy among weary bones.

Uprisen betimes, our journey we renewed,
Led by the Stream, ere noon-day magnified
Into a lordly River, broad and deep,
Dimpling along in silent majesty,
With mountains for its neighbours, and in view
Of distant mountains and their snowy tops,
And thus proceeding to Locarno's Lake,
Fit resting-place for such a Visitant.
—Locarno, spreading out in width like Heaven,
And Como, thou, a treasure by the earth
Kept to itself, a darling bosomed up
In Abyssinian privacy, I spake
Of thee, thy chestnut woods, and garden plots
Of Indian corn tended by dark-eyed Maids,

Locarno's Lake] Lake Maggiore

Thy lofty steeps, and pathways roofed with vines
Winding from house to house, from town to town,
Sole link that binds them to each other, walks
League after league, and cloistral avenues
Where silence is, if music be not there:
While yet a Youth, undisciplined in Verse,
Through fond ambition of my heart, I told
Your praises; nor can I approach you now
Ungreeted by a more melodious Song,
Where tones of learned Art and Nature mixed
May frame enduring language. Like a breeze
Or sunbeam over your domain I passed
In motion without pause; but Ye have left
Your beauty with me, an impassioned sight
Of colours and of forms, whose power is sweet
And gracious, almost might I dare to say,
As virtue is, or goodness, sweet as love,
Or the remembrance of a noble deed,
Or gentlest visitations of pure thought
When God, the Giver of all joy, is thanked
Religiously, in silent blessedness,
Sweet as this last herself, for such it is.

    Through those delightful pathways we advanced
Two days, and still in presence of the Lake,
Which, winding up among the Alps, now changed
Slowly its lovely countenance, and put on
A sterner character. The second night
(In eagerness, and by report misled
Of those Italian Clocks that speak the time
In fashion different from ours) we rose
By moonshine, doubting not that day was near,
And that, meanwhile, coasting the Water's edge
As hitherto, and with as plain a track
To be our guide, we might behold the scene
In its most deep repose.—We left the Town
Of Gravedona with this hope, but soon
Were lost, bewildered among woods immense,
Where, having wandered for a while, we stopped
And on a rock sate down, to wait for day.
An open place it was, and overlooked
From high, the sullen water underneath,
On which a dull red image of the moon
Lay bedded, changing oftentimes its form
Like an uneasy snake: long time we sate,
For scarcely more than one hour of the night,
Such was our error, had been gone, when we

Renewed our journey. On the rock we lay
And wished to sleep but could not, for the stings
Of insects, which with noise like that of noon
Filled all the woods. The cry of unknown birds,
The mountains, more by darkness visible
And their own size, than any outward light,
The breathless wilderness of clouds, the clock
That told with unintelligible voice
The widely-parted hours, the noise of streams
And sometimes rustling motions nigh at hand
Which did not leave us free from personal fear,
And lastly the withdrawing Moon, that set
Before us while she still was high in heaven,
These were our food, and such a summer's night
Did to that pair of golden days succeed,
With now and then a doze and snatch of sleep,
On Como's Banks, the same delicious Lake.

GEORGE GORDON, LORD BYRON
1788–1824

67   from *Childe Harold's Pilgrimage*

I stood in Venice on the Bridge of Sighs,
A palace and a prison on each hand:
I saw from out the wave her structures rise
As from the stroke of the enchanter's wand;
A thousand years their cloudy wings expand
Around me, and a dying glory smiles
O'er the far times, when many a subject land
Looked to the wingèd Lion's marble piles,
Where Venice sat in state, throned on her hundred isles!

She looks a sea Cybele, fresh from ocean,
Rising with her tiara of proud towers
At airy distance, with majestic motion,
And such she was; her daughters had their dowers
From spoils of nations, and the exhaustless East
Poured in her lap all gems in sparkling showers:
In purple was she robed, and of her feast
Monarchs partook, and deemed their dignity increased.

---

67 Lion] emblem of St Mark, patron saint of Venice   Cybele] a nature goddess

In Venice Tasso's echoes are no more,
And silent rows the songless gondolier;
Her palaces are crumbling to the shore,
And music meets not always now the ear:
Those days are gone, but Beauty still is here;
States fall, arts fade, but Nature doth not die,
Nor yet forget how Venice once was dear,
The pleasant place of all festivity,
The revel of the earth, the masque of Italy!

But unto us she hath a spell beyond
Her name is story, and her long array
Of mighty shadows, whose dim forms despond
Above the Dogeless city's vanished sway:
Ours is a trophy which will not decay
With the Rialto; Shylock and the Moor,
And Pierre, cannot be swept or worn away,—
The keystones of the arch!—though all were o'er,
For us repeopled were the solitary shore.

PERCY BYSSHE SHELLEY
1792–1822

68   from *Julian and Maddalo*

I rode one evening with Count Maddalo
Upon the bank of land which breaks the flow
Of Adria towards Venice: a bare strand
Of hillocks, heaped from ever-shifting sand,
Matted with thistles and amphibious weeds.
Such as from earth's embrace the salt ooze breeds,
Is this; an uninhabited sea-side,
Which the lone fisher, when his nets are dried,
Abandons; and no other object breaks
The waste, but one dwarf tree and some few stakes
Broken and unrepaired, and the tide makes
A narrow space of level sand thereon.
Where 'twas our wont to ride while day went down.

Tasso's echoes] pairs of gondoliers once sang alternate stanzas from Tasso's *Gerusalemme liberata*. The custom died out when Venice lost her independence to Napoleon

68 bank of land] the sands of the Lido   Adria] the Adriatic Sea

This ride was my delight. I love all waste
And solitary places; where we taste
The pleasure of believing what we see
Is boundless, as we wish our souls to be:
And such was this wide ocean, and this shore
More barren than its billows; and yet more
Than all, with a remembered friend I love
To ride as then I rode;—for the winds drove
The living spray along the sunny air
Into our faces; the blue heavens were bare,
Stripped to their depths by the awakening north;
And, from the waves, sound like delight broke forth
Harmonising with solitude, and sent
Into our hearts aëreal merriment.
So, as we rode, we talked; and the swift thought,
Winging itself with laughter, lingered not,
But flew from brain to brain,—such glee was ours.
Charged with light memories of remembered hours,
None slow enough for sadness: till we came
Homeward, which always makes the spirit tame.
This day had been cheerful but cold, and now
The sun was sinking, and the wind also.
Our talk grew somewhat serious, as may be
Talk interrupted with such raillery
As mocks itself, because it cannot scorn
The thoughts it would extinguish:—'twas forlorn,
Yet pleasing, such as once, so poets tell,
The devils held within the dales of Hell
Concerning God, freewill and destiny:
Of all that earth has been or yet may be,
All that vain men imagine or believe,
Or hope can paint or suffering may achieve,
We descanted, and I (for ever still
Is it not wise to make the best of ill?)
Argued against despondency, but pride
Made my companion take the darker side.
The sense that he was greater than his kind
Had struck, methinks, his eagle spirit blind
By gazing on its own exceeding light.
Meanwhile the sun paused ere it should alight,
Over the horizon of the mountains;—Oh,
How beautiful is sunset, when the glow
Of Heaven descends upon a land like thee,
Thou Paradise of exiles, Italy!
Thy mountains, seas, and vineyards, and the towers
Of cities they encircle!—it was ours

To stand on thee, beholding it: and then,
Just where we had dismounted, the Count's men
Were waiting for us with the gondola.—
As those who pause on some delightful way
Though bent on pleasant pilgrimage, we stood
Looking upon the evening, and the flood
Which lay between the city and the shore,
Paved with the image of the sky . . . the hoar
And aëry Alps towards the North appeared
Through mist, an heaven-sustaining bulwark reared
Between the East and West; and half the sky
Was roofed with clouds of rich emblazonry
Dark purple at the zenith, which still grew
Down the steep West into a wondrous hue
Brighter than burning gold, even to the rent
Where the swift sun yet paused in his descent
Among the many-folded hills: they were
Those famous Euganean hills, which bear,
As seen from Lido thro' the harbour piles,
The likeness of a clump of peakèd isles—
And then—as if the Earth and Sea had been
Dissolved into one lake of fire, were seen
Those mountains towering as from waves of flame
Around the vaporous sun, from which there came
The inmost purple spirit of light, and made
Their very peaks transparent. 'Ere it fade,'
Said my companion, 'I will show you soon
A better station'—so, o'er the lagune
We glided; and from that funereal bark
I leaned, and saw the city, and could mark
How from their many isles, in evening's gleam,
Its temples and its palaces did seem
Like fabrics of enchantment piled to Heaven.

JOHN HENRY NEWMAN
1801–1890

69   *The Good Samaritan*

Palermo, 13 June 1833

Oh that thy creed were sound!
For thou dost soothe the heart, thou Church of Rome,
 By thy unwearied watch and varied round
Of service, in thy Saviour's holy home.
 I cannot walk the city's sultry streets,
 But the wide porch invites to still retreats,
Where passion's thirst is calmed, and care's unthankful gloom.

 There, on a foreign shore,
The homesick solitary finds a friend:
 Thoughts, prisoned long for lack of speech, outpour
Their tears; and doubts in resignation end.
 I almost fainted from the long delay
 That tangles me within this languid bay,
When comes a foe, my wounds with oil and wine to tend.

ELIZABETH BARRETT BROWNING
1806–1861

70   from *Aurora Leigh*

I felt the wind soft from the land of souls;
The old miraculous mountains heaved in sight,
One straining past another along the shore,
The way of grand dull Odyssean ghosts,
Athirst to drink the cool blue wine of seas
And stare on voyagers. Peak pushing peak
They stood: I watched, beyond that Tyrian belt
Of intense sea betwixt them and the ship,
Down all their sides the misty olive-woods
Dissolving in the weak, congenial moon
And still disclosing some brown convent tower
That seems as if it grew from some brown rock,
Or many a little lighted village, dropped
Like a fallen star upon so high a point,

You wonder what can keep it in its place
From sliding headlong with the waterfalls
Which powder all the myrtle and orange groves
With spray of silver. Thus my Italy
Was stealing on us. Genoa broke with day,
The Doria's long pale palace striking out,
From green hills in advance of the white town,
A marble finger dominant to ships,
Seen glimmering through the uncertain grey of dawn.

And then I did not think, 'My Italy',
I thought 'My father!' O my father's house,
Without his presence!—Places are too much,
Or else too little, for immortal man—
Too little, when love's May o'ergrows the ground;
Too much, when that luxuriant robe of green
Is rustling to our ankles in dead leaves.
'Tis only good to be or here or there,
Because we had a dream on such a stone,
Or this or that,—but, once being wholly waked
And come back to the stone without the dream,
We trip upon't,—alas, and hurt ourselves;
Or else it falls on us and grinds us flat,
The heaviest gravestone on this burying earth.

.   .   .   .

I found a house at Florence on the hill
Of Bellosguardo. 'Tis a tower which keeps
A post of double observation o'er
That valley of Arno (holding as a hand
The outspread city) straight toward Fiesole
And Mount Morello and the setting sun,
The Vallombrosan mountains opposite,
Which sunrise fills as full as crystal cups
Turned red to the brim because their wine is red.
No sun could die nor yet be born unseen
By dwellers at my villa: morn and eve
Were magnified before us in the pure
Illimitable space and pause of sky,
Intense as angels' garments blanched with God,
Less blue than radiant. From the outer wall
Of the garden, drops the mystic floating grey
Of olive-trees (with interruptions green
From maize and vine), until 'tis caught and torn
Upon the abrupt black line of cypresses
Which signs the way to Florence. Beautiful
The city lies along the ample vale,

Cathedral, tower and palace, piazza and street,
The river trailing like a silver cord
Through all, and curling loosely, both before
And after, over the whole stretch of land
Sown whitely up and down its opposite slopes
With farms and villas.

RICHARD MONCKTON MILNES
1809–1885

71   *Sir Walter Scott at the Tomb of the Stuarts in*
St Peter's

Eve's tinted shadows slowly fill the fane
Where Art has taken almost Nature's room,
While still two objects clear in light remain,
An alien pilgrim at an alien tomb.—

—A sculptured tomb of regal heads discrowned,
Of one heart-worshipped, fancy-haunted, name,
Once loud on earth, but now scarce else renowned
Than as the offspring of that stranger's fame.

There lie the Stuarts!—There lingers Walter Scott!
Strange congress of illustrious thoughts and things!
A plain old moral, still too oft forgot,—
The power of Genius and the fall of Kings.

The curse on lawless Will high-planted there,
A beacon to the world, shines not for him;
He is with those who felt their life was sere,
When the full light of loyalty grew dim.

He rests his chin upon a sturdy staff,
Historic as that sceptre, theirs no more;
His gaze is fixed; his thirsty heart can quaff,
For a short hour the spirit-draughts of yore.

Each figure in its pictured place is seen,
Each fancied shape his actual vision fills,
From the long-pining, death-delivered Queen,
To the worn Outlaw of the heathery hills.

O grace of life, which shame could never mar!
O dignity, that circumstance defied!
Pure is the neck that wears the deathly scar,
And sorrow has baptised the front of pride.

But purpled mantle, and blood-crimsoned shroud,
Exiles to suffer and returns to woo,
Are gone, like dreams by daylight disallowed;
And their historian,—he is sinking too!

A few more moments and that labouring brow
Cold as those royal busts and calm will lie;
And, as on them his thoughts are resting now,
His marbled form will meet the attentive eye.

Thus, face to face, the dying and the dead,
Bound in one solemn ever-living bond,
Communed; and I was sad that ancient head
Ever should pass those holy walls beyond.

ALFRED, LORD TENNYSON
1809–1892

72   *'Frater Ave atque Vale'*

Row us out from Desenzano, to your Sirmione row!
So they rowed, and there we landed—'O venusta Sirmio!'
There to me thro' all the groves of olive in the summer glow,
There beneath the Roman ruin where the purple flowers grow,
Came that 'Ave atque Vale' of the Poet's hopeless woe,
Tenderest of Roman poets nineteen-hundred years ago,
'Frater Ave atque Vale'—as we wandered to and fro
Gazing at the Lydian laughter of the Garda Lake below
Sweet Catullus's all-but-island, olive-silvery Sirmio!

'*Frater Ave atque Vale*'] 'Brother, hail and farewell'

ROBERT BROWNING
1812–1889

73   *The Englishman in Italy*

Piano di Sorrento

Fortù, Fortù, my beloved one,
   Sit here by my side,
On my knees put up both little feet!
   I was sure, if I tried,
I could make you laugh spite of Scirocco.
   Now, open your eyes,
Let me keep you amused till he vanish
   In black from the skies,
With telling my memories over
   As you tell your beads;
All the Plain saw me gather, I garland
   —The flowers or the weeds.

Time for rain! for your long hot dry Autumn
   Had net-worked with brown
The white skin of each grape on the bunches,
   Marked like a quail's crown,
Those creatures you make such account of,
   Whose heads,—speckled white
Over brown like a great spider's back,
   As I told you last night,—
Your mother bites off for her supper.
   Red-ripe as could be,
Pomegranates were chapping and splitting
   In halves on the tree:
And betwixt the loose walls of great flintstone,
   Or in the thick dust
On the path, or straight out of the rockside,
   Wherever could thrust
Some burnt sprig of bold hardy rock-flower
   Its yellow face up,
For the prize were great butterflies fighting,
   Some five for one cup.
So, I guessed, ere I got up this morning,
   What change was in store,
By the quick rustle-down of the quail-nets
   Which woke me before

Scirocco] hot wind from Northern Africa that causes languor and depression

I could open my shutter, made fast
   With a bough and a stone,
And look thro' the twisted dead vine-twigs,
   Sole lattice that's known.
Quick and sharp rang the rings down the net-poles,
   While, busy beneath,
Your priest and his brother tugged at them,
   The rain in their teeth.
And out upon all the flat house-roofs
   Where split figs lay drying,
The girls took the frails under cover:
   Nor use seemed in trying
To get out the boats and go fishing,
   For, under the cliff,
Fierce the black water frothed o'er the blindrock.
   No seeing our skiff
Arrive about noon from Amalfi,
   —Our fisher arrive,
And pitch down his basket before us,
   All trembling alive
With pink and grey jellies, your sea-fruit;
   You touch the strange lumps,
And mouths gape there, eyes open, all manner
   Of horns and of humps,
Which only the fisher looks grave at,
   While round him like imps
Cling screaming the children as naked
   And brown as his shrimps;
Himself too as bare to the middle
   —You see round his neck
The string and its brass coin suspended,
   That saves him from wreck.
But to-day not a boat reached Salerno,
   So back, to a man,
Came our friends, with whose help in the vineyards
   Grape-harvest began.
In the vat, halfway up in our house-side,
   Like blood the juice spins,
While your brother all bare-legged is dancing
   Till breathless he grins
Dead-beaten in effort on effort
   To keep the grapes under,
Since still when he seems all but master,
   In pours the fresh plunder

Amalfi] small town on the Gulf of Salerno in southern Italy   Salerno] port in southern
Italy

From girls who keep coming and going
    With basket on shoulder,
And eyes shut against the rain's driving;
    Your girls that are older,—
For under the hedges of aloe,
    And where, on its bed
Of the orchard's black mould, the love-apple
    Lies pulpy and red,
All the young ones are kneeling and filling
    Their laps with the snails
Tempted out by this first rainy weather,—
    Your best of regales,
As to-night will be proved to my sorrow,
    When, supping in state,
We shall feast our grape-gleaners (two dozen,
    Three over one plate)
With lasagne so tempting to swallow
    In slippery ropes,
And gourds fried in great purple slices,
    That colour of popes.
Meantime, see the grape bunch they've brought you:
    The rain-water slips
O'er the heavy blue bloom on each globe
    Which the wasp to your lips
Still follows with fretful persistence:
    Nay, taste, while awake,
This half of a curd-white smooth cheese-ball
    That peels, flake by flake,
Like an onion, each smoother and whiter;
    Next, sip this weak wine
From the thin green glass flask, with its stopper,
    A leaf of the vine;
And end with the prickly-pear's red flesh
    That leaves thro' its juice
The stony black seeds on your pearl-teeth.
    Scirocco is loose!
Hark, the quick, whistling pelt of the olives
    Which, thick in one's track,
Tempt the stranger to pick up and bite them,
    Tho' not yet half black!
How the old twisted olive trunks shudder,
    The medlars let fall
Their hard fruit, and the brittle great fig-trees
    Snap off, figs and all,
For here comes the whole of the tempest!
    No refuge, but creep
Back again to my side and my shoulder,

And listen or sleep.
O how will your country show next week,
    When all the vine-boughs
Have been stripped of their foliage to pasture
    The mules and the cows?
Last eve, I rode over the mountains;
    Your brother, my guide,
Soon left me, to feast on the myrtles
    That offered, each side,
Their fruit-balls, black, glossy and luscious,—
    Or strip from the sorbs
A treasure, or, rosy and wondrous,
    Those hairy gold orbs!
But my mule picked his sure sober path out,
    Just stopping to neigh
When he recognized down in the valley
    His mates on their way
With the faggots and barrels of water;
    And soon we emerged
From the plain, where the woods could scarce follow;
    And still as we urged
Our way, the woods wondered, and left us,
    As up still we trudged
Though the wild path grew wilder each instant,
    And place was e'en grudged
'Mid the rock-chasms and piles of loose stones
    Like the loose broken teeth
Of some monster which climbed there to die
    From the ocean beneath—
Place was grudged to the silver-grey fume-weed
    That clung to the path,
And dark rosemary ever a-dying
    That, 'spite the wind's wrath,
So loves the salt rock's face to seaward,
    And lentisks as staunch
To the stone where they root and bear berries,
    And . . . what shows a branch
Coral-coloured, transparent, with circlets
    Of pale seagreen leaves;
Over all trod my mule with the caution
    Of gleaners o'er sheaves,
Still, foot after foot like a lady,
    Till, round after round,
He climbed to the top of Calvano,
    And God's own profound
Was above me, and round me the mountains,
    And under, the sea,

And within me my heart to bear witness
    What was and shall be.
Oh, heaven and the terrible crystal!
    No rampart excludes
Your eye from the life to be lived
    In the blue solitudes.
Oh, those mountains, their infinite movement!
    Still moving with you;
For, ever some new head and breast of them
    Thrusts into view
To observe the intruder; you see it
    If quickly you turn
And, before they escape you surprise them.
    They grudge you should learn
How the soft plains they look on, lean over
    And love (they pretend)
—Cower beneath them, the flat sea-pine crouches,
    The wild fruit-trees bend,
E'en the myrtle-leaves curl, shrink and shut:
    All is silent and grave:
'Tis a sensual and timorous beauty,
    How fair! but a slave.
So, I turned to the sea; and there slumbered
    As greenly as ever
Those isles of the siren, your Galli;
    No ages can sever
The Three, nor enable their sister
    To join them,—halfway
On the voyage, she looked at Ulysses
    No farther to-day,
Tho' the small one, just launched in the wave,
    Watches breast-high and steady
From under the rock, her bold sister
    Swum halfway already.
Fortù, shall we sail there together
    And see from the sides
Quite new rocks show their faces, new haunts
    Where the siren abides?
Shall we sail round and round them, close over
    The rocks, tho' unseen,
That ruffle the grey glassy water
    To glorious green?
Then scramble from splinter to splinter,
    Reach land and explore,
On the largest, the strange square black turret
    With never a door,
Just a loop to admit the quick lizards;

Then, stand there and hear
The birds' quiet singing, that tells us
    What life is, so clear?
—The secret they sang to Ulysses
    When, ages ago,
He heard and he knew this life's secret
    I hear and I know.

Ah, see! The sun breaks o'er Calvano;
    He strikes the great gloom
And flutters it o'er the mount's summit
    In airy gold fume.
All is over. Look out, see the gipsy,
    Our tinker and smith,
Has arrived, set up bellows and forge,
    And down-squatted forthwith
To his hammering, under the wall there;
    One eye keeps aloof
The urchins that itch to be putting
    His jews'-harps to proof,
While the other, thro' locks of curled wire,
    Is watching how sleek
Shines the hog, come to share in the windfall
    —Chew, abbot's own cheek!
All is over. Wake up and come out now,
    And down let us go,
And see the fine things got in order
    At church for the show
Of the Sacrament, set forth this evening.
    To-morrow's the Feast.
Of the Rosary's Virgin, by no means
    Of Virgins the least,
As you'll hear in the off-hand discourse
    Which (all nature, no art)
The Dominican brother, these three weeks,
    Was getting by heart.
Not a pillar nor post but is dizened
    With red and blue papers;
All the roof waves with ribbons, each altar
    A-blaze with long tapers;
But the great masterpiece is the scaffold
    Rigged glorious to hold
All the fiddlers and fifers and drummers
    And trumpeters bold,
Not afraid of Bellini nor Auber,

Bellini] Vincenzo Bellini (1801–35), composer of opera   Auber] Daniel François Esprit
Auber (1782–1871), composer of *opéra comique*

Who, when the priest's hoarse,
Will strike us up something that's brisk
    For the feast's second course.
And then will the flaxen-wigged Image
    Be carried in pomp
Thro' the plain, while in gallant procession
    The priests mean to stomp.
All round the glad church lie old bottles
    With gunpowder stopped,
Which will be, when the Image re-enters,
    Religiously popped;
And at night from the crest of Calvano
    Great bonfires will hang,
On the plain will the trumpets join chorus,
    And more poppers bang.
At all events, come—to the garden
    As far as the wall;
See me tap with a hoe on the plaster
    Till out there shall fall
A scorpion with wide angry nippers!

    —'Such trifles!' you say?
Fortù, in my England at home,
    Men meet gravely to-day
And debate, if abolishing Corn-laws
    Be righteous and wise
—If 'twere proper, Scirocco should vanish
    In black from the skies!

74   from *'De Gustibus—'*

What I love best in all the world
Is a castle, precipice-encurled,
In a gash of the wind-grieved Apennine.
Or look for me, old fellow of mine,
(If I get my head from out the mouth
O' the grave, and loose my spirit's bands,
And come again to the land of lands)—
In a sea-side house to the farther South,
Where the baked cicala dies of drouth,
And one sharp tree—'tis a cypress—stands,
By the many hundred years red-rusted,
Rough iron-spiked, ripe fruit-o'ercrusted,
My sentinel to guard the sands
To the water's edge. For, what expands

Before the house, but the great opaque
Blue breadth of sea without a break?
While, in the house, for ever crumbles
Some fragment of the frescoed walls,
From blisters where a scorpion sprawls.
A girl bare-footed brings, and tumbles
Down on the pavement, green-flesh melons,
And says there's news to-day—the king
Was shot at, touched in the liver-wing,
Goes with his Bourbon arm in a sling:
—She hopes they have not caught the felons.
Italy, my Italy!
Queen Mary's saying serves for me—
    (When fortune's malice
    Lost her—Calais)—
Open my heart and you will see
Graved inside of it, 'Italy'.
Such lovers old are I and she:
So it always was, so shall ever be!

75   *Up at a Villa—Down in the City*

As Distinguished by an Italian Person of Quality

I

Had I but plenty of money, money enough and to spare,
The house for me, no doubt, were a house in the city-square;
Ah, such a life, such a life, as one leads at the window there!

II

Something to see, by Bacchus, something to hear, at least!
There, the whole day long, one's life is a perfect feast;
While up at a villa one lives, I maintain it, no more than a beast.

III

Well now, look at our villa! stuck like the horn of a bull
Just on a mountain-edge as bare as the creature's skull,
Save a mere shag of a bush with hardly a leaf to pull!
—I scratch my own, sometimes, to see if the hair's turned wool.

IV

But the city, oh the city—the square with the houses! Why?
They are stone-faced, white as a curd, there's something to take the
    eye!

Houses in four straight lines, not a single front awry;
You watch who crosses and gossips, who saunters, who hurries by;
Green blinds, as a matter of course, to draw when the sun gets high;
And the shops with fanciful signs which are painted properly.

V

What of a villa? Though winter be over in March by rights,
'Tis May perhaps ere the snow shall have withered well off the heights:
You've the brown ploughed land before, where the oxen steam and
    wheeze,
And the hills over-smoked behind by the faint grey olive-trees.

VI

Is it better in May, I ask you? You've summer all at once;
In a day he leaps complete with a few strong April suns.
'Mid the sharp short emerald wheat, scarce risen three fingers well,
The wild tulip, at end of its tube, blows out its great red bell
Like a thin clear bubble of blood, for the children to pick and sell.

VII

Is it ever hot in the square? There's a fountain to spout and splash!
In the shade it sings and springs; in the shine such foam-bows flash
On the horses with curling fish-tails, that prance and paddle and pash
Round the lady atop in her conch—fifty gazers do not abash,
Though all that she wears is some weeds round her waist in a sort of
    sash.

VIII

All the year long at the villa, nothing to see though you linger,
Except yon cypress that points like death's lean lifted forefinger.
Some think fireflies pretty, when they mix i' the corn and mingle,
Or thrid the stinking hemp till the stalks of it seem a-tingle.
Late August or early September, the stunning cicala is shrill,
And the bees keep their tiresome whine round the resinous firs on the
    hill.
Enough of the seasons,—I spare you the months of the fever and chill.

IX

Ere you open your eyes in the city, the blessed church-bells begin:
No sooner the bells leave off than the diligence rattles in:
You get the pick of the news, and it costs you never a pin.
By-and-by there's the travelling doctor gives pills, lets blood, draws
    teeth;
Or the Pulcinello-trumpet breaks up the market beneath.
At the post-office such a scene-picture—the new play, piping hot!
And a notice how, only this morning, three liberal thieves were shot.

Above it, behold the Archbishop's most fatherly of rebukes,
And beneath, with his crown and his lion, some little new law of the
    Duke's!
Or a sonnet with flowery marge, to the Reverend Don So-and-so
Who is Dante, Boccaccio, Petrarca, Saint Jerome and Cicero,
'And moreover,' (the sonnet goes rhyming), 'the skirts of Saint Paul has
    reached,
Having preached us those six Lent-lectures more unctuous than ever he
    preached.'
Noon strikes,—here sweeps the procession! our Lady borne smiling and
    smart
With a pink gauze gown all spangles, and seven swords stuck in her
    heart!
Bang-whang-whang goes the drum, *tootle-te-tootle* the fife;
No keeping one's haunches still: it's the greatest pleasure in life.

X

But bless you, it's dear—it's dear! fowls, wine, at double the rate.
They have clapped a new tax upon salt, and what oil pays passing the
    gate
It's a horror to think of. And so, the villa for me, not the city!
Beggars can scarcely be choosers: but still—ah, the pity, the pity!
Look, two and two go the priests, then the monks with cowls and
    sandals,
And the penitents dressed in white shirts, a-holding the yellow candles;
One, he carries a flag up straight, and another a cross with handles
And the Duke's guard brings up the rear, for the better prevention of
    scandals:
Bang-whang-whang goes the drum, *tootle-te-tootle* the fife.
Oh, a day in the city-square, there is no such pleasure in life!

ARTHUR HUGH CLOUGH
1819–1861

76   from *Amours de Voyage*

Claude to Eustace

I

Dear Eustatio, I write that you may write me an answer,
Or at the least to put us again *en rapport* with each other.
Rome disappoints me much,—St Peter's, perhaps, in especial
Only the Arch of Titus and view from the Lateran please me:

This, however, perhaps is the weather, which truly is horrid.
Greece must be better, surely; and yet I am feeling so spiteful,
That I could travel to Athens, to Delphi, and Troy, and Mount Sinai,
Though but to see with my eyes that these are vanity also.

Rome disappoints me much; I hardly as yet understand, but
Rubbishy seems the word that most exactly would suit it.
All the foolish destructions, and all the sillier savings,
All the incongruous things of past incompatible ages,
Seem to be treasured up here to make fools of present and future.
Would to Heaven the old Goths had made a cleaner sweep of it!
Would to Heaven some new ones would come and destroy these
    churches!
However, one can live in Rome as also in London.
It is a blessing, no doubt, to be rid, at least for a time, of
All one's friends and relations,—yourself (forgive me!) included,—
All the *assujettissement* of having been what one has been,
What one thinks one is, or thinks that others suppose one;
Yet, in despite of all, we turn like fools to the English.
Vernon has been my fate; who is here the same that you knew him
Making the tour, it seems, with friends of the name of Trevellyn.

II

Rome disappoints me still; but I shrink and adapt myself to it.
Somehow a tyrannous sense of a superincumbent oppression
Still, wherever I go, accompanies ever, and makes me
Feel like a tree (shall I say?) buried under a ruin of brickwork.
Rome, believe me, my friend, is like its own Monte Testaceo,
Merely a marvellous mass of broken and castaway wine-pots.
Ye gods! what do I want with this rubbish of ages departed,
Things that Nature abhors, the experiments that she has failed in?
What do I find in the Forum? An archway and two or three pillars.
Well, but St Peter's? Alas, Bernini has filled it with sculpture!
No one can cavil, I grant, at the size of the great Coliseum.
Doubtless the notion of grand and capacious and massive amusement,
This the old Romans had; but tell me, is this an idea?
Yet of solidity much, but of splendour little is extant:
'Brickwork I found thee, and marble I left thee!' their Emperor
    vaunted;
'Marble I thought thee, and brickwork I find thee!' the Tourist may
    answer.

THOMAS HARDY
1840–1928

77   *In the Old Theatre, Fiesole*

I traced the Circus whose gray stones incline
Where Rome and dim Etruria interjoin,
Till came a child who showed an ancient coin
That bore the image of a Constantine.

She lightly passed; nor did she once opine
How, better than all books, she had raised for me
In swift perspective Europe's history
Through the vast years of Caesar's sceptred line.

For in my distant plot of English loam
'Twas but to delve, and straightway there to find
Coins of like impress. As with one half blind
Whom common simples cure, her act flashed home
In that mute moment to my opened mind
The power, the pride, the reach of perished Rome.

OSCAR WILDE
1854–1900

78   *The Grave of Shelley*

Like burnt-out torches by a sick man's bed
    Gaunt cypress-trees stand round the sun bleached stone;
    Here doth the little night-owl make her throne,
And the slight lizard show his jewelled head.
And, where the chaliced poppies flame to red,
    In the still chamber of yon pyramid
    Surely some Old-World Sphinx lurks darkly hid,
Grim warder of this pleasaunce of the dead.

Ah! sweet indeed to rest within the womb
    Of Earth, great mother of eternal sleep,
But sweeter far for thee a restless tomb
    In the blue cavern of an echoing deep,
Or where the tall ships founder in the gloom
    Against the rocks of some wave-shattered steep.

77 Fiesole] a Tuscan hilltop village with a Roman amphitheatre, overlooking Florence

D. H. LAWRENCE
1885–1930

79   *Bat*

At evening, sitting on this terrace,
When the sun from the west, beyond Pisa, beyond the mountains of
   Carrara
Departs, and the world is taken by surprise . . .

When the tired flower of Florence is in gloom beneath the glowing
Brown hills surrounding . . .

When under the arches of the Ponte Vecchio
A green light enters against stream, flush from the west,
Against the current of obscure Arno . . .

Look up, and you see things flying
Between the day and the night;
Swallows with spools of dark thread sewing the shadows together.

A circle swoop, and a quick parabola under the bridge arches
Where light pushes through;
A sudden turning upon itself of a thing in the air.
A dip to the water.

And you think:
'The swallows are flying so late!'

Swallows?

Dark air-life looping
Yet missing the pure loop . . .
A twitch, a twitter, an elastic shudder in flight
And serrated wings against the sky,
Like a glove, a black glove thrown up at the light,
And falling back.

Never swallows!
Bats!
The swallows are gone.

At a wavering instant the swallows gave way to bats
By the Ponte Vecchio . . .
Changing guard.

Bats, and an uneasy creeping in one's scalp
As the bats sweep overhead!
Flying madly.

Pipistrello!
Black piper on an infinitesimal pipe.
Little lumps that fly in air and have voices indefinite, wildly vindictive;

Wings like bits of umbrella.

Bats!

Creatures that hang themselves up like an old rag, to sleep;
And disgustingly upside down.
Hanging upside down like rows of disgusting old rags
And grinning in their sleep.
Bats!

In China the bat is symbol of happiness

Not for me!

80   *Bare Almond-Trees*

Wet almond-trees, in the rain,
Like iron sticking grimly out of earth;
Black almond trunks, in the rain,
Like iron implements twisted, hideous, out of the earth,
Out of the deep, soft fledge of Sicilian winter-green,
Earth-grass uneatable,
Almond trunks curving blackly, iron-dark, climbing the slopes.

Almond-tree, beneath the terrace rail,
Black, rusted, iron trunk,
You have welded your thin stems finer,
Like steel, like sensitive steel in the air,
Grey, lavender, sensitive steel, curving thinly and brittly up in a
    parabola.

What are you doing in the December rain?
Have you a strange electric sensitiveness in your steel tips?
Do you feel the air for electric influences
Like some strange magnetic apparatus?
Do you take in messages, in some strange code,

From heaven's wolfish, wandering electricity, that prowls so constantly
    round Etna?
Do you take the whisper of sulphur from the air?
Do you hear the chemical accents of the sun?
Do you telephone the roar of the waters over the earth?
And from all this, do you make calculations?

Sicily, December's Sicily in a mass of rain
With iron branching blackly, rusted like old, twisted implements
And brandishing and stooping over earth's wintry fledge, climbing the
    slopes
Of uneatable soft green!

SIEGFRIED SASSOON
1886–1967

81   *Villa d'Este Gardens*[1]

'Of course you saw the Villa d'Este Gardens',
Writes one of my Italianistic friends.
Of course; of course; I saw them in October,
Spired with pinaceous ornamental gloom
Of that arboreal elegy the cypress.

Those fountains, too, 'like ghosts of cypresses';—
(The phrase occurred to me while I was leaning
On an old balustrade; imbibing sunset;
Wrapped in my verse vocation)—how they linked me
With Byron, Landor, Liszt, and Robert Browning! . . .
A *Liebestraum* of Liszt cajoled my senses.

My language favoured Landor, chaste and formal.
My intellect (though slightly in abeyance)
Functioned against a Byronistic background.
Then Browning jogged my elbow; bade me hob-nob
With some forgotten painter of dim frescoes
That haunt the Villa's intramural twilight.

While roaming in the Villa d'Este Gardens
I felt like that . . . and fumbled for my note-book.

---

[1] Villa d'Este Gardens, begun in 1550, are at Tivoli just east of Rome.

LOUIS MacNEICE
1907–1963

82   *Ravenna*

What do I remember of my visit to Ravenna? Firstly,
That I had come from Venice where I had come from Greece
So that my eyes seemed dim and the world flat. Secondly,
That after Tintoretto's illusory depth and light
The mosaics knocked me flat. There they stood. The geese
Had hissed as they pecked the corn from Theodora's groin,
Yet here she stands on the wall of San Vitale, as bright
As life and a long shot taller, self-made empress,
Who patronized the monophysites and the Greens
And could have people impaled. There was also and thirdly the long
Lost naval port of Caesar, surviving now in the name
In Classe: the sea today is behind the scenes
Like his Liburnian galleys. What went wrong
With Byzantium as with Rome went slowly, their fame
Sunk in malarial marsh. The flat lands now
Are ruled by a sugar refinery and a church,
Sant' Apollinare in Classe. What do I remember of Ravenna?
A bad smell mixed with glory, and the cold
Eyes that belie the tessellated gold.

DYLAN THOMAS
1914–1953

83   In a shuttered room I roast
Like a pumpkin in a serra
And the sun like buttered toast
Drips upon the classic terra,
Upon swimming pool and pillar,
Loggia, lemon, pineclad pico,
And this quite enchanting villa
That isn't worth a fico,
Upon terrace and frutteto
Of this almost a palazzo
Where the people talk potato
And the weather drives me pazzo—

GAVIN EWART

1916–

84   *On First Looking into Michael Grant's* Cities of
Vesuvius

In battledress, yes, I was there. That dramatic great wartime eruption
    spewed out the red-hot shit; it looked very splendid at night
crushing the villas and trees, and the ash came down, a red-purple,
    to the depth of an old-fashioned foot. We moved the trucks and
        the guns
for safety. But our letters home were security-minded. No mention.
    You needed a four-wheel drive to churn through that stuff on the
        road.
This was in March '44 (as the clubland talks would remind you),
    of Europe's one active volcano the last recorded display.

Before this happened, I took, on an outing, a party of gunners
    (we weren't operational then) to Pompeii; they wanted the church,
the wine-shops, the cheap souvenirs. I opted, alone, for the *Scavi.*
    I had one guide to myself—and paid with a tin of corned beef.
We covered a lot of the ground. His English was good but not
        perfect—
    I was pleased to hear of a king whose name seemed to be Charles
        the Turd.
Although I went there three times—with a friend on two visits—
    and the guide remarked with a grin, as we looked at the rough
        plaster thighs,
how it was obvious enough that the body we saw was a woman.
    We went round the brothel as well. He lit up the paintings on
        walls
with a candle held high; you could see where each girl's speciality,
        pictured
    above the door of her room, enticed you inside to her skill.
He unlocked for us, too, with his key, that famous and frivolous fresco
    which shows the soldier who weighs his huge uncircumcised cock
on the scales, and the gold goes up—for pleasure's more precious than
        money.
    Behind us, by accident, there (for this is inside a house door)
an American nurse walked by. She gave a great 'Oo!' and fled, shaken.
    I don't know what it's like now. But *Off Limits* would, then, be the
        words;

Scavi] excavations

and the delicate souls of the girls were protected, the brothel was
         banned; though
    plain enough in the road you could see a large bas-relief tool
to point the vernacular way to the house dedicated to Venus.
    With a naked foot, on dark nights, it must have been useful, at
        that.
Herculaneum wasn't so good. The best thing of all was the statue
    that shows Pan at work on a goat. This was our verdict, at least.

So, Grant, you swim into my ken. With your writing, so large and clear,
        telling
    of thirty-three years ago now—more or less, give or take, to the
        day
when the boil on the neck of the land burst, on the warlike eighteenth
    and we stood with our drinks, there, to watch, on the roof of the
        officers' mess,
how the lava rolled down in the dark, a slow raw mass on the skyline.
    We didn't think so much, then, of the suffering; how those who
        died
choked in the chemical fumes—like the brave and inquisitive Pliny,
    like the dog at the end of its chain. That's one of the things about
        war.
The dying was commonplace, then. It was interesting, more than
        distressing.
    And of course you're entirely right, the gladiatorial shows
were disgusting (as Seneca said); more so than the drinking and fucking.
    Dr Arnold, the father, who wrote that the Bay of Naples was one
long drama (and 'fearsome' too) of Sin and Death, and, yes, Pleasure,
    got it wrong in his Puritan way—and so did his talented son.
Why should there be shame? No one lived (as you say) to be much over
        forty—
    over most of the world, to this day, that's an average life.

We are exceptions, aloof and well-dressed in our self-conscious cities.
    If any small British town, perhaps a resort like Torquay,
were quickly hermetically sealed, volcanoed and covered for ever,
    would archaeologists find such a high standard of art?
Architecture, as well. I think you make a good point there.
    I know they crucified slaves. There was cruelty, but easiness too;
the easiness of a land where the passions could be quite volcanic
    but with the blue sea and sky there was always benevolent sun.

ELIZABETH JENNINGS
1926–

85   *Men Fishing in the Arno*

I do not know what they are catching,
I only know that they stand there, leaning
A little like lovers, eager but not demanding,
Waiting and hoping for a catch, money,
A meal tomorrow but today, still there, steady.

And the river also moves as calmly
From the waterfall slipping to a place
A mind could match its thought with
And above, the cypresses with cool gestures
Command the city, give it formality.

It is like this every day but more especially
On Sundays; every few yards you see a fisherman,
Each independent, none
Working with others and yet accepting
Others. From this one might, I think,

Build a whole way of living—men in their mazes
Of secret desires yet keeping a sense
Of order outwardly, hoping
Not too flamboyantly, satisfied with little
Yet not surprised should the river suddenly
Yield a hundredfold, every hunger appeased.

PETER PORTER
1929–

86   *The Cats of Campagnatico*

Since a harebrained Devil has changed the world
To scenes from a Nature Documentary,
There are those of us who will forever seek
Rational landscapes, dotted with walled cemeteries,
Unquestioned rivers of familiar fords
And an efficient bus from which adulteresses

86 Campagnatico] small mountain village/town in lower Tuscany, north-east of Grosseto

Alight before the ascent to the neighbour village.
Not that His blocked thumb is absent: those
English families tooting along the scatty road
(Our fifteen-year-old crunching the clutch
of the little Fiat) are outside the cemetery
Before anyone notices the just-widowed blob
At the armorial gates—the regret, the shame
The silence—she at the gardens of death which need
A constant tending, and us hurrying
To lunch at the hydrophilic villa—
The Oldest Presence of All will be well pleased.
Not just a vignette, we reflect, this shadowless day
In Southern Tuscany, more a looking for shades
Which match the petrified intelligence of time:
One sees the small bends which history makes
In the lanes of scarcely-visited villages.
True, this one is in Dante, and that oleander-screened wall
You take for the headquarters of the Carabinieri
Might be an out-station of the Piccolomini,
If only you could remember which is which
Among the towers that mark the lesions of the sky.
Siena is as far away as London; life as far away
As last night's dream whose every promontory
Is in the present. Now, coming through the gate,
The view is a pastoral benediction for those
Who have never lived in Arcadia. *Thank God,
Grace à Dieu, Gott sei dank*—we are
As international as an opera festival,
We who love Italy. We have no home
And come from nowhere, a marvellous patrimony.
Then before the laying of the table in the arbour,
The helpful barefoot girls from good schools,
The gossip and the wine, a sudden vision
Of belonging. The cats of Campagnatico,
Which are never fully grown and have never
Been kittens, will not move for the honking motorist
But expect to be gone round. Thin and cared-for,
Fat and neglected, watchful and hardly seen awake,
Cool-haired in the sun and warm in shadow,
Embodying Nature's own perversity,
They lie on this man-made floor, the dialectic
Of survival. O God, we cry, help us through
Your school of adaptation—between the fur of the cat
And the cement of extinction, there are only
Cypress moments lingering and the long tray of the sky.

Piccolomini] a great Sienese family (which included Pope Pius II) who have a provincial
residence in Campagnatico

GREECE AND THE BALKANS

JOHN MILTON
1608–1674

87   from *Paradise Regained*

Look once more ere we leave this specular mount
Westward, much nearer by south-west, behold
Where on the Aegean shore a city stands
Built nobly, pure the air, and light the soil,
Athens the eye of Greece, Mother of Arts
And Eloquence, native to famous wits
Or hospitable, in her sweet recess,
City or suburban, studious walks and shades;
See there the olive grove of Academe,
Plato's retirement, where the Attic bird
Trills her thick-warbled notes the summer long,
There flowery hill Hymettus with the sound
Of bees' industrious murmur oft invites
To studious musing; there Ilissus rolls
His whispering stream; within the walls then view
The schools of ancient sages; his who bred
Great Alexander to subdue the world,
Lyceum there, and painted Stoa next:
There thou shalt hear and learn the secret power
Of harmony in tones and numbers hit
By voice or hand, and various-measured verse,
Aeolian charms and Dorian Lyric odes,
And his who gave them breath, but higher sung,
Blind Melesigenes thence Homer called,
Whose poem Phoebus challenged for his own.
Thence what the lofty grave tragedians taught
In Chorus or Iambic, teachers best
Of moral prudence, with delight received
In brief sententious precepts, while they treat
Of fate, and chance, and change in human life;
High actions, and high passions best describing.
Thence to the famous orators repair,
Those ancient, whose resistless eloquence
Wielded at will that fierce democratie,
Shook the Arsenal and fulmined over Greece,
To Macedon, and Artaxerxes' throne;
To sage philosophy next lend thine ear,

From heaven descended to the low-roofed house
Of Socrates, see there his tenement,
Whom well inspired the Oracle pronounced
Wisest of men; from whose mouth issued forth
Mellifluous streams that watered all the schools
Of academics old and new, with those
Surnamed Peripatetics, and the sect
Epicurean, and the Stoic severe;
These here revolve, or, as thou lik'st, at home,
Till time mature thee to a kingdom's weight;
These rules will render thee a king complete
Within thy self, much more with empire joined.

MARK AKENSIDE

1721–1770

88   from *The Pleasures of Imagination*

Genius of ancient Greece! whose faithful steps
Well-pleased I follow through the sacred paths
Of nature and of science; nurse divine
Of all heroic deeds and fair desires!
O! let the breath of thy extended praise
Inspire my kindling bosom to the height
Of this untempted theme. Nor be my thoughts
Presumptuous counted, if, amid the calm
That sooths this vernal evening into smiles,
I steal impatient from the sordid haunts
Of strife and low ambition, to attend
Thy sacred presence in the sylvan shade,
By their malignant footsteps ne'er profaned.
Descend, propitious! to my favoured eye;
Such in thy mien, thy warm, exalted air,
As when the Persian tyrant, foiled and stung
With shame and desperation, gnashed his teeth
To see thee rend the pageants of his throne;
And at the lightning of thy lifted spear
Crouched like a slave. Bring all thy martial spoils,
Thy palms, thy laurels, thy triumphal songs,
Thy smiling band of arts, thy godlike sires
Of civil wisdom, thy heroic youth
Warm from the schools of glory. Guide my way
Through fair Lyceum's walk, the green retreats

Of Academus, and the thymy vale,
Where oft enchanted with Socratic sounds,
Ilissus pure devolved his tuneful stream
In gentler murmurs. From the blooming store
Of these auspicious fields, may I unblamed
Transplant some living blossoms to adorn
My native clime: while far above the flight
Of fancy's plume aspiring, I unlock
The springs of ancient wisdom; while I join
Thy name, thrice honoured! with th' immortal praise
Of nature; while to my compatriot youth
I point the high example of thy sons,
And tune to Attic themes the British lyre.

WALTER SAVAGE LANDOR
1775–1864

89   *Corinna, to Tanagra, from Athens*

Tanagra! think not I forget
    Thy beautifully storeyed streets;
Be sure my memory bathes yet
    In clear Thermodon, and yet greets
The blythe and liberal shepherd-boy
Whose sunny bosom swells with joy
When we accept his matted rushes
Upheaved with sylvan fruit; away he bounds, and blushes.

I promise to bring back with me
    What thou with transport wilt receive,
The only proper gift for thee,
    Of which no mortal shall bereave
In later times thy mouldering walls,
Until the last old turret falls;
A crown, a crown from Athens won,
A crown no God can wear, beside Latona's son.

There may be cities who refuse
    To their own child the honours due,
And look ungently on the Muse;
    But ever shall those cities rue

89 Corinna] a Boeotian poetess of the third century BC   Tanagra] town in Boeotia
Latona's son] Apollo

The dry, unyielding, niggard breast,
Offering no nourishment, no rest,
To that young head which soon shall rise
Disdainfully, in might and glory, to the skies.

Sweetly where caverned Dirce flows
    Do white-armed maidens chaunt my lay,
Flapping the while with laurel-rose
    The honey-gathering tribes away;
And sweetly, sweetly Attick tongues
Lisp your Corinna's early songs;
To her with feet more graceful come
The verses that have dwelt in kindred breasts at home.

O let thy children lean aslant
    Against the tender mother's knee,
And gaze into her face, and want
    To know what magic there can be
In words that urge some eyes to dance,
While others as in holy trance
Look up to heaven: be such my praise!
Why linger? I must haste, or lose the Delphic bays.

WILLIAM HAYGARTH

fl. early 19th century

90   from *Greece*

    Genius of Greece! thou livest, though thy domes
Are fallen; here, in this thy loved abode,
Thine Athens, as I breathe the clear pure air
Which thou hast breathed, climb the dark mountain's side
Which thou hast trod, or in the temple's porch
Pause on the sculptured beauties which thine eye
Has often viewed delighted, I confess
Thy nearer influence; I feel thy power,
Exalting every wish to virtuous hope;
I hear thy solemn voice amidst the crash
Of fanes hurled prostrate by barbarian hands,
Calling me forth to tread with thee the paths
Of wisdom, or to listen to thy harp
Hymning immortal strains. Genius of Greece!
Lead me, O lead me to thy deep retreats,

Where the loud savage yell that mocks thy woes
May never reach us; then with aspect mild
Unfold the treasures of thine ample page;
Instruct my reason; guide my fancy's flight,
And bear me back along the stream of time,
To those bright days when thou wert great and free.
     The sultry rage is passed, and the broad orb
Of day descending in a vap'rous flood
Of golden light, leans on th' horizon's verge.
Now whilst the rays of ev'ning slumb'ring rest
Upon the mountain's bosom—whilst her soft
And fragrant moisture floats along the sky,
Let us ascend yon craggy eminence,
And view the glorious scene which opens round
Far as the eye can wander. From the plain
Cecropia's citadel uprears its brow,
Rugged, and crowned with circumambient walls
And glitt'ring temples; at its rocky base
The shattered wrecks of ancient days repose,
Half-sunk in shadow, capitals and shafts,
Porches and monuments, the sculptured pomp
Of pediments, towers and triumphal arcs,
And marble fanes, and mould'ring theatres.
Imagination, kindling at the view,
Throws o'er the varied prospect the clear light
Of former ages; the still solitudes
Once more are peopled, and the sacred bands
Of poets and of sages seek again
Their shady groves and marble porticos.
Here, from the rocky Pnyx, the eloquence
Of Athens lightened over Greece, and winged
Her thunders; I behold her orators
Gath'ring their robes, and pointing to the shores
Whose billows lave the tombs of those who bled
For liberty. Here, ling'ring on the banks
Of pure Ilissus, underneath the shade
Of aged planes, the philosophic few
Apart retire, to hang upon the lips
Of Wisdom's son. There, on the marble steps
Of the vast stadium's mound, range over range,
Assembled multitudes gaze silently,
In breathless expectation, on the throng
Of combatants striving for mastery
In fight, in wrestling, or in fervid course.

Pnyx] amphitheatre cut out of rock, west of the Acropolis; used for assemblies
Wisdom's son] Socrates held many of his philosophical conversations on the banks of the Ilissus

There soars Hymettus, flinging far around
His dark arms to the main, whilst at his feet
I trace a gleaming line of steeds and cars,
And mailed warriors guiding with their spears
The serried phalanxes to Marathon.
Now westward turn your gaze, and see amidst
Yon olive woods, whose broad and verdant belt
Invests the plain, the consecrated groves
Of Academus, where Philosophy,
With finger pressed upon his withered lip,
Leads by the hand a stole-clad group to hear
From Plato's mouth his Heav'nly eloquence.
Thence further glancing, let your eye repose
Upon the distant mountains whose dark range
Bounds the wide prospect, and exulting flash
When on yon pointed peak, Aegaleos,
It views, or seems to view, the Persian king
Thrice leaping from his throne, as he beholds
His shattered navy dark'ning the broad wave
Of Salamis. Now strain your utmost sight
To Corinth, and the hills of Pelops' isle,
Which on the amber sky of ev'ning float
Like summer clouds, thence homeward turning, view
The wide Saronic sea, broken in capes,
In headlands, and in gulfs, Piraeus' Bay,
And bleak Munychia; mark its golden breast
Studded with purple isles, and overhung
With marble temples, to the level ray
Of sunset gleaming, till it melts in gloom
Beyond the shadows of Aegina's rocks,
Amidst the dark Aegean's distant surge.

91   from *Greece*

Mournful is the remembrance which awakes
Within my breast, as I ascend thy heights,
O Oeta! nor can thy majestic scenes,
Thy woody fastnesses, thy naked cliffs
Sinking in precipice, or shooting bold
In towered masses, charm my mind from thoughts

Hymettus] range of hills to south and south-east of Athens   Aegaleos] mountain on the
north-east of the bay of Salamis   Pelops' isle] Peloponnesus   Munychia] remains of
the naval dockyard built in the fourth century BC.

91 Oeta] mountain range extending from Thermopylae to the Ambracian gulf

Of former deeds, and glories now no more.
Bulwark of Greece, whilst Greece had still a name,
How awful did thy rocky barriers rise
To the invader, when from far he viewed
Thy rugged form imprinted on the sky
Of ev'ning glowing with its golden tints:
He vaunted not when, on thy highest point,
He saw unnumbered fires streaking the gloom
Of night with ruddy gleams, and darting wide
From peak to peak in one long stream of light,
The silent signal that the foe was nigh:
He vaunted not when, with a nearer glance,
Down thy rough sides he traced a glitt'ring line
Of radiant panoply, and watched the rays
Of morning playing on the helm and spear
Of warriors, marching with firm tread to sounds
Of Doric flute; but now amidst thy glens
No sound is heard, save when the loosened rock
Thund'ring down the torrent, breaks on the ear
Of silence, or the robber, from his lone
And ruined watch-tower gathering his bands,
Wakens the echoes with his whistle shrill.
  Heavily rise the long blue clouds of smoke
From yonder hamlet, and in wavy folds
Unrolling slowly to the moon's pale ray,
Streak the deep shades of night; the kindling fire,
At first half-smothered, casts a livid glare
Upon the lowest wreaths, till bursting forth
In one o'erwhelming blaze it upward shoots
Its pointed spires, and with a bloody tint
Stains every object; crag, and tree, and mosque,
And tap'ring pinnacle, reflect the light,
And glow more vivid 'midst th' impending gloom.
Wide spreads the deadly ravage; every cot
Pours forth its inmates; youth and hoary age,
Roused from their slumbers, crowd in haste along,
Tearing their locks and garments, as they gaze
On the devouring flame; but hark! a cry
Of louder woe appals the ear, a shriek
Of female agony, and now the shouts
As of contending hosts—they come, they come,
The robbers of the mountains,[1] and amidst
The wild uproar, rush on their trembling prey,
Tear the young daughter from the aged sire,

[1] On our arrival at Zetouni we found the town in much confusion. A party of robbers had descended in the night from the neighbouring mountains, attacked the houses of some poor Greeks, carried off three men, and killed another' (W.H.).

And from her lover drag the weeping bride;
The night re-echoes with the voice of grief,
And shrieks and wailings load the mournful breeze.
     His forehead veiled in wreaths of mist, his brow
White with the age of an eternal snow,
His giant form, furrowed with channels deep
By wintry torrents worn, Parnassus bursts
The twilight gloom which slumbers at his feet,
And meets the rising ray.—Ye Delphian shades,
Ye dreary solitudes, ye terrors stern,
Of cave and yawning dell, where Silence holds
Her empire unmolested, save by sounds
Of savage melody, the wild beasts' roar,
Or rush of distant waters; ye grey rocks,
Cleft by the midnight tempest, shooting high
Your rugged tops, with grass and lichen wreathed,
To Heav'n; ye olive groves, which wave your boughs
To the hoarse blast that sweeps the mountain's breast,
With pleasing dread I view you, and confess
An awe which overpow'rs, yet charms the soul.

GEORGE GORDON, LORD BYRON
1788–1824

92   *Written after Swimming from Sestos to Abydos*

1

If, in the month of dark December,
     Leander, who was nightly wont
(What maid will not the tale remember?)
     To cross thy stream, broad Hellespont!

2

If, when the wintry tempest roared,
     He sped to Hero, nothing loth,
And thus of old thy current poured,
     Fair Venus! how I pity both!

3

For *me*, degenerate modern wretch,
     Though in the genial month of May
My dripping limbs I faintly stretch,
     And think I've done a feat to-day.

4

But since he crossed the rapid tide,
  According to the doubtful story,
To woo,—and—Lord knows what beside,
  And swam for Love, as I for Glory;

5

'Twere hard to say who fared the best:
  Sad mortals! thus the Gods still plague you!
He lost his labour, I my jest:
  For he was drowned, and I've the ague.

93   ## from *Don Juan*

1

The Isles of Greece, the Isles of Greece!
  Where burning Sappho loved and sung,
Where grew the arts of War and Peace,
  Where Delos rose, and Phoebus sprung!
Eternal summer gilds them yet,
But all, except their Sun, is set.

2

The Scian and the Teian muse,
  The Hero's harp, the Lover's lute,
Have found the fame your shores refuse:
  Their place of birth alone is mute
To sounds which echo further west
Than your Sires' 'Islands of the Blest'.[1]

3

The mountains look on Marathon—
  And Marathon looks on the sea;
And musing there an hour alone,
  I dreamed that Greece might still be free;
For standing on the Persians' grave,
I could not deem myself a slave.

---

[1] The classical poets believed the Μακάρων νῆσοι to be the Cape Verde Islands or the Canaries.

4

A King sat on the rocky brow
  Which looks o'er sea-born Salamis;
And ships, by thousands, lay below,
  And men in nations;—all were his!
He counted them at break of day—
And, when the Sun set, where were they?

5

And where are they? and where art thou,
  My country? On thy voiceless shore
The heroic lay is tuneless now—
  The heroic bosom beats no more!
And must thy Lyre, so long divine,
Degenerate into hands like mine?

6

'Tis something, in the dearth of Fame,
  Though linked among a fettered race,
To feel at least a patriot's shame,
  Even as I sing, suffuse my face;
For what is left the poet here?
For Greeks a blush—for Greece a tear.

7

Must *we* but weep o'er days more blest?
  Must *we* but blush?—Our fathers bled.
Earth! render back from out thy breast
  A remnant of our Spartan dead!
Of the three hundred grant but three,
To make a new Thermopylae!

8

What, silent still? and silent all?
  Ah! no;—the voices of the dead
Sound like a distant torrent's fall,
  And answer, 'Let one living head,
But one arise,—we come, we come!'
'Tis but the living who are dumb.

9

In vain—in vain: strike other chords;
  Fill high the cup with Samian wine!
Leave battles to the Turkish hordes,
  And shed the blood of Scio's vine!

Hark! rising to the ignoble call—
How answers each bold Bacchanal!

10

You have the Pyrrhic dance as yet,
   Where is the Pyrrhic phalanx gone?
Of two such lessons, why forget
   The nobler and the manlier one?
You have the letters Cadmus gave—
Think ye he meant them for a slave?

11

Fill high the bowl with Samian wine!
   We will not think of themes like these!
It made Anacreon's song divine:
   He served—but served Polycrates—
A Tyrant; but our masters then
Were still, at least, our countrymen.

12

The Tyrant of the Chersonese
   Was Freedom's best and bravest friend;
That tyrant was Miltiades!
   Oh! that the present hour would lend
Another despot of the kind!
Such chains as his were sure to bind.

13

Fill high the bowl with Samian wine!
   On Suli's rock, and Parga's shore,
Exists the remnant of a line
   Such as the Doric mothers bore;
And there, perhaps, some seed is sown,
The Heracleidan blood might own.

14

Trust not for freedom to the Franks—
   They have a king who buys and sells;
In native swords, and native ranks,
   The only hope of courage dwells;
But Turkish force, and Latin fraud,
Would break your shield, however broad.

15

Fill high the bowl with Samian wine!
  Our virgins dance beneath the shade—
I see their glorious black eyes shine;
  But gazing on each glowing maid,
My own the burning tear-drop laves,
To think such breasts must suckle slaves.

16

Place me on Sunium's marbled steep,
  Where nothing, save the waves and I,
May hear our mutual murmurs sweep;
  There, swan-like, let me sing and die:
A land of slaves shall ne'er be mine—
Dash down yon cup of Samian wine!

Farewell to Malta

94

Adieu, ye joys of La Valette!
Adieu, sirocco, sun, and sweat!
Adieu, thou palace rarely entered!
Adieu, ye mansions where—I've ventured!
Adieu, ye cursed streets of stairs!
(How surely he who mounts you swears!)
Adieu, ye merchants often failing!
Adieu, thou mob for ever railing!
Adieu, ye packets—without letters!
Adieu, ye fools—who ape your betters!
Adieu, thou damned'st quarantine,
That gave me fever, and the spleen!
Adieu that stage which makes us yawn, Sirs,
Adieu, his Excellency's dancers!
Adieu to Peter—whom no fault's in,
But could not teach a colonel waltzing;
Adieu, ye females fraught with graces!
Adieu red coats, and redder faces!
Adieu the supercilious air
Of all that strut 'en militaire'!
I go—but God knows when, or why,
To smoky towns and cloudy sky,
To things (the honest truth to say)
As bad—but in a different way.

Farewell to these, but not adieu,
Triumphant sons of truest blue!

While either Adriatic shore,
And fallen chiefs, and fleets no more,
And nightly smiles, and daily dinners,
Proclaim you war and women's winners.
Pardon my Muse, who apt to prate is,
And take my rhyme—because 'tis 'gratis'.

And now I've got to Mrs Fraser,
Perhaps you think I mean to praise her—
And were I vain enough to think
My praise was worth this drop of ink,
A line—or two—were no hard matter,
As here, indeed, I need not flatter:
But she must be content to shine
In better praises than in mine,
With lively air, and open heart,
And fashion's ease, without its art;
Her hours can gaily glide along,
Nor ask the aid of idle song.

And now, O Malta! since thou'st got us,
Thou little military hothouse!
I'll not offend with words uncivil,
And wish thee rudely at the Devil,
But only stare from out my casement,
And ask, for what is such a place meant?
Then, in my solitary nook,
Return to scribbling, or a book,
Or take my physic while I'm able
(Two spoonfuls hourly by the label),
Prefer my nightcap to my beaver,
And bless the gods—I've got a fever.

RICHARD MONCKTON MILNES
1809–1885

95   from *The Ionian Islands*
Corfou

Thou pleasant island, whose rich garden-shores
Have had a long-lived fame of loveliness;
Recorded in the historic song, that framed

95 historic song] *Odyssey*, vii. 79 (Σχερίην ἐρατεινήν)

The unknown poet of an unknown time,
Illustrating his native Ithaca,
And all her bright society of isles,—
Most pleasant land! To us, who journeying come
From the far west, and fall upon thy charms,
Our earliest welcome to Ionian seas,
Thou art a wonder and a deep delight,
Thy usual habitants can never know.
Thou art a portal, whence the Orient,
The long-desired, long-dreamt-of Orient,
Opens upon us, with its stranger forms,
Outlines immense and gleaming distances,
And all the circumstance of faery-land.
Not only with a present happiness,
But taking from anticipated joys
An added sense of actual bliss, we stand
Upon thy cliffs, or tread the slopes that leave
No interval of shingle, rock, or sand,
Between their verdure and the Ocean's brow,—
Whose olive-groves (unlike the darkling growth,
That earns on western shores the traveller's scorn)
Can wear the grey that on their foliage lies,
As but the natural hoar of lengthened days,—
Making, with their thick-bossed and fissured trunks,
Bases far-spread and branches serpentine,
Sylvan cathedrals, such as in old times
Gave the first life to Gothic art, and led
Imagination so sublime a way.
Then forth advancing, to our novice eyes
How beautiful appears the concourse clad
In that which, of all garbs, may best befit
The grace and dignity of manly form:
The bright red open vest, falling upon
The white thick-folded kirtle, and low cap
Above the high-shorn brow.
                                        Nor less than these,
With earnest joy, and not injurious pride,
We recognise of Britain and her force
The wonted ensigns and far-known array;
And feel how now the everlasting sea,
Leaving his old and once imperious spouse,
To faint, in all the beauty of her tears,
On the dank footsteps of a mouldering throne,
Has taken to himself another mate,
Whom his uxorious passion has endowed,
Not only with her antient properties,
But with all other gifts and privilege,

Within the circle of his regal hand.
Now forward,—forward on a beaming path,
But be each step as fair as hope has feigned it,
For me, the memory of the little while,
That here I rested happily, within
The close-drawn pale of English sympathies,
Will bear the fruit of many an after-thought,
Bright in the dubious track of after-years.

SIR OWEN SEAMAN
1861–1936

96   *The Schoolmaster Abroad*

(*The steam yacht* Argonaut *was chartered from Messrs Perowne & Lunn by a body of public
school masters for the purposes of an educative visit to the Levant*)

O 'Isles' (as Byron said) 'of Greece!'
    For which the firm of Homer sang,
Especially that little piece
    Interpreted by Mr Lang;
Where the unblushing Sappho wrote
The hymns we hardly like to quote;—

I cannot share his grave regret
    Who found your fame had been and gone;
There seems to be a future yet
    For Tenedos and Marathon;
Fresh glory gilds their deathless sun,
And this is due to Dr Lunn!

What though your harpers twang no more?
    What though your various lyres are dumb?
See where by Cirrha's sacred shore,
    Bold Argonauts, the Ushers come!
All bring their maps and some their wives,
And at the vision Greece revives!

The Delphic oracles are off,
    But still the site is always there;
The fumes that made the Pythian cough
    Still permeate the conscious air;

96 Mr Lang] Andrew Lang (1844–1912), man of letters, translated the *Odyssey* and the
Iliad and wrote *World of Homer*   Cirrha] town at the foot of Mt. Parnassus

Parnassus, of the arduous 'grade',
May still be climbed, with local aid.

Lunching upon the self-same rock
  Whence Xerxes viewed the wine-red frith,
They realize with vivid shock
  The teachings of 'the smaller Smith';
With bated breath they murmur—'This
Is actually Salamis!'

They visit where Penelope
  Nightly unwove the work of day,
Staving her suitors off till he,
  Ulysses, let the long-bow play,
And on his brave grass-widow's breast
Forgot Calypso and the rest.

In Crete, where Theseus first embraced
  His Ariadne, they explore
(Just now authentically traced)
  The footprints of the Minotaur;
And follow, to the maze's source,
The thread of some profound discourse.

That isle where Leto, sick with fright,
  So scandalized her mortal kin,
Where young Apollo, lord of light,
  Commenced his progress as a twin—
Fair Delos, they shall get to know,
And Paros, where the marbles grow.

Not theirs the course of crude delight
  On which the common tourist wends;
From faith they move, by way of sight,
  To knowledge meant for noble ends;
'Twill be among their purest joys
To work it off upon the boys.

One hears the travelled teacher call
  Upon the Upper Fifth to note
(Touching the Spartan counter-wall)
  How great the lore of Mr Grote;
And tell them, 'His are just the views
I formed myself—at Syracuse!'

Mr Grote] George Grote, author of the famous eight-volume *History of Greece* (1846–56)

When Jones is at a loss to show
  Where certain islands ought to be,
How well to whack him hard and low
  And say, 'The pain is worse for me,
To whom the Cyclades are quite
Familiar, like the Isle of Wight.'

And then the lecture after prep.!
  The Magic Lantern's lurid slide!
The speaker pictured on the step
  Of some old shrine, with no inside;
Or groping on his reverent knees
For Eleusinian mysteries!

Hellas defunct? O say not so,
  While Public School-boys faint to hear
The tales of antique love or woe,
  Brought home and rendered strangely clear
With instantaneous Kodak-shots
Secured by Ushers on the spots!

GEOFFREY GRIGSON

1905–1985

97   *And Forgetful of Europe*

(Mlina 1935 to 1937)

Think now about all the things which made up
That place: you noticed first
Under the plane tree, where the red
And white canoes were, the green peppers
And the black figs on the stall: the countess then
(slightly red when we came close
Between the brown of her body
And her white bathing dress),
Her blonde hair pulled off her smart
Old face, her crimson nails, and not
A quiver in the guarded bust, as she rose
With Bull-dog Drummond from her wicker
Chair: then from the Countess
To the chapel, under the pink and the white

97 Mlina] now called Mlini; near Cavtat and Dubrovnik

Oleanders, up the path between the white walls
And the soft agrimony: the orchard with
Scarlet pomegranate flowers, the very deep
Stream full of light in its curved
Silk-stocking-coloured limestone bed.
A sulphur wagtail balanced, where it moved
Under the mill-house.
                 And then came
The first fall, where the water bellied out
Over a limestone hood (remember, my darling,
The cave behind the hood, and the way
The limestone coated the roots of the trees there):
And the second fall seen for a dinar,
So high the water just poured from
The intensest heaven, through the figs on the lime-
Stone precipice.
             I think there were doves
Sounding among the figs. Certainly
There were swallows all around, more
Wagtails, and two black and white
Dippers there.
             And when we came down
Again through the leaves it was obvious
That the chapel tower was new, that
The stones were machine-cut and too regular;
But then the sun was going down
Behind Cavtat: the sea turned a quieter blue
Crossed with catches of yellow, and
The pink and white of those two vast
Oleanders caught just the slight china-
Tea colour of the sun.

How we were hungry then: how we felt
We enjoyed the fish, the olives, and the chocolate
Cake, under the miniature emerald grapes!
How vigorously we talked of nothing with
The countess and old white and pink and
Wicked Strozzi! How we enjoyed our bridge with them,
The scarlet nails drumming *Tisch, Tisch,*
When the lead was wrong! And after
Our two rubbers at ten dinars
A hundred, you and I fifty dinars and
Five hundred to the bad, how we marked
The lights of the fish-spearers and wished
There was a moon over the cypresses,
And forgetful of Europe, walked to bed
In the warm wind from the mountain.

LAWRENCE DURRELL
1912–

98 *Sarajevo*

Bosnia. November. And the mountain roads
Earthbound but matching perfectly these long
And passionate self-communings counter-march,
Balanced on scarps of trap, ramble or blunder
Over traverses of cloud: and here they move,
Mule-teams like insects harnessed by a bell
Upon the leaf-edge of a winter sky.

And down at last into this lap of stone
Between four cataracts of rock: a town
Peopled by sleepy eagles, whispering only
Of the sunburnt herdsman's hopeless ploy:
A sterile earth quickened by shards or rock
Where nothing grows, not even in his sleep,

Where minarets have twisted up like sugar
And a river, curdled with blond ice, drives on
Tinkling among the mule-teams and the mountaineers,
Under the bridges and the wooden trellises
Which tame the air and promise us a peace
Harmless with nightingales. None are singing now.

No history much? Perhaps. Only this ominous
Dark beauty flowering under veils,
Trapped in the spectrum of a dying style:
A village like an instinct left to rust,
Composed around the echo of a pistol-shot.[1]

99 *At Epidaurus*

The islands which whisper to the ambitious,
Washed all winter by the surviving stars
Are here hardly recalled: or only as
Stone choirs for the sea-bird,
Stone chairs for the statues of fishermen.

[1] Gavrilo Princip assassinated Ferdinand, Archduke of Austria, on 28 June 1914.

This civilized valley was dedicated to
The cult of the circle, the contemplation
And correction of famous maladies
Which the repeating flesh has bred in us also
By a continuous babyhood, like the worm in meat.

The only disorder is in what we bring here:
Cars drifting like leaves over the glades,
The penetration of clocks striking in London.
The composure of dolls and fanatics,
Financed migrations to the oldest sources:
A theatre where redemption was enacted,
Repentance won, the stones heavy with dew.
The olive signs the hill, signifying revival,
And the swallow's cot in the ruin seems how
Small yet defiant an exaggeration of love!

Here we can carry our own small deaths
With the resignation of place and identity;
A temple set severely like a dice
In the vale's Vergilian shade; once apparently
Ruled from the whitest light of the summer:
A formula for marble when the clouds
Troubled the architect, and the hill spoke
Volumes of thunder, the sibyllic god wept.
Here we are safe from everything but ourselves,
The dying leaves and the reports of love.

The land's lie, held safe from the sea,
Encourages the austerity of the grass chambers,
Provides a context understandably natural
For men who could divulge the forms of gods.
Here the mathematician entered his own problem,
A house built round his identity,
Round the fond yet mysterious seasons
Of green grass, the teaching of summer-astronomy.
Here the lover made his calculations by ferns,
And the hum of the chorus enchanted.

We, like the winter, are only visitors,
To prosper here the breathing grass,
Encouraging petals on a terrace, disturbing
Nothing, enduring the sun like girls
In a town window. The earth's flowers
Blow here original with every spring,
Shines in the rising of a man's age
Into cold texts and precedents for time.

Everything is a slave to the ancestor, the order
Of old captains who sleep in the hill.

Then smile, my dear, above the holy wands,
Make the indefinite gesture of the hands,
Unlocking this world which is not our world.
The somnambulists walk again in the north
With the long black rifles, to bring us answers.
Useless a morality for slaves: useless
The shouting at echoes to silence them.
Most useless inhabitants of the kind blue air,
Four ragged travellers in Homer.
All causes end within the great Because.

PATRICK LEIGH-FERMOR

1915–

100   *Greek Archipelagoes*

Crete
Smoulders on sea, half-way to Africa,
Solitary phœnix of the Ægean brood.
Songs, shouts echo in a lunar wilderness
Where blood flowers on the knuckles of the mountains.
High in the ilex woods the black riflemen stalk
Waking the din of bells; their jangling shots
Uncoil interminable echoes. Here the hands of friends
Grasp yours for ever.

Stone warrior up to the waist in sea
Blue as an eye and circled by the blood
Of minotaur and janissary and german!
The wild goat leaps from biceps to armoured shoulder,
And fossilized whiskers are a perch for eagles.
The iron eye of Ida
Looks towards Africa, the empty road
Where no ship travels and the Libyan moon
Only moves: the liquid desert
That hides with the hazard of an excavation
Forests of sponges, ringed by the tunnelling plunge

---

99 Four ragged travellers] Odysseus, Telemachus, Eumaeus, and Philoetius (*Iliad*, xxii)

Of men from Kalymnos, who, taut as miners,
Work underwater.

*   *   *

Count Spiridion and the noble Dionysios,
Gonfaloniers of the Doge, halt on a silver stair,
Falter a moment by the looking-glass
To lisp a rumour of the Mocenigo.
They puff their lace out, poising fastidious fingers
On hilts of swords they never draw. The flicker
Of paste buckles underneath a scutcheon
Marks their way through barley-sugar columns
Into the grape-green evening. There
Lanterns in olive trees cast spokes of shade
On lawns that slope to the sea. The lanterned boats
Scatter the sound of mandolines on pearl-smooth water.

These are Corfu and Zante. Their balustrades,
Magnolias and aloe-flowers are pale as snow
Under a benevolent zodiac.
These islands float like aloe petals
On the Ionian, as though a south wind might
Blow them away, baring the western sea
Of the italianate septinsular galaxy;
All but that dismal and preposterous mountain,
Those villages peopled by statues of shipowners,
Where, on the limestone crags, gesticulate
The lunatics of Cephalonia.

*   *   *

Nothing seems older than the Cyclades,
Worn by the world's earliest winds, thumbed smooth by legend,
They are the seamarks of history,
Offering columns like an instrument
To the wind's mouth; and these oleanders once gave shade
To kings and philosophers that have left
Not even, or nothing but, a name.
Bargains were struck by merchants on the quays
While the first heroes snored in the stifling marble
Awaiting the sculptor's chisel, the tap of a bird's beak
To hatch them.

They were stepping-stones to Troy
Trireme-harbours, milestones to Odysseys

Mocenigo] old Venetian family who gave many doges to the Republic and were great warriors
against the Turks   italianate septinsular galaxy] the Ionian Islands, long subjected to
Venetian rule and still in small measure Italianate in their customs

A night's sleep for argonauts.
Their thoroughfares are stale with a million keels
Weaving and looping their course like wool-winders
Round the porous, the salty fingertips
Of a gigantic and drowned skeleton, jutting here
A bleached knee or a rib; or charred eye-socket
Like Santorin.
Santorin,
Curling and smoky and satanic,
Fires a spiral ladder in the air
And balances a town among the birds.

* * *

'Εν ἀρχῇ ἦν ὁ Λόγος
From the north
The autumn wind carries the storks over Patmos
From Kiev and Bukovina, Rila and the Euxine,
Mystra and Athos and the hanging Meteora,
Stretching their necks for Sinai. The slow armada
Tangles the passage of the Word of God:
A load of plumed and shifting fruit
Bends the branches of the only tree.

The Word of God split the rocks here
And built this battlemented monastery
On rocks that are Magians cast down and turned to stone,
To hide the Word, the leisure of the monks
From scimitars of the corsairs, a stone casket
For treasure of Constantinople and the Russias,
Mitres and flasks and chrysobuls and scrolls,
Gifts of half-legendary voivodes, and the crosiers
Of bishops who became saints.
(Foreheads of parchment seen in silver coffins,
Palimpsests where the flourishes of mortality have faded
Under the calligraphy of beatitude.)

The wind in the soaking darkness winds
Through rocks and roofs, lifting the unwilling wing
Of huddling storks.
Thunder explodes, and the shuddering apocalypse
Of lightning bares the shapes of cupolas,
The mountain-side, and rain-logged wings
And tethered caïques that rear like frightened horses.

* * *

'Εν ἀρχῆ ἦν ὁ Λόγος] In the beginning was the Word

On an Ægean rock compound of salt
And oil and lizards, the bent mastick-tree
Under the sun's tread spills a lingering tear.
The press destroys the olive. A gold tooth
Sparkles in the dark under a tired forehead
Striped like a tiger with the wipe of fingers
Where the oil clings. Fingers that are fossils
Roll a cigarette; juice streams from ankles
Into the trodden vine-stalks among the jars
And the must grumbles and hits, sending fumes as startling
Into the vaults, as the sudden movement of the heart's
Split-second scaffolding of a poem
Assembling in the skull's archways.

        The spite of the sun
Splinters the discs of shade the olives cast,
Crumples the fetishes of the carob-tree
That hang in haze and dazzles the track of the eye
Under the ilex to the sea
That gasps for sunset.
These stones and thorns, that stone without a shadow,
Are ambiguous emblems, they are
Half-decipherable runes, notes in a tune
That can't be memorized. (The unrancorous
Moon will rise over an unsolved problem.)

The donkey waiting under a load of jars,
Under the prickly-pear and the white walls
Of this necropolis, brays without an echo
To stir the rare blue waterfalls of shade.
There is nothing here, nothing at all,
Only, perhaps, a question or a mood
A reference or a suggestion,
Rocks and the sun, and pastures for dolphins
Scattered with other islands, old and bare
As jutting bones, recent as thunderbolts.

Unfathomable wells
Tunnel the heart of the pumice. Like a hand
The fig leaf lays a shadow on the dust.

JOHN HEATH-STUBBS
1918–

101   *The Parthenon*

Where they tamed the wild Libyan
Unmarried war-goddess, goatskin-aproned;
Transmuted the owl-shrieking bugaboo
Into an image of Wisdom—[1]

A dash in a reckless and exorbitant taxi
Will get you there; then climb
Above the esurient, lively, and stuffy city,
Feet slipping on loose stones.

Suddenly it stands there; like a familiar quotation
From dusty oleographs, the model
Of every second-rate 'classical' building—
Church or museum—

Off-white like a sea-worn shell,
Like a bird's skull,
Under remorseless light;
Denuded the colour and gold

Long since; the centaurs and heroes
Shanghaied to Bloomsbury.
It seems very small:
And She has departed.

So that's all. There is nothing to do
But stand and gape like any other
Romantic tourist; and then go.

But turn your back, and stumble
Down the steep track—then suddenly
The mathematical candour,
Neither over- nor under-statement,

Owl-clawed, hooks to the heart.

---

[1] Minerva [Athena], goddess of war, wisdom, chastity, and the arts, was patron goddess of Athens and Attica.

DAVID CONSTANTINE
1944–

102   *Watching for Dolphins*

In the summer months on every crossing to Piraeus
One noticed that certain passengers soon rose
From seats in the packed saloon and with serious
Looks and no acknowledgement of a common purpose
Passed forward through the small door into the bows
To watch for dolphins. One saw them lose

Every other wish. Even the lovers
Turned their desires on the sea, and a fat man
Hung with equipment to photograph the occasion
Stared like a saint, through sad bi-focals; others,
Hopeless themselves, looked to the children for they
Would see dolphins if anyone would. Day after day

Or on their last opportunity all gazed
Undecided whether a flat calm were favourable
Or a sea the sun and the wind between them raised
To a likeness of dolphins. Were gulls a sign, that fell
Screeching from the sky or over an unremarkable place
Sat in a silent school? Every face

After its character implored the sea.
All, unaccustomed, wanted epiphany,
Praying the sky would clang and the abused Aegean
Reverberate with cymbal, gong and drum.
We could not imagine more prayer, and had they then
On the waves, on the climax of our longing come

Smiling, snub-nosed, domed like satyrs, oh
We should have laughed and lifted the children up
Stranger to stranger, pointing how with a leap
They left their element, three or four times, centred
On grace, and heavily and warm re-entered,
Looping the keel. We should have felt them go

Further and further into the deep parts. But soon
We were among the great tankers, under their chains
In black water. We had not seen the dolphins
But woke, blinking. Eyes cast down
With no admission of disappointment the company
Dispersed and prepared to land in the city.

EUROPE OF THE NORTH
THE LOW COUNTRIES

SAMUEL BUTLER
1613–1680

103   *Description of Holland*

A country that draws fifty foot of water
In which men live, as in the hold of nature;
And when the sea does in upon them break
And drown a province, does but spring a leak;
That always ply the pump, and never think
They can be safe, but at the rate they sink;
That live as if they have been run on ground
And when they die, are cast away and drowned;
That dwell in ships like swarms of rats, and prey
Upon the goods all nations' fleets convey
And, when their merchants are blown up and cracked,
Whole towns are cast away in storms and wracked;
That feed like cannibals on other fishes
And serve their cousin Germans up in dishes:
A land that rides at anchor, and is moored
In which they do not live, but go aboard.

ANDREW MARVELL
1621–1678

104   *The Character of Holland*

Holland, that scarce deserves the name of land,
As but the off-scouring of the British sand;
And so much earth as was contributed
By English pilots when they heaved the lead;
Or what by th' ocean's slow alluvion fell
Of shipwrecked cockle and the mussel shell;
This indigested vomit of the sea
Fell to the Dutch by just propriety.

Glad then, as miners that have found the ore,
They with mad labour fished the land to shore,
And dived as desperately for each piece
Of earth, as if't had been of ambergris,
Collecting anxiously small loads of clay,
Less than what building swallows bear away,
Or than those pills which sordid beetles roll,
Transfusing into them their dunghill soul.
  How did they rivet, with gigantic piles,
Thorough the centre their new-catchèd miles,
And to the stake a struggling country bound,
Where barking waves still bait the forcèd ground,
Building their watery Babel far more high
To reach the sea, than those to scale the sky.
  Yet still his claim the injured ocean laid,
And oft at leap-frog o'er their steeples played:
As if on purpose it on land had come
To show them what's their *Mare Liberum*.
A daily deluge over them does boil;
The earth and water play at level-coil;
The fish oft-times the burger dispossessed,
And sat not as a meat but as a guest.
And oft the tritons and the sea nymphs saw
Whole shoals of Dutch served up for cabillau;
Or as they over the new level ranged
For pickled herring, pickled *Heeren* changed.
Nature, it seemed, ashamed of her mistake,
Would throw their land away at duck and drake.
  Therefore necessity, that first made kings,
Something like government among them brings.
For as with pygmies, who best kills the crane,
Among the hungry, he that treasures grain,
Among the blind, the one-eyed blinkard reigns,
So rules among the drownèd, he that drains.
Not who first sees the rising sun commands,
But who could first discern the rising lands.
Who best could know to pump an earth so leak
Him they their Lord and country's Father speak.
To make a bank was a great plot of state;
Invent a shovel, and be magistrate.
Hence some small dyke-grave unperceived invades
The power, and grows, as 'twere, a King of Spades.
But for less envy some joint states endures,
Who look like a Commission of the Sewers.
For these Half-anders, half wet, and half dry,
Nor bear strict service, nor pure liberty.

'Tis probable religion after this
Came next in order, which they could not miss.
How could the Dutch but be converted, when
The Apostles were so many fishermen?
Besides, the waters of themselves did rise,
And, as their land, so them did re-baptize,
Though herring for their god few voices missed,
And Poor-John to have been the Evangelist.
Faith, that could never twins conceive before,
Never so fertile, spawned upon this shore,
More pregnant than their Margaret, that laid down
For *Hans-in-Kelder* of a whole Hans-town.

Sure when religion did itself embark,
And from the East would Westward steer its ark,
It struck, and splitting on this unknown ground,
Each one thence pillaged the first piece he found:
Hence Amsterdam, Turk-Christian-Pagan-Jew,
Staple of sects and mint of schism grew,
That bank of conscience, where not one so strange
Opinion but finds credit, and exchange.
In vain for Catholics ourselves we bear;
The Universal Church is only there.

Nor can civility there want for tillage,
Where wisely for their court they chose a village.
How fit a title clothes their governors,
Themselves the *Hogs*, as all their subjects *Bores*!

Let it suffice to give their country fame
That it had one Civilis called by name,
Some fifteen hundred and more years ago;
But surely never any that *was* so.

See but their mermaids with their tails of fish,
Reeking at church over the chafing-dish:
A vestal turf enshrined in earthen ware
Fumes through the loopholes of a wooden square.
Each to the temple with these altars tend
(But still does place it at her western end),
While the fat steam of female sacrifice
Fills the priest's nostrils and puts out his eyes.

Or what a spectacle the skipper gross,
A water-Hercules butter-coloss,
Tunned up with all their several towns of *Beer*,
When staggering upon some land, snick and sneer,
They try, like statuaries, if they can
Cut out each other's Athos to a man:

Margaret] Dutch countess said to have given birth to 365 children in one delivery
Hans-in-Kelder] unborn child

And carve in their large bodies, where they please,
The arms of the United Provinces.
   But when such amity at home is showed,
What then are their confederacies abroad?
Let this one court'sy witness all the rest:
When their whole navy they together pressed—
Not Christian captives to redeem from bands,
Or intercept the Western golden sands –
No, but all ancient rights and leagues must vail,
Rather than to the English strike their sail;
To whom their weather-beaten province owes
Itself—when as some greater vessel tows
A cockboat tossed with the same wind and fate—
We buoyed so often up their sinking state.
   Was this *Jus Belli & Pacis*? Could this be
Cause why their burgomaster of the sea
Rammed with gun powder, flaming with brand wine,
Should raging hold his linstock to the mine,
While, with feigned treaties, they invade by stealth
Our sore new circumcisèd Commonwealth?
   Yet of his vain attempt no more he sees
Than of case-butter shot and bullet-cheese.
And the torn navy staggered with him home,
While the sea laughed itself into a foam.
'Tis true since that (as fortune kindly sports),
A wholesome danger drove us to our ports,
While half their banished keels the tempest tossed,
Half, bound at home in prison to the frost:
That ours meantime at leisure might careen,
In a calm winter, under skies serene,
As the obsequious air and waters rest,
Till the dear halcyon hatch out all its nest.
The Commonwealth doth by its losses grow;
And, like its own seas, only ebbs to flow.
Besides, that very agitation laves,
And purges out the corruptible waves.
   And now again our armèd *Bucentore*
Doth yearly their sea nuptials restore.
And now their hydra of seven provinces
Is strangled by our infant Hercules.
Their tortoise wants its vainly stretchèd neck;
Their navy all our conquest or our wreck;
Or, what is left, their Carthage overcome
Would render fain unto our better Rome,

Bucentore] State galley originally used by the Doge in the annual nuptials of Venice and the Adriatic, here appropriated by Marvell on behalf of the English navy

Unless our Senate, lest their youth disuse
The war (but who would?), peace, if begged, refuse.
   For now of nothing may our state despair,
Darling of heaven, and of men the care;
Provided that they be what they have been,
Watchful abroad, and honest still within.
For while our Neptune doth a trident shake,
Steeled with those piercing heads—Deane, Monck, and Blake--
And while Jove governs in the highest sphere,
Vainly in Hell let Pluto domineer.

MATTHEW PRIOR

1664–1721

105   *Verses Written at The Hague. Anno 1696*

While with labour assid'ous due pleasure I mix,
And in one day atone for the business of six,
In a little Dutch-chaise on a Saturday night,
On my left hand my Horace, a nymph on my right.
No memoire to compose, and no post-boy to move,
That on Sunday may hinder the softness of love;
For her, neither visits, nor parties of tea,
Nor the long-winded cant of a dull refugee.
This night and the next shall be hers, shall be mine,
To good or ill fortune the third we resign:
Thus scorning the world, and superior to fate,
I drive on my car in processional state;
So with Phya through Athens Pisistratus[1] rode,
Men thought her Minerva, and him a new God.
But why should I stories of Athens rehearse,
Where people knew love, and were partial to verse,
Since none can with justice my pleasures oppose,
In Holland half drowned in interest and prose:
By Greece and past ages, what need I be tried,
When the Hague and the present, are both on my side,
And is it enough, for the joys of the day;
To think what Anacreon, or Sappho would say.

[1] In 546 BC the tyrant Pisistratus returned to Athens with a beautiful woman, Phya, disguised as Athena (Lat. Minerva); there were proclamations that the goddess herself was restoring him to power.

---

104 Deane, Monck, and Blake] Generals-at-Sea from November 1652 until June 1653

When good Vandergoes, and his provident Vrough,
As they gaze on my triumph, do freely allow,
That search all the province, you'd find no man there is
So blessed as the *Englishen Heer SECRETARIS*.

MARK AKENSIDE

1721–1770

106   from *On Leaving Holland*

Farewell to Leyden's lonely bound,
The Belgian Muse's sober seat;
Where dealing frugal gifts around
To all the favourites at her feet,
She trains the body's bulky frame
For passive, persevering toils;
And lest, from any prouder aim,
The daring mind should scorn her homely spoils,
She breathes maternal fogs to damp its restless flame.

Farewell the grave, pacific air,
Where never mountain-zephyr blew:
The marshy levels lank and bare,
Which Pan, which Ceres never knew:
The naiads, with obscene attire,
Urging in vain their urns to flow;
While round them chant the croking choir,
And haply soothe some lover's prudent woe,
Or prompt some restive bard and modulate his lyre.

Farewell, ye nymphs, whom sober care of gain
Snatched in your cradles from the god of Love:
She rendered all his boasted arrows vain;
And all his gifts did he in spite remove.
Ye too, the slow-eyed fathers of the land,
With whom dominion steals from hand to hand,
Unowned, undignified by public choice,
I go where liberty to all is known,
And tells a monarch on his throne,
He reigns not but by her preserving voice.

WILLIAM PARSONS
?1758–1828

107   *Epigram on the Play-House at Amsterdam*

*Being shut on Saturday night on account of the Communion being
administered the next day*

Bigots at home, and infidels abroad,
Traitors to man, and hypocrites to God!
Who here with seeming piety can tease us,
And shut the Play-House for the love of Jesus,
Yet at Japan, this fiery zeal grown cold,
Sell with your wares your very faith for gold,
Christians no more,[1] but Dutchmen then and scoffers,
You trample on the cross—to fill your coffers.
Vile race!—could I your sacrament ordain,
Those lips should neither bread nor wine profane,
But all your manners keep consistent union,
And pipes and gin should be your sole Communion!

WILLIAM WORDSWORTH
1770–1850

108   *Incident at Bruges*

In Brugès town is many a street
    Whence busy life hath fled;
Where, without hurry, noiseless feet
    The grass-grown pavement tread.
There heard we, halting in the shade
    Flung from a Convent-tower,
A harp that tuneful prelude made
    To a voice of thrilling power.

The measure, simple truth to tell,
    Was fit for some gay throng;
Though from the same grim turret fell
    The shadow and the song.

---

[1] 'There being a law in the kingdom of Japan, that no Christians are to be admitted there, it is said this indefatigable people evade it by trampling on the cross and declaring they are not Christians but Dutchmen' (W.P.).

When silent were both voice and chords
    The strain seemed doubly dear,
Yet sad as sweet, for *English* words
    Had fallen upon the ear.

It was a breezy hour of eve;
    And pinnacle and spire
Quivered and seemed almost to heave,
    Clothed with innocuous fire;
But where we stood, the setting sun
    Showed little of his state;
And, if the glory reached the Nun,
    'Twas through an iron grate.

Not always is the heart unwise,
    Nor pity idly born,
If even a passing Stranger sighs
    For them who do not mourn.
Sad is thy doom, self-solaced dove,
    Captive, whoe'er thou be!
Oh! what is beauty, what is love,
    And opening life to thee?

Such feeling pressed upon my soul,
    A feeling sanctified
By one soft trickling tear that stole
    From the Maiden at my side;
Less tribute could she pay than this,
    Borne gaily o'er the sea,
Fresh from the beauty and the bliss
    Of English liberty?

GEORGE CANNING

1770–1827

109   *The Dutch*

In matters of commerce the fault of the Dutch
Is offering too little and asking too much.
The French are with equal advantage content,
So we clap on Dutch bottoms just 20 per cent.

SAMUEL TAYLOR COLERIDGE
1772–1834

110　　*The Netherlands*

Water and windmills, greenness, Islets green;—
Willows whose Trunks beside the shadows stood
Of their own higher half, and willowy swamp:—
Farmhouses that at anchor seemed—in the inland sky
The fog-transfixing Spires—
Water, wide water, greenness and green banks,
And water seen—

THOMAS HOOD
1799–1845

111　　*To* *******

I gaze upon a city,
A city new and strange;
Down many a wat'ry vista
My fancy takes a range;
From side to side I saunter,
And wonder where I am;—
And can *you* be in England,
And I at Rotterdam!

Before me lie dark waters,
In broad canals and deep,
Whereon the silver moonbeams
Sleep, restless in their sleep:
A sort of vulgar Venice
Reminds me where I am,—
Yes, yes, you are in England,
And I'm at Rotterdam.

Tall houses with quaint gables,
Where frequent windows shine,
And quays that lead to bridges,
And trees in formal line,

And masts of spicy vessels,
From distant Surinam,
All tell me you're in England,
And I'm in Rotterdam.

Those sailors,—how outlandish
The face and garb of each!
They deal in foreign gestures,
And use a foreign speech;
A tongue not learned near Isis,
Or studied by the Cam,
Declares that you're in England,
But I'm at Rotterdam.

And now across a market
My doubtful way I trace,
Where stands a solemn statue,
The Genius of the place;
And to the great Erasmus
I offer my salaam,—
Who tells me you're in England,
And I'm at Rotterdam.

The coffee-room is open,
I mingle in its crowd;
The dominoes are rattling,
The hookahs raise a cloud;
A flavour, none of Fearon's,
That mingles with my dram,
Reminds me you're in England,
But I'm in Rotterdam.

Then here it goes, a bumper,—
The toast it shall be mine,
In Schiedam, or in Sherry,
Tokay, or Hock of Rhine,—
It well deserves the brightest
Where sunbeam ever swam,—
'The girl I love in England,'
I drink at Rotterdam!

DANTE GABRIEL ROSSETTI
1828–1882

112   *Antwerp and Bruges*

I climbed the stair in Antwerp church,
  What time the circling thews of sound
  At sunset seem to heave it round.
Far up, the carillon did search
The wind, and the birds came to perch
  Far under, where the gables wound.

In Antwerp harbour on the Scheldt
  I stood alone, a certain space
  Of night. The mist was near my face;
Deep on, the flow was heard and felt.
The carillon kept pause, and dwelt
  In music through the silent place.

John Memmeling and John van Eyck
  Hold state at Bruges. In sore shame
  I scanned the works that keep their name.
The carillon, which then did strike
Mine ears, was heard of theirs alike:
  It set me closer unto them.

I climbed at Bruges all the flight
  The belfry has of ancient stone.
  For leagues I saw the east wind blown;
The earth was grey, the sky was white.
I stood so near upon the height
  That my flesh felt the carillon.

113   from *A Trip to Paris and Belgium*

Antwerp to Ghent

We are upon the Scheldt. We know we move
Because there is a floating at our eyes
Whatso they seek; and because all the things
Which on our outset were distinct and large
Are smaller and much weaker and quite grey,
And at last gone from us. No motion else.

THOMAS HOOD
1799–1845

123   Ye Tourists and Travellers, bound to the Rhine,
Provided with passport, that requisite docket,
First listen to one little whisper of mine—
Take care of your pocket!—take care of your pocket!

Don't wash or be shaved—go like hairy wild men,
Play dominoes, smoke, wear a cap and smock-frock it,
But if you speak English, or look it, why then
Take care of your pocket!—take care of your pocket!

You'll sleep at great inns, in the smallest of beds,
Find charges as apt to mount up as a rocket,
With thirty per cent as a tax on your heads,
Take care of your pocket!—take care of your pocket!

You'll see old Cologne,—not the sweetest of towns,—
Wherever you follow your nose you will shock it;
And you'll pay your three dollars to look at three crowns,
Take care of your pocket!—take care of your pocket!

You'll count Seven Mountains, and see Roland's Eck,
Hear legends veracious as any by Crockett;
But oh! to the tone of romance what a cheek,
Take care of your pocket!—take care of your pocket!

Old Castles you'll see on the vine-covered hill,—
Fine ruins to rivet the eye in its socket—
Once haunts of Baronial Banditti, and still
Take care of your pocket!—take care of your pocket!

You'll stop at Coblenz, with its beautiful views,
But make no long stay with your money to stock it,
Where Jews are all Germans, and Germans all Jews,
Take care of your pocket!—take care of your pocket!—

A Fortress you'll see, which, as people report,
Can never be captured, save famine should block it—
Ascend Ehrenbreitstein—but that's not their *forte*,
Take care of your pocket!—take care of your pocket!

Roland's Eck] ruined castle just north of Oberwinter   Ehrenbreitstein] castle opposite
Coblenz

You'll see an old man who'll let off an old gun,
And Lurley, with her hurly-burly, will mock it;
But think that the words of the echo thus run—
Take care of your pocket!—take care of your pocket!

You'll gaze on the Rheingau, the soil of the Vine!
Of course you will freely Moselle it and Hock it—
P'raps purchase some pieces of Humbugheim wine—
Take care of your pocket!—take care of your pocket!

Perchance you will take a frisk off to the Baths—
Where some to their heads hold a pistol and cock it;
But still mind the warning, wherever your paths,
Take care of your pocket!—take care of your pocket!

And Friendships you'll swear, most eternal of pacts,
Change rings, and give hair to be put in a locket;
But still, in the most sentimental of acts,
Take care of your pocket!—take care of your pocket!

In short, if you visit that stream or its shore,
Still keep at your elbow one caution to knock it,
And where Schinderhannes was Robber of yore,—
Take care of your pocket!—take care of your pocket!

GEORGE MEREDITH
1828–1909

124   *Pictures of the Rhine*

I

The spirit of Romance dies not to those
Who hold a kindred spirit in their souls:
Even as the odorous life within the rose
Lives in the scattered leaflets and controls
Mysterious adoration, so there glows
Above dead things a thing that cannot die;
Faint as the glimmer of a tearful eye,
Ere the orb fills and all the sorrow flows.
Beauty renews itself in many ways;
The flower is fading while the new bud blows;

---

123 Schinderhannes] nickname of Johann Bückler (1783–1803), head of a gang of robbers active in central Rhineland

And this dear land as true a symbol shows,
While o'er it like a mellow sunset strays
The legendary splendour of old days,
In visible, inviolate repose.

II

About a mile behind the viny banks,
How sweet it was, upon a sloping green,
Sunspread, and shaded with a branching screen,
To lie in peace half-murmuring words of thanks!
To see the mountains on each other climb,
With spaces for rich meadows flowery bright;
The winding river freshening the sight
At intervals, the trees in leafy prime;
The distant village-roofs of blue and white,
With intersections of quaint-fashioned beams
All slanting crosswise, and the feudal gleams
Of ruined turrets, barren in the light;—
To watch the changing clouds, like clime in clime;
Oh! sweet to lie and bless the luxury of time.

III

Fresh blows the early breeze, our sail is full;
A merry morning and a mighty tide.
Cheerily O! and past St Goar we glide,
Half hid in misty dawn and mountain cool.
The river is our own! and now the sun
In saffron clothes the warming atmosphere;
The sky lifts up her white veil like a nun,
And looks upon the landscape blue and clear;—
The lark is up; the hills, the vines in sight;
The river broadens with his waking bliss
And throws up islands to behold the light;
Voices begin to rise, all hues to kiss;—
Was ever such a happy morn as this!
Birds sing, we shout, flowers breathe, trees shine with one delight!

IV

Between the two white breasts of her we love,
A dewy blushing rose will sometimes spring;
Thus Nonnenwerth like an enchanted thing
Rises mid-stream the crystal depths above.
On either side the waters heave and swell,
But all is calm within the little Isle;
Content it is to give its holy smile,
And bless with peace the lives that in it dwell.

Most dear on the dark grass beneath its bower
Of kindred trees embracing branch and bough,
To dream of fairy foot and sudden flower;
Or haply with a twilight on the brow,
To muse upon the legendary hour,
And Roland's lonely love and Hildegard's sad vow.

V

Hark! how the bitter winter breezes blow
Round the sharp rocks and o'er the half-lifted wave,
While all the rocky woodland branches rave
Shrill with the piercing cold, and every cave,
Along the icy water-margin low,
Rings bubbling with the whirling overflow;
And sharp the echoes answer distant cries
Of dawning daylight and the dim sunrise,
And the gloom-coloured clouds that stain the skies
With pictures of a warmth, and frozen glow
Spread over endless fields of sheeted snow;
And white untrodden mountains shining cold,
And muffled footpaths winding thro' the wold,
O'er which those wintry gusts cease not to howl and blow.

VI

Rare is the loveliness of slow decay!
With youth and beauty all must be desired,
But 'tis the charm of things long past away,
They leave, alone, the light they have inspired:
The calmness of a picture; Memory now
Is the sole life among the ruins grey,
And like a phantom in fantastic play
She wanders with rank weeds stuck on her brow,
Over grass-hidden caves and turret-tops,
Herself almost as tottering as they;
While, to the steps of Time, her latest props
Fall stone by stone, and in the Sun's hot ray
All that remains stands up in rugged pride,
And bridal vines drink in his juices on each side.

Roland] heroic nephew to Charlemagne; he never made love to a woman and his 'lonely love'
was honour   Hildegard] Abbess Hildegard (1098–1179), visionary and poet who took the
veil at the age of 15; she was known as the 'Sibyl of the Rhine'

RUPERT BROOKE
1887–1915

125   *In Freiburg Station*

In Freiburg station, waiting for a train,
I saw a Bishop in puce gloves go by.
Now God may thunder furious from the sky,
Shattering all my glory into pain,
And joy turn stinking rotten, hope be vain,
Night fall on little laughters, little loves,
And better Bishops don more glorious gloves,
While I go down in darkness; what care I?

There is one memory God can never break,
There is one splendour more than all the pain,
There is one secret that shall never die,
Star-crowned I stand and sing, for that hour's sake.
In Freiburg station, waiting for a train,
I saw a Bishop with puce gloves go by.

BERNARD SPENCER
1909–1963

126   *The Empire Clock*

Muted wood-wind is one noise of the traffic, and there is a second
when trams manœuvre the bend, the muffled grinding and wail
of steel turned on steel.

The River drifts its ice under no stars towards
the Black Sea (and what winter cities?). The long-silent
Empire clock with its pediment

Abruptly intones once. Rather than a chime, a stirring,
a gruffness. And instantly I am conscious of the young man
from the war in nineteen-fifteen

Who cut on the back door in this house his 'goodbye'
to his girl, and the date.
                    Fifty-odd winters it stayed, that thought,

Which we painted out. Which we painted out.

C. H. SISSON

1914–

127   *Over the Wall: Berlin, May 1975*

I

He will go over and tell the king
Or whoever is top dog in that country
How there is feasting here, the wastes are empty
The nine governors sleeping

Not a prophetic sleep, with the lids opening
Upon passion, dreaming of conflict
But the eyes turned inwards so that the whites
Gaze upon the world, and the heart ticks steadily
To the combustion of a strange engine
Not in the heart, more like a bee
Buzzing in the neighbourhood. Over the wall,
Knives drawn, teeth drawn back,
Swallowing the rattle they make in case the night
Should interpret their wishes.
Here in the west, far west, slumber
While death collects his paces.

I am not warlike but, once the frontiers are falling
Each man must put on his belt; it has been done before
And the whimpering must stop, Death being the kingdom
Of this world.

2

I have seen the doomed city, it was not my own
Love has no city like this, with barred hatreds
All bitterness, all shames. I do not think there is any
Feast to be eaten or long shawls
Trailed in the dust before the fanatic mob
Only quiet people live here, eating their sandwiches
Under the lilac while the boats go by,
Interminable imitation of reality
Which is not to be had, and should the frost fall
Should the eagle turn its head
The city of too many desperate adventures
I have seen them all, or so it seems, the Uhlans . . .

Uhlans] originally cavalry regiments, converted into lancers in 1889

And now from the steppes
It is as if the Dalmatian horsemen came back,
Yet they do not stir, or make themselves visible . . .
One street I remember
There is no majesty in its lost endeavours
Speak to me no more, I have heard only
The marching men.
Sleep comes to those who deserve
Funerals under the chipped archways.

3

I do not think this is the end of the story
There are battalions enough behind the wall.
The tall policeman bent over me like the priest
Of an evil religion, as if I were the elements
And he the emissary who was empowered to transform me.
That was not the same
Dream-ridden solitude I had known before
Where a flame climbed the walls there was no one by.

4

I know only aspen, beech, oak
But here in these wastes the turtle
Sang among the sands, sitting upon a pine-tree
No man has meditated this regress
Yet the afternoon sun falls upon faces
Less tame than tigers.

PETER PORTER

1929–

128   *Vienna*

This Imperial city
Needs no Empire: turks, saints, huge nineteenth-
    Century geniuses,

Poets with the tic, the spade
Bearded patriarch who raised to the nth
    The power of love, these came

Here like spokes to their axle.
Europe needed a capital—tenth
    Sons needed to be Civil

Servants: such imagined strength
Focused on a style. The statued squares
    Don't know that wet Hungary

Isn't theirs. Their birds can fly
To Balaton. The attic's story
    Is that Haydn was beaten

There. An old lady who liked
Hitler's voice says Schubert's family
    Lived fourteen to a room. Now

The tall Minnesotan will
Tell his wife 'we wash too much, you can't be
    A genius in America'.

At Whitsun cars and buses
Carry large dragonflies, God can fly
    In this architecture. Dreams

Adorned like cream cakes fatten
The citizens; they wake to abuses
    That need icing. Smiling men

Arrive at work at seven
a.m. and a tourist confesses
    To his unknown neighbour he

Was unfaithful on the boat.
Grapes grow up to the tram terminuses,
    Nature is one of the boasts

Of lost prestige. History
Which puts the pop singer and the iron-
    haired conductor in the same

Plane crash has kept this city
To vindicate its geniuses.
    The trivial is immortal.

    Balaton] vast lake in the west of Hungary

SWITZERLAND

LADY MARY WORTLEY MONTAGU
1689–1762

129   Such soft ideas all my pains beguile,
The Alps are levelled, and the deserts smile;
These pendant rocks and ever 'during snow,
These rolling torrents that eternal flow,
Amidst this chaos that around me lies,
I only hear your voice, and see your eyes.

OLIVER GOLDSMITH
?1730–1774

130   from *The Traveller*

          . . . turn we to survey
Where rougher climes a nobler race display,
Where the bleak Swiss their stormy mansions tread,
And force a churlish soil for scanty bread;
No product here the barren hills afford,
But Man and steel, the soldier and his sword.
No vernal blooms their torpid rocks array,
But winter ling'ring chills the lap of May;
No Zephyr fondly sues the mountain's breast,
But meteors glare, and stormy glooms invest.
   Yet still, even here, content can spread a charm,
Redress the clime, and all its rage disarm.
Though poor the peasant's hut, his feasts though small,
He sees his little lot the lot of all;
Sees no contiguous palace rear its head
To shame the meanness of his humble shed;
No costly lord the sumptuous banquet deal
To make him loathe his vegetable meal;
But calm, and bred in ignorance and toil,
Each wish contracting, fits him to the soil.
Cheerful at morn he wakes from short repose,
Breasts the keen air, and carols as he goes;

With patient angle trolls the finny deep,
Or drives his venturous ploughshare to the steep;
Or seeks the den where snow-tracks mark the way,
And drags the struggling savage into day.
At night returning, every labour sped,
He sits him down the monarch of a shed;
Smiles by his cheerful fire, and round surveys
His children's looks, that brighten at the blaze;
While his loved partner, boastful of her hoard,
Displays her cleanly platter on the board:
And haply too some pilgrim, thither led,
With many a tale repays the nightly bed.

Thus every good his native wilds impart,
Imprints the patriot passion on his heart,
And even those ills, that round his mansion rise,
Enhance the bliss his scanty fund supplies.
Dear is that shed to which his soul conforms,
And dear that hill which lifts him to the storms;
And as a child, when scaring sounds molest,
Clings close and closer to the mother's breast,
So the loud torrent, and the whirlwind's roar,
But bind him to his native mountains more.

WILLIAM PARSONS
?1758–1828

131   *Ode to the Lake of Geneva*

Written at the Château de Chillon, near Vevey, after a tour to the Glaciers of
Chamonix and through the lower Valais

From Alpine heights where clad in snow
Mont Blanc uprears his monarch brow,
Where chamois on the ridgy rock
The hunter's daring efforts mock,
To grasp each bare dry crag who strains,
And opes in fell despair his veins.[1]

[1] 'It is a fact mentioned by many travellers, and verified by the Author's own enquiries, that
the Chamois hunters in the hot season when the sliding dust makes the points of the rocks
unsafe to hold by, are sometimes obliged, after all other moisture fails, to wound themselves and
moisten them with their blood' (W.P.).

From where in indolence supine
The sluggish Valaisans recline,
Where, as I trod the marshy plain,
I pitying saw the listless swain,
Bent by the goitre's tumid load,
Scarce lift his hand to point the road.

To thee returned, enchanting Lake!
With thy pure wave my thirst I slake,
Thy wave whose crystal pride disdains
The furious Rhône's polluting stains,
And all his turbid stream refines[2]
Till like thyself serene it shines.

Too soon, as men, reformed in vain,
Meet vice and grow corrupt again,
Foul as before he rolls allied
With sallow Arve's contagious tide;
Mourns he forsook thy chaster bed,
And hides in earth his conscious head.

On scenes of dread I gaze no more,
Nor hear the tumbling glaciers roar,
Thy mild expanse of sapphire hue
Shall now far more delight my view,
Thy gentle tide's soft murmurs cheer
With soothing melody my ear.

Fair Queen of Lakes! neglected long,
Unhonoured in Ausonian song,
Yet not the wave that Dian loves
O'erhung by Nemi's nodding groves,
Nor bright Blandusia raised so high
In Flaccus' strain with thee can vie.

And while I cast my eyes around
They yet shall stray o'er classic ground,
For here Rousseau's expressive power
Commands the visionary hour;
The well-marked scenes his tale renew,
And fancy fondly thinks it true.

---

[2] 'The Rhone is extremely muddy when it enters the Lake, and preserves its foul course distinct from the deep azure of the latter for some distance till in its progress all the slime is deposited, it comes out at Geneva perfectly clear ...' (W.P.).

My glowing thought attempts to trace
Each charm that dwelt on Julia's[1] face,
Views the frail damsel's altered will
The matron's chaste devoirs fulfil;
'Twas here, with frantic sorrow wild,
She leaped to save her sinking child.

If Chablais' cliffs attract my eye.
The suffering peasants claim a sigh,
Who leave untilled the fertile soil
Envying their happier neighbour's toil,
So wondrous strong the marks appear
Of Slavery there, and Freedom here.

O Freedom! at thine honoured name
I kindle with congenial flame,
For not to Albion's scenes alone
Her sons can wish thy blessings known,
More rapturous far were their delight
Could all partake the common right!

SAMUEL ROGERS
1763–1855

132   *The Great St Bernard*

Night was again descending, when my mule,
That all day long had climbed among the clouds,
Higher and higher still, as by a stair
Let down from heaven itself, transporting me,
Stopped, to the joy of both, at that low door,
That door which ever, as self-opened, moves
To them that knock, and nightly sends abroad
Ministering Spirits. Lying on the watch,
Two dogs of grave demeanour welcomed me,
All meekness, gentleness, though large of limb;
And a lay-brother of the Hospital,

[1] Julie, heroine of Rousseau's *Julie, ou la Nouvelle Héloïse* (1761), threw herself into the water at the Château de Chillon, thereby occasioning her last illness.

---

132 St Bernard] Alpine pass from Switzerland into Italy on which stands the hospice founded by St Bernard of Menthon (932–1009). The huge St Bernard dog is bred there and trained to track and help travellers lost in the snow

Who, as we toiled below, had heard by fits
The distant echoes gaining on his ear,
Came and held fast my stirrup in his hand
While I alighted. Long could I have stood,
With a religious awe contemplating
That House, the highest in the Ancient World,
And destined to perform from age to age
The noblest service, welcoming as guests
All of all nations and of every faith;
A temple, sacred to Humanity!
It was a pile of simplest masonry,
With narrow windows and vast buttresses,
Built to endure the shocks of time and chance;
Yet showing many a rent, as well it might,
Warred on for ever by the elements,
And in an evil day, nor long ago,
By violent men—when on the mountain-top
The French and Austrian banners met in conflict.
    On the same rock beside it stood the church,
Reft of its cross, not of its sanctity;
The vesper-bell, for 'twas the vesper-hour,
Duly proclaiming through the wilderness,
'All ye who hear, whatever be your work,
Stop for an instant—move your lips in prayer!'
And, just beneath it, in that dreary dale,
If dale it might be called, so near to heaven,
A little lake, where never fish leaped up,
Lay like a spot of ink amid the snow;
A star, the only one in that small sky,
On its dead surface glimmering. 'Twas a place
Resembling nothing I had left behind,
As if all worldly ties were now dissolved;—
And, to incline the mind still more to thought,
To thought and sadness, on the eastern shore
Under a beetling cliff stood half in gloom
A lonely chapel destined for the dead,
For such as, having wandered from their way,
Had perished miserably. Side by side,
Within they lie, a mournful company,
All in their shrouds, no earth to cover them;
Their features full of life yet motionless
In the broad day, nor soon to suffer change,
Though the barred windows, barred against the wolf,
Are always open!—But the North blew cold;
And, bidden to a spare but cheerful meal,
I sat among the holy brotherhood
At their long board. The fare indeed was such

As is prescribed on days of abstinence,
But might have pleased a nicer taste than mine;
And through the floor came up, an ancient crone
Serving unseen below; while from the roof
(The roof, the floor, the walls of native fir),
A lamp hung flickering, such as loves to fling
Its partial light on Apostolic heads,
And sheds a grace on all. Theirs Time as yet
Had changed not. Some were almost in the prime;
Nor was a brow o'ercast. Seen as they sat,
Ranged round their ample hearth-stone in an hour
Of rest, they were as gay, as free from guile,
As children; answering, and at once, to all
The gentler impulses, to pleasure, mirth;
Mingling, at intervals, with rational talk
Music; and gathering news from them that came,
As of some other world. But when the storm
Rose, and the snow rolled on in ocean-waves,
When on his face the experienced traveller fell,
Sheltering his lips and nostrils with his hands,
Then all was changed; and, sallying with their pack
Into that blank of nature, they became
Unearthly beings. 'Anselm, higher up,
Just where it drifts, a dog howls loud and long,
And now, as guided by a voice from Heaven,
Digs with his feet. That noble vehemence
Whose can it be, but his who never erred?[1]
A man lies underneath! Let us to work!—
But who descends Mont Velan? 'Tis La Croix.
Away, away! if not, alas, too late.
Homeward he drags an old man and a boy,
Faltering and falling, and but half awaked,
Asking to sleep again.' Such their discourse.

  Oft has a venerable roof received me;
St Bruno's once—where, when the winds were hushed,
Nor from the cataract the voice came up,
You might have heard the mole work underground,
So great the stillness of that place; none seen,
Save when from rock to rock a hermit crossed
By some rude bridge—or one at midnight tolled
To matins, and white habits, issuing forth,
Glided along those aisles interminable,

---

[1] 'Alluding to Barri, a dog of great renown in his day... His skin is stuffed, and preserved in
the Museum of Berne' (S.R.).

St Bruno's] the Grande Chartreuse

All, all observant of the sacred law
Of Silence. Nor is that sequestered spot,
Once called 'Sweet Waters', now 'The Shady Vale',
To me unknown; that house so rich of old,
So courteous, and, by two that passed that way,
Amply requited with immortal verse,
The Poet's payment. But, among them all,
None can with this compare, the dangerous seat
Of generous, active Virtue. What though Frost
Reign everlastingly, and ice and snow
Thaw not, but gather—there is that within,
Which, where it comes, makes Summer; and, in thought,
Oft am I sitting on the bench beneath
Their garden-plot, where all that vegetates
Is but some scanty lettuce, to observe
Those from the South ascending, every step
As though it were their last,—and instantly
Restored, renewed, advancing as with songs,
Soon as they see, turning a lofty crag,
That plain, that modest structure, promising
Bread to the hungry, to the weary rest.

PERCY BYSSHE SHELLEY

1792–1822

133   *Mont Blanc*

Lines written in the Vale of Chamonix

I

The everlasting universe of things
Flows through the mind, and rolls its rapid waves,
Now dark—now glittering—now reflecting gloom—
Now lending splendour, where from secret springs
The source of human thought its tribute brings
Of waters,—with a sound but half its own,
Such as a feeble brook will oft assume
In the wild woods, among the mountains lone,
Where waterfalls around it leap for ever,

---

132 The Shady Vale] Vallombrosa, originally the site of the hermitage of Santa Maria of
Acqua Bella, and later a Benedictine monastery, twenty-one miles south-east of
Florence   by two that passed that way] Ariosto and Milton

Where woods and winds contend, and a vast river
Over its rocks ceaselessly bursts and raves.

II

Thus thou, Ravine of Arve—dark, deep Ravine—
Thou many-coloured, many-voicèd vale,
Over whose pines, and crags, and caverns sail
Fast cloud-shadows and sunbeams: awful scene,
Where Power in likeness of the Arve comes down
From the ice-gulfs that gird his secret throne,
Bursting through these dark mountains like the flame
Of lightning through the tempest;—thou dost lie,
Thy giant brood of pines around thee clinging,
Children of elder time, in whose devotion
The chainless winds still come and ever came
To drink their odours, and their mighty swinging
To hear—an old and solemn harmony;
Thine earthly rainbows stretched across the sweep
Of the aethereal waterfall, whose veil
Robes some unsculptured image; the strange sleep
Which when the voices of the desert fail
Wraps all in its own deep eternity;—
Thy caverns echoing to the Arve's commotion,
A loud, lone sound no other sound can tame;
Thou art pervaded with that ceaseless motion,
Thou art the path of that unresting sound—
Dizzy Ravine! and when I gaze on thee
I seem as in a trance sublime and strange
To muse on my own separate fantasy,
My own, my human mind, which passively
Now renders and receives fast influencings,
Holding an unremitting interchange
With the clear universe of things around;
One legion of wild thoughts, whose wandering wings
Now float above thy darkness, and now rest
Where that or thou art no unbidden guest,
In the still cave of the witch Poesy,
Seeking among the shadows that pass by
Ghosts of all things that are, some shade of thee,
Some phantom, some faint image; till the breast
From which they fled recalls them, thou art there!

III

Some say that gleams of a remoter world
Visit the soul in sleep,—that death is slumber,
And that its shapes the busy thoughts outnumber

Of those who wake and live.—I look on high;
Has some unknown omnipotence unfurled
The veil of life and death? or do I lie
In dream, and does the mightier world of sleep
Spread far around and inaccessibly
Its circles? For the very spirit fails,
Driven like a homeless cloud from steep to steep
That vanishes among the viewless gales!
Far, far above, piercing the infinite sky,
Mont Blanc appears,—still, snowy, and serene—
Its subject mountains their unearthly forms
Pile around it, ice and rock; broad vales between
Of frozen floods, unfathomable deeps,
Blue as the overhanging heaven, that spread
And wind among the accumulated steeps;
A desert peopled by the storms alone,
Save when the eagle brings some hunter's bone,
And the wolf tracks her there—how hideously
Its shapes are heaped around! rude, bare, and high,
Ghastly, and scarred, and riven.—Is this the scene
Where the old Earthquake-daemon taught her young
Ruin? Were these their toys? or did a sea
Of fire envelop once this silent snow?
None can reply—all seems eternal now.
The wilderness has a mysterious tongue
Which teaches awful doubt, or faith so mild,
So solemn, so serene, that man may be,
But for such faith, with nature reconciled;
Thou hast a voice, great Mountain, to repeal
Large codes of fraud and woe; not understood
By all, but which the wise, and great, and good
Interpret, or make felt, or deeply feel.

IV

The fields, the lakes, the forests, and the streams,
Ocean, and all the living things that dwell
Within the daedal earth; lightning, and rain,
Earthquake, and fiery flood, and hurricane,
The torpor of the year when feeble dreams
Visit the hidden buds, or dreamless sleep
Holds every future leaf and flower;—the bound
With which from that detested trance they leap;
The works and ways of man, their death and birth,
And that of him and all that his may be;
All things that move and breathe with toil and sound
Are born and die; revolve, subside, and swell.

Power dwells apart in its tranquillity,
Remote, serene, and inaccessible:
And *this*, the naked countenance of earth,
On which I gaze, even these primaeval mountains
Teach the adverting mind. The glaciers creep
Like snakes that watch their prey, from their far fountains,
Slow rolling on; there, many a precipice,
Frost and the Sun in scorn of mortal power
Have piled: dome, pyramid, and pinnacle,
A city of death, distinct with many a tower
And wall impregnable of beaming ice.
Yet not a city, but a flood of ruin
Is there, that from the boundaries of the sky
Rolls its perpetual stream; vast pines are strewing
Its destined path, or in the mangled soil
Branchless and shattered stand; the rocks, drawn down
From yon remotest waste, have overthrown
The limits of the dead and living world,
Never to be reclaimed. The dwelling-place
Of insects, beasts, and birds, becomes its spoil;
Their food and their retreat for ever gone,
So much of life and joy is lost. The race
Of man flies far in dread; his work and dwelling
Vanish, like smoke before the tempest's stream,
And their place is not known. Below, vast caves
Shine in the rushing torrents' restless gleam,
Which from those secret chasms in tumult welling
Meet in the vale, and one majestic River,
The breath and blood of distant lands, for ever
Rolls its loud waters to the ocean-waves,
Breathes its swift vapours to the circling air.

                              v

Mont Blanc yet gleams on high:—the power is there,
The still and solemn power of many sights,
And many sounds, and much of life and death.
In the calm darkness of the moonless nights,
In the lone glare of day, the snows descend
Upon that Mountain; none beholds them there,
Nor when the flakes burn in the sinking sun,
Or the star-beams dart through them:—Winds contend
Silently there, and heap the snow with breath
Rapid and strong, but silently! Its home
The voiceless lightning in these solitudes
Keeps innocently, and like vapour broods
Over the snow. The secret Strength of things

Which governs thought, and to the infinite dome
Of Heaven is as a law, inhabits thee!
And what were thou, and earth, and stars, and sea,
If to the human mind's imaginings
Silence and solitude were vacancy?

THOMAS LOVELL BEDDOES
1803–1849

134   *Alpine Spirit's Song*

I

O'er the snow, through the air, to the mountain,
　　With the antelope, with the eagle, ho!
　　With a bound, with a feathery row,
To the side of the icy fountain,
　　Where the gentians blue-belled blow.
Where the storm-sprite, the rain-drops counting,
　　Cowers under the bright rainbow,
　　　　Like a burst of midnight fire,
　　　　Singing shoots my fleet desire,
　　　　Winged with the wing of love,
　　　　Earth below and stars above.

II

Let me rest on the snow, never pressed
　　But by chamois light and by eagle fleet,
　　Where the hearts of the antelope beat
'Neath the light of the moony cresset,
　　Where the wild cloud rests his feet,
And the scented airs caress it
　　From the alpine orchis sweet;
　　　　And about the Sandalp lone
　　　　Voices airy breathe a tone,
　　　　Charming, with the sense of love,
　　　　Earth below and stars above.

III

Through the night, like a dragon from Pilate
　　Out of murky cave, let us cloudy sail
　　Over lake, over bowery vale,

---

134 Sandalp] Sandalpthal runs out of Linthal in the canton of Uri　　　　Pilate] Mons
Pileatus ('hooded peak') above the Lake of Lucerne

As a chime of bells, at twilight
In the downy evening gale,
Passes swimming tremulously light;
Till we reach yon rocky pale
    Of the mountain crowning all,
    Slumber there by waterfall,
Lonely like a spectre's love,
Earth beneath, and stars above.

ARTHUR HUGH CLOUGH
1819–1861

135   from *Mari Magno*

Have you the Giesbach seen? a fall
In Switzerland you say, that's all;
That, and an inn, from which proceeds
A path that to the Faulhorn leads,
From whence you see the world of snows.
Few see how perfect in repose,
White green, the lake lies deeply set,
Where, slowly purifying yet,
The icy river-floods retain
A something of the glacier stain.
Steep cliffs arise the waters o'er,
The Giesbach leads you to a shore,
And to one still sequestered bay
I found elsewhere a scrambling way.
Above, the loftier heights ascend,
And level platforms here extend
The mountains and the cliffs between,
With firs and grassy spaces green,
And little dips and knolls to show
In part or whole the lake below;
And all exactly at the height
To make the pictures exquisite.
Most exquisite they seemed to me,
When, a year after my degree,
Passing upon my journey home
From Greece, and Sicily, and Rome,

135 Giesbach] stream in the Bernese Oberland famous for its seven waterfalls
Faulhorn] mountain (8,806 ft.) east of Interlaken in the Bernese Oberland

I stayed at that minute hotel
Six days, or eight, I cannot tell.
Twelve months had led me fairly through
The old world surviving in the new.
From Rome with joy I passed to Greece,
To Athens and the Peloponnese;
Saluted with supreme delight
The Parthenon-surmounted height;
In huts at Delphi made abode,
And in Arcadian valleys rode;
Counted the towns that lie like slain
Upon the wide Boeotian plain;
With wonder in the spacious gloom
Stood of the Mycenaean tomb;
From the Acrocorinth watched the day
Light the eastern and the western bay.
Constantinople then had seen,
Where, by her cypresses, the queen
Of the East sees flow through portals wide
The steady streaming Scythian tide;
And after, from Scamander's mouth,
Went up to Troy, and to the South,
To Lycia, Caria, pressed, atwhiles
Outvoyaging to Egean isles.
    To see the things, which, sick with doubt
And comment, one had learnt about,
Was like clear morning after night,
Or raising of the blind to sight.
Aware it might be first and last,
I did it eagerly and fast,
And took unsparingly my fill.
The impetus of travel still
Urged me, but laden, half oppressed,
Here lighting on a place of rest,
I yielded, asked not if 'twere best.
Pleasant it was, reposing here,
To sum the experience of the year,
And let the accumulated gain
Assort itself upon the brain.
Travel's a miniature life,
Travel is evermore a strife,
Where he must run who would obtain.
'Tis a perpetual loss and gain;
For sloth and error dear we pay,
By luck and effort win our way,
And both have need of every day.

Each day has got its sight to see,
Each day must put to profit be;
Pleasant, when seen are all the sights,
To let them think themselves to rights.
I on the Giesbach turf reclined,
Half watched this process in my mind;
Watched the stream purifying slow,
In me and in the lake below;
And then began to think of home,
And possibilities to come.

Brienz, on our Brienzer See
From Interlaken every day
A steamer seeks, and at our pier
Lets out a crowd to see things here;
Up a steep path they pant and strive;
When to the level they arrive,
Dispersing, hither, thither, run,
For all must rapidly be done,
And seek, with questioning and din,
Some the cascade, and some the inn,
The waterfall, for if you look,
You find it printed in the book
That man or woman, so inclined,
May pass the very fall behind;
So many feet there intervene
The rock and flying jet between;
The inn, 'tis also in the plan
(For tourist is a hungry man),
And a small *salle* repeats by rote
A daily task of *table d'hôte*,
Where broth and meat, and country wine,
Assure the strangers that they dine;
Do it they must while they have power,
For in three-quarters of an hour
Back comes the steamer from Brienz,
And with one clear departure hence
The quietude is more intense.

MATTHEW ARNOLD
1822–1888

136   *A Dream*

Was it a dream? We sailed, I thought we sailed,
Martin and I, down a green Alpine stream,
Bordered, each bank, with pines; the morning sun,
On the wet umbrage of their glossy tops,
On the red pinings of their forest-floor,
Drew a warm scent abroad; behind the pines
The mountain-skirts, with all their sylvan change
Of bright-leafed chestnuts and mossed walnut-trees
And the frail scarlet-berried ash, began.
Swiss chalets glittered on the dewy slopes,
And from some swarded shelf, high up, there came
Notes of wild pastoral music—over all
Ranged, diamond-bright, the eternal wall of snow.
Upon the mossy rocks at the stream's edge,
Backed by the pines, a plank-built cottage stood,
Bright in the sun; the climbing gourd-plant's leaves
Muffled its walls, and on the stone-strewn roof
Lay the warm golden gourds; golden, within,
Under the eaves, peered rows of Indian corn.
We shot beneath the cottage with the stream.
On the brown, rude-carved balcony, two forms
Came forth—Olivia's, Marguerite! and thine.
Clad were they both in white, flowers in their breast;
Straw hats bedecked their heads, with ribbons blue,
Which danced, and on their shoulders, fluttering, played.
They saw us, they conferred; their bosoms heaved,
And more than mortal impulse filled their eyes.
Their lips moved; their white arms, waved eagerly,
Flashed once, like falling streams; we rose, we gazed.
One moment, on the rapid's top, our boat
Hung poised—and then the darting river of Life
(Such now, methought, it was), the river of Life,
Loud thundering, bore us by; swift, swift it foamed,
Black under cliffs it raced, round headlands shone.
Soon the planked cottage by the sun-warmed pines
Faded—the moss—the rocks; us burning plains,
Bristled with cities, us the sea received.

Martin] possibly Wyndham Slade   Marguerite] a French girl whom Arnold met at
Thun in 1848 and 1849, subject of his Marguerite poems

137   *The Terrace at Berne*

Ten years! and to my waking eye
Once more the roofs of Berne appear;
The rocky banks, the terrace high,
The stream!—and do I linger here?

The clouds are on the Oberland,
The Jungfrau snows look faint and far;
But bright are those green fields at hand,
And through those fields comes down the Aar,

And from the blue twin-lakes it comes,
Flows by the town, the churchyard fair;
And 'neath the garden-walk it hums,
The house!—and is my Marguerite there?

Ah, shall I see thee, while a flush
Of startled pleasure floods thy brow,
Quick through the oleanders brush,
And clap thy hands, and cry: *'Tis thou!*

Or hast thou long since wandered back,
Daughter of France! to France, thy home;
And flitted down the flowery track
Where feet like thine too lightly come?

Doth riotous laughter now replace
Thy smile; and rouge, with stony glare,
Thy cheek's soft hue; and fluttering lace
The kerchief that enwound thy hair?

Or is it over?—art thou dead?
Dead!—and no warning shiver ran
Across my heart, to say thy thread
Of life was cut, and closed thy span!

Could from earth's ways that figure slight
Be lost, and I not feel 'twas so?
Of that fresh voice the gay delight
Fail from earth's air, and I not know?

Or shall I find thee still, but changed,
But not the Marguerite of thy prime?
With all thy being re-arranged,
Passed through the crucible of time;

twin-lakes] Lakes Thun and Brienz   garden-walk] of the Hotel Bellevue at Thun

With spirit vanished, beauty waned,
And hardly yet a glance, a tone,
A gesture—anything—retained
Of all that was my Marguerite's own?

I will not know! For wherefore try,
To things by mortal course that live,
A shadow durability,
For which they were not meant, to give?

Like driftwood spars, which meet and pass
Upon the boundless ocean-plain,
So on the sea of life, alas!
Man meets man—meets, and quits again.

I knew it when my life was young;
I feel it still, now youth is o'er.
—The mists are on the mountain hung,
And Marguerite I shall see no more.

THOMAS HARDY
1840–1928

138   *Lausanne*

In Gibbon's Old Garden

11–12 p.m., 27 June 1897

A spirit seems to pass,
Formal in pose, but grave withal and grand:
He contemplates a volume in his hand,
And far lamps fleck him through the thin acacias.

Anon the book is closed,
With 'It is finished!' And at the alley's end
He turns, and when on me his glances bend
As from the Past comes speech—small, muted, yet composed.

'How fares the Truth now?—Ill?
—Do pens but slyly further her advance?
May one not speed her but in phrase askance?
Do scribes aver the Comic to be Reverend still?

'Still rule those minds on earth
At whom sage Milton's wormwood words were hurled:
"*Truth like a bastard comes into the world
Never without ill-fame to him who gives her birth*"?'

A. D. GODLEY

1856–1925

139   *Switzerland*

In the steamy, stuffy Midlands, 'neath an English summer sky,
When the holidays are nearing with the closing of July,
And experienced Alpine stagers and impetuous recruits
Are renewing with the season their continual disputes—
      Those inveterate disputes
      On the newest Alpine routes—
And inspecting the condition of their mountaineering boots:

You may stifle your reflections, you may banish them afar,
You may try to draw a solace from the thought of 'Nächstes Jahr'—
But your heart is with those climbers, and you'll feverishly yearn
To be crossing of the Channel with your luggage labelled 'Bern',
      Leaving England far astern
      With a ticket through to Bern,
And regarding your profession with a lordly unconcern!

They will lie beside the torrent, just as you were wont to do,
With the woodland green around them and a snowfield shining
   through:
They will tread the higher pastures, where celestial breezes blow,
While the valley lies in shadow and the peaks are all aglow—
      Where the airs of heaven blow
      'Twixt the pine woods and the snow,
And the shades of evening deepen in the valley far below:

They will scale the mountain strongholds that in days of old you won,
They will plod behind a lantern ere the rising of the sun,
On a 'grat' or in a chimney, on the steep and dizzy slope,
For a foothold or a handhold they will diligently grope—
      On the rocky, icy slope
      (Where we'll charitably hope
'Tis assistance only Moral that they're getting from a rope);

They will dine on mule and marmot, and on mutton made of goats,
They will face the various horrors of Helvetian table-d'hôtes:
But whate'er the paths that lead them, and the food whereon they fare,
They will taste the joy of living, as you only taste it there,
      As you taste it Only There
      In the higher, purer air,
Unapproachable by worries and oblivious quite of care!

Place me somewhere in the Valais, 'mid the mountains west of Binn,
West of Binn and east of Savoy, in a decent kind of inn,
With a peak or two for climbing, and a glacier to explore,—
Any mountains will content me, though they've all been climbed
  before—
      Yes! I care not any more
      Though they've all been done before,
And the names they keep in bottles may be numbered by the score!

Though the hand of Time be heavy: though your ancient comrades fail:
Though the mountains you ascended be accessible by rail:
Though your nerve begin to weaken, and you're gouty grown and fat,
And prefer to walk in places which are reasonably flat—
      Though you grow so very fat
      That you climb the Gorner Grat
Or perhaps the Little Scheideck,—and are rather proud of that:
      Yet I hope that till you die
      You will annually sigh
For a vision of the Valais with the coming of July,
For the Oberland or Valais and the higher, purer air,
And the true delight of living, as you taste it only there!

ANTHONY THWAITE

1930–

140   *Switzerland*

In a valley in Switzerland a brass band marches.
The dapper chalets twinkle in the sun
Among the meadows and the well-drilled larches
And watercourses where streams briskly run.

Bravely the little drums pretend their thunder
To far-off crags whose melting snow brings down
A rattle of small pebbles buried under
Drifts deeper than the church spire in the town.

The soldier-citizens of the canton practise
Before an audience of sheep and cows.
As for the real thing, the simple fact is
Each keeps a well-oiled rifle in his house.

Duchies and principalities have fathered
These drums and cornets under angrier skies,
Bucolic bellicosities which gathered
The Ruritanian airs of paradise

Into a clockwork joke envious Europe
Could laugh at, play in, patronize, ignore,
As, poised between the saddle and the stirrup,
The Switzer was acknowledged as a bore.

The peaceable kingdom rests on marks and dollars
Beside the lake at Zurich, lined with banks,
Far from the towns draped with insurgent colours
Whose dawn breaks with the grinding tread of tanks.

The Alpine avalanche holds back this summer
Its fragile tons, and watches from the height
The nimble piper and the strutting drummer
Putting the valley's herbivores to flight.

BEYOND THE IRON CURTAIN

GEORGE TURBERVILLE

*c.*1544–*c.*1597

141   *To Parker*

My Parker, paper, pen, and ink were made to write,
And idle heads, that little do, have leisure to indite:
Wherefore, respecting these, and thine assured love,
If I would write no news to thee, thou might'st my pen reprove.
And sithence fortune thus hath shoved my ship on shore:
And made me seek another realm unseen of me before:
The manners of the men I purpose to declare,
And other private points besides, which strange and geazon are.
The Russie men are round of bodies, fully faced,
The greatest part with bellies big that overhang the waist,

141 geazon] amazing

Flat-headed for the most, with faces nothing fair,
But brown, by reason of the stove, and closeness of the air:
It is their common use to shave or else to shear
Their heads, for none in all the land long lolling locks doth wear,
Unless perhaps he have his sovereign prince displeased,
For then he never cuts his hair, until he be appeased.
A certain sign to know who in displeasure be,
For every man that views his head, will say, 'Lo this is he.'
And during all the time he lets his locks to grow,
Dares no man for his life to him a face of friendship show.
Their garments be not gay, nor handsome to the eye,
A cap aloft their heads they have, that standeth very high,
Which Colpack they do term. They wear no ruffs at all:
The best have collars set with pearl, which they Rubasca call.
Their shirts in Russie long, they work them down before,
And on the sleeves with coloured silks, two inches good and more.
Aloft their shirts they wear a garment jacket-wise
Hight Onoriadka, and about his burly waist he ties
His portkies, which instead of better breeches be:
Of linen cloth that garment is, no codpiece is to see.
A pair of yarnen stocks to keep the cold away,
Within his boots the Russie wears, the heels they underlay
With clouting clamps of steel, sharp-pointed at the toes,
And over all a Shuba furd, and thus the Russie goes.
Well buttoned is the Shube, according to his state,
Some silk, of silver other some: but those of poorest rate
Do wear no Shubs at all, but grosser gowns to sight,
That reachest down beneath the calf, and that Armacha hight:
These are the Russies' robes. The richest use to ride
From place to place, his servant runs, and follows by his side.
The Cassacke bears his felt, to force away the rain:
Their bridles are not very brave, their saddles are but plain.
No bits but snaffles all, of birch their saddles be,
Much fashioned like the Scottish seats, broad flakes to keep the
    knee
From sweating of the horse, the panels larger far
And broader be than ours, they use short stirrups for the war:
For when the Russie is pursued by cruel foe,
He rides away, and suddenly betakes him to his bow,
And bends me but about in saddle as he sits,
And therewithal amids his face his following foe he hits.
Their bows are very short, like Turkie bows outright,
Of sinews made with birchen bark, in cunning manner dight.
Small arrows, cruel heads, that fell and forked be,
Which being shot from out those bows, a cruel way will flee.

Colpack] a felt cap of triangular form   Shuba furd, Shube, Shubs] fur gown or greatcoat

They seldom use to shoe their horse, unless they ride
In post upon the frozen floods, then cause they shall not slide,
He sets a slender calk, and so he rides his way.
The horses of the country go good fourscore versts a day,
And all without the spur, once prick them and they skip,
But go not forward on their way, the Russie hath his whip
To rap him on the ribs, for though all booted be,
Yet shall you not a pair of spurs in all the country see.
The common game is chess, almost the simplest will
Both give a check and eke a mate, by practice comes their skill.
Again they dice as fast, the poorest rogues of all
Will sit them down in open field, and there to gaming fall.
Their dice are very small, in fashion like to those
Which we do use, he takes them up, and over thumb he throws
Not shaking them a whit, they cast suspiciously,
And yet I deem them void of art that dicing most apply.
At play when silver lacks, goes saddle, horse and all,
And each thing else worth silver walks, although the price be small.
Because thou lovest to play friend Parker other while,
I wish thee there the weary day with dicing to beguile.
But thou wert better far at home, I wist it well,
And wouldest be loathe among such louts so long a time to dwell.
Then judge of us thy friends, what kind of life we had,
That near the frozen pole to waste our weary days were glad.
In such a savage soil, where laws do bear no sway,
But all is at the king his will, to save or else to slay.
And that sans cause, God wot, if so his mind be such.
But what mean I with kings to deal? we ought no saints to touch.
Conceive the rest your self, and deem what lives they lead,
Where lust is law, and subjects live continually in dread.
And where the best estates have none assurance good
Of lands, of lives, nor nothing falls unto the next of blood.
But all of custom doeth unto the prince redown,
And all the whole revenue comes unto the king his crown.
Good faith I see thee muse at what I tell thee now,
But true it is, no choice, but all at prince's pleasure bow.
So Tarquin ruled Rome as thou remembrest well,
And what his fortune was at last, I know thyself canst tell.
Where will in common weal doth bear the only sway,
And lust is law, the prince and realm must needs in time decay.
The strangeness of the place is such for sundry things I see,
As if I would I cannot write each private point to thee.
The cold is rare, the people rude, the prince so full of pride,
The realm so stored with monks and nuns, and priests on every side:

calk] a pointed piece of iron on a horseshoe to prevent slipping   versts] a verst is approximately two-thirds of a mile

The manners are so Turkie like, the men so full of guile,
The women wanton, temples stuffed with idols that defile
The seats that sacred ought to be, the customs are so quaint,
As if I would describe the whole, I fear my pen would faint.
In sum, I say I never saw a prince that so did reign,
Nor people so beset with saints, yet all but vile and vain.
Wild Irish are as civil as the Russies in their kind,
Hard choice which is the best of both, each bloody, rude and blind.
If thou be wise, as wise thou art, and wilt be ruled by me,
Live still at home, and covet not those barbarous coasts to see.
No good befalls a man that seeks, and finds no better place,
No civil customs to be learned, where God bestows no grace.
And truly ill they do deserve to be beloved of God,
That neither love nor stand in awe of his assured rod:
Which though be long, yet plagues at last the vile and beastly sort
Of sinful wights, that all in vice do place their chiefest sport.
  A dieu friend Parker, if thou list, to know the Russes well,
To Sigismundus' book repair, who all the truth can tell:
For he long erst in message went unto that savage king,
Sent by the Pole, and true report in each respect did bring,
To him I recommend my self, to ease my pen of pain,
And now at last do wish thee well, and bid farewell again.

142   *To Spencer*

If I should now forget, or not remember thee,
Thou Spencer might'st a foul rebuke, and shame impute to me.
For I to open show did love thee passing well,
And thou wert he at parture, whom I loathed to bid farewell.
And as I went thy friend, so I continue still,
No better proof thou canst than this desire of true good will.
I do remember well when needs I should away,
And that the post would license us, no longer time to stay:
Thou wrungst me by the fist, and holding fast my hand,
Didst crave of me to send thee news, and how I liked the land.
It is a sandy soil, no very fruitful vein,
More waste and woody grounds there are, than closes fit for grain.
Yet grain there growing is, which they untimely take,
And cut or e'er the corn be ripe, they mow it on a stack.

Sigismundus' book] probably *De vetustatibus Polonorum: De Sigismundi Regis temporibus Liber*
(Cracow, 1521), which was written by Jodocus Ludovicus Decius (Jodok Decjus) for Sigismund
I (the Old), 1467–1548

And laying sheaf by sheaf, their harvest so they dry,
They make the greater haste, for fear the frost the corn destroy.
For in the winter time, so glary is the ground,
As neither grass, nor other grain, in pastures may be found.
In comes the cattle then, the sheep, the colt, the cow,
Fast by his bed the Mowsike then a lodging doth allow,
Whom he with fodder feeds, and holds as dear as life:
And thus they wear the winter with the Mowsike and his wife.
Seven months the winter dures, the glare it is so great,
As it is May before he turn his ground to sow his wheat.
The bodies eke that die unburied lie they then,
Laid up in coffins made of fir, as well the poorest men,
As those of greater state: the cause is lightly found,
For that in winter-time, they cannot come to break the ground.
And wood so plenteous is, quite throughout all the land,
As rich, and poor, at time of death assured of coffins stand.
Perhaps thou musest much, how this may stand with reason,
That bodies dead can uncorrupt abide so long a season.
Take this for certain troth, as soon as heat is gone,
The force of cold the body binds as hard as any stone,
Without offence at all to any living thing:
And so they lie in perfect state, till next return of spring.
Their beasts be like to ours, as far as I can see,
For shape and show, but somewhat less of bulk and bone they be,
Of wat'rish taste, the flesh not firm, like English beef,
And yet it serves them very well, and is a good relief:
Their sheep are very small, sharp singled, handful long,
Great store of fowl on sea and land, the moorish reeds among.
The greatness of the store doth make the prices less,
Besides in all the land they know not how good meat to dress.
They use neither broach nor spit, but when the stove they heat,
They put their victuals in a pan, and so they bake their meat.
No pewter to be had, no dishes but of wood;
No use of trenchers, cups cut out of birch are very good.
They use but wooden spoons, which hanging in a case
Each Mowsike at his girdle ties, and thinks it no disgrace.
With whittles two or three, the better man the mo,
The chiefest Russies in the land, with spoon and knives do go.
Their houses are not huge of building, but they say,
They plant them in the loftiest ground, to shift the snow away,
Which in the winter-time, each where full thick doth lie:
Which makes them have the more desire, to set their houses high.
No stonework is in use, their roofs of rafters be,
One linked in another fast, their walls are all of tree.

glary] frozen   Mowsike peasant (R. *muzhik*)   glare] frost

Of masts both long, and large, with moss put in between,
To keep the force of weather out, I never erst have seen
A gross device so good, and on the roof they lay
The burthen bark, to rid the rain, and sudden showers away.
In every room a stove, to serve the winter turn,
Of wood they have sufficient store, as much as they can burn.
They have no English glass, of slices of a rock
Hight Sluda they their windows make, that English glass doth mock.
They cut it very thin, and sow it with a thread
In pretty order like to panes, to serve their present need.
No other glass, good faith, doth give a better light:
And sure the rock is nothing rich, the cost is very slight.
The chiefest place is that, where hangs the god by it,
The owner of the house himself doth never sit,
Unless his better come, to whom he yields the seat:
The stranger bending to the god, the ground with brow must beat.
And in that very place which they most sacred deem,
The stranger lies: a token that his guest he doth esteem.
Where he is wont to have a bear's skin for his bed,
And must, instead of pillow, clap his saddle to his head.
In Russia other shift there is not to be had,
For where the bedding is not good, the bolsters are but bad.
I mused very much, what made them so to lie,
Sith in their country down is rife, and feathers out of cry:
Unless it be because the country is so hard,
They fear by niceness of a bed their bodies would be marred,
I wished thee oft with us save that I stood in fear
Thou wouldst have loathed to have laid thy limbs upon a bear,
As I and Stafford did, that was my mate in bed:
And yet (we thank the God of heaven) we both right well have sped.
Lo thus I make an end: none other news to thee,
But that the country is too cold, the people beastly be.
I write not all I know, I touch but here and there,
For if I should, my pen would pinch, and eke offend I fear.
Who so shall read this verse, conjecture of the rest,
And think by reason of our trade, that I do think the best.
But if no traffic were, then could I boldly pen
The hardness of the soil, and eke the manners of the men.
They say the lion's paw gives judgement of the beast:
And so may you deem of the great, by reading of the least.

Sluda] Russian mica

143 *Unable by Long and Hard Travel to Banish Love,*
       Returns her Friend

Wounded with love and piercing deep desire
Of your fair face, I left my native land
With Russia snow to slack mine English fire;
But well I see no cold can quench the brand
That Cupid's coals enkindle in the breast,
Frost hath no force where friendship is possessed.
  The ocean sea, for all his fearful flood,
The perils great of passage, not prevail,
To banish love the rivers do no good,
The mountains high cause Cupid not to quail,
Wight are his wings, and fancy flies as fast
As any ship, for all his sails and mast.
  The river Dwina cannot wash away
With all his waves the love I bear to thee,
Nor Suchan swift love's raging heat delay,—
Good will was graffed upon so sure a tree.
Sith travel then, nor frost, can cool this fire,
From Moscow I thy friend will home retire.

JOHN TAYLOR
?1578–1653

144   from *Taylor's Travels from London to Prague*

I come from Bohem, yet no news I bring
Of business 'twixt the Kaiser and the King:
My Muse dares not ascend the lofty stairs
Of state, or write of princes' great affairs.
And as for news of battles or of war,
Were England from Bohemia thrice as far,
Yet we do know (or seem to know) more here
Than was, is, or will be ever known there.
At ordinaries, and at barber-shops,
There tidings vented are, as thick as hops:

Wight] strong, rapid   Dwina] (Northern) Dvina, river that flows north from Kotlas into
the White Sea   Suchan] Sukhona, tributary of the Northern Dvina

144 ordinaries] eating-houses or taverns

How many thousands such a day were slain,
What men of note were in the battle ta'en,
When, where, and how the bloody fight begun,
And how such sconces and such towns were won;
How so and so the armies bravely met,
And which side glorious victory did get;
The month, the week, the day, the very hour
And time they did oppose each other's power:
These things in England prating fools do chatter,
When all Bohemia knows of no such matter.
For all this summer that is gone and past,
Until the first day of October last,
The armies never did together meet,
Nor scarce their eyesight did each other greet.
The fault is neither in the foot or horse
Of the right valiant brave Bohemian force;
From place to place they daily seek the foe,
They march and remarch, watch, ward, ride, run, go,
And grieving so to waste the time away,
Thirst for the hazard of a glorious day.
But still the enemy doth play bo-peep
And thinks it best in a whole skin to sleep,
For neither martial policy, or might,
Or any means can draw the foe to fight;
And now and then they conquer, spoil and pillage
Some few thatched houses or some pelting village,
And to their trenches run away again
Where they like foxes in their holes remain,
Thinking by ling'ring out the wars in length
To weaken and decay the Beamish strength.
This is the news, which now I mean to book,
He that will needs have more, must needs go look.
Thus leaving wars, and matters of high state
To those that dare, and knows how to relate,
I'll only write how I passed here and there,
And what I have observed everywhere.
I'll truly write what I have heard and eyed,
And those that will not so be satisfied,
I (as I meet them) will some tales devise,
And fill their ears (by word of mouth) with lies.

pelting] paltry   Beamish] Bohemian

145 from *Taylor's Travels from London to Prague*

Prague is a famous, ancient, kingly seat,
In situation and in state complete,
Rich in abundance of the earth's best treasure,
Proud and high-minded beyond bounds or measure,
In architecture, stately; in attire
Beizonians plebeians do aspire
To be apparelled with the stately port
Of worship, honour, or the royal court.
Their coaches and caroches are so rife,
They do attend on every tradesman's wife,
Whose husbands are but in a mean regard
And get their living by the ell or yard.
However their estates may be defended,
Their wives like demi-ladies are attended.
I there a chimney-sweeper's wife have seen
Habilimented like the Diamond Queen,
Most gaudy garish, as a fine Maid Marian,
With breath as sweet as any sugar carrion,
With satin cloak, lined through with budge or sable
Or cunny fur (or what her purse is able),
With velvet hood, with tiffanies and purls,
Rebatoos, frizzlings, and with powdered curls,
And (lest her hue or scent should be attainted)
She's antidoted, well perfumed and painted;
She's furred, she's fringed, she's laced, and at her waist
She's with a massy chain of silver braced;
She's yellow starched, and ruffed, and cuffed, and muffed,
She's ringed, she's braceleted, she's richly tuffed,
Her petticoat good silk as can be bought,
Her smock about the tail laced round and wrought.
Her gadding legs are finely Spanish booted,
The whilst her husband like a slave all sooted
Looks like a courtier to infernal Pluto,
And knows himself to be a base cornuto.
Then since a man that lives by chimney sweep,
His wife so gaudy richly clad doth keep,
Think then but how a merchant's wife may go,
Or how a burgomaster's wife doth show.

Beizonians] beggars or knaves   port] bearing   budge] a kind of fur,
consisting of lamb's skin with the wool dressed outwards   cunny fur] rabbit's skin
tiffanies] 'Epiphany silk', thin transparent silks or muslins   Rebatoos] stiff collars
frizzlings] frizzled hair   tuffed] furnished with bunches of flowers or feathers
cornuto] cuckold

There (by a kind of topsy-turvy use),
The women wear the boots, the men the shoes.
I know not if't be profit or else pride,
But sure they're oft'ner ridden than they ride.
These females seem to be most valiant there:
Their painting shows they do no colours fear,
Most art-like plast'ring Nature's imperfections
With sublimated, white and red complexions.
    So much for pride I have observed there;
    Their other faults are almost everywhere.

DANIEL DEFOE
1660–1731

146   from *The Diet of Poland, A Satire*

In northern climes where furious tempests blow,
And men more furious raise worse storms below,
At nature's elbow, distant and remote,
Happy for Europe had she been forgot,
The world's proboscis, near the globe's extremes,
For barb'rous men renowned, and barb'rous names,
There Poland lies too much her maker's care,
And shares the mod'rate blessings of the air,
Just as far off from heav'n as we are here:
    Under the arctic circle of the sky,
Where virtue's streams run low, and nature's high,
For heat of clime too far, of blood too nigh,
Tempered for plenty, plenteously supplied
With men advanced in ev'ry grace but pride.
    A mighty nation throngs the groaning land,
Rude as the climate, num'rous as the sand:
Uncommon monstrous virtues they possess,
Strange odd prepost'rous Polish qualities;
Mysterious contraries they reconcile,
The pleasing frown and the destroying smile;
Precisely gay, and most absurdly grave,
Most humbly high, and barbarously brave;
Debauch'dly civil and profanely good,
And filled with gen'rous brave ingratitude,
By bounty disobliged, by hatred won,
Bold in their danger, cowards when 'tis gone;

To their own ruin they're the only tools,
Wary of knaves, and eas'ly choused by fools;
Profoundly empty, yet declar'dly wise,
And fond of blind impossibilities;
Swelled with conceit, they boast of all they do,
First praise themselves, then think that praise their due:
So fond of flatt'ring words, so vain in pride,
The world mocks them, and they the world deride;
Value themselves upon their nation's merit,
In spite of all the vices they inherit;
So wedded to the country where they dwell,
They think that's heav'n, and all the world's a hell.
Their frozen Vistula they'd not forgo
For fruitful Danube, or the flow'ry Po.
Rapid Boristhenes delights them more
Than pearly streams, or a Peruvian shore:
And Russian Dwina dwells upon their song,
Hurried by barb'rous steeps and hills, and pushed along.
    The land too happy would the people bless,
Could they agree to know their happiness;
Nature with very liberal hand supplies
Her situation-insufficiencies:
The temperate influence revolves of course,
And spite of climate nature works by force.
The bounteous spring the winter's waste repairs,
And makes the world grow young in spite of years.
The fruitful earth uncommon freedom shows,
And foreign wealth by foreign commerce flows.
    But peopled with a hardened thankless race,
Whose crimes add horror to the milder place,
The bounties by indulgent Heav'n bestowed
Corrode the mischief and debauch the blood.
That native fierceness which in Christian lands
Makes heroes, and their poets' praise commands,
Here 'tis a vice, which rankles up to feud,
And nourishes the gust of vile ingratitude.
Pride, plenty's handmaid, deeply taints their blood,
And seeds of faction mix the crimson flood.
Eternal discords brood upon the soil,
And universal strifes the state embroil,
In every family the temper reigns,
In every action seed of gall remains.
The very laws of peace create dispute,
And makes them quarrel who shall execute.
Their valued constitutions are so lame,
That governing the governments inflame.

    choused] duped   Boristhenes] river Dnieper

Wild aristocracy torments the state,
And people their own miseries create.
    In vain has Heav'n its choicer gifts bestowed,
And strives in vain to do a wilful nation good:
Such is the people's folly, such their fate,
As all decrees of peace anticipate.
Immortal jars in ev'ry class appear,
Conceived in strife, and nursed to civil war.
    Such, Poland, is thy people, such thy name,
Yet still thy sons our panegyrics claim,
Because their partial genius is inclined
To think they merit more than all mankind.
    Imaginary happiness will do
For near as many uses as the true:
And if the Poles in their own plagues delight,
Wise Heaven's too just to let them thrive in spite.

EDWIN MUIR

1887–1959

147   *The Cloud*

One late spring evening in Bohemia,
Driving to the Writers' House, we lost our way
In a maze of little winding roads that led
To nothing but themselves,
Weaving a rustic web for thoughtless travellers.
No house was near, nor sign or sound of life:
Only a chequer-board of little fields,
Crumpled and dry, neat squares of powdered dust.
At a sudden turn we saw
A young man harrowing, hidden in dust; he seemed
A prisoner walking in a moving cloud
Made by himself for his own purposes;
And there he grew and was as if exalted
To more than man, yet not, not glorified:
A pillar of dust moving in dust; no more.
The bushes by the roadside were encrusted
With a hard sheath of dust.
We looked and wondered; the dry cloud moved on
With its interior image.
                        Presently we found
A road that brought us to the Writers' House,

And there a preacher from Urania
(Sad land where hope each day is killed by hope)
Praised the good dust, man's ultimate salvation,
And cried that God was dead. As we drove back
Late to the city, still our minds were teased
By the brown barren fields, the harrowing,
The figure walking in its cloud, the message
From far Urania. This was before the change;
And in our memory cloud and message fused,
Image and thought condensed to a giant form
That walked the earth clothed in its earthly cloud,
Dust made sublime in dust. And yet it seemed unreal
And lonely as things not in their proper place.
And thinking of the man
Hid in his cloud we longed for light to break
And show that his face was the face once broken in Eden,
Beloved, world-without-end lamented face;
And not a blindfold mask on a pillar of dust.

HUGH MacDIARMID
1892–1978

148   *The Skeleton of the Future*

(At Lenin's Tomb)

Red granite and black diorite, with the blue
Of the labradorite crystals gleaming like precious stones
In the light reflected from the snow; and behind them
The eternal lightning of Lenin's bones.

DONALD DAVIE
1922–

149   *A Meeting of Cultures*

Iced with a vanilla
Of dead white stone, the Palace
Of Culture is a joke

147 Urania] the Muse of Astronomy, and thus of wisdom in the highest senses; so, by
transference, the Land of Wisdom.

Or better, a vast villa
In some unimaginable suburb
Of Perm or Minsk.

Ears wave and waggle
Over the poignant Vistula,
Horns of a papery stone,

Not a wedding-cake but its doily!
The Palace of Culture sacks
The centre, the dead centre

Of Europe's centre, Warsaw.
The old town,
Rebuilt, is a clockwork toy.

I walked abroad in it,
Charmed and waylaid
By a nursery joy:

Hansel's and Gretel's city!
Their house of gingerbread
That lately in

Horrific forest glooms
Of Germany
Bared its ferocity

Anew, resumes its gilt
For rocking-horse rooms
In Polish rococo.

Diseased imaginations
Extant in Warsaw's stone
Her air makes sanative.

How could a D.S.O.
Of the desert battles live,
If it were otherwise,

In his wooden cabin
In a country wood
In the heart of Warsaw

As the colonel did, who for
The sake of England took
Pains to be welcoming!

More jokes then. And the wasps humming
Into his lady's jam
That we ate with a spoon

Out in the long grass. Shades,
Russian shades out of old slow novels,
Lengthened the afternoon.

GERDA MAYER

1927–

150 *Small Park in East Germany: 1969*

Crumbling and weathered, their features half-erased,
they stand gracefully in these gardens under the quiet sun,
satyrs and goddesses, some in niches of leaves;
now they're returning to stone, they are more real
than when—what ages ago?—they were wheeled in
and put up, looking too white and too newly chiselled.

Once all was gay and decorous; children white-beribboned
and sailor-suited drove their hoops before them, the white
whipped cream topped aromatic coffee, and the band
played in the open air to the prosperous and the bourgeois.

The band is silent, the café locked up, the too
prosperous have departed. And departed too is
that later and crooked time that fouled Germany's air.
Now is the time of unyielding ideals; the egalitarian
walk here but without conviction and feel out of place.

But whose place was it ever? The happy complacent
once owned it perhaps but in a different way;
then came the blackly hysterical, then the quietly out-of-sorts.
It seems to belong to itself and is growing towards Arcadia;
a half-forgotten garden full of dense leaves and sun,
and nymphs and satyrs breaking from weathered stone.

TONY HARRISON

1937–

151   *Prague Spring*

on my birthday, 30 April

A silent scream? The madrigal's top note?
Puking his wassail on the listening throng?
Mouthfuls of cumulus, then cobalt throat.
Medusa must have hexed him in mid-song.

The finest vantage point in all of Prague's
this gagging gargoyle's with the stone-locked lute,
leaning over cherries, blow-ups of Karl Marx
the pioneers 'll march past and salute.

Tomorrow's May but still a North wind scuffs
the plated surface like a maced cuirass,
lays on, lays off, gets purchase on and roughs
up the Vltava, then makes it glass.

The last snow of this year's late slow thaw
dribbles as spring saliva down his jaw.

SCANDINAVIA WITH ICELAND

AMBROSE PHILIPS

1674–1749

152   *A Winter-Piece*

Epistle to Lord Dorset

Copenhagen, 9 March 1709

From frozen climes, and endless tracks of snow,
From streams that northern winds forbid to flow;
What present shall the Muse to Dorset bring;
Or how, so near the pole, attempt to sing?

151 Vltava] river that runs through Prague

The hoary winter here conceals from sight
All pleasing objects that to verse invite.
The hills and dales, and the delightful woods,
The flow'ry plains, and silver streaming floods,
By snow disguised, in bright confusion lie,
And with one dazzling waste fatigue the eye.
   No gentle breathing breeze prepares the spring,
No birds within the Desert region sing.
The ships unmoved the boist'rous winds defy,
While rattling chariots o'er the ocean fly.
The vast Leviathan wants room to play,
And spout his waters in the face of day.
The starving wolves along the main sea prowl,
And to the moon in icy valleys howl.
For many a shining league the level main
Here spreads itself into a glassy plain:
There solid billows of enormous size,
Alps of green ice, in wild disorder rise.
   And yet but lately have I seen, e'en here,
The winter in a lovely dress appear.
E'er yet the clouds let fall the treasured Snow,
Or winds begun through hazy skies to blow.
At ev'ning a keen eastern breeze arose;
And the descending rain unsullied froze.
Soon as the silent shades of night withdrew,
The ruddy morn disclosed at once to view
The face of nature in a rich disguise,
And brightened ev'ry object to my eyes.
For ev'ry shrub, and ev'ry blade of grass,
And ev'ry pointed thorn, seemed wrought in glass.
In pearls and rubies rich the hawthorns show,
While through the ice the crimson berries glow.
The thick-sprung reeds the wat'ry marshes yield,
Seem polished lances in a hostile field.
The stag in limpid currents with surprise
Sees crystal branches on his forehead rise.
The spreading oak, the beech, and tow'ring pine,
Glazed over, in the freezing ether shine.
The frighted birds the rattling branches shun,
That wave and glitter in the distant sun.
   When if a sudden gust of wind arise,
The brittle forest into atoms flies:
The crackling wood beneath the tempest bends,
And in a spangled shower the prospect ends.
Or if a southern gale the region warm,
And by degrees unbind the wintry charm;

The traveller a miry country sees,
And journeys sad beneath the dropping trees.
   Like some deluded Peasant, Merlin leads
Through fragrant bow'rs, and through delicious meads;
While here enchanted gardens to him rise,
And airy fabrics there attract his eyes,
His wand'ring feet the magic paths pursue;
And while he thinks the fair illusion true,
The trackless scenes disperse in fluid air,
And woods and wilds, and thorny ways appear:
A tedious road the weary wretch returns,
And, as he goes, the transient vision mourns.

SIR JOHN CARR
1732–1807

153   *Sonnet upon a Swedish Cottage,*

Written on the Road,
Within a Few Miles of Stockholm

Here, far from all the pomp ambition seeks,
   Much sought, but only whilst untasted praised,
Content and innocence, with rosy cheeks,
   Enjoy the simple shed their hands have raised.

On a grey rock it stands, whose fretted base
   The distant cat'ract's murm'ring waters lave,
Whilst o'er its mossy roof, with varying grace,
   The slender branches of the white birch wave.

Around the forest-fir is heard to sigh,
   On which the pensive ear delights to dwell,
Whilst, as the gazing trav'ller passes by,
   The grey goat, starting, sounds his tinkling bell.
Oh! in my native land, ere life's decline,
May such a spot, so wild, so sweet, be mine!

WILLIAM MORRIS
1834–1896

154   *Iceland First Seen*

Lo from our loitering ship
a new land at last to be seen;
Toothed rocks down the side of the firth
on the east guard a weary wide lea,
And black slope the hillsides above,
striped adown with their desolate green:
And a peak rises up on the west
from the meeting of cloud and of sea,
Foursquare from base unto point
like the building of Gods that have been,
The last of that waste of the mountains
all cloud-wreathed and snow-flecked and grey,
And bright with the dawn that began
just now at the ending of day.

Ah! what came we forth for to see
that our hearts are so hot with desire?
Is it enough for our rest,
the sight of this desolate strand,
And the mountain-waste voiceless as death
but for winds that may sleep not nor tire?
Why do we long to wend forth
through the length and breadth of a land,
Dreadful with grinding of ice,
and record of scarce hidden fire,
But that there 'mid the grey grassy dales
sore scarred by the ruining streams
Lives the tale of the Northland of old
and the undying glory of dreams?

O land, as some cave by the sea
where the treasures of old have been laid,
The sword it may be of a king
whose name was the turning of fight:
Or the staff of some wise of the world
that many things made and unmade.
Or the ring of a woman maybe
whose woe is grown wealth and delight.
No wheat and no wine grows above it,
no orchard for blossom and shade;

The few ships that sail by its blackness
but deem it the mouth of a grave;
Yet sure when the world shall awaken,
this too shall be mighty to save.

Or rather, O land, if a marvel
it seemeth that men ever sought
Thy wastes for a field and a garden
fulfilled of all wonder and doubt,
And feasted amidst of the winter
when the fight of the year had been fought,
Whose plunder all gathered together
was little to babble about;
Cry aloud from thy wastes, O thou land,
'Not for this nor for that was I wrought
Amid waning of realms and of riches
and death of things worshipped and sure,
I abide here the spouse of a God,
and I made and I make and endure.'

O Queen of the grief without knowledge,
of the courage that may not avail,
Of the longing that may not attain,
of the love that shall never forget,
More joy than the gladness of laughter
thy voice hath amidst of its wail:
More hope than of pleasure fulfilled
amidst of thy blindness is set;
More glorious than gaining of all
thine unfaltering hand that shall fail:
For what is the mark on thy brow
but the brand that thy Brynhild doth bear?
Lone once, and loved and undone
by a love that no ages outwear.

Ah! when thy Balder comes back,
and bears from the heart of the Sun
Peace and the healing of pain,
and the wisdom that waiteth no more;
And the lilies are laid on thy brow
'mid the crown of the deeds thou hast done;
And the roses spring up by thy feet
that the rocks of the wilderness wore.
Ah! when thy Balder comes back
and we gather the gains he hath won,

Balder] beautiful, wise, and gentle Norse god who will return from the dead after the all-consuming conflict of Ragnarok

Shall we not linger a little
to talk of thy sweetness of old,
Yea, turn back awhile to thy travail
whence the Gods stood aloof to behold?

155   *Gunnar's Howe above the House at Lithend*[1]

Ye who have come o'er the sea
to behold this grey minster of lands,
Whose floor is the tomb of time past,
and whose walls by the toil of dead hands
Show pictures amidst of the ruin
of deeds that have overpast death,
Stay by this tomb in a tomb
to ask of who lieth beneath.
Ah! the world changeth too soon,
that ye stand there with unbated breath,
As I name him that Gunnar of old,
who erst in the haymaking tide
Felt all the land fragrant and fresh,
as amidst of the edges he died.
Too swiftly fame fadeth away,
if ye tremble not lest once again
The grey mound should open and show him
glad-eyed without grudging or pain.
Little labour methinks to behold him
but the tale-teller laboured in vain.
Little labour for ears that may hearken
to hear his death-conquering song,
Till the heart swells to think of the gladness
undying that overcame wrong.
O young is the world yet meseemeth
and the hope of it flourishing green,
When the words of a man unremembered
so bridge all the days that have been,
As we look round about on the land
that these nine hundred years he hath seen.

Dusk is abroad on the grass
of this valley amidst of the hill:

---

[1] Hliðarendi ('Farm at the End of the Hillside') is in the south of Iceland. It is the site of the farm of Gunnar who, as described in *Njal's Saga*, defied a sentence of exile and so faced death: 'He happened to glance up towards his home and the slopes of Hlidarend. "How lovely the slopes are,", he said, "more lovely than they have ever seemed to be before, golden cornfield and new-mown hay. I am going back home and I will not go away." '

Dusk that shall never be dark
till the dawn hard on midnight shall fill
The trench under Eyiafell's snow,
and the grey plain the sea meeteth grey.
White, high aloft hangs the moon
that no dark night shall brighten ere day,
For here day and night toileth the summer
lest deedless his time pass away.

'JOHN'

late 19th century

156   *Ode to the Last Pot of Marmalade*

To the fishers of Gjendin the bold Skipper spoke:
'There is one two-pound pot that as yet is unbroke;
So rouse ye, my gallants, and after our tea
Let us "go for" our Keiller's own Bonnie Dundee.'

    (*Chorus*)

  Come! up with the Smör! Come! out with the Brod,
  We'll have one more Spise that's fit for a god;
  Come, whip off the paper and let it gae free,
  And we'll wade into Keiller's own Bonnie Dundee.

You may talk of your mölte with sugar and milk,
Your blueberry pasties, and jam of that ilk;
They are all very well in the wilds, don't you see?
But they can't hold a candle to Bonnie Dundee.
                                  Chorus as before.

Oh! the pies they were good, and the oven baked true,
With its door of green sod, and its sinuous flue.
Oh! the curry was toothsome as curry can be,
But where is the equal of Bonnie Dundee?
                             Chorus again, gentlemen.

There are ryper on Glopit as fleet as the wind,
And the Stor Bock roams on the Skagastolstind;
There are trout, teal, and woodcock, a sight for to see,
But what meal can be perfect without our Dundee?
                               Chorus, if you please.

Eyiafell's snow] the glacier of Eyjafjall

156 Keiller's] brand of marmalade   Smör] butter   Brod] bread   Spise] a
meal   mölte] cloudberry (orange-red fruit related to the blackberry)   Glopit] mountain between Gjendin and Rus Vand   Stor] big

Pandecagos are tasty, and omelettes are good;
Our eggs, though antique, not unsuited for food;
You can always be sure of at least one in three,
But blue mould cannot ruin our Bonnie Dundee.

Chorus, only more so.

Take my soup, though 'tis luscious, my öl, though 'tis rare,
My whisky, though scanty, beyond all compare;
Take my baccy, take all that is dearest to me,
But leave me one spoonful of Bonnie Dundee.

Chorus ad lib.

HUMBERT WOLFE
1886–1940

157   *Denmark*

I left Warnemünde and Germany with a sense of little ease,
because of the trees in Germany, because of the wounded trees
that muttered together sullenly in a dark conspiring crowd,
and when the wind went among them sullenly cried aloud—
But the small first tree of Denmark was a verse (I knew) that had
  strayed,
a little apart from the others, out of a serenade,
where the slim pink stems were only a note, and the easy stir
of the wind in the needles only the dark musicianer,
and out of the carriage window I suddenly saw (I swear!)
how over the lower branches of my fir-tree there leaped a hare.

I had crossed over to Denmark with the most exalted plans
of writing a Danish epic—why did you slip in, Hans,
with your hare, and your little fir-tree, and your dead-red sand, and
  then
with all the loves of my childhood and my dreams, Hans Andersen!
It was an Epic poet, that carelessly offered ten mark
to a discontented porter, as he stepped on the shores of Denmark;
—why did you take him, and change him (confess the whole business
  and own up!)

Pandecagos] pancakes   öl] ale

157 Warnemünde] town on the Baltic, now in East Germany

into the ghost of his boyhood, who had meant to be far more than
   grown up!
Ah, well! I surrendered at random, and made no attempt to be too coy
to be caught, and be held, and be dazzled by the old enchanter—
   Luke-oie.
O little fir-tree of Denmark, I passed you by, but I guessed
what star of an unborn Christmas waited against your breast—
somewhere the glass-balls are waiting, and the unlit candles glisten
somewhere, and somewhere the children unborn are singing! oh, listen!
And though, when your Christmas is over, you must lie despoiled in the
   garden,
yet there is nothing to rail at, fir-tree, nothing to pardon.
For, while you lie there, (it is written) playing his little drum
down through the pipe of the wash-house the lead soldier will come—
Yes, and the darning-needle will boast to the old street-lamp
that she alone is a lady, but the soldier an idle scamp.
All this as the train swept onwards I dreamed, I saw, I heard,
till out of the deep of the forest, as the night came down, a bird,
an unseen bird in the forest sang, like the light of a star
clean through the stems of the fir-trees where no twigs or branches are,
of the great lord in the castle, who only answered 'P'
(which, as you know, means nothing) to folk like you and me,
of the little kitchen-maiden, who, though she had scrubbed the floor,
was a better judge of music than a Chinese Emperor.
He sang, as he has been singing this thousand years, again
the tale of the fir, and the water, and the quiet heart of the Dane,
the fir, and the glass-cool water, and the night-sun-haunted sky,
and how we come with the morning, and how with the night we die.

I have seen great Kronborg standing in the red king's robes he wore
when Hamlet, Prince of Denmark, was a prince at Helsingor—
I have seen Fredensborg whiter than the pale white hand of a queen,
and—a water-lily floating—Frederichsborg I have seen.
And yet these castles are shadows, lovely they were and are,
but all their man-made beauty fades by the light of the star,
that struck through the stems of the fir-trees—the evening star, the pale
cool-throated star, that rises with the Danish nightingale.

     Luke-oie] Luk-oie, Hans Andersen's magician-storyteller

LOUIS MacNEICE
1907–1963

Letter to Graham and Anna

Reykjavik, 16 August 1936

To Graham and Anna: from the Arctic Gate
I send this letter to N.W.8,
Hoping that Town is not the usual mess,
That Pauli is rid of worms, the new cook a success.
I have got here, you see, without being sick
On a boat of eight hundred tons to Reykjavik.
Came second-class—no air but many men;
Having seen the first-class crowd would do the same again.
Food was good, mutton and bits of fishes,
A smart line-up of Scandinavian dishes—
Beet, cheese, ham, jam, smoked salmon, gaffalbitar,
Sweet cucumber, German sausage, and Ryvita.
So I came here to the land the Romans missed,
Left for the Irish saint and the Viking colonist.
But what am I doing here? Qu'allais-je faire
Among these volcanic rocks and this grey air?
Why go north when Cyprus and Madeira
De jure if not de facto are much nearer?
The reason for hereness seems beyond conjecture,
There are no trees or trains or architecture,
Fruits and greens are insufficient for health,
Culture is limited by lack of wealth,
The tourist sights have nothing like Stonehenge,
The literature is all about revenge.
And yet I like it if only because this nation
Enjoys a scarcity of population
And cannot rise to many bores or hacks
Or paupers or poor men paying Super-Tax.
Yet further, if you can stand it, I will set forth
The obscure but powerful ethics of Going North.
Morris did it before, dropping the frills and fuss,
Harps and arbours, Tristram and Theseus,
For a land of rocks and sagas. And certain unknown
Old Irish hermits, holy skin and bone,
Camped on these crags in order to forget
Their blue-black cows in Kerry pastures wet.
Those Latin-chattering margin-illuminating monks
Fled here from home without kit-bags or trunks

gaffalbitar] snacks eaten with the fork

To mortify their flesh—but we must mortify
Our blowsy intellects before we die,
Who feed our brains on backchat and self-pity
And always need a noise, the radio or the city,
Traffic and changing lights, crashing the amber,
Always on the move and so do not remember
The necessity of the silence of the islands,
The glacier floating in the distance out of existence,
The need to grip and grapple the adversary,
Knuckle on stony knuckle, to dot and carry
One and carry one and not give up the hunt
Till we have pinned the Boyg down to a point.
In England one forgets—in each performing troupe
Forgets what one has lost, there is no room to stoop
And look along the ground, one cannot see the ground
For the feet of the crowd, and the lost is never found.
I dropped something, I think, but I am not sure what
And cannot say if it mattered much or not,
So let us get on or we shall be late, for soon
The shops will close and the rush-hour be on.
This is the fret that makes us cat-like stretch
And then contract the fingers, gives the itch
To open the French window into the rain,
Walk out and never be seen at home again.
But where to go? No oracle for us,
Bible or Baedeker, can tell the terminus.
The songs of jazz have told us of a moon country
And we like to dream of a heat which is never sultry,
Melons to eat, champagne to drink, and a lazy
Music hour by hour depetalling the daisy.
Then Medici manuscripts have told of places
Where common sense was wedded to the graces,
Doric temples and olive-trees and such,
But broken marble no longer goes for much.
And there are some who scorn this poésie de départs
And say 'Escape by staying where you are;
A man is what he thinks he is and can
Find happiness within.' How nice to be born a man.
The tourist in space or time, emotion or sensation,
Meets many guides but none have the proper orientation.
We are not changing ground to escape from facts
But rather to find them. This complex world exacts
Hard work of simplifying; to get its focus
You have to stand outside the crowd and caucus.
This all sounds somewhat priggish. You and I
Know very well the immediate reason why

I am in Iceland. Three months ago or so
Wystan said that he was planning to go
To Iceland to write a book and would I come too;
And I said yes, having nothing better to do.
But all the same we never make any choice
On such a merely mechanical stimulus.
The match is not the cause of fire, so pause
And look for the formal as well as the efficient cause.
Aristotle's pedantic phraseology
Serves better than common sense or hand-to-mouth psychology
ἔσχε τὴν φύσιν—'found its nature'; the crude
Embryo rummages every latitude
Looking for itself, its nature, its final pattern,
Till the fairy godmother's wand touches the slattern
And turns her to a princess for a moment
Beyond definition or professorial comment.
We find our nature daily or try to find it,
The old flame gutters, leaves red flames behind it.
An interval of tuning and screwing and then
The symphony restarts, the creature lives again—
Blake's arabesques of fire; the subtle creature
Swings on Ezekiel's wheels, finding its nature.
In short we must keep moving to keep pace
Or else drop into Limbo, the dead place.
I have come north, gaily running away
From the grinding gears, the change from day to day,
The creaks of the familiar room, the smile
Of the cruel clock, the bills upon the file,
The excess of books and cushions, the high heels
That walk the street, the news, the newsboys' yells,
The flag-days and the cripple's flapping sleeve.
The ambushes of sex, the passion to retrieve
Significance from the river of passing people,
The attempt to climb the ever-climbing steeple
And no one knows what is at the top of it,
All is a raffle for caps which may not fit,
But all take tickets, keep moving; still we may
Move off from movement or change it for a day;
Here is a different rhythm, the juggled balls
Hang in the air—the pause before the soufflé falls.
Here we can take a breath, sit back, admire
Stills from the film of life, the frozen fire;
Among these rocks can roll upon the tongue
Morsels of thought, not jostled by the throng,
Or morsels of un-thought, which is still better,
(Thinking these days makes a suburban clatter).

Wystan] W. H. Auden

Here we can practise forgetfulness without
A sense of guilt, fear of the tout and lout,
And here—but Wystan has butted in again
To say we must go out in the frightful rain
To see a man about a horse and so
I shall have to stop. For we soon intend to go
Around the Langjökull, a ten-days' ride,
Gumboots and stockfish. Probably you'll deride
This sissy onslaught on the open spaces.
I can see the joke myself; however the case is
Not to be altered, but please remember us
So high up here in this vertiginous
Crow's-nest of the earth. Perhaps you'll let us know
If anything happens in the world below?

W. H. AUDEN
1907–1973

159   *Journey to Iceland*

Each traveller prays *Let me be far from any
physician*, every port has its name for the sea,
    the citiless, the corroding, the sorrow,
        and North means to all *Reject*.

These plains are for ever where cold creatures are hunted
and on all sides: white wings flicker and flaunt;
    under a scolding flag the lover
        of islands may see at last,

in outline, his limited hope, as he nears a glitter
of glacier, sterile immature mountains intense
    in the abnormal northern day, and a river's
        fan-like polyp of sand.

Here let the citizen, then, find natural marvels,
a horse-shoe ravine, an issue of steam from a cleft
    in the rock, and rocks, and waterfalls brushing
        the rocks, and among the rocks birds;

158 Langjökull] large glacier in the west of Iceland

the student of prose and conduct places to visit,
the site of a church where a bishop was put in a bag,
    the bath of a great historian, the fort where
        an outlaw dreaded the dark,

remember the doomed man thrown by his horse and crying
Beautiful is the hillside. I will not go,
    the old woman confessing *He that I loved the*
        best, to him I was worst.

Europe is absent: this is an island and should be
a refuge, where the affections of its dead can be bought
    by those whose dreams accuse them of being
        spitefully alive, and the pale

from too much passion of kissing feel pure in its deserts.
But is it, can they, as the world is and can lie?
    A narrow bridge over a torrent,
        a small farm under a crag

are natural settings for the jealousies of a province:
a weak vow of fidelity is made at a cairn,
    within the indigenous figure on horseback
        on the bridle-path down by the lake

his blood moves also by furtive and crooked inches,
asks all our questions: *Where is the homage? When*
    shall justice be done? Who is against me?
        Why am I always alone?

Our time has no favourite suburb, no local features
are those of the young for whom all wish to care;
    its promise is only a promise, the fabulous
        country impartially far.

Tears fall in all the rivers: again some driver
pulls on his gloves and in a blinding snowstorm starts
    upon a fatal journey, again some writer
        runs howling to his art.

NORMAN NICHOLSON

1914–

Glacier

Its hectares of white
Out of sight from below,
It gropes with one green paw
The rim of the rock-fall.
Each claw
A crunching of bottle-glass,
Opaque and raw,
Splinters as big as a cottage
Cracked between tongs:
A malevolent, rock-crystal
Precipitate of lava,
Corroded with acid,
Inch by inch erupting
From volcanoes of cold.

Slow
Paws creak downwards,
Annexing no
Extra acreage of stone—
For each hooked talon
Is pruned back and pared
By mid-June sun,
And a hundred sluicings
Ooze down the inclined plane
To a wizened, terminal
Half-cone of snow.

The ebb and flow
Of becks that live for a minute
Swishes bath-salt icebergs
Through a shingle moraine—
Where the dandy, grey-rust
Fieldfare rattles
Pebbles in its crop,
And the dwarf cornel
Blinks like a black-eyed buttercup
On the brink of the milk of melting.

Summer now
Out-spills the corrie

With a swill of willow,
But winter's overhang
Retreats not a centimetre—
No fractured knuckle, no
Refrigerated bone
Relinquishes grasp,
Lets slip a finger-hold
To the bland noon's seepage.

For behind black
Rock-terraces and tiers
Slumped winter waits—
For a tilt of earth's axis,
A stretching-out of the polar cold,
To restore the normal, to correct
The climate's misdirection,
Corroborate and order
Mean average temperature
For the last million years.

FRANCIS BERRY

1915–

161   *Gudveig*

ᛏᚠᛏᛁ : ᛘᚾᛁ᛬ᚾᛁᚠ᛬ᛘᚠᚨ᛬ᚠᛁᚱᛁ᛬ᛒᛁᚱᚦᛁ᛬ᚠᚱᛅᛘ
ᛘᚼ : ᚼᛁᚠᛁ᛬ ᛏᚱ᛬ ᚠᚢᚦᚾᛁᚴ᛬ᚼᛁᛏ

Þæs: kona: uar: lagþ: firi-borð: i: grøna
lanȝ: hafi; ær: guðuih: het

This: woman: was: laid: overboard: in: Green
land's: sea: is: Gudveig: hight

So runed on a rune-stick, and the rune-stick put
In a coffin with another's body, and the coffin found
By Nörlund, in the churchyard of Herjolfsnes, and
On the ground, over the grave, was a stone
Enormous, one and a half ton, and it took
Eight men to shift it.

161 Nörlund] Poul Nörlund, Danish archaeologist, excavated the churchyard at Herjolfsnes
in 1921

Stone there to keep down
The ghost of Gudveig: to keep quiet, keep bound
The ghost of a woman, her body overboard
Laid, in the waters around

GREENLAND.

MICHAEL DENNIS BROWNE
1940–

162   *The Visitor*

For Alex and Hanna Quaade

A fine rain falls, greening their garden.
The ladder into the apple tree drips beads of silk.
Silk rolls from the roof.

They do not play at owning.
The house is screwed well into the earth,
it holds firmly,
the foundations are good,
the earth is black and gripping.

Silk rolls from the roof.

The baby is an electric piece in their hands,
is a portion of their own exactness.
is an ease of them,
passes between them like a blueness.
Love is exact. They fit. They are three soft locks.

They have a kitchen and an orchard
and this good plot of love,
this twined intrigue of a straight marriage.

A fine Danish rain falls.

And I the guest, the friend, the foreigner,
with strange suitcase and unused energy
causing my hands to violate the slow peace
of their house.
On a darkened wet August afternoon that has simply given up.

Red books on their shelves, and purple.
The clock in the hall
springs into the pool of its sound.
A walk of ten minutes would bring me to the beech woods
which are near.

To note them is an envy.
This cannot be earned.
It comes to the hands like a cloth. It is given.

What may it be then, and what shall I take
with me tomorrow on the flight to London?
The idea of your marriage in my case?
Like a piece of wood Alex has found and painted?
Do I borrow this Danish idea?

What they have is very difficult.
Not a harbour.
Not silk. It will not swallow.

Greened is the garden, silked by the rain.
The ladder drips like a silver engine.
The apples are hard but glamorous.

I would take a scissors to my own clouds if I could,
weary of playing a Falstaff on quick visits.
I am a thin thin man.

No peace like the peace of this darkened house
in the Danish afternoon.
Christian has one tooth and sleeps.
Alex has a red book with his own Danish poems written in it.
Hanna cooks and has a hundred real skills.

A fine rain falls,
greened is their garden.

IRELAND

Attributed to ALDFRITH
reigned 685–705

163   *Prince Aldfrith's Itinerary through Ireland*

I found in Innisfail the fair,
In Ireland, while in exile there,
Women of worth, both grave and gay men,
Many clerics and many laymen.

I travelled its fruitful provinces round,
And in every one of the five[1] I found,
Alike in church and in palace hall,
Abundant apparel, and food for all.

Gold and silver I found, and money,
Plenty of wheat and plenty of honey;
I found God's people rich in pity,
Found many a feast and many a city.

I also found in Armagh, the splendid,
Meekness, wisdom, and prudence blended,
Fasting, as Christ hath recommended,
And noble councillors untranscended.

I found in each great church, moreo'er,
Whether on island or on shore,
Piety, learning, fond affection,
Holy welcome and kind protection.

I found the good lay monks and brothers
Ever beseeching help for others,
And in their keeping the holy word
Pure as it came from Jesus the Lord.

I found in Munster, unfettered of any,
Kings, and queens, and poets a many,—
Poets well skilled in music and measure,
Prosperous doings, mirth and pleasure.

---

[1] The two Meaths then formed a distinct province.

I found in Connaught the just, redundance
Of riches, milk in lavish abundance;
Hospitality, vigour, fame,
In Cruachan's land of heroic name.

I found in the country of Connall the glorious,
Bravest heroes, ever victorious;
Fair-complexioned men and warlike,
Ireland's lights, the high, the starlike!

I found in Ulster, from hill to glen,
Hardy warriors, resolute men;
Beauty that bloomed when youth was gone,
And strength transmitted from sire to son.

I found in the noble district of Boyle
        [*MS here illegible*]
Brehon's, Erenachs, weapons bright,
And horsemen bold and sudden in fight.

I found in Leinster the smooth and sleek,
From Dublin to Slewmargy's peak,
Flourishing pastures, valour, health,
Long-living worthies, commerce, wealth.

I found, besides, from Ara to Glea,
In the broad rich country of Ossorie,
Sweet fruits, good laws for all and each,
Great chess-players, men of truthful speech.

I found in Meath's fair principality,
Virtue, vigour, and hospitality,
Candour, joyfulness, bravery, purity,
Ireland's bulwark and security.

I found strict morals in age and youth,
I found historians recording truth;
The things I sing of in verse unsmooth,
I found them all,—I have written sooth.

Translated from the Irish by James Mangan

Cruachan] Croghan, the royal palace of Connaught   Connall] Tyrconnell, the present
Donegal   Brehon] law judge   Erenachs] rulers or archdeacons   Slewmargy] a
mountain in Co. Leix

JOHN DERRICKE
fl. 1578

164   from *The Image of Irelande*

No table there is spread,
  they have no courtlike guise,
The earth sometimes stands them in stead
  whereon their victual lies.
Their cushions are of straw,
  of rushes or of hay,
Made banksetwise with withies,
  their tails to underlay.
Their platters are of wood
  by cunning turners made,
But not of pewter (credit me)
  as is our English trade.
Now ere the lord sits down
  with concubine or wife
(Whereof he often makes exchange
  in compass of his life),[1]
Before he takes his room
  a friar doth begin
To bless the rebel and his wife,
  the place and thieves therein;
Which when he blessèd hath
  in highest place of all,
The chieftain then this trait'rous knave
  like honest man doth stall.
And next his surgeon he
  doth set at friar's side,
And then himself his room enjoy'th
  adornèd with his bride.
In sin the hellish rout
  like lucky fellows met
Do sit them down on straw or ground
  their victuals for to get.
Long stabbers pluck they forth
  instead of handsome knives:
And with the same they slash me out,
  good God, what pretty shives!

---

[1] 'Irishe Karne [foot-soldiers] every yeare once or twise peradventure make exchaunge of their wives, as thei like them so will thei keepe them, for thei will not be bounde to them' (J.D.).

---

shives] slices

Not shives of bread I mean,
    for that were very rare,
But gobs of flesh not boiled enough,
    which is their common fare.
Their chiefest drink is milk;
    for want of milk, the broth:
They take which thing the surgeon swears
    is physic by his troth.
And if that broth be scant,
    yet water is at hand:
for every river yields enough
    within that goodly land.
Again if Fortune fawn'th,
    or on them chance to smile
She fills them then with usquebaugh,
    and wine another while.
O that is cheer in bowls,
    it beautifieth the feast:
And makes them look with drunken nolls,
    from most unto the least.
Now when their guts be full,
    then comes the pastime in:
The bard and harper melody
    unto them do begin.
This bard he doth report
    the noble conquests done,
And eke in rhymes shows forth at large
    their glory thereby won.
Thus he at random runn'th,
    he pricks the rebels on,
And shows by such external deeds
    their honour lies upon;
And more to stir them up
    to prosecute their ill,
What great renown their fathers got
    they show by rhyming skill.
And they most gladsome are,
    to hear of parents' name:
As how by spoiling honest men
    they won such endless fame.
Wherefore like graceless grafts
    sprung from a wicked tree,
They grow through daily exercise
    to all iniquity.

usquebaugh] aqua vitae, whiskey   nolls] heads

WILLIAM KING
1663–1712

165   from *Mully of Mountown*

Mountown! thou sweet retreat from Dublin cares,
Be famous for thy apples and thy pears;
For turnips, carrots, lettuce, beans, and pease;
For Peggy's butter, and for Peggy's cheese.
May clouds of pigeons round about thee fly!
But condescend sometimes to make a pie.
May fat geese gaggle with melodious voice,
And ne'er want gooseberries or apple-sauce!
Ducks in thy ponds, and chicken in thy pens,
And be thy turkeys numerous as thy hens!
May thy black pigs lie warm in little sty,
And have no thought to grieve them till they die!
Mountown! the Muses' most delicious theme;
Oh! may thy codlins ever swim in cream!
Thy rasp- and straw-berries in Bourdeaux drown,
To add a redder tincture to their own!
Thy white-wine, sugar, milk, together club,
To make that gentle viand syllabub.
Thy tarts to tarts, cheese-cakes to cheese-cakes join,
To spoil the relish of the flowing wine.
But to the fading palate bring relief,
By thy Westphalian ham, or Belgic beef;
And, to complete thy blessings, in a word,
May still thy soil be generous as its lord!

MARY ALCOCK
?1742–1798

166   *Written in Ireland*

How blest would be Iërne's isle,
Were bigotry and all its guile
     Chased as a cloud away;
Then would Religion rear her head,
And sweet Contentment round her spread,
     Like a new dawn of day.

165 Mountown] country house and estate south of Dublin   its lord] Judge Upton

Come then, oh come, thou Truth divine!
With double radiance deign to shine,
    Thy heavenly light expand;
'Tis thine to chase these clouds of night,
Which darken and confound the sight
    In this divided land.

Attendant on thy prosp'rous train
I see sweet Peace with honest gain
    Spread wide her liberal hand,
While Discord, masked in deep disguise,
Abashed from forth her presence flies,
    Struck by her magic wand.

Around, where now in ruins lie
Thy sacred altars, I espy
    Fair Order rear each pile,
Whilst o'er thy wilds forlorn and waste,
Lo, Industry with nimble haste
    Makes hill and valley smile.

No more thy sons in fell despite,
A murderous band *arrayed in white*,[1]
    Shall deal destruction round;
Each man beneath his vine shall rest,
No more by bigotry oppressed,
    But Truth by Peace be crowned.

Then shall Iërne tune her lyre,
And with united voice conspire
    To hail her happy state;
All hail, Iërne, Nature's pride,
No more shall wars thy land divide,
    Wert thou as good as great.

---

[1] 'Whiteboys', members of agrarian secret societies formed in Connaught and Munster in about 1760 as a result of evictions.

WILLIAM MAKEPEACE THACKERAY
1811–1863

167   *Peg of Limavaddy*

Riding from Coleraine
  (Famed for lovely Kitty),
Came a Cockney bound
  Unto Derry city;
Weary was his soul,
  Shivering and sad he
Bumped along the road
  Leads to Limavaddy.

*

Mountains stretched around,
  Gloomy was their tinting,
And the horse's hoofs
  Made a dismal clinting;
Wind upon the heath
  Howling was and piping,
On the heath and bog,
  Black with many a snipe in:
'Mid the bogs of black,
  Silver pools were flashing,
Crows upon their sides
  Picking were and splashing.
Cockney on the car
  Closer folds his plaidy,
Grumbling at the road
  Leads to Limavaddy.

Through the crashing woods
  Autumn brawled and blustered,
Tossing round about
  Leaves the hue of mustard;
Yonder lay Lough Foyle,
  Which a storm was whipping,
Covering with mist
  Lake, and shores, and shipping.
Up and down the hill
  (Nothing could be bolder),
Horse went with a raw,
  Bleeding on his shoulder.

'Where are horses changed?'
    Said I to the laddy
Driving on the box:
    'Sir, at Limavaddy.'

*

Limavaddy inn's
    But a humble baithouse,
Where you may procure
    Whiskey and potatoes;
Landlord at the door
    Gives a smiling welcome
To the shivering wights
    Who to his hotel come.
Landlady within
    Sits and knits a stocking,
With a wary foot
    Baby's cradle rocking.

To the chimney nook,
    Having found admittance,
There I watch a pup
    Playing with two kittens;
(Playing round the fire,
    Which of blazing turf is,
Roaring to the pot
    Which bubbles with the murphies);
And the cradled babe
    Fond the mother nursed it,
Singing it a song
    As she twists the worsted!

Up and down the stair
    Two more young ones patter
(Twins were never seen
    Dirtier nor fatter);
Both have mottled legs,
    Both have snubby noses,
Both have—Here the Host
    Kindly interposes:
'Sure you must be froze
    With the sleet and hail, sir,
So will you have some punch,
    Or will you have some ale, sir?'

Presently a maid
   Enters with the liquor,
(Half a pint of ale
   Frothing in a beaker).
Gods! I didn't know
   What my beating heart meant,
Hebe's self I thought
   Entered the apartment.
As she came she smiled,
   And the smile bewitching,
On my word and honour,
   Lighted all the kitchen!

With a curtsey neat
   Greeting the new comer,
Lovely, smiling Peg
   Offers me the rummer;
But my trembling hand
   Up the beaker tilted,
And the glass of ale
   Every drop I spilt it:
Spilt it every drop
   (Dames, who read my volumes,
Pardon such a word),
   On my whatd'ycall 'ems!

Witnessing the sight
   Of that dire disaster,
Out began to laugh
   Missis, maid, and master;
Such a merry peal,
   'Specially Miss Peg's was,
(As the glass of ale
   Trickling down my legs was),
That the joyful sound
   Of that ringing laughter
Echoed in my ears
   Many a long day after.

Such a silver peal!
   In the meadows listening,
You who've heard the bells
   Ringing to a christening;
You who ever heard
   Caradori pretty,

Hebe] goddess of youth, and cup-bearer to the gods

Smiling like an angel
   Singing 'Giovinetti',
Fancy Peggy's laugh,
   Sweet, and clear, and cheerful,
At my pantaloons
   With half a pint of beer full!

When the laugh was done,
   Peg, the pretty hussy,
Moved about the room
   Wonderfully busy;
Now she looks to see
   If the kettle keeps hot,
Now she rubs the spoons,
   Now she cleans the teapot;
Now she sets the cups
   Trimly and secure,
Now she scours a pot
   And so it was I drew her.

Thus it was I drew her
   Scouring of a kettle,
(Faith! her blushing cheeks
   Reddened on the metal!)
Ah! but 'tis in vain
   That I try to sketch it;
The pot perhaps is like,
   But Peggy's face is wretched.
No: the best of lead,
   And of Indian-rubber,
Never could depict
   That sweet kettle-scrubber!

See her as she moves!
   Scarce the ground she touches,
Airy as a fay,
   Graceful as a duchess;
Bare her rounded arm,
   Bare her little leg is,
Vestris never showed
   Ankles like to Peggy's;
Braided is her hair.
   Soft her look and modest,
Slim her little waist
   Comfortably bodiced.

Vestris] Vestris Gaetano (1729–1808), the finest male ballet dancer of his time

This I do declare,
  Happy is the laddy
Who the heart can share
  Of Peg of Limavaddy;
Married if she were,
  Blest would be the daddy
Of the children fair
  Of Peg of Limavaddy;
Beauty is not rare
  In the land of Paddy,
Fair beyond compare
  Is Peg of Limavaddy.

Citizen or squire,
  Tory, Whig, or Radi-
cal would all desire
  Peg of Limavaddy.
Had I Homer's fire,
  Or that of Sergeant Taddy,
Meetly I'd admire
  Peg of Limavaddy.
And till I expire,
  Or till I grow mad, I
Will sing unto my lyre
  Peg of Limavaddy!

GEOFFREY GRIGSON
1905–1985

168   *Glen Lough*
                     (Co. Donegal)

'We are the dead,' we shouted up in fun,
Standing between the brown lake and the falling sun—
We are the dead; then, frightened at the sound
As the three times echo in the mountains rolled it round
And round, the Dead, the Dead, the Dead—
And the wide sunset turned the Atlantic red
And the light below us yellowed from the farm,
With hair on end we stumbled through the fern
Down to the red-quilted bed,
Low stools, and richly carboned roof,
And powdery-glowing, scented fire of turf,

That never has been out, the farmer said,
A hundred years;
And company, and warmth, replaced our pointless fears,
And Dan Ward's awkward, Irish-speaking, silent wife,
In the close warmth, pale light, and sudden life,
Was setting spuds in a bowl, and trout we'd taken in the lake,
And milk, and eggs, and a hot orange cake
Of maize, and the lifting ears
Of the lazing dog
Accepted us. Two signs of God,
A niche of holy water with a tiny light,
A pale cross of rushes up in the thatch's night,
Told us once more the country we were in;
And sitting in the past, we waited for the farmer to begin
His tales of Maoris, seals, and poteen-making in the fog,
And murdered men:
He warmed his brown feet in the silent glow, and then,
Free and happy, under the black thatch, or in the next day's
Gilded air, how little thought we of the curious ways
And fears our world was turning to; out in the glen
Corn-marigold and loose-strife mixed into a flame,
The mountains that had cried the dead were not the same,
But pink and blue above the blue unrippled lake:
We lay on the warm and gentle turf, watching the easy gannets make
Splashes of white in the deep sea, then,
In the summer morning of that day,
Upon the bar of skull-like stones we sat and sang,
Until the immense cliffs rang.
And curious seals pushed out their whiskered heads and came
Closer and closer to us, neither wild nor tame,
To see who made those ringing noises in that summer bay.

SIR JOHN BETJEMAN
1906–1984

169   *The Small Towns of Ireland*

Public houses in Irish country towns are very often general merchants as well. You
drink at a counter with bacon on it. Brooms and plastic dustpans hang from the
ceiling. Loaves of new bread are stacked on top of fuse wire and, over all, there is a
deep, delicious silence that can be found only in Ireland, in the midlands of Ireland in
particular—the least touristed and profoundest part of that whole sad, beautiful
country. Much that is native and traditional goes on, including the printing of ballads
in metres derived from the Celts via Tom Moore. These ballads are called hedge

poetry and their authors are the last descendants of the Gaelic bards. It was in just such a general shop as I have described that I might have found, pinned up among the notices for a local Feis, Gaelic football matches and Government proclamations, the following ballad, printed on emerald paper in a border of shamrocks.

The small towns of Ireland by bards are neglected,
    They stand there, all lonesome, on hilltop and plain.
The Protestant glebe house by beech trees protected
    Sits close to the gates of his Lordship's demesne.

But where is his Lordship, who once in a phaeton
    Drove out twixt his lodges and into the town?
Of his tragic misfortunes I will not dilate on;
    His mansion's a ruin, his woods are cut down.

His impoverished descendant is dwelling in Ealing,
    His daughters must type for their bread and their board,
O'er the graves of his forebears the nettle is stealing
    And few will remember the sad Irish Lord.

Yet still stands the Mall where his agent resided,
    The doctor, attorney and such class of men.
The elegant fanlights and windows provided
    A Dublin-like look for the town's Upper Ten.

'Twas bravely they stood by the Protestant steeple
    As over the town rose their roof-trees afar.
Let us slowly descend to the part where the people
    Do mingle their ass-carts by Finnegan's bar.

I hear it once more, the soft sound of those voices,
    When fair day is filling with farmers the Square,
And the heart in my bosom delights and rejoices
    To think of the dealing and drinking done there.

I see thy grey granite, O grim House of Sessions!
    I think of the judges who sat there in state
And my mind travels back to our monster processions
    To honour the heroes of brave Ninety-Eight.

The barracks are burned where the Redcoats oppressed us,
    The gaol is broke open, our people are free.
Though Cromwell once cursed us, Saint Patrick has blessed us—
    The merciless English have fled o'er the sea.

Look out where yon cabins grow smaller to smallest,
   Straw-thatched and one-storey and soon to come down,
To the prominent steeple, the newest and tallest
   Of Saint Malachy's Catholic Church in our town:

The fine architecture, the wealth of mosaic,
   The various marbles on altars within—
To attempt a description were merely prosaic,
   So, asking your pardon, I will not begin.

O my small town of Ireland, the raindrops caress you,
   The sun sparkles bright on your field and your Square
As here on your bridge I salute you and bless you,
   Your murmuring waters and turf-scented air.

LOUIS MacNEICE
1907–1963

170   from *The Closing Album*
Dublin

Grey brick upon brick,
Declamatory bronze
On sombre pedestals—
O'Connell, Grattan, Moore—
And the brewery tugs and the swans
On the balustraded stream
And the bare bones of a fanlight
Over a hungry door
And the air soft on the cheek
And porter running from the taps
With a head of yellow cream
And Nelson on his pillar
Watching his world collapse.

This was never my town,
I was not born nor bred
Nor schooled here and she will not
Have me alive or dead
But yet she holds my mind
With her seedy elegance,
With her gentle veils of rain

And all her ghosts that walk
And all that hide behind
Her Georgian façades—
The catcalls and the pain,
The glamour of her squalor,
The bravado of her talk.

The lights jig in the river
With a concertina movement
And the sun comes up in the morning
Like barley-sugar on the water
And the mist on the Wicklow hills
Is close, as close
As the peasantry were to the landlord,
As the Irish to the Anglo-Irish,
As the killer is close one moment
To the man he kills,
Or as the moment itself
Is close to the next moment.

She is not an Irish town
And she is not English,
Historic with guns and vermin
And the cold renown
Of a fragment of Church latin,
Of an oratorical phrase.
But oh the days are soft,
Soft enough to forget
The lesson better learnt,
The bullet on the wet
Streets, the crooked deal,
The steel behind the laugh,
The Four Courts burnt.

Fort of the Dane,
Garrison of the Saxon,
Augustan capital
Of a Gaelic nation,
Appropriating all
The alien brought,
You give me time for thought
And by a juggler's trick
You poise the toppling hour—
O greyness run to flower,
Grey stone, grey water,
And brick upon grey brick.

THE LEVANT

FYNES MORYSON
1566–1630

171 To thee, dear Henry Morison,
Thy brother Phines, here left alone,
Hath left this fading memory.
For monuments and all must die.

WILLIAM LITHGOW
1582–?1645

172   [Of Constantinople]

A painted whore, the mask of deadly sin,
Sweet fair without, and stinking foul within.

173 Still this, still that I would! all I surmise
is cruelly stopped: at last my scopes devise
To make a boat, to bear me down alone
With drudges two, to ground-changed Babylon:
That could not be, the charges were too great,[1]
And eke the stream, did naught but dangers threat:
My conduct still deceived me, made it square
Another caravan, O! would come there
From Aleppe, or Damascus: till in end
Most of my moneys did his knavery spend:
Thus was I tossed long five weeks, and four days
With struggling doubts: O strange were these delays!
At last a Chelfane came, a Christian kind
Who by my grief soon understood my mind;
And told me flat, the Janizary's drift
Was to extort me with a ling'ring shift.

---

[1] Travellers paid tolls to local tribes as well as to the Turkish government.

---

173 Chelfane] Armenian

'Come, come', said he, 'the Sanzack here is just,
Let us complain, for now complain you must':
He with me went, and for a trencherman served
And told the Ruler, how my conduct swerved:
He's called, and soon convinced, and with command
Forced to transport me back to Syria's land:
I'm there arrived, and eftsoons made me bound
For the Venetian Consul: there to sound
My great abuses, by this villain done.
Which soon were heard, and eke repaired as soon:
The Bassaw was upright, and for time's sake
He did me more, than conscience willed me take.
My plaint preferred, he was in prison laid
And all my gold, to give me back was made.
Thus leaving him, I with the consul bode,
Full forty days, or I went thence abroad.

LADY MARY WORTLEY MONTAGU
1689–1762

174 *Verses Written in the Chiosk at Pera, Overlooking Constantinople*

Give me, great God! said I, a little farm,
In summer shady, and in winter warm;
Where a clear spring gives birth to murm'ring brooks,
By nature gliding down the mossy rocks.
Not artfully by leaden pipes conveyed,
Or greatly falling in a forced cascade,
Pure and unsullied winding through the shade.
All bounteous Heaven has added to my prayer,
A softer climate and a purer air.
Our frozen isle now chilling winter binds,
Deformed by rains, and rough with blasting winds;
The withered woods grow white with hoary frost,
By driving storms their verdant beauty lost;
The trembling birds their leafless covert shun,
And seek in distant climes a warmer sun:
The water-nymphs their silent urns deplore,
Ev'n Thames, benumbed, 's a river now no more:
The barren meads no longer yield delight,
By glist'ning snows made painful to the sight.

173 Sanzack] administrative district, part of an eyalet or vilayet   Bassaw] an earlier
form of *pasha*, Turkish officer of high rank

Here summer reigns with one eternal smile,
Succeeding harvests bless the happy soil;
Fair fertile fields, to whom indulgent Heaven
Has ev'ry charm of ev'ry season given.
No killing cold deforms the beauteous year,
The springing flowers no coming winter fear.
But as the parent rose decays and dies,
The infant buds with brighter colour rise,
And with fresh sweets the mother's scent supplies.
  Near them the violet grows with odours blessed,
And blooms in more than Tyrian purple dressed;
The rich jonquils their golden beams display,
And shine in glory's emulating day;
The peaceful groves their verdant leaves retain,
The streams still murmur undefiled with rain,
And tow'ring greens adorn the fruitful plain.
The warbling kind interrupted sing,
Warmed with enjoyments of perpetual spring.
  Here, at my window, I at once survey
The crowded city and resounding sea;
In distant views the Asian mountains rise,
And lose their snowy summits in the skies;
Above these mountains proud Olympus tow'rs,
The parliamental seat of heavenly pow'rs.
New to the sight my ravished eyes admire
Each gilded crescent and each antique spire,
The marble mosques, beneath whose ample domes
Fierce warlike sultans sleep in peaceful tombs;
Those lofty structures, once the Christian's boast,
Their names, their beauty, and their honours lost;
Those altars bright with gold and sculpture graced,
By barb'rous zeal of savage foes defaced;
Soph'a alone, her ancient name retains,
Though th' unbeliever now her shrine profanes;
Where holy saints have died in sacred cells,
Where monarchs prayed, the frantic dervise dwells.
How art thou fall'n, imperial city, low!
Where are thy hopes of Roman glory now?
Where are thy palaces by prelates raised?
Where Grecian artists all their skill displayed,
Before the happy sciences decayed;
So vast, that youthful kings might here reside,
So splendid, to content a patriarch's pride;
Convents where emperors professed of old,
The laboured pillars that their triumphs told;

Soph'a] Santa Sophia, the great metropolitan cathedral of the Greek Orthodox Church, has
been used as a mosque since the Turks captured Constantinople in 1453

Vain monuments of them that once were great,
Sunk undistinguished by one common fate;
One little spot the tenure small contains,
Of Greek nobility the poor remains;
Where other Helens, with like powerful charms,
Had once engaged the warring world in arms;
Those names which royal ancestors can boast,
In mean mechanic arts obscurely lost;
Those eyes a second Homer might inspire,
Fixed at the loom, destroy their useless fire:
Grieved at a view, which struck upon my mind
The short-lived vanity of humankind.

   In gaudy objects I indulge my sight,
And turn where Eastern pomp gives gay delight;
See the vast train in various habits dressed,
By the bright scimitar and sable vest
The proud vizier distinguished o'er the rest!
Six slaves in gay attire his bridle hold,
His bridle rich with gems, and stirrups gold:
His snowy steed adorned with costly pride,
Whole troops of soldiers mounted by his side,
These top the plumy crest Arabian courtiers guide.
With artful duty all decline their eyes,
No bellowing shouts of noisy crowds arise;
Silence, in solemn state, the march attends,
Till at the dread divan the slow procession ends.

   Yet not these prospects all profusely gay,
The gilded navy that adorns the sea,
The rising city in confusion fair,
Magnificently formed, irregular,
Where woods and palaces at once surprise,
Gardens on gardens, domes on domes arise,
And endless beauties tire the wand'ring eyes,
So soothe my wishes, or so charm my mind,
As this retreat secure from humankind.
No knave's successful craft does spleen excite,
No coxcomb's tawdry splendour shocks my sight,
No mob-alarm awakes my female fear,
No praise my mind, nor envy hurts my ear,
Ev'n fame itself can hardly reach me here;
Impertinence, with all her tattling train,
Fair-sounding flattery's delicious bane;
Censorious folly, noisy party rage,
The thousand tongues with which she must engage
Who dares have virtue in a vicious age.

THOMAS LISLE
1709–1767

175 *Letter from Smyrna to his Sisters at Crux-Easton,*
1733

The hero who to Smyrna bay
From Easton, Hants, pursued his way,
Who traversed seas, and hills and vales,
To fright his sisters with his tales,
Sing heavenly Muse; for what befell
Thou saw'st, and only thou canst tell.
Say first (but one thing I premise,
I'll not be chid for telling lies;
Besides, my grannum used to say
I always had a knack that way,
So, if the love of truth be in ye,
Read Strabo, Diodorus, Pliny—
But like some authors I could name,
Wrapped in myself I lose my theme.)
Say first, those very rocks we spied,
But left 'em on the starboard side,
Where Juno urged the Trojan's fate.
Shield us, ye Gods, from female hate!
Then how precarious was the doom
Of Caesar's line, and mighty Rome,
Snatched from the very jaws of ruin,
And saved poor Die, for thy undoing,
What saw we on Sicilian ground?
(A soil in ancient verse renowned)
The selfsame spot, or Virgil lied,
On which the good Anchises died;
The fields where Ceres' daughter sported,
And where the pretty Cyclops courted.
The nymph hard-hearted as the rocks,
Refused the monster, scorned his flocks,
And took a shepherd in his stead,
With naught but love and worth to plead:
An instance of a generous mind
That does much honour to your kind,
But in an age of fables grew,
So possibly it may'nt be true.

Die] Dido

While on the summit Etna glows,
His shivering sides are chilled with snows.
Beneath, the painted landskip charms;
Here infant spring in winter's arms
Wantons secure; in youthful pride
Stands summer laughing by her side;
Ev'n autumn's yellow robes appear,
And one gay scene discloses all the year.
    Hence to rude Cerigo we came,
Known once by Cytherea's name;
When Ocean first the goddess bore,
She rose on this distinguished shore.
Here first the happy Paris stopped,
When Helen from her lord eloped.
With pleased reflection I surveyed
Each secret grot, each conscious shade;
Envied his choice, approved his flame,
And fondly wished my lot the same.
O were the cause revived again!
For charming Queensbury lived not then,
The radiant fruit, had she been there,
Would scarce have fallen to Venus' share;
Saturnia's self had waived her claim,
And modest Pallas blushed for shame;
All had been right: the Phrygian swain
Had sighed for her, but sighed in vain;
The fair Oenone joyed to find,
The pains she felt repaid in kind;
No rape revenged, no room for strife,
Atrides might have kept his wife,
Old Troy in peace and plenty smiled—
But the best poem had been spoiled.
    How did my heart with joy run o'er,
When to the famed Cecropian shore,
Wafted by gentle breezes, we
Came gliding through the smooth still sea!
While backward roved my busy thought
On deeds in distant ages wrought;
On tyrants gloriously withstood;
On seas distained with Persian blood;
On trophies raised o'er hills of slain
In Marathon's unrivalled plain.
Then, as around I cast my eye,
And viewed the pleasing prospect nigh,

the best poem] the *Iliad*

The land for arms and arts renowned,
Where wit was honoured, poets crowned;
Whose manners and whose rules refined
Our souls, and civilized mankind;
Or (yet a loftier pitch to raise
Our wonder, and complete its praise)
The land that Plato's master bore—
How did my heart with joy run o'er!
    Now coasting on the eastern side,
We peeped where Peneus rolls his tide:
Where Arethusa came t'appease
The shepherd that had lost his bees,
And led him to Cyrene's grot;
'Tis a long tale, and matters not.
Dryden will tell you all that passed;
See Virgil's Georgics, book the last.
I speak on't, but to let you know
This grot still stands in statu quo;
Of which if any doubts remain,
I've proof, as follows, clear and plain.
Here, sisters, we such honours met!
Such honour I shall ne'er forget.
The Goddess (no uncommon case)
Proud, I suppose, to shew her place,
Or piqued perhaps at your renown,
Sent Boreas to invite us down;
And he so pressed it, that we used
Some pains to get ourselves excused.
My brother shipmates, all in haste
Declared, that shells were not their taste;
And I had somewhere seen, you know,
A finer grot than she could show.
    Hence let the Muse to Delos roam,
Or Nio, famed for Homer's tomb;
To Naxos, known in ancient time
For Bacchus' love, for Theseus' crime.
Can she the Lesbian vine forget
Whence Horace reinforced his wit?
Where the famed harp Arion strung
Nor played more sweet than Sappho sung?
Could the old bards revive again,
How would they mourn th' inverted scene!
Scarce with the barren waste acquainted,
They once so beautifully painted.

Plato's master] Socrates   somewhere seen] at Crux-Easton

And here, 'twixt friends, I needs must say,
But let it go no farther, pray,
These sung-up, cried-up countries are
Displeasing, rugged, black and bare;
And all I've yet beheld or known
Serve only to endear my own.
  The matters I shall next disclose,
'Tis likely may be wrapped in prose;
But verse methought would suit these better,
Besides, it lengthens out my letter.
Read then, dear girls, with kind regard,
What comes so far, what comes so hard;
And to our mother too make known,
How travelling has improved her son.
  Let not malicious critics join
Pope's homespun rhymes in rank with mine,
Formed on that very spot of earth,
Where Homer's self received his birth;
Add, as I said, t'enhance their worth,
The pains they cost in bringing forth;
While his, as all mankind agrees,
Though wrote with care, are wrote with ease.

WILLIAM LISLE BOWLES
1762–1850

176   *An Egyptian Tomb*

Pomp of Egypt's elder day,
Shade of the mighty passed away,
Whose giant works still frown sublime
Mid the twilight shades of time;
Fanes, of sculpture vast and rude,
That strew the sandy solitude,
Lo! before our startled eyes,
As at a wizard's wand, ye rise,
Glimmering larger through the gloom!
While on the secrets of the tomb,
Rapt in other times, we gaze,
The Mother Queen of ancient days,
Her mystic symbol in her hand,
Great Isis, seems herself to stand.

From mazy vaults, high-arched and dim,
Hark! heard ye not Osiris' hymn?
And saw ye not in order dread
The long procession of the dead?
Forms that the night of years concealed,
As by a flash, are here revealed;
Chiefs who sang the victor song;
Sceptred kings,—a shadowy throng,—
From slumber of three thousand years
Each, as in light and life, appears,
Stern as of yore! Yes, vision vast,
Three thousand years have silent passed,
Sums of empire risen and set,
Whose story Time can ne'er forget,
Time, in the morning of her pride
Immense, along the Nile's green side,
The City of the Sun appeared,
And her gigantic image reared.

As Memnon, like a trembling string
When the sun, with rising ray,
Streaked the lonely desert gray,
Sent forth its magic murmuring,
That just was heard,—then died away;
So passed, O Thebes! thy morning pride!
Thy glory was the sound that died!
Dark city of the desolate,
Once thou wert rich, and proud, and great!
This busy-peopled isle was then
A waste, or roamed by savage men
Whose gay descendants now appear
To mark thy wreck of glory here.

Phantom of that city old,
Whose mystic spoils I now behold,
A kingdom's sepulchre, O, say,
Shall Albion's own illustrious day
Thus darkly close! Her power, her fame,
Thus pass away, a shade, a name!
The Mausoleum murmured as I spoke;
A spectre seemed to rise, like towering smoke;
It answered not, but pointed as it fled
To the black carcass of the sightless dead.
Once more I heard the sounds of earthly strife,
And the streets ringing to the stir of life.

City of the Sun] Thebes　　Memnon] see footnote to no. 180

RICHARD HENGIST HORNE
1802–1884

177   *Pelters of Pyramids*

Nought loves another as itself,
Nor venerates another so;
Nor is it possible to thought
A greater than itself to know.

(Blake)

A shoal of idlers, from a merchant craft
Anchored off Alexandria, went ashore,
And mounting asses in their headlong glee,
Round Pompey's Pillar rode with hoots and taunts,—
As men oft say 'What are thou more than we?'
Next in a boat they floated up the Nile,
Singing and drinking, swearing senseless oaths,
Shouting, and laughing most derisively
At all majestic scenes. A bank they reached,
And clambering up, played gambols among tombs;
And in portentous ruins (through whose depths—
The mighty twilight of departed Gods—
Both sun and moon glanced furtive, as in awe)
They hid, and whooped, and spat on sacred things.

At length, beneath the blazing sun they lounged
Near a great Pyramid. Awhile they stood
With stupid stare, until resentment grew,
In the recoil of meanness from the vast;
And gathering stones, they with coarse oaths and jibes,
(As they would say, 'What art thou more than we?')
Pelted the Pyramid! But soon these men,
Hot and exhausted, sat them down to drink—
Wrangled, smoked, spat, and laughed, and drowsily
Cursed the bald Pyramid, and fell asleep.

Night came:—a little sand went drifting by—
And morn again was in the soft blue heavens.
The broad slopes of the shining Pyramid
Looked down in their austere simplicity
Upon the glistening silence of the sands
Whereon no trace of mortal dust was seen.

THOMAS LOVELL BEDDOES
1803–1849

178   *A Crocodile*

Hard by the lilied Nile I saw
A duskish river dragon stretched along.
The brown habergeon of his limbs enamelled
With sanguine alamandines and rainy pearl:
And on his back there lay a young one sleeping,
No bigger than a mouse; with eyes like beads,
And a small fragment of its speckled egg
Remaining on its harmless, pulpy snout;
A thing to laugh at, as it gaped to catch
The baulking merry flies. In the iron jaws
Of the great devil-beast, like a pale soul
Fluttering in rocky hell, lightsomely flew
A snowy trochilus, with roseate beak
Tearing the hairy leeches from his throat.

RICHARD MONCKTON MILNES
1809–1885

179   from *The Burden of Egypt*

Tranquil above the rapids, rocks, and shoals,
The Tivoli of Egypt, Philae lies;
No more the frontier-fortress that controls
The rush of Ethiopian enemies,—
No more the Isle of Temples to surprise,
With hierophantic courts and porticos,
The simple stranger, but a scene where vies
Dead Art with living Nature, to compose
For that my pilgrimage a fit and happy close.

There I could taste without distress of thought
The placid splendours of a Nubian night,
The sky with beautiful devices fraught
Of suns and moons and spaces of white light:

While on huge gateways rose the forms of might,
Awful as when the people's heart they swayed,
And the grotesque grew solemn to my sight;
And earnest faces thronged the colonnade,
As if they wailed a faith forgotten or betrayed.

There too, in calmer mood, I sent aflight
My mind through realms of marvel stretching far,
O'er Abyssinian Alps of fabled height,
O'er deserts where no paths or guidance are,
Save when, by pilotage of some bright star,
As on the ocean, wends the caravan;[1]
And then I almost mourned the mythic bar
That in old times along that frontier ran,
When gods came down to feast with Ethiopian man.

For I remembered races numberless,
Whom still those latitudes in mystery fold,
And asked, what does the Past, my monitress,
For them within her genial bosom hold?
Where is for them the tale of history told?
How is their world advancing on its way?
How are they wiser, better, or more bold,
That they were not created yesterday?
Why are we life-taught men, why poor ephemerals they?

J. W. BURGON
1813–1888

180   *Written on the Plain of Thebes*[2]

Our boats were moored where Luxor throws
    A seven-fold image in the stream:
In the pale east the morning rose,
    And guided by that slanting beam

---

[1] 'Canopus, the ornament of the Southern hemisphere, is called by the Arabs, "the caravan-seducer"—a large caravan having been lost in the desert by the driver taking it for Venus' (R.M.M.).
[2] 'The writer and a friend one morning visited the Vocal Memnon at sunrise, in order to listen for the marvellous sounds which that statue was anciently said to emit when it encounters the beams of the rising sun' (J.W.B.).

We made our way across the plain
 Where Thebes once owned a hundred gates,
With eager eye and slackened rein,
 Like men who know that Memnon waits.

We reached the statue with the sun.
 We listened for the wished-for sound.
In vain, in vain! 'twas heard by none.
 Deep silence brooded all around.
When lo, a lark with wings outspread
 Soared O how joyfully along,
And poised, it seemed, above my head
 Dissolved herself in sweetest song.

O God (thought I), *Thy* works abide
 While Man's inventions haste away:
Or if these stem awhile the tide,
 Their nobler uses,—where are they?
Thy works not so! These mock at Time.
 The music of the heavenly lute
Will still flow on in strain sublime
 When stones, and even men, are mute.

SIR EDWIN ARNOLD
1832–1904

181   *To a Pair of Egyptian Slippers*

Tiny slippers of gold and green,
 Tied with a mouldering golden cord!
What pretty feet they must have been
 When Caesar Augustus was Egypt's lord!
Somebody graceful and fair you were!
 Not many girls could dance in these!
When did your shoemaker make you, dear,
 Such a nice pair of Egyptian 'threes'?

Where were you measured? In Saïs, or On,
 Memphis, or Thebes, or Pelusium?
Fitting them neatly your brown toes upon,
 Lacing them deftly with finger and thumb,

I seem to see you!—so long ago,
   Twenty-one centuries, less or more!
And here are your sandals: yet none of us know
   What name, or fortune, or face you bore.

Your lips would have laughed, with a rosy scorn,
   If the merchant, or slave-girl, had mockingly said,
'The feet will pass, but the shoes they have worn
   Two thousand years onward Time's road shall tread,
And still be footgear as good as new!'
   To think that calf-skin, gilded and stitched,
Should Rome and the Pharaohs outlive—and you
   Be gone, like a dream, from the world you bewitched!

Not that we mourn you! 'Twere too absurd!
   You have been such a long while away!
Your dry spiced dust would not value one word
   Of the soft regrets that my verse could say.
Sorrow and Pleasure, and Love and Hate,
   If you ever felt them, have vaporized hence
To this odour—so subtle and delicate—
   Of myrrh, and cassia, and frankincense.

Of course they embalmed you! Yet not so sweet
   Were aloes and nard, as the youthful glow
Which Amenti stole when the small dark feet
   Wearied of treading our world below.
Look! it was flood-time in valley of Nile,
   Or a very wet day in the Delta, dear!
When your slippers tripped lightly their latest mile—
   The mud on the soles renders that fact clear.

You knew Cleopatra, no doubt! You saw
   Antony's galleys from Actium come.
But there! if questions could answers draw
   From lips so many a long age dumb,
I would not teaze you with history,
   Nor vex your heart for the men that were;
The one point to learn that would fascinate me
   Is, where and what are you to-day, my dear!

You died, believing in Horus and Pasht,
   Isis, Osiris, and priestly lore;
And found, of course, such theories smashed
   By actual fact on the heavenly shore.

What next did you do? Did you transmigrate?
　　Have we seen you since, all modern and fresh?
Your charming soul—so I calculate—
　　Mislaid its mummy, and sought new flesh.

Were you she whom I met at dinner last week,
　　With eyes and hair of the Ptolemy black,
Who still of this find in the Fayoum would speak,
　　And to Pharaohs and scarabs still carry us back?
A scent of lotus about her hung,
　　And she had such a far-away wistful air
As of somebody born when the Earth was young;
　　And she wore of gilt slippers a lovely pair.

Perchance you were married? These might have been
　　Part of your *trousseau*—the wedding shoes;
And you laid them aside with the garments green,
　　And painted clay Gods which a bride would use;
And, may be, to-day, by Nile's bright waters
　　Damsels of Egypt in gowns of blue—
Great-great-great—very great—grand-daughters
　　Owe their shapely insteps to you!

But vainly I beat at the bars of the Past,
　· Little green slippers with golden strings!
For all you can tell is that leather will last
　　When loves, and delightings, and beautiful things
Have vanished, forgotten—No! not quite that!
　　I catch some gleam of the grace you wore
When you finished with Life's daily pit-a-pat,
　　And left your shoes at Death's bedroom door.

You were born in the Egypt which did not doubt;
　　You were never sad with our new-fashioned sorrows:
You were sure, when your play-days on Earth ran out,
　　Of play-times to come, as we of our morrows!
Oh, wise little Maid of the Delta! I lay
　　Your shoes in your mummy-chest back again,
And wish that one game we might merrily play
　　At 'Hunt the Slippers'—to see it all plain.

the Fayoum] province of Upper Egypt west of the Nile covered with Pharaonic architecture

WILFRID SCAWEN BLUNT
1840–1922

182　　　　*The Oasis of Sidi Khaled*

How the earth burns! Each pebble underfoot
Is as a living thing with power to wound.
The white sand quivers, and the footfall mute
Of the slow camels strikes but gives no sound,
As though they walked on flame, not solid ground.
'Tis noon, and the beasts' shadows even have fled
Back to their feet, and there is fire around
And fire beneath, and overhead the sun.
Pitiful heaven! What is this we view?
Tall trees, a river, pools, where swallows fly,
Thickets of oleander where doves coo,
Shades, deep as midnight, greenness for tired eyes.
Hark, how the light winds in the palm-tops sigh.
Oh this is rest. Oh this is paradise.

G. K. CHESTERTON
1874–1936

183　　　　*Sonnet*

High on the wall that holds Jerusalem
I saw one stand under the stars like stone.
And when I perish it shall not be known
Whether he lived, some strolling son of Shem,
Or was some great ghost wearing the diadem
Of Solomon or Saladin on a throne:
I only know, the features being unshown,
I did not dare draw near and look on them.

Did ye not guess . . . the diadem might be
Plaited in stranger style by hands of hate . . .
But when I looked, the wall was desolate
And the grey starlight powdered tower and tree
And vast and vague beyond the Golden Gate
Heaved Moab of the mountains like a sea.

DOROTHY WELLESLEY,
DUCHESS OF WELLINGTON
1889—1956

184   *Camels in Persia*

Along the caravan routes go the camels tall:
Forward-flung friezes of night, for they travel at nightfall,
Outward going, onward,
And the sound of their bells thrown forward
Makes a rhythm no man can recall
To his ears in the silences afterward.

But he knows that the camels stride
Hunched up on a night scarce purple for many stars;
He knows that the camels are tied
Together in strings, are padding their way to Fars.

The leading camel is great, has a long underlip,
A rank red beard on his throat, and a suretiship,
A manner of turning his head to look at a stranger
Who grinds in his Ford to Fars;
He sneers as all camels sneer as he passes the dead
Arched white ribs of his kind, and nothing said,
Caring for nothing but excellent leadership.

The camel is sullen and proud, he is not my friend,
Will have none of my fellowship.
Soon he knows he will fail, he will fall by the way
And his caravan pass, and leave him to vultures, but now
He knows he will drink his fill at the journey's end,
And be at peace by the palms in the heat of the day.

He knows he will fall by the way,
And lie as all camels lie when he comes to die,
With the insolent pride of the camel,
Watching his caravan wend toward the evening end
In beautiful dignity onward,
                    The sound of the bells flung forward—
Over the Plain of Passagardae where the black irises
Spring from the shale and slate—

Fars] region situated on the Persian Gulf; the original home of the Persians, who derive their
name from it

Past the tall stone tomb where once King Cyrus lay,
Who carved a maxim for all he would subjugate:
'Traveller, pause! For you will pass this way;
I was Cyrus the Great.'

REX WARNER

1905–

185   *Palm Trees*

These bottle-washer trees that give no shade,
with silly topknot, poles stuck in the ground,
ringed like muddy embalmed caterpillars,
irritating, foolish, absurd trees,
are yet by night invested with curious beauty
when, like strange weeds, fronds flow into the air
as though that were liquid and they submarine
deep sea growths shifted and shaken by purple tides.

So savagely plumed, wafted on the warm wind,
they wave and flap among stars, and the solid earth
seems as they shift to shift, seems downy, swimming
trackless in space, drifting among resistless winds
aimless unenterprising inanely beautiful
across the tremendous oceans of the Milky Way.

LAWRENCE DURRELL

1912–

186   *Levant*

Gum, oats and syrup
The Arabians bore.
Evoking nothing from the sea but more
And more employ to christen them
With whips of salt and glittering spray,
Their wooden homes rocked on the chastening salt.

184 Cyrus the Great] Cyrus II the Great, 590/580–529 BC

Lamps on altars, breath of children;
So coming and going with their talk of bales,
Lading and enterprises marked out
And fell on this rusty harbour
Where tills grew fat with cash
And the quills of Jews invented credit,
And in margins folded up
Bales, gum-arabic, and syrup;
Syrian barley in biffed coracles
Hugging the burking gulf or blown
As cargoes from the viny breath
Of mariners, the English or the Dutch.
In manners taught them nothing much
Beyond the endurance in the vile.
Left in history words like
Portuguese or Greek
Whose bastards can still speak and smile.

After this, lamps
Confused the foreigners;
Boys, women and drugs
Built this ant-hill for grammarians
Who fed upon the fathers fat with cash,
Turned oats and syrup here
To ribbons and wands and rash
Patents for sex and feathers,
Sweets for festivals and deaths.

Nothing changes. The indifferent
Or the merely good died off, but fixed
Here once the human type 'Levant'.
Something fine of tooth and with the soft
Hanging lashes to the eye,
Given once by Spain and kept
In a mad friendship here and sadness
By the promiscuous sea upon this spit of sand.

Something money or promises can buy.

TERENCE TILLER
1916–

187   *Egyptian Dancer*

Slowly, with intention to tempt, she sidles out
      (a smile and a shake of bells)
in silver, tight as a fish's, and a web
of thin-flame veils, and her brown buttery flesh
(but she is a mermaid with twelve metal tails)
      glimpsed or guessed by seconds.

Slowly the insidious unison sucks her in,
      and the rhythm of the drums,
the mournful feline quavering whose pulse
runs through her limbs; shivering like a bride
she lifts her arms into a lyre; there comes
      a sense of nakedness

as the red gauze floats off; and of release.
      She is all silver-finned:
it hangs from wrist and ankle, she is silver-
feather-crowned, tight silver across the breasts;
skirt of bright strips; and where in the fat forced up
      her navel winks like a wound.

The dance begins: she ripples like a curtain;
      her arms are snakes
—she is all serpent, she coils on her own loins
and shakes the bells; her very breasts are alive
and writhing, and around the emphatic sex
      her thighs are gimlets of oil.

All the half-naked body, as if tortured
      or loving with a ghost,
labours; the arms are lifted to set free
atrocious lust or anguish, and the worms
that are fingers crack as croupe or bust
      or belly rolls to the drums.

Wilder: the drift of the sand-spout the wavering
      curve of the legs grow a blaze
and a storm while the obsession of music hammers and wails
to her dim eyes to her shrieking desire of the flesh
that is dumb with an ecstasy of movement and plays
      fiercely the squirming act

and sweat breaks out she is bright as metal while the skirt
         spins like a flower at her hips
into the last unbearable glorious agony
between the lips and suddenly, it is over;
a last groan of the drum, panting she drops
         into the darkness of past love.

KEITH DOUGLAS

1920–1944

188   *Behaviour of Fish in an Egyptian Tea Garden*

As a white stone draws down the fish
she on the seafloor of the afternoon
draws down men's glances and their cruel wish
for love. Her red lip on the spoon

slips-in a morsel of ice-cream. Her hands
white as a shell, are submarine
fronds, sink with spread fingers, lean
along the table, carmined at the ends.

A cotton magnate, an important fish
with great eyepouches and a golden mouth
through the frail reefs of furniture swims out
and idling, suspended, stays to watch.

A crustacean old man clamped to his chair
sits near her and might coldly see
her charms through fissures where the eyes should be;
or else his teeth are parted in a stare.

Captain on leave, a lean dark mackerel,
lies in the offing, turns himself and looks
through currents of sound. The flat-eyed flatfish sucks
on a straw, staring from its repose, laxly.

And gallants in shoals swim up and lag,
circling and passing near the white attraction—
sometimes pausing, opening a conversation—
fish pause so to nibble or tug.

Now the ice-cream is finished, is
paid for. The fish swim off on business
and she sits alone at the table, a white stone
useless except to a collector, a rich man.

D. J. ENRIGHT

1920–

189   *Deir El Bahari: Temple of Hatshepsut*

How did she come here, when it was new and sparkling,
White and immaculate against the huge and spongy cliffs,
The great Queen, how did she come, in the cool of winter,
To review her voyages, perhaps, or admire her politics?
Not like the tourist, with his camera and serious weary step,
Not like the dragoman, with his sideways twist, poised in a revelatory
     date,
Not like the archaeologist, brisk, with a fly-whisk . . .

Grand destination, deserving a green and pleasant air-field,
Or a royal station, garnished with banners and carpets—
How did she arrive, the peaceful Queen, to smile discreetly over her
     portraits—
Her masculine beard, being man, or her marvellous birth, being god?
To study her exotic wonders, the Red Sea fishes, the fat queen of
     Punt?
Not like the tourist, homesick on a hell-bred donkey,
Not like the dragoman, informed yet obsequious,
Not like the archaeologist, in a jeep, with new theories . . .

How did she reach here? Kohl-eyed and henna-stained?
Across her breast the whip and the crozier? The desert
Is old and democratic, rude and unpolished the rocks.
The figures of this landscape? During the season,
Gentlemen in shorts and sun-glasses, ladies with tweeds and twisted
     ankles,
And all the year, the little denizens, with leather feet and tattered
     gallabiehs,
The wide-striding village women, their drab and dusty dress . . .

189 Hatshepsut] Hatshepsut (*fl.* 1500 BC), daughter of Tuthmosis I, ruled Egypt until her
son, Tuthmosis III, came of age. In 1841 her tomb was found on a cliff in the Valley of the Kings;
on her monuments she wears a masculine garb   the fat queen of Punt] a figure Hatshepsut brought back as tribute or souvenir from her great expedition to Punt, the land of aromatics
and incense   gallabiehs] long loose garb worn by Egyptian men

But what of a Queen, and one who built this temple, so clean and deep
    and sure,
Curling inside the clenched and hanging cliff? What magic carpet
Drawn by bright and flying lions? What cloudburst of gold dust?
Between her treasures, incense trees and ivory, panther skins and
    ebony—
What laid her gently upon those sculptured steps?

AFRICA

THOMAS CAMPBELL
1777–1844

190   *Epistle, from Algiers, to Horace Smith*

Dear Horace! be melted to tears,
　For I'm melting with heat as I rime;
Though the name of the place is Algiers
　'Tis no joke to fall in with its clime.

With a shaver from France who came o'er,
　To an African inn I ascend;
I am cast on a barbarous shore,
　Where a barber alone is my friend.

Do you ask me the sights and the news
　Of this wonderful city to sing?
Alas! my hotel has its mews,
　But no muse of the Helicon's spring.

My windows afford me the sight
　Of a people all diverse in hue;
They are black, yellow, olive, and white,
　Whilst I in my sorrow look blue.

Here are groups for the painter to take,
　Whose figures jocosely combine,—
The Arab disguised in his haik,
　And the Frenchman disguised in his wine.

In his breeches of petticoat size
　You may say, as the Mussulman goes,
That his garb is a fair compromise
　'Twixt a kilt and a pair of small-clothes.

The Mooresses, shrouded in white,
　Save two holes for their eyes to give room,
Seem like corpses in sport or in spite
　That have slily whipped out of their tomb.

haik] mantle

The old Jewish dames make me sick:
    If I were the devil—I declare
Such hags should not mount a broom-stick
    In my service to ride through the air.

But hipped and undined as I am,
    My hippogriff's course I must rein—
For the pain of my thirst is no sham,
    Though I'm bawling aloud for Champagne.

Dinner's brought; but their wines have no pith—
    They are flat as the statutes at law;
And for all that they bring me, dear Smith!
    Would a glass of brown stout they could draw!

O'er each French trashy dish as I bend,
    My heart feels a patriot's grief!
And the round tears, O England! descend
    When I think on a round of thy beef.

Yes, my soul sentimentally craves
    British beer.—Hail, Britannia, hail!
To thy flag on the foam of the waves,
    And the foam on thy flagons of ale.

Yet I own, in this hour of my drought,
    A dessert has most welcomely come;
Here are the peaches that melt in the mouth,
    And grapes blue and big as a plum.

There are melons too, luscious and great,
    But the slices I eat shall be few,
For from melons incautiously eat
    Melancholic effects may ensue.

Horrid pun! you'll exclaim; but be calm,
    Though my letter bears date, as you view,
From the land of the date-bearing palm,
    I will palm no more puns upon you.

191   *The Dead Eagle*

Fallen as he is, this king of birds still seems
Like royalty in ruins. Though his eyes
Are shut, that look undazzled on the sun,
He was the sultan of the sky, and earth

Paid tribute to his eyry. It was perched
Higher than human conqueror ever built
His bannered fort. Where Atlas' top looks o'er
Zahara's desert to the equator's line—
From thence the winged despot marked his prey,
Above the encampments of the Bedouins, ere
Their watchfires were extinct, or camels knelt
To take their loads, or horsemen scoured the plain;
And there he dried his feathers in the dawn,
Whilst yet the unwakened world was dark below.

There's such a charm in natural strength and power
That human fancy has for ever paid
Poetic homage to the bird of Jove.
Hence 'neath his image Rome arrayed her turms
And cohorts for the conquest of the world.
And, figuring his flight, the mind is filled
With thoughts that mock the pride of wingless man.
True the carred aeronaut can mount as high;
But what's the triumph of his volant art?
A rash intrusion on the realms of air.
His helmless vehicle a silken toy,
A bubble bursting in the thunder-cloud—
His course has no volition, and he drifts
The passive plaything of the winds. Not such
Was this proud bird: he clove the adverse storm,
And cuffed it with his wings. He stopped his flight
As easily as the Arab reins his steed,
And stood at pleasure 'neath heaven's zenith, like
A lamp suspended from its azure dome,
Whilst underneath him the world's mountains lay
Like molehills, and her streams like lucid threads.
Then downward, faster than a falling star,
He neared the earth until his shape distinct
Was blackly shadowed on the sunny ground,
And deeper terror hushed the wilderness
To hear his nearer whoop. Then up again
He soared and wheeled. There was an air of scorn
In all his movements, whether he threw round
His crested head to look behind him, or
Lay vertical and sportively displayed
The inside whiteness of his wing declined
In gyres and undulations full of grace,
An object beautifying heaven itself.

He—reckless who was victor, and above
The hearing of their guns—saw fleets engaged

In flaming combat. It was nought to him
What carnage, Moor or Christian, strewed their decks.
But, if his intellect had matched his wings,
Methinks he would have scorned man's vaunted power
To plough the deep. His pinions bore him down
To Algiers the warlike, or the coral groves
That blush beneath the green of Bona's waves,
And traversed in an hour a wider space
Than yonder gallant ship, with all her sails
Wooing the winds, can cross from morn till eve.
His bright eyes were his compass, earth his chart;
His talons anchored on the stormiest cliff,
And on the very lighthouse rock he perched
When winds churned white the waves.
                                        The earthquake's self
Disturbed not him that memorable day
When o'er yon tableland, where Spain had built
Cathedrals, cannoned forts, and palaces,
A palsy-stroke of Nature shook Oran,
Turning her city to a sepulchre,
And strewing into rubbish all her homes;
Amidst whose traceable foundations now,
Of streets and squares, the hyaena hides himself.
That hour beheld him fly as careless o'er
The stifled shrieks of thousands buried quick
As lately when he pounced the speckled snake,
Coiled in yon mallows and wide nettle-fields
That mantle o'er the dead old Spanish town.

Strange is the imagination's dread delight
In objects linked with danger, death, and pain!
Fresh from the luxuries of polished life,
The echo of these wilds enchanted me;
And my heart beat with joy when first I heard
A lion's roar come down the Libyan wind
Across yon long, wide, lonely inland lake,
Where boat ne'er sails from homeless shore to shore.

And yet Numidia's landscape has its spots
Of pastoral pleasantness—though far between.
The village planted near the Maraboot's
Round roof has aye its feathery palm-trees
Paired, for in solitude they bear no fruits.
Here nature's hues all harmonize—fields white
With alasum or blue with bugloss—banks

Bona's waves] Bona is an Algerian seaport   Maraboot] Muhammadan hermit

Of glossy fennel, blent with tulips wild
And sunflowers like a garment prankt with gold—
Acres and miles of opal asphodel,
Where sports and couches the black-eyed gazelle.
Here, too, the air's harmonious—deep-toned doves
Coo to the fife-like carol of the lark;
And, when they cease, the holy nightingale
Winds up his long, long shakes of ecstasy,
With notes that seem but the protracted sounds
Of glassy runnels bubbling over rocks.

THOMAS PRINGLE
1789–1834

192   *The Hottentot*

Mild, melancholy, and sedate, he stands,
Tending another's flock upon the fields,
His father's once, where now the White Man builds
His home, and issues forth his proud commands.
His dark eye flashes not; his listless hands
Lean on the shepherd's staff; no more he wields
The Libyan bow—but to th' oppressor yields
Submissively his freedom and his lands.
Has he no courage? Once he had—but, lo!
Harsh Servitude hath worn him to the bone.
No enterprise? Alas! the brand, the blow,
Have humbled him to dust—even *hope* is gone!
'He's a base-hearted hound—not worth his food'—
His Master cries—'he has no *gratitude*!'[1]

193   *The Lion-Hunt*

Mount—mount for the hunting—with musket and spear!
Call our friends to the field—for the Lion is near!
Call Arend[2] and Ekhard and Groepe to the spoor;
Call Muller and Coetzer and Lucas Van Vuur.

[1] 'Such was the common allegation of the colonists regarding the Hottentots, and frequently have I heard it repeated. My own experience enables me totally to deny its truth.' (T.P.).
[2] These and all the following names were some of Thomas Pringle's neighbours, mulatto tenants, and Hottentot servants. 'The brothers Diederik and Christian Muller, two of our Dutch African neighbours ... were among the most intrepid lion-hunters in South Africa' (T.P.).

Side up Eildon-Cleugh, and blow loudly the bugle:
Call Slinger and Allie and Dikkop and Dugal;
And George with the elephant-gun on his shoulder—
In a perilous pinch none is better or bolder.

In the gorge of the glen lie the bones of my steed,
And the hoofs of a heifer of fatherland's breed:
But mount, my brave boys! if our rifles prove true,
We'll soon make the spoiler his ravages rue.

Ho! the Hottentot lads have discovered the track—
To his den in the desert we'll follow him back;
But tighten your girths, and look well to your flints,
For heavy and fresh are the villain's foot-prints.

Through the rough rocky kloof into grey Huntly-Glen,
Past the wild-olive clump where the wolf has his den,
By the black-eagle's rock at the foot of the fell,
We have tracked him at length to the buffalo's well.

Now mark yonder brake where the blood-hounds are howling;
And hark that hoarse sound—like the deep thunder growling;
'Tis his lair—'tis his voice!—from your saddles alight;
He's at bay in the brushwood preparing for fight.

Leave the horses behind—and be still every man:
Let the Mullers and Rennies advance in the van:
Keep fast in your ranks;—by the yell of yon hound,
The savage, I guess, will be out—with a bound.

He comes! the tall jungle before him loud crashing,
His mane bristled fiercely, his fiery eyes flashing;
With a roar of disdain, he leaps forth in his wrath,
To challenge the foe that dare 'leaguer his path.

He couches—ay now we'll see mischief, I dread:
Quick—level your rifles—and aim at his head:
Thrust forward the spears, and unsheath every knife—
St George! he's upon us!—Now fire, lads, for life!

He's wounded—but yet he'll draw blood ere he falls—
Ha! under his paw see Bezuidenhout sprawls—
Now Diederik! Christian! right in the brain
Plant each man his bullet—Hurra! he is slain!

Bezuidenhout—up man!—'tis only a scratch—
(You were always a scamp, and have met with your match!)
What a glorious lion!—what sinews—what claws—
And seven-feet-ten from the rump to the jaws!

His hide, with the paws and the bones of his skull,
With the spoils of the leopard and buffalo bull,
We'll send to Sir Walter.[1]—Now, boys, let us dine,
And talk of our deeds o'er a flask of old wine.

194   *The Desolate Valley*

Far up among the forest-belted mountains,
Where Winterberg, stern giant old and grey,
Looks down the subject dells, whose gleaming fountains
To wizard Kat their virgin tribute pay,
A valley opens to the noontide ray,
With green savannahs shelving to the brim
Of the swift River, sweeping on his way
To where Umtóka hies to meet with him,
Like a blue serpent gliding through the acacias dim.

Round this secluded region circling rise
A billowy waste of mountains, wild and wide;
Upon whose grassy slopes the pilgrim spies
The gnu and quagga, by the greenwood side,
Tossing their shaggy manes in tameless pride;
Or troop of elands near some sedgy fount;
Or kùdù fawns, that from the thicket glide
To seek their dam upon the misty mount;
With harts, gazelles, and roes, more than the eye may count.

And as we journeyed up the pathless glen,
Flanked by romantic hills on either hand,
The boschbok oft would bound away—and then
Beside the willows, backward gazing, stand.

---

[1] Sir Walter Scott used his influence to secure Pringle a Civil Service appointment in South Africa.

---

194 Umtóka] a tributary of the Kat River   kùdù] a kind of antelope (*Tragelaphus strepsiceros*)   harts, gazelles, and roes] hartebeests, gazelles, and reeboks   boschbok] a kind of antelope (*Tragelaphus scriptus*)

And where old forests darken all the land
From rocky Katberg to the river's brink,
The buffalo would start upon the strand,
Where, 'mid palmetto flags, he stooped to drink,
And, crashing through the brakes, to the deep jungle shrink.

Then, couched at night in hunter's wattled shieling,
How wildly beautiful it was to hear
The elephant his shrill *réveillé* pealing,
Like some far signal-trumpet on the ear!
While the broad midnight moon was shining clear,
How fearful to look forth upon the woods,
And see those stately forest-kings appear,
Emerging from their shadowy solitudes—
As if that trump had woke Earth's old gigantic broods!

Such the majestic, melancholy scene
Which 'midst that mountain-wilderness we found;
With scarce a trace to tell where man had been,
Save the old Caffer cabins crumbling round.
Yet this lone glen (Sicána's ancient ground),
To Nature's savage tribes abandoned long,
Had heard, erewhile, the Gospel's joyful sound,
And low of herds mixed with the Sabbath song.
But all is silent now. The Oppressor's hand was strong.

Now the blithe loxia hangs her pensile nest
From the wild-olive, bending o'er the rock,
Beneath whose shadow, in grave mantle drest,
The Christian Pastor taught his swarthy flock.
A roofless ruin, scathed by flame and smoke,
Tells where the decent Mission-chapel stood;
While the baboon with jabbering cry doth mock
The pilgrim, pausing in his pensive mood
To ask—'Why is it thus? Shall Evil baffle Good?'

Yes—for a season Satan may prevail,
And hold, as if secure, his dark domain;
The prayers of righteous men may seem to fail,
And Heaven's Glad Tidings be proclaimed in vain.
But wait in faith: ere long shall spring again
The seed that seemed to perish in the ground;
And, fertilised by Zion's latter rain,
The long-parched land shall laugh, with harvests crowned,
And through those silent wastes Jehovah's praise resound.

Katberg] a ridge of mountains east of the Kat River   Sicána] Sicána was the chief of a
Kaffir hamlet converted to Christianity

Look round that Vale: behold the unburied bones
Of Ghona's children withering in the blast:
The sobbing wind, that through the forest moans,
Whispers—'The spirit hath for ever passed!'
Thus, in the Vale of Desolation vast,
In moral death dark Afric's myriads lie;
But the Appointed Day shall dawn at last,
When, breathed on by a Spirit from on High,
The dry bones shall awake, and shout—'Our God is nigh!'

MARTIN FARQUHAR TUPPER
1810–1889

195   from *The African Desert*
                         The Simoom

It comes, the blast of death! that sudden glare
Tinges with purple hues the stagnant air:
Fearful in silence, o'er the heaving strand
Sweeps the wild gale, and licks the curling sand,
While o'er the vast Sahara from afar
Rushes the tempest in his wingèd car:
Swift from their bed the flame-like billows rise
Whirling and surging to the copper skies,
As when Briareus lifts his hundred arms,
Grasps at high heaven, and fills it with alarms;
In eddying chaos madly mixt on high
Gigantic pillars dance along the sky,
Or stalk in awful slowness through the gloom,
Or track the coursers of the dread simoom,
Or clashing in mid air, to ruin hurled,
Fall as the fragments of a shattered world!

Hushed is the tempest, desolate the plain,
Stilled are the billows of that troubled main;
As if the voice of death had checked the storm,
Each sandy wave retains its sculptured form:
And all is silence, save the distant blast
That howled, and mocked the desert as it passed;
And all is solitude, for where are they,
That o'er Sahara wound their toilsome way?

195 Simoom] a hot, dry, suffocating wind that blows across the desert in spring and
summer   Briareus] also Aegaeon, a Greek giant with fifty heads and one hundred hands

Ask of the heavens above, that smile serene,
Ask that burnt spot, no more of lovely green,
Ask of the whirlwind in its purple cloud,
The desert is their grave, the sand their shroud.

SIR ALFRED LYALL
1835–1911

196   *A Night in the Red Sea*

The strong hot breath of the land is lashing
    The wild sea-horses, they rear and race;
The plunging bows of our ships are dashing
    Full in the fiery south wind's face.

She rends the water, it foams and follows,
    And the silvery jet of the towering spray,
And the phosphor sparks in the deep wave hollows,
    Lighten the line of our midnight way.

The moon above, with its full-orbed lustre,
    Lifting the veil of the slumberous land,
Gleams o'er a desolate island cluster,
    And the breakers white on the lonely sand.

And a bare hill-range in the distance frowning
    Dim wrapt in haze like a shrouded ghost,
With its jagged peaks the horizon crowning,
    Broods o'er the stark Arabian coast.

See, on the edge of the waters leaping,
    The lamp, far flashing, of Perim's strait
Glitters and grows, as the ship goes sweeping
    Fast on its course for the Exile's Gate.

And onward still to the broadening ocean
    Out of the narrow and perilous seas,
Till we rock with a large and listless motion
    In the moist soft air of the Indian breeze.

196 Exile's Gate] the strait known as Bab el Mandeb (Gate of Tears) which links the Red Sea
and the Gulf of Aden

And the Southern Cross, like a standard flying,
   Hangs in the front of the tropic night,
But the Great Bear sinks, like a hero dying,
   And the Pole-star lowers its signal light;

And the round earth rushes toward the morning,
   And the waves grow paler and wan the foam,
Misty and dim, with a glance of warning,
   Vanish the stars of my northern home.

Let the wide waste sea for a space divide me,
   Till the close-coiled circles of time unfold,
Till the stars rise westward to greet and guide me,
   When the exile ends, and the years are told.

RUDYARD KIPLING
1865–1936

197   *Stellenbosch*

(Composite Columns)

The General 'eard the firin' on the flank,
   An' 'e sent a mounted man to bring 'im back
The silly, pushin' person's name an' rank
   'Oo'd dared to answer Brother Boer's attack:
For there might 'ave been a serious engagement,
   An' 'e might 'ave wasted 'alf a dozen men;
So 'e ordered 'im to stop 'is operations round the kopjes,
   An' 'e told 'im off before the Staff at ten!

     And it all goes into the laundry,
     But it never comes out in the wash,
     'Ow we're sugared about by the old men
     ('Eavy-sterned amateur old men!)
     That 'amper an' 'inder an' scold men
     For fear o' Stellenbosch!

197 Stellenbosch] incompetent commanders used to be sent to the town of Stellenbosch.
The name became a verb

The General 'ad 'produced a great effect',
　The General 'ad the country cleared—almost;
The General ''ad no reason to expect',
　And the Boers 'ad us bloomin' well on toast!
For we might 'ave crossed the drift before the twilight,
　Instead o' sitting down an' takin' root;
But we was now allowed, so the Boojers scooped the crowd,
　To the last survivin' bandolier an' boot.

The General saw the farm'ouse in 'is rear,
　With its stoep so nicely shaded from the sun;
Sez 'e, 'I'll pitch my tabernacle 'ere,'
　An' 'e kept us muckin' round till 'e 'ad done.
For 'e might 'ave caught the confluent pneumonia
　From sleepin' in his gaiters in the dew;
So 'e took a book an' dozed while the other columns closed,
　And De Wet's commando out an' trickled through!

The General saw the mountain-range ahead,
　With their 'elios showin' saucy on the 'eight,
So 'e 'eld us to the level ground instead,
　An' telegraphed the Boojers wouldn't fight.
For 'e might 'ave gone an' sprayed 'em with a pompom,
　Or 'e might 'ave slung a squadron out to see—
But 'e wasn't takin' chances in them 'igh an' 'ostile kranzes—
　He was markin' time to earn a K.C.B.

The General got 'is decorations thick
　(The men that backed 'is lies could not complain),
The Staff 'ad D.S.O.'s till we was sick,
　An' the soldier—'ad the work to do again!
For 'e might 'ave known the District was an 'otbed,
　Instead of 'andin' over, upside-down,
To a man 'oo 'ad to fight 'alf a year to put it right,
　While the General sat an' slandered 'im in town!

　　An' it all went into the laundry,
　　But it never came out in the wash.
　　We were sugared about by the old men
　　(Panicky, perishin' old men)
　　That 'amper an' 'inder an' scold men
　　For fear o' Stellenbosch!

ROY FULLER

1912–

198   *The Green Hills of Africa*

The green, humped, wrinkled hills: with such a look
Of age (or youth) as to erect the hair.
They crouch above the ports or on the plain,
Beneath the matchless skies; are like a strange
Girl's shoulders suddenly against your hands.
What covers them so softly, vividly?
They break at the sea in a cliff, a mouth of red:
Upon the plain are unapproachable,
Furrowed and huge, dramatically lit.

And yet one cannot be surprised at what
The hills contain. The girls run up the slope,
Their oiled and shaven heads like caramels.
Behind, the village, with its corrugated
Iron, the wicked habit of the store.
The villagers cough, the sacking blows from the naked
Skin of a child, a white scum on his lips.
The youths come down in feathers from the peak.
And over all a massive frescoed sky.

The poisoner proceeds by tiny doses,
The victim weaker and weaker but uncomplaining.
Soon they will only dance for money, will
Discover more and more things can be sold.
What gods did you expect to find here, with
What healing powers? What subtle ways of life?
No, there is nothing but the forms and colours,
And the emotion brought from a world already
Dying of what starts to infect the hills.

JAMES RUSSELL GRANT
1928–

199   *Africa*

Africa.
Skull with a golden chin,
Brimful of flies.

Jungle and veldt.
Elephant scent.
Doe eyes.

ANTHONY THWAITE
1930–

200   *Arabic Script*

Like a spider through ink, someone says, mocking: see it
Blurred on the news-sheets or in neon lights
And it suggests an infinitely plastic, feminine
Syllabary, all the diacritical dots and dashes
Swimming together like a shoal of minnows,
Purposive yet wayward, a wavering measure
Danced over meaning, obscuring vowels and breath.
But at Sidi Kreibish, among the tombs,
Where skulls lodge in the cactus roots,
The pink claws breaking headstone, cornerstone,
Each fleshy tip thrusting to reach the light,
Each spine a hispid needle, you see the stern
Edge of the language, Kufic, like a scimitar
Curved in a lash, a flash of consonants
Such as swung out of Medina that day
On the long flog west, across ruins and flaccid colonials,
A swirl of black flags, white crescents, a language of swords.

---

200 Sidi Kreibish] old Islamic cemetery in Benghazi   Medina] Medina, in western
Saudi Arabia, is seen here as the source of Islam because that is where the Prophet went when he
fled from Mecca   long flog west] military campaign led by Amr Ibn el-As which spread
Islam from the borders of Egypt to Morocco and the Atlantic

DAVID GILL

1934–

201   *The Kaleidoscope*

You do not know this Byaruhanga: he is short
and his belly swells like a toffee-apple above
his spindly legs, and he is black and wants
to go to school.
You would not understand the wonder quite
when one day he got a kaleidoscope and peered
gingerly down it,
if you knew nothing of his lustreless mornings
among the maize and beans, beneath
an unkempt thatch with rain
brown as tobacco juice
oozing through,
his hours of cockroach boredom.
And rare the patterns in his brain: the seasons' repetitions,
the red and black mosaics of drying coffee beans
in murram forecourts,
weave of birds in flight, of mats on floors.
So when he poked the tube against the sun
the siliceous patterns dazzled,
dazzled and danced and left him dazed
staring at us with the linings of his pockets out
for similes he does not have:
rose-windows, snow-flakes, molecules, mosaics,
a glimpse of vast complexities, of puzzling constellations,
a hint of Beauty's structures, of subtle thought
and delicate engineering.
A glimpse, no more.
Submerged keel of this racing generation,[1]
he'll never catch the breeze, nor flutter brightly from the mast,
nor read the compass for the course.
He'll never start.

---

[1] The children of Uganda in the years following independence (1962) when 'there was a great deal of optimism and talk of nation-building about' (D.G. to K.C.-H.).

Byaruhanga] a proper name (fairly common in the district of Toro in Western Uganda)

DONALD THOMAS
1935–

202
Tangier: Hotel Rif

Pale pink and green lights flush on white
Façades and balconies. All questions are
Steps on dead carpets here: the high-stooled blonde
Imposes on a chromium bar.

As carp in an abandoned pool,
Her slow thoughts turn; through olive waves
Their golden snouts distil the light
In images of deep sky's architraves.

As light from the emerald glass she holds,
Her morning images run waste:
Tired fashions of the mind commend
The wide-paved avenues of taste.

Faint winds fall in a hiss upon
Plumes of the palms: the brown wind stirs
Neat cypress by the hillside tombs,
White marble promenade of fears.

At sand's white rim, on cobalt wave's
Trim verge, sky in slack water blends
With shifting, effluence of decay,
Takings and leavings of the sense.

Shells, amber weed, a late tide's scum
Like habit's shrivelled flotsam ride:
No needle fine enough to etch
Such deliquescence of the mind.

Beyond the sun's striped awnings
And coloured bulbs in slack festoons,
Hull-down the bilge-sprung tankers limp
To pale Atlantic afternoons.

STEWART BROWN

1951–

203   *Anthropology: Cricket at Kano*

Cerulean and jet, the Tuareg
from the Sahel with his bow and arrow
stalks the dusty outfield
which is his heritage, his history,
like a wraith from an Absurd drama,

squats at deep mid-wicket
to watch the strange Bature ritual,
the inexplicable dances
of the white men in their bleached
ceremonial robes.

Soon play continues,
the intruding spectator ignored,
merely a local hazard
like the gully-oak at Brook,
or the boundary stream at Carnon Downs,

and with eyes closed, behind
mosquito screens, the pavilion's
ceiling fan rustling an artificial breeze,
the sounds of leather on willow,
of 'come one', 'no wait',

and 'How-was-that-umpire?'
appeal to racial memories,
recall the ancestors and holy places
of the tribe's formation . . .
Canterbury, Lords, the County Ground at York.

Such reverie would explain
our dancing to the nomad from Niger,
but neither he nor we will probe
beneath the fictions that our eyes create,
our shared humanity obscured

Kano] city in northern Nigeria   Tuareg] desert tribesman   Sahel] semi-desert
scrubland that borders the southern fringe of the Sahara   Bature] Hausa word for
Europeans/white men

by vocabularies of such conflict
that their lexicon is silence.
So, at stumps, nomad and exile
pursue their disparate paths,
amicably separate, rooted in certainties

centuries old, our rootlessness
a fragile bond that will not bear embrace.

ASIA

The Indian Subcontinent

ANONYMOUS
late 18th–early 19th century

204   *[Graffito inscribed on a wall of the Taj Mahal]*

Oh! thou—whose great imperial mind could raise
This splendid trophy to a woman's praise!
If love or grief inspired the bold design,
No mortal's joy or sorrow equals thine.—
Sleep on secure—this monument shall stand,
When desolation's wings sweep o'er the land,
By death again in one wide ruin hurled,
The last triumphant wonder of the world!

RICHARD OWEN CAMBRIDGE
1717–1802

The Fakir

205

A fakir (a religious well known in the East,
Not much like a parson, still less like a priest)
With no canting, no sly Jesuitical arts,
Field-preaching, hypocrisy, learning or parts;
By a happy refinement in mortification,
Grew the oracle, saint, and the pope of his nation.
But what did he do this esteem to acquire?
Did he torture his head or his bosom with fire?
Was his neck in a portable pillory cased?
Did he fasten a chain to his leg or his waist?
No. His holiness rose to this sovereign pitch
By the merit of running long nails in his breech.
   A wealthy young Indian, approaching the shrine,
Thus in banter accosts the prophetic divine:
'This tribute accept for your interest with Fo,
Whom with torture you serve, and whose will you must know;

205 Fo] the Chinese word for Buddha, here used very loosely

To your suppliant disclose his immortal decree;
Tell me which of the Heavens is allotted for me.'

FAKIR

Let me first know your merits.

INDIAN

                                        I strive to be just:
To be true to my friend, to my wife, to my trust:
In religion I duly observe every form:
With a heart to my country devoted and warm:
I give to the poor, and I lend to the rich . . .

FAKIR

But how many nails do you run in your breech?

INDIAN

With submission I speak to your reverence's tail;
But mine has no taste for a tenpenny nail.

FAKIR

Well! I'll pray to our prophet and get you preferred;
Though no farther expect than to Heaven the third.
With me in the thirtieth your seat to obtain,
You must qualify duly with hunger and pain.

INDIAN

With you in the thirtieth! You impudent rogue!
Can such wretches as you give to madness a vogue!
Though the priesthood of Fo on the vulgar impose,
By squinting whole years at the end of their nose;
Though with cruel devices of mortification
They adore a vain idol of modern creation;
Does the God of the Heavens such a service direct?
Can his mercy approve a self-punishing sect?
Will his wisdom be worshipped with chains and with nails?
Or e'er look for his rites in your noses and tails?
Come along to my house and these penances leave,
Give your belly a feast, and your breech a reprieve.

This reasoning unhinged each fanatical notion;
And staggered our saint, in his chair of promotion.
At length with reluctance he rose from his seat:
And resigning his nails and his fame for retreat;

Two weeks his new life he admired and enjoyed:
The third he with plenty and quiet was cloyed.
To live undistinguished to him was the pain,
An existence unnoticed he could not sustain.
In retirement he sighed for the fame-giving chair;
For the crowd to admire him, to reverence and stare:
No endearments of pleasure and ease could prevail:
He the saintship resumed, and new larded his tail.

Our Fakir represents all the votaries of fame:
Their ideas, their means, and their end is the same;
The sportsman, the buck; all the heroes of vice,
With their gallantry, lewdness, the bottle and dice;
The poets, the critics, the metaphysicians,
The courtier, the patriot, all politicians;
The statesman begirt with th' importunate ring,
(I had almost completed my list with the king)
All labour alike to illustrate my tale;
All tortured by choice with th' invisible nail.

REGINALD HEBER

1783–1826

206   *An Evening Walk in Bengal*

Our task is done! on Gunga's breast
The sun is sinking down to rest;
And, moored beneath the tamarind bough,
Our bark has found its harbour now.
With furled sail and painted side
Behold the tiny frigate ride.
Upon her deck, 'mid charcoal gleams,
The Moslem's savoury supper steams;
While all apart beneath the wood,
The Hindoo cooks his simpler food.

Come walk with me the jungle through.
If yonder hunter told us true,
Far off in desert dank and rude,
The tiger holds its solitude;
Nor (taught by recent harm to shun
The thunders of the English gun)

206 Gunga] Ganges

A dreadful guest but rarely seen,
Returns to scare the village green.
Come boldly on! no venomed snake
Can shelter in so cool a brake.
Child of the Sun! he loves to lie
'Midst Nature's embers, parched and dry,
Where o'er some tower in ruin laid,
The peepul spreads its haunted shade;
Or round a tomb his scales to wreathe
Fit warder in the gate of Death.
Come on! yet pause! Behold us now
Beneath the bamboo's arched bough,
Where gemming oft that sacred gloom
Glows the geranium's scarlet bloom,
And winds our path through many a bower
Of fragrant tree and giant flower;
The ceiba's crimson pomp displayed
O'er the broad plantain's humbler shade,
And dusk anana's prickly glade;
While o'er the brake, so wild and fair
The betel waves his crest in air.
With pendent train and rushing wings
Aloft the gorgeous peacock springs;
And he the bird of hundred dyes,
Whose plumes the dames of Ava prize.
So rich a shade, so green a sod
Our English fairies never trod!
Yet who in Indian bowers has stood,
But thought on England's 'good greenwood'!
And blessed, beneath the palmy shade,
Her hazel and her hawthorn glade,
And breathed a prayer (how oft in vain!)
To gaze upon her oaks again?
A truce to thought,—the jackal's cry
Resounds like sylvan revelry;
And through the trees yon failing ray
Will scantly serve to guide our way.
Yet mark, as fade the upper skies,
Each thicket opes ten thousand eyes.
Before, beside us, and above,
The fire-fly lights his lamp of love,
Retreating, chasing, sinking, soaring,
The darkness of the copse exploring.
While to this cooler air confest,
The broad Dhatura bares her breast,

geranium's scarlet bloom] shrub called the Indian geranium   bird of hundred dyes] the
mucharunga

Of fragrant scent and virgin white,
A pearl around the locks of night!
Still as we pass in softened hum
Along the breezy alleys come
The village song, the horn, the drum.
Still as we pass, from bush and briar,
The shrill cigala strikes his lyre;
And, what is she whose liquid strain
Thrills through yon copse of sugar-cane?
I know that soul-entrancing swell,
It is—it must be—Philomel!
Enough, enough, the rustling trees
Announce a shower upon the breeze,
The flashes of the summer sky
Assume a deeper, ruddier dye;
Yon lamp that trembles on the stream,
From forth our cabin sheds its beam;
And we must early sleep to find
Betimes the morning's healthy wind.
But oh! with thankful hearts confess
E'en here there may be happiness;
And He, the bounteous Sire, has given
His peace on earth,—his hope of Heaven!

THOMAS SKINNER

fl. 1830s

207   *The Suttee*

The evening sun-beams threw their golden light,
And smiling ushered in the bridal night;
The gay procession wound its happy way
In colours brilliant as the jocund day.
The pipe, the viol, and unceasing drum,
Proclaim to all, the blooming bride is come!
Light dancing maids the gaudy train prolong,
And Gunga's banks are startled, too, with song.
Thousands rush forth the joyous scene to hail,
And lend their voices—lest the music fail;
The bride reclined, in costly jewels dressed—
Jewels less bright than hope within her breast;

207 Gunga] Ganges

Of sweetly-scented flowers, a snowy braid,
Pure as the fancies of th' espousèd maid,
In her black hair a striking contrast show,
While o'er her neck the sable ringlets flow.
The bride reclined; a crimson litter bore
Her blushing charms along the sacred shore.
What joy is breaking from her large dark eye—
The vivid lightnings of a tropic sky!
The rosy veil is archly drawn aside
To show the glances she affects to hide.
'Tis all a modest maiden dare betray—
The sudden sparkle of a meteor's play.
No hand may give those features to the light,
Save his who takes her to his hall tonight.
    Hark, from that hall what happy spirits break!
What joyous revelry the echoes make!
Lo, the young lord awaits her at the porch,
While mid-day bursts from each attending torch.
The maid has reached her bridegroom's home at last:—
The morning came, and all her joy had passed;
Death had gone over like a wild simoom,
And marked her youthful husband for the tomb.
And must he only suffer? Still the pride
Of youth and beauty lives, the lovely bride.
She, too, must die: some savage god, unknown
To Christian climes, demands her for his own.
    The pile now rears aloft its awful head,
Where late the bride her gay procession led:
Still ring the notes of merriment: the strain
Of mirth still sweeps along the crowded plain.
Why rush the thousands? Why this grand display
Of pomp and pride? A widow burns today!
Must the same mirth, the same bright hues appear
To grace the bridal, and to deck the bier?
Is there no sorrow in the hurrying throng?
Will the wild herd still pour the maddening song?
No breast to sympathize, no tear to fall,
No trembling hand to elevate the pall?
It is some jubilee;—it cannot be,
That death is hailed with such a savage glee.
Another bridal! see the gathering fire;
The altar stands upon that burning pyre!
There, in still death, the bridegroom waits his spouse:
To bind their union, and renew her vows,
Calmly she stands, and gazes o'er the scene,
Unnerved by thoughts of what she might have been.

How changed that day, on which, almost from birth,
Arose the star of all her hopes on earth!
For, pledged in childhood, all her charms had grown
(So fondly thought she) for that day alone;
To bless his sight, whose name was wont to share
In every wish and every childish prayer,
Since first she lisped the mighty Bramah's name!
Yet now unawed she views the spreading flame;
With false devotion gazes on the pile
And moves to die—with a contented smile;
Waves a farewell; and, steadfast to the last,
Scorns on this world one lingering look to cast.

  Yes! she rejects this world without one thought
Of all the bliss but yesterday had brought;
Sees unconcerned an aged father stand,
And scarcely owns the pressure of his hand;
Hears a loved brother urge her on to die
With cold indifference: not a rebel sigh
Bursts to declare that yet one pulse remains,
Against her will to throb at human pains.
Beyond this transient earth her heart is set;
She dreams that happiness may meet her yet;
Thinks, like a phoenix, 'tis her fate to rise
Pure from her ashes, to adorn the skies;
And bear (for all her torments seek but this)
Her husband with her to divide her bliss.
For this she suffers, and for this she dies;
Disowns, for this, all nature's dearest ties.

  O noble spirit! In a Christian's cause,
A martyr's crown, and a whole world's applause,
To bury the hopes, and mitigate the pain,
Have oft displayed their tempting lures in vain:
Heroes have shrunk before the torture's wheel,
And e'en in martyrdom have stooped to feel.
Yet here, each day, in agonizing fires,
For sinful man some gentle dame expires,
Gentle and pure, with every tender fear
A woman knows, yet all forgotten here.

  A cheerful victim, lo, she mounts the pile,
While the flame quickens in the fragrant oil:
The thickening smoke now circles o'er her head;
Her husband's bosom forms an easy bed.
Here she reclines, nor seeks a safer rest;
No couch so sweet as his unconscious breast.
While the fire wreathes around each quiv'ring limb,
She feels it not, she slumbers upon him;—

A fleeting rest: with him she makes, to reach
Eternal joy, for thus the Vedahs teach.
Too fatal error! Oh! that such a mind
To truth divine should still continue blind!
She will not doubt: devoted to her creed,
She claims the glory, and demands the meed;
Courts the proud triumph of a Hindoo bride,
Betrothed in life, in death to be allied.

EDWARD LEAR

1812–1888

208
The Cummerbund

An Indian Poem

I

She sate upon her Dobie,
  To watch the Evening Star,
And all the Punkahs as they passed,
  Cried, 'My! how fair you are!'
Around her bower, with quivering leaves,
  The tall Kamsamahs grew,
And Kitmutgars in wild festoons
  Hung down from Tchokis blue.

II

Below her home the river rolled
  With soft meloobious sound,
Where golden-finned Chuprassies swam,
  In myriads circling round.
Above, on tallest trees remote
  Green Ayahs perched alone,
And all night long the Mussak moaned
  Its melancholy tone.

III

And where the purple Nullahs threw
  Their branches far and wide,—
And silvery Goreewallahs flew
  In silence, side by side,—

The little Bheesties' twittering cry
  Rose on the flagrant air,
And oft the angry Jampan howled
  Deep in his hateful lair.

IV

She sate upon her Dobie,—
  She heard the Nimmak hum,—
When all at once a cry arose,—
  'The Cummerbund is come!'
In vain she fled:—with open jaws
  The angry monster followed,
And so (before assistance came)
  That Lady Fair was swollowed.

V

They sought in vain for even a bone
  Respectfully to bury,—
They said,—'Hers was a dreadful fate!'
  (And Echo answered 'Very'.)
They nailed her Dobie to the wall,
  Where last her form was seen,
And underneath they wrote these words,
  In yellow, blue, and green:—

Beware, ye Fair! Ye Fair, beware!
  Nor sit out late at night,—
Lest horrid Cummerbunds should come,
  And swollow you outright.

H. G. KEENE
1825–1915

209   *The Taj*

White, like a spectre seen when night is old
Yet stained with hues of many a tear and smart,
Cornelian, blood-stone, matched in callous art:
Aflame, like passion, like dominion cold,
Bed of imperial consorts whom none part
For ever (domed with glory, heart to heart)
Still whispering to the ages, 'Love is bold
And seeks the height, though rooted in the mould':

Touched, when the dawn floats in an opal mist
By fainter blush than opening roses own;
Calm in the evening's lucent amethyst;
Pearl-crowned, when midnight airs aside have blown
The clouds that rising moonlight faintly kissed;
—An aspiration fixed, a sigh made stone.

SIR EDWIN ARNOLD

1832–1904

210   from *The Light of Asia*

The painted streets alive with hum of noon,
The traders cross-legged 'mid their spice and grain,
The buyers with their money in the cloth,
The war of words to cheapen this or that,
The shout to clear the road, the huge stone wheels,
The strong slow oxen and their rustling loads,
The singing bearers with the palanquins,
The broad-necked hamals sweating in the sun,
The housewives bearing water from the well
With balanced chatties, and athwart their hips
The black-eyed babes; the fly-swarmed sweetmeat shops,
The weaver at his loom, the cotton-bow
Twanging, the millstones grinding meal, the dogs
Prowling for orts, the skilful armourer
With tong and hammer linking shirts of mail,
The blacksmith with a mattock and a spear
Reddening together in his coals, the school
Where round their Guru, in a grave half-moon,
The Sâkya children sang the mantras through,
And learned the greater and the lesser gods;
The dyers stretching waistcloths in the sun
Wet from the vats—orange, and rose, and green;
The soldiers clanking past with swords and shields,
The camel-drivers rocking on the humps,
The Brahman proud, the martial Kshatriya,
The humble toiling Sudra; here a throng
Gathered to watch some chattering snake-tamer
Wind round his wrist the living jewellery

210 Sâkya] sect of Tibetan Buddhists   Kshatriya] military or governing class
Sudra] menials and artisans

Of asp and nâg, or charm the hooded death
To angry dance with drone of beaded gourd;
There a long line of drums and horns, which went,
With steeds gay painted and silk canopies,
To bring the young bride home; and here a wife
Stealing with cakes and garlands to the god
To pray her husband's safe return from trade,
Or beg a boy next birth; hard by the booths
Where the swart potters beat the noisy brass
For lamps and lotas; thence, by temple walls
And gateways, to the river and the bridge
Under the city walls.

SIR ALFRED LYALL
1835–1911

211 *Studies at Delhi, 1876*

I. THE HINDU ASCETIC

Here as I sit by the Jumna bank,
    Watching the flow of the sacred stream,
Pass me the legions, rank on rank,
    And the cannon roar, and the bayonets gleam.

Is it a god or a king that comes?
    Both are evil, and both are strong;
With women and worshipping, dancing and drums,
    Carry your gods and your kings along.

Fanciful shapes of a plastic earth,
    These are the visions that weary the eye;
These I may 'scape by a luckier birth,
    Musing, and fasting, and hoping to die.

When shall these phantoms flicker away?
    Like the smoke of the guns on the windswept hill,
Like the sounds and colours of yesterday:
    And the soul have rest, and the air be still.

210 nâg] *nâga*, snake   lotas] *lota*, water-pot, usually made of brass

II. BADMINTON

Hardly a shot from the gate we stormed,
   Under the Moree battlement's shade;
Close to the glacis our game was formed,
   There had the fight been, and there we played.

Lightly the demoiselles tittered and leapt,
   Merrily capered the players all;
North, was the garden where Nicholson slept,
   South, was the sweep of a battered wall.

Near me a Musalmán, civil and mild,
   Watched as the shuttlecocks rose and fell;
And he said, as he counted his beads and smiled,
   'God smite their souls to the depths of hell.'

212   *Rajpoot Rebels*

On the Sardah, 1858

Where the mighty cliffs are frowning
   Far o'er the torrents fall,
And the pine and the oak stand crowning
   The ridges of high Nepaul,

Sat twenty Rajpoot rebels,
   Haggard and pale and thin,
Lazily chucking the pebbles
   Into the foaming lynn.

Their eyes were sunken and weary,
   With a sort of listless woe
They looked from their desolate eyrie
   Over the plains below.

They turned from the mountain breezes
   And shivered with cold and damp,
They were faint with the fierce diseases
   Of the deadly jungle swamp.

211 Nicholson] John Nicholson (1822–53), soldier and administrator, who did more than any other man to keep the Punjab loyal and bring about the fall of Delhi during the Indian Mutiny. He was killed in action

212 Sardah] the Sarda or Kali river, which rises in the Himalayas and flows along the Indian–Nepali border

Two had wounds from a sabre
  And one from an Enfield ball,
But no one cared for his neighbour,
  There was sickness or wounds on all.

The Rajpoot leader rose then
  Stiffly and slow from the ground,
He looked at the camp of his foes then,
  And he looked at his brethren round;

And he said: 'From my country driven
  With the last of my hunted band,
My home to another given,
  On a foreign soil I stand.

'They have burnt every roof in the village,
  They have slain the best of my kin,
They have ruined and burnt and pillaged,
  And yet we had done no sin;

'Our clans were heady and rude,
  Our robbers many and tall,
But our fighting never shed English blood,
  Nor harried an English hall.

'The king took tithe if he might;
  He was paid by a knave or a fool;
For we held our lands on a firmer right
  Than is given by parchment rule;

'Our fathers of old had cleared it
  From the jungle with axe and sword,
Our ancient rights had endeared it
  To him who was chief and lord.

'Our father's curse with our father's land,
  Like the wrath of a great god's blow
May it fall on the head and the iron hand
  And the heart of our English foe.

'As our fathers fought, we fight;
  But a sword and a matchlock gun,
'Gainst the serried line of bayonets bright
  A thousand moving like one!

'From the banks of Ganges holy,
   From the towers of fair Lucknow,
They have driven us surely and slowly,
   They have crushed us blow on blow.

        *   *   *

'When the army has slain its fill,
   When they bid the hangman cease;
They will beckon us down from the desert hill
   To go to our homes in peace.

'To plough with a heavy heart,
   And, of half our fields bereft,
'Gainst the usurer's oath, and the lawyer's art
   To battle that some be left.

'At the sight of an English face
   Loyally bow the head,
And cringe like slaves to the surly race
   For pay and a morsel of bread;

'Toil like an ox or a mule
   To earn the stranger his fee—
Our sons may brook the Feringhee's rule,
   There is no more life for me!'

THOMAS FRANK BIGNOLD.
?1839–1888

213   *The Holiday*

Port Blair

Embalm, O Muse, in an appropriate lay
The worn Civilian's well-earned holiday;
Touch lightly on the hours of weary pain
And wasting sickness combated in vain;
Tell how the leech exhausted all his store,
Tell how the sufferer murmured 'Hold! No more!'
Till wife and leech and patient did agree
To trust Dame Nature and a trip to sea.

Feringhee's rule] European's rule
213 Port Blair] town in the Andaman and Nicobar Islands; penal colony until 1921

A trip to sea! but whither, gentle Muse?
The waves are all before us, where to choose;
Bound for what port, of all the ports that are?
Ceylon is muggy, and Hongkong too far;
So let me rather, whose judicial care
Has quartered many a convict on Port Blair,
Sign my own warrant with my own consent
Affirming thus my proper precedent.

Next to arrange the details of my plan;
Shall I set sail, a solitary man—
I, round whose neck some seventy fingers twine
The pleasant tendrils of the clustered vine?—
No! 'tis not good for man to live alone,
And Adam needed Eve, and Darby Joan;
And I with wife and children will embark
A band two short of Noah's in the ark.
So said so done; selecting as our scene
The eastern alias of our gracious Queen,
Anon to Hastings jetty we repair,
Cast by kind Fate on kindly Burleigh's care.

Him had his sire with clear prophetic view
Named from the God of sinew and of thew
Who, in the early days when Earth was young,
Strangled the snakes that on his cradle hung.
His waxing might be plighted to the seas,
And here he stands—a burly Hercules.

How fair are strength and beauty when allies!
Love in her smile, and laughter in her eyes,
For Burleigh is her idol, who but he?
His fair fond Florence sails in company;
Nor only she; their cabin is the home
Of two wee fairies, daughters of the foam.

A son of Mars, whose skilful pen portrays
All that his just theodolite surveys—
A man of peace, who plucks from India's field
A leaf more fragrant than Cathay may yield—
These are our party, well equipped and found
In pluck and all good humour for the round.

*   *   *   *   *   *   *

O favoured isles of Heaven! O lovely scene!
Whose wooded heights slope down to seas as green,
Save where the wave, dashed on some reef below,
Lights the long base with clouds of wreathed snow.

The eastern alias of our gracious Queen] SS *Maharani*   Hastings] district of Calcutta on
the river Hooghly, north of Tolly's Nullah. It used to be a Government colony

Here, Mercy tempering Justice, for a time
Britannia gathers India's sons of crime.
Not theirs to pine in dungeons or in chains,
Chilled in the cold, or mouldering in the rains;
Here must they toil, but free, or all but free,
Their only prison-wall the girdling sea!
Toil, but in hope; for wisdom bids them learn
The sweets of honest effort, and to earn
The stipend of their labour, until time
Fill the full tale of years that expiates their crime.

   Aye, all may hope! for even he whose knife
Has dealt a death-blow to another's life,
He whose own life were forfeit, knows that he
When twenty years have rolled, shall yet be free;
Seek the dear village where a boy he played,
The little temple and the banyan-shade,
Rejoin his children grown to man's estate
And early friends still mourning for his fate;
Pluck the rich harvest of the mangoe groves,
And breathe his last among the scenes he loves.

   O brothers of the ermine, who in Ind
Award their fate to thousands who have sinned,
Deem not that doom vindictive or severe
Which saves a wretch from Jail, and sends him here!
But grant henceforth (what thoughtful Judge would not?)
The more deterrent but the milder lot.

   Here convicts clear the jungle, plant the tea;
Yon coral pier that breaks the angry sea
Was piled by convict hands; the cargo boats,
This busy fleet that round our steamer floats,
Were built, are manned by convicts; convict toil
Your linen laves, and fills your lamp with oil.

   Turn we from crimes and convicts, Muse, awhile,
And hymn the social honours of the isle.

   Soon as the anchor thunders to its bed
A swift boat glances from the jetty-head;
Twelve sturdy rowers of Panjabi race
Bend to the oar and urge the speed apace.
No prisoners they; since Mayo, good and great,
Fell less by convict than fanatic hate,
These towering Sikhs, broad-chested, iron-hard
Ply the Chief's oars, and form his body-guard.
And none need ask a doughtier following
Than this, the gallant band of Teja Singh.

Mayo] Richard Southwell Bourke, Earl of Mayo (1822–72), Viceroy of India, assassinated by
a convict at Port Blair on 8 February 1872

These, from his seat of Government on Ross
Speed the Chief near us; whom Victoria's Cross
Adorns, for deeds of mark in days gone by,
When India travailed in the Mutiny.

The boat alongside, prompt the Chief appears,
Not fifty yet, and younger than his years;
If any doubt, lawn-tennis be my witness
Of youth and pluck and energy and fitness.

What is his errand as he mounts our deck?
—To place his gig, launch, escort at our beck;
And, last and best, fair welcome to afford
To his most choice and hospital board.

Here in his sea-girt realm, mid balmy gales,
Teased by no wire and only monthly mails,
High in his tree-clad seat above the wave
He holds such court as crowned kings might crave;
While ladies fair, though few, with fitting grace
Share and refine the genius of the place.
Here Cadell's converse, Tuson's liquid song
Enhance the charm and speed the hours along;
Where all were glad and making others glad—
Years will not dim the pleasant time we had.

Right well his Captains seconded their Chief;
There at the ebb we visited the reef,
Plucked the fair coral blossoms where they grew
So pink, so white, so delicately blue.
We saw the little jail on Viper's shore
For those who, once admonished, erred once more;
(It seemed to need the few who were not free
To emphasise the general liberty);
We saw some natives, half reclaimed and rude,
Adorned with shells, but desperately nude;
There bought we bows and sea-shells one and all,
And sheaves of arrows, trophies for the hall;
We saw the tea-house, drank the fragrant tea
From plants that were but seeds in '83;
While every reach and every headland passed
Revealed some vista lovelier than the last.

Thence to Camorta, where I fished in vain;
A monster broke me and was off again;
Alas! I have no details of the trip
For illness held me prisoner by the ship.
Yet did I shake a friendly hand with Man
Who anthropologizeth when he can,
And knows and almost loves the Andaman.

Camorta] one of the Nicobar Islands

(He vowed by all the Andaman religions
He'd send me up a pair of bronze-winged pigeons.)
I have his book, and contemplate the pleasure
Of mastering the language—at my leisure.

Back to Port Blair, and onward to Rangoon
Athirst for war news; and we heard full soon
The loud salute resounding through the bay
For Theebaw caught and taken Mandalay.

Ashore I found my friend of early years
Now judging in Rangoon, my trusty Meres;
While kind MacEwen opened his abode
And held high hospital in Halpin Road.

There Griffiths, master of the healing art,
Most patient man of ear, and kind of heart,
Did something like a miracle display—
He all but cured me in a single day.
Long may he flourish in his chosen line!
The thanks be his; the benefit is mine.

So to Port Blair once more. Nay, do not pout!
My Muse, like you, fair reader, is tired out;
I will but note the kindness and good-will
That all untiring lighted on us still
And urge on all who need a change of air
The round,—Rangoon, Camorta, and Port Blair;
And to that end as swiftly as I can
Shall take this copy to the 'Englishman'.

RUDYARD KIPLING
1865–1936

214   *Gunga Din*

You may talk o' gin and beer
When you're quartered safe out 'ere,
An' you're sent to penny-fights an' Aldershot it;
But when it comes to slaughter
You will do your work on water,
An' you'll lick the bloomin' boots of 'im that's got it.
Now in Injia's sunny clime,
Where I used to spend my time
A-servin' of 'Er Majesty the Queen,
Of all them blackfaced crew
The finest man I knew

Was our regimental bhisti, Gunga Din,
      He was 'Din! Din! Din!
   You limpin' lump o' brick-dust, Gunga Din!
      Hi! Slippy *hitherao*!
      Water, get it! *Panee lao*,
   You squidgy-nosed old idol, Gunga Din.'

The uniform 'e wore
Was nothin' much before,
An' rather less than 'arf o' that be'ind,
For a piece o' twisty rag
An' a goatskin water-bag
Was all the field-equipment 'e could find.
When the sweatin' troop-train lay
In a sidin' through the day,
Where the 'eat would make your bloomin' eyebrows crawl,
We shouted 'Harry By!'
Till our throats were bricky-dry,
Then we wopped 'im 'cause 'e couldn't serve us all.
      It was 'Din! Din! Din!
   You 'eathen, where the mischief 'ave you been?
      You put some *juldee* in it
      Or I'll *marrow* you this minute
   If you don't fill up my helmet, Gunga Din!'

'E would dot an' carry one
Till the longest day was done;
An' 'e didn't seem to know the use o' fear.
If we charged or broke or cut,
You could bet your bloomin' nut,
'E'd be waitin' fifty paces right flank rear.
With 'is mussick on 'is back,
'E would skip with our attack,
An' watch us till the bugles made 'Retire',
An' for all 'is dirty 'ide
'E was white, clear white, inside
When 'e went to tend the wounded under fire!
      It was 'Din! Din! Din!'
   With the bullets kickin' dust-spots on the green.
      When the cartridges ran out,
      You could hear the front-ranks shout,
   'Hi! ammunition-mules an' Gunga Din!'

Panee lao] Bring water swiftly   *juldee*] be quick   *marrow*] hit   mussick
'' water-skin

I shan't forgit the night
When I dropped be'ind the fight
With a bullet where my belt-plate should 'a' been.
I was chokin' mad with thirst,
An' the man that spied me first
Was our good old grinnin', gruntin' Gunga Din.
'E lifted up my 'ead,
An' he plugged me where I bled,
An' 'e guv me 'arf-a-pint o' water green.
It was crawlin' and it stunk.
But of all the drinks I've drunk,
I'm gratefullest to one from Gunga Din.
    It was 'Din! Din! Din!
  'Ere's a beggar with a bullet through 'is spleen;
    'E's chawin' up the ground,
    An' 'e's kickin' all around:
  For Gawd's sake git the water, Gunga Din!'

'E carried me away
To where a dooli lay,
An' a bullet come an' drilled the beggar clean.
'E put me safe inside,
An' just before 'e died,
'I 'ope you liked your drink', sez Gunga Din.
So I'll meet 'im later on
At the place where 'e is gone—
Where it's always double drill and no canteen.
'E'll be squattin' on the coals
Givin' drink to poor damned souls,
An' I'll get a swig in hell from Gunga Din!
    Yes, Din! Din! Din!
  You Lazarushian-leather Gunga Din!
    Though I've belted you and flayed you,
    By the livin' Gawd that made you,
  You're a better man than I am, Gunga Din!

215 *Mandalay*

By the old Moulmein Pagoda, lookin' lazy at the sea,
There's a Burma girl a-settin', and I know she thinks o' me;
For the wind is in the palm-trees, and the temple-bells they say:
'Come you back, you British soldier; come you back to Mandalay!'
    Come you back to Mandalay,
    Where the old Flotilla lay:

Can't you 'ear their paddles chunkin' from Rangoon to
    Mandalay?
On the road to Mandalay,
Where the flyin'-fishes play,
An' the dawn comes up like thunder outer China 'crost the
    Bay!

'Er petticoat was yaller an' 'er little cap was green,
An' 'er name was Supi-yaw-lat—jes' the same as Theebaw's Queen,
An' I seed her first a-smokin' of a whackin' white cheroot,
An' a-wastin' Christian kisses on an 'eathen idol's foot;
    Bloomin' idol made o' mud—
    Wot they called the Great Gawd Budd—
    Plucky lot she cared for idols when I kissed 'er where she stud!
    On the road to Mandalay . . .

When the mist was on the rice-fields an' the sun was droppin' slow,
She'd git 'er little banjo an' she'd sing '*Kulla-lo-lo!*'
With 'er arm upon my shoulder an' 'er cheek agin my cheek
We useter watch the steamers an' the *hathis* pilin' teak.
    Elephints a-pilin' teak
    In the sludgy, squdgy creek,
    Where the silence 'ung that 'eavy you was 'arf afraid to speak!
    On the road to Mandalay . . .

But that's all shove be'ind me—long ago an' fur away,
An' there ain't no 'buses runnin' from the Bank to Mandalay;
An' I'm learnin' 'ere in London what the ten-year soldier tells:
'If you've 'eard the East a-callin', you won't never 'eed naught else.'
    No! you won't 'eed nothin' else
    But them spicy garlic smells,
    An' the sunshine an' the palm-trees an' the tinkly
        temple-bells;
    On the road to Mandalay . . .

I am sick o' wastin' leather on these gritty pavin'-stones,
An' the blasted English drizzle wakes the fever in my bones;
Tho' I walks with fifty 'ousemaids outer Chelsea to the Strand,
An' they talks a lot o' lovin', but wot do they understand?
    Beefy face an' grubby 'and—
    Law! wot do they understand?
    I've a neater, sweeter maiden in a cleaner, greener land!
    On the road to Mandalay . . .

Ship me somewheres east of Suez, where the best is like the worst,
Where there aren't no Ten Commandments an' a man can raise a
   thirst;

For the temple-bells are callin', an' it's there that I would be—
By the old Moulmein Pagoda, looking lazy at the sea;
      On the road to Mandalay,
      Where the old Flotilla lay,
      With our sick beneath the awnings when we went to
        Mandalay!
      On the road to Mandalay,
      Where the flyin'-fishes play,
      An' the dawn comes up like thunder outer China 'crost the
        Bay!

GEORGE ORWELL

1903–1950

216   *The Lesser Evil*

Empty as death and slow as pain
The days went by on leaden feet;
And parson's week had come again
As I walked down the little street.

Without, the weary doves were calling,
The sun burned on the banks of mud;
Within, old maids were caterwauling
A dismal tale of thorns and blood.

I thought of all the church bells ringing
In towns that Christian folks were in;
I heard the godly maidens singing;
I turned into the house of sin.

The house of sin was dark and mean,
With dying flowers round the doors;
They spat the betel juice between
The rotten bamboo of the floors.

Why did I come, the woman cried
So seldom to her bed of ease?
When I was not, her spirit died
And would I give her ten rupees.

The weeks went by, and many a day
That black-haired woman did implore
Me as I hurried on my way
To come more often than before.

The days went by like dead leaves falling,
And parson's week came round again.
Once more devout old maids were bawling
Their ugly rhymes of death and pain.

The woman waited for me there
As down the little street I trod;
And musing on her oily hair,
I turned into the house of God.

LOUIS MacNEICE
1907–1963

217   *Mahabalipuram*

All alone from his dark sanctum the lingam fronts, affronts the sea,
The world's dead weight of breakers against sapling, bull and candle
          Where worship comes no more,
Yet how should these cowherds and gods continue to dance in the rock
All the long night along ocean in this lost border between
That thronging gonging mirage of paddy and toddy and dung
          And this uninhabited shore?

Silent except for the squadrons of water, the dark grim chargers
     launched from Australia,
Dark except for their manes of phosphorus, silent in spite of the
     rockhewn windmill
          That brandishes axe and knife—
The many-handed virgin facing, abasing the Oaf, the Demon;
Dark in spite of the rockhewn radiance of Vishnu and Shiva and silent
In spite of the mooing of Krishna's herds; yet in spite of this darkness
     and silence
          Behold what a joy of life—

Which goes with an awe and a horror; the innocence which surmounted
     the guilt
Thirteen centuries back when an artist eyeing this litter of granite
          Saw it for waste and took

Mahabalipuram] the site (35 miles south of Madras) of a complex of Pallava (seventh-century
AD) temples and of the enormous bas-relief of 'Arjuna's Penance', a rock wall incised with one
thousand humans and animals   lingam] phallus, emblem of the god Shiva   the
rockhewn windmill / That brandishes axe and knife] Kali, the four-armed goddess of death and
destruction

A header below the rockface, found there already like a ballet of fishes
Passing, repassing each other, these shapes of gopi and goblin,
Of elephant, serpent and antelope, saw them and grasped his mallet
         And cried with a clear stroke: Look!

And now we look, we to whom mantra and mudra mean little,
And who find in this Hindu world a zone that is ultra-violet
         Balanced by an infra-red,
Austerity and orgy alike being phrased, it seems, in a strange dead
   language
But how that we look without trying to learn and only look in the act of
   leaping
After the sculptor into the rockface, now we can see, if not hear, those
   phrases
         To be neither strange nor dead.

Not strange for all their farouche iconography, not so strange as our
   own dreams
Because better ordered, these are the dreams we have needed
         Since we forgot how to dance;
This god asleep on the snake is the archetype of the sleep that we lost
When we were born, and these wingless figures that fly
Merely by bending the knee are the earnest of what we aspire to
         Apart from science and chance.

And the largest of all these reliefs, forty foot high by a hundred,
Is large in more senses than one, including both heaven and the animal
   kingdom
         And a grain of salt as well
For the saint stands always above on one leg fasting
Acquiring power while the smug hypocritical cat beneath him
Stands on his hindlegs too admired by the mice
         Whom the sculptor did not tell.

Nor did he tell the simple and beautiful rustics
Who saved from their doom by Krishna are once more busy and happy
         Absorbed in themselves and Him,
That trapped in this way in the rock their idyl would live to excite
And at once annul the lust and the envy of tourists
Taking them out of themselves and to find themselves in a world
         That has neither rift nor rim:

A monochrome world that has all the indulgence of colour,
A still world whose every harmonic is audible,
         Largesse of spirit and stone;

god asleep on the snake] Vishnu slept on a coiled snake between the cycles of creation

Created things for once and for all featured in full while for once and
    never
The creator who is destroyer stands at the last point of land
Featureless; in a dark cell, a phallus of granite, as abstract
        As the North Pole; as alone.

But the visitor must move on and the waves assault the temple,
Living granite against dead water, and time with its weathering action
        Make phrase and feature blurred;
Still from today we know what an avatar is, we have seen
God take shape and dwell among shapes, we have felt
Our ageing limbs respond to those ageless limbs in the rock
        Reliefs. Relief is the word.

ALUN LEWIS

1915–1944

218   *The Mahratta Ghats*

    The valleys crack and burn, the exhausted plains
    Sink their black teeth into the horny veins
    Straggling the hills' red thighs, the bleating goats
    —Dry bents and bitter thistles in their throats—
    Thread the loose rocks by immemorial tracks.
    Dark peasants drag the sun upon their backs.

    High on the ghat the new turned soil is red,
    The sun has ground it to the finest red,
    It lies like gold within each horny hand.
    Siva has spilt his seed upon this land.

    Will she who burns and withers on the plain
    Leave, ere too late, her scraggy herds of pain,
    The cow-dung fire and the trembling beasts,
    The little wicked gods, the grinning priests,
    And climb, before a thousand years have fled,
    High as the eagle to her mountain bed
    Whose soil is fine as flour and blood-red?

avatar] incarnation of a Hindu deity

218 Mahratta Ghats] the northern end (in Maharashtra, home of the Mahratta peoples) of
the mountain range known as the Western Ghats

But no! She cannot move. Each arid patch
Owns the lean folk who plough and scythe and thatch
Its grudging yield and scratch its stubborn stones.
The small gods suck the marrow from their bones.

Who is it climbs the summit of the road?
Only the beggar bumming his dark load.
Who was it cried to see the falling star?
Only the landless soldier lost in war.

And did a thousand years go by in vain?
And does another thousand start again?

KEVIN CROSSLEY-HOLLAND

1941–

219   *Postcards from Kodai*

Kodaikanal is a hill station in the Western Ghats. More than seven thousand feet
high, it was developed as a retreat by the English who frequented it during the
summer months when life became unbearably hot on the plains.

Here I am once more. Do you remember
the castanets of toads at dusk, thousands
of them? The veil, diaphanous, that drifts
over the glaze of the five-fingered lake?
This will bring it back if anything will.
Colonel Edgcumbe is here again and sends
regards—we two are the last survivors.

*

Have you ever stood higher than the clouds
and watched them smoking, lifting from valleys?
This is the eyrie of the Western Ghats.
From the verandah of this bungalow
I can survey the whole apparent world,
everything, my dear, trapped in place or time,
hazy or shining. Godlike, powerless!

*

Down at the Carlton the new head waiter
is called Joseph! Is that a requirement
for the post? They still fold all the napkins

in unexpected ways and trick them out
with wildflowers. A log fire in the grate
and, outside, the cool air close with pinesmoke,
the improving smell of eucalyptus
(only this would seem the least out of place
in an Alpine resort). Dear old Kodai!
There are changes here, but not as elsewhere.

*

You'd laugh, Emily. The Carlton Hotel—
I went there for tea with Colonel Edgcumbe—
still has the books we combed through as children:
Just Patty, True Tilda and *Bawbee Jock.*
Does that ring a bell or two? They're wrapped now
in parcel paper, and kept behind glass.
As if they were quite irreplaceable.

*

Big changes in the air at the golf club!
A 'high water rise tank and sump' have been
installed; they mean to replace all the browns
with greens. What was good enough for us . . .
But no, they must always go one better.
It all seems a dreadful waste of money.
Are these the highest golf links anywhere?
I asked the new secretary but he does
not know. Typical! Hope this card gets through!

*

Light is a generous discoverer.
Like God, it finds itself. The sleeping lake
wakes, stretches, slips into its newfound shape
as if all its life had been the darkness
of dream and illusion. A countenance
liquid, empty, impassive; one bird sings . . .

*

I can't quite explain it but I feel free
to ride my own tides: it is a certain
glory in all my thoughts and emotions,
the ego's representatives. They are
my coat of many colours on this earth.
The same force that fathers inhibition
and denial changes course within me:
here I can become the song of myself.

*

You'd think little or nothing of the sound
of rain falling on outstretched leaves, falling
from leaf to leaf. You hear it every day
almost. But this soft rainmusic, my dear,
always at my ear with how it will be,
how it was: this is really why I come
to this dreaming hill station. I suppose
it is the nearest I will get to home.

THE FAR EAST

JOHN LEYDEN
1775–1811

220   *Address to my Malay Krees*

Written while pursued
by a French privateer off Sumatra

Where is the arm I well could trust
    To urge the dagger in the fray?
Alas! how powerless now its thrust,
    Beneath Malay's burning day!

The sun has withered in their prime
    The nerves that once were strong as steel:
Alas! in danger's venturous time
    That I should live their loss to feel!

Yet still my trusty Krees prove true,
    If e'er thou serv'dst at need the brave,
And thou shalt wear a crimson hue,
    Or I shall win a watery grave.

Now let thine edge like lightning glow,
    And, second but thy master's will,
Malay ne'er struck a deadlier blow,
    Though practised in the art to kill.

220 Krees] dagger

O! by thy point! for every wound
   Where trace of Frankish blood hath been,
A golden circle shall surround
   Thy hilt of agate smooth and green.

My trusty Krees now play thy part,
   And second well thy master's will!
And I will wear thee next my heart,
   And many a life-blood owe thee still.

221   *Christmas in Penang*

   Dear Nona, Christmas comes from far
   To seek us near the eastern star,
   But wears not, in this orient clime,
   Her wintry wreaths and ancient thyme.—
   What flowerets must we strew to thee,
   For glossy bay or rosemary?

     Champaca flowers for thee we strew,
   To drink the merry Christmas dew:
   Though hailed in each Malayan grove
   The saffron-tinted flower of love,
   Its tulip-buds adorn the hair
   Of none more loved amid the fair.

     Banana leaves their ample screen
   Shall spread, to match the holly green.
   Well may their glossy softness please,
   Sweet emblem of the soul at ease,
   The heart expanding frank and free,
   Like the still-green Banana tree.

     Nona, may all the woodland powers
   That stud Malaya's clime with flowers,
   Or on the breeze their fragrance fling,
   Around thee form an angel ring,
   To guard thee ever gay and free,
   Beneath thy green Banana tree!

FRANCIS HASTINGS DOYLE
1810—1888

222 *The Private of the Buffs; or, the British Soldier in China*

Last night, among his fellow roughs,
    He jested, quaffed, and swore;
A drunken private of the Buffs,
    Who never looked before.
Today, beneath the foeman's frown,
    He stands in Elgin's place,
Ambassador from Britain's crown,
    And type of all her race.

Poor, reckless, rude, low-born, untaught,
    Bewildered, and alone,
A heart, with English instinct fraught,
    He yet can call his own.
Ay, tear his body limb from limb,
    Bring cord, or axe, or flame,
He only knows that not through him
    Shall England come to shame.

Far Kentish hop-fields round him seemed,
    Like dreams, to come and go;
Bright leagues of cherry-blossom gleamed,
    One sheet of living snow;
The smoke above his father's door
    In grey soft eddyings hung;
Must he then watch it rise no more,
    Doomed by himself, so young?

Yes, honor calls!—with strength like steel
    He put the vision by;
Let dusky Indians whine and kneel,
    An English lad must die.
And thus, with eyes that would not shrink,
    With knee to man unbent,
Unfaltering on its dreadful brink,
    To his red grave he went.

Buffs] the Royal East Kent Regiment, the 3rd Foot

Vain, mightiest fleets of iron framed,
   Vain, those all-shattering guns,
Unless proud England keep, untamed,
   The strong heart of her sons;
So let his name through Europe ring,—
   A man of mean estate,
Who died, as firm as Sparta's king,
   Because his soul was great.

SIR EDWIN ARNOLD
1832–1904

223   *The Musmee*

The Musmee has brown-velvet eyes,
   Curtained with satin, sleepily;
You wonder if those lids would rise
   The newest, strangest sight to see!
Yet, when she chatters, laughs, or plays
   Koto, or lute, or samisen—
No jewel gleams with brighter rays
   Than flash from those dark lashes then.

The Musmee has a small brown face—
   Musk-melon seed its perfect shape—
Arched, jetty eyebrows; nose to grace
   The rosy mouth beneath; a nape,
And neck, and chin; and smooth soft cheeks,
   Carved out of sun-burned ivory;
With teeth which, when she smiles or speaks,
   Pearl merchants might come leagues to see!

The Musmee's hair could teach the night
   How to grow dark, the raven's wing
How to seem ebon; grand the sight
   When in rich masses towering.
She builds each high black-marble coil,
   And binds the gold and scarlet in,
And thrusts, triumphant, through the toil
   The *Kanzâshi*, her jewelled pin.

223 Musmee] an unmarried Japanese girl

The Musmee has small, faultless feet,
  With snow-white tabi trimly decked,
Which patter down the city street
  In short steps, slow and circumspect;
A velvet string between her toes
  Holds to its place the unwilling shoe,
Pretty and pigeon-like she goes,
  And on her head a hood of blue.

The Musmee wears a wondrous dress—
  Kimôno, obi, imogi—
A rose-bush in spring-loveliness
  Is not more color-glad to see!
Her girdle holds her silver pipe,
  And heavy swing her long silk sleeves
With cakes, love-letters, *mikans* ripe,
  Small change, musk-box, and writing leaves.

The Musmee's heart is slow to grief
  And quick to pleasure, love, and song;
The Musmee's pocket-handkerchief,
  A square of paper! All day long
Gentle, and sweet, and debonair
  Is—rich or poor—this Asian lass,
Heaven have her in its tender care!
  O medeto gozarimas!

RUDYARD KIPLING
1865–1936

224   *Buddha at Kamakura*

'And there is a Japanese idol at Kamakura'

O ye who tread the Narrow Way
By Tophet-flare to Judgment Day,
Be gentle when 'the heathen' pray
  To Buddha at Kamakura!

mikans] mandarin oranges   *O medeto gozarimas!*] May it be prosperous with you!

224 Kamakura] town just south of Yokohama on Honshu

To him the Way, the Law, apart,
Whom Maya held beneath her heart,
Ananda's Lord, the Bodhisat,
   The Buddha of Kamakura.

For though he neither burns nor sees,
Nor hears ye thank your Deities,
Ye have not sinned with such as these,
   His children at Kamakura,

Yet spare us still the Western joke
When joss-sticks turn to scented smoke
The little sins of little folk
   That worship at Kamakura—

The grey-robed, gay-sashed butterflies
That flit beneath the Master's eyes.
He is beyond the Mysteries
   But loves them at Kamakura.

And whoso will, from Pride released,
Contemning neither creed nor priest,
May feel the Soul of all the East
   About him at Kamakura.

Yea, every tale Ananda heard,
Of birth as fish or beast or bird,
While yet in lives the Master stirred,
   The warm wind brings Kamakura.

Till drowsy eyelids seem to see
A-flower 'neath her golden *htee*
The Shwe-Dagon flare easterly
   From Burmah to Kamakura,

And down the loaded air there comes
The thunder of Thibetan drums,
And droned—'*Om mane padme hums*'—
   A world's-width from Kamakura.

htee] dome   Shwe-Dagon] pagoda in Rangoon which is the centre of Buddhist worship
in Burma   *Om mane padme hums*] mystic Buddhist invocation: 'Om, the jewel, is in the
lotus: amen'. The last word is spelt *hum*, but Kipling was pluralizing it

Yet Brahmans rule Benares still,
Buddh-Gaya's ruins pit the hill,
And beef-fed zealots threaten ill
    To Buddha and Kamakura.

A tourist-show, a legend told,
A rusting bulk of bronze and gold,
So much, and scarce so much, ye hold
    The meaning of Kamakura?

But when the morning prayer is prayed,
Think, ere ye pass to strife and trade,
Is God in human image made
    No nearer than Kamakura?

OSMAN EDWARDS
fl. 1894–1912

225   from *Residential Rhymes*

(i) *The Merchant at Yokohama*

Air: 'When I first put this uniform on' (Sullivan)

When I first came to live in Japan,
    My duty was simple and plain:
To dazzle the nation with civilization
    Implying more money than brain;
In a mansion as big as the Bluff
I had servants and horses enough,
While the native possessions
Outside the concessions
    Appeared to me very poor stuff.
I shall live on a different plan,
When I mix with authentic Japan.

(*Refrain*)
You may have guessed
That East and West
    Have a difficult gulf to span;
We shall cross on a golden bridge,
    When we mix with the Real Japan.

(ii) *The Missionary at Karnizawa*

Air: 'From Greenland's icy mountains' (Heber)

When summer strikes Tsukiji
    With rays, which turn to gold
That glory of Meiji,
    Our complex Christian fold,
To colder heights and calmer
    Each missionary flies;
He loves Asama-yama
    For nearer heaven it lies.

Should residential mixture
    Make men more kind and true,
This philanthropic fixture
    Will certainly ensue:—
Each year the sheep will hasten
    Where mountain-breezes blow,
While shepherds' voices chasten
    Deserted Tokyo.

(iii) *The Minister at Chiuzenji*

Air: 'The policeman's lot is not a happy one' (Sullivan)

When the tourists cease from calling, and the heat is,
                and the heat is,
What none but a mosquito can support,
                can support,
When the minister is sick of signing treaties,
                signing treaties,
Or snubbing an audacious treaty-port,
                (treaty-port,)
He loves to read *Kojiki* or the *Guenji*,
                (or the *Guenji*,)
And prays in Japanese to Tō-shō-gū,
                (Tō-shō-gū,)

Karnizawa] principal town in the Prefecture of Tshikawa in north-west Honshu   Tsukiji] part of Tokyo and site of the Tsukiji Honganji Temple (in Edwards's time the original 1680 building)   Meiji] the current (1868–1912) Emperor   Asama-yama] volcano in central Honshu   Chiuzenji] now Chuzenji, beautiful lake in Tochigi Prefecture, near Nikko; favourite summer resort for rich Japanese, foreign diplomats, etc. *Kojiki*] history (largely mythological) of Japan written in AD 712, usually translated as *Chronicles of Ancient Matters*; the earliest complete work in Japanese extant   *Guenji*] *The Tale of Genji*, by Lady Murasaki Shikibu (?978–?1026), is the earliest of all novels and the greatest work of literature in Japanese

And wishes by the waters of Chiuzenji,
                                        (of Chiuzenji,)
That both Moses and Confucius were true,
                                        (true—)

(*Refrain*)

He will never leave the country any more,
                                        (any more,)

Japonicis jam japonicior.

(iv) *The Professor in Nirvana*

Air: 'In old Madrid'

I draw the breath of Old Japan,
New vistas fade and modern voices cease;
    My soul on wings cerulean
Attains to perfect wisdom, perfect peace.
In vain the self-deluded students prate
    In accents loud of Western lore;
In vain of commerce and of rights debate;
    Forgetting what they learned of yore.
Let them spurn an alien creed,
    Shun the European fold,
Unless, of course, they chance to need
    Mere, perishable gold.

(*Refrain*)

Far above see Shaka shining,
    Fugen dreaming,
    Monju gleaming,
Jizo, on his staff reclining:
Brother-gods, they wait for me!

EDMUND BLUNDEN
1896–1974

226   *The Cottage at Chigasaki*

That well you drew from is the coldest drink
In all the country Fuji looks upon;
And me, I never come to it but I think
The poet lived here once who one hot noon

---

225 *Japonicis jam japonicior*] 'more Catholic than the Pope!'   Shaka] Buddha
Fugen, Monju, Jizo] Buddhist gods

Came dry and eager, and with wonder saw
The morning-glory about the bucket twined,
Then with a holy heart went out to draw
His gallon where he might;[1] the poem's signed
By him and Nature. We need not retire,
But freely dip, and wash away the salt
And sand we've carried from the sea's blue fire;
Discuss a melon; and without great fault,
Though comfort is not poetry's best friend,
We'll write a poem too, and sleep at the end.

WILLIAM EMPSON
1906–1984

227   *China*

The dragon hatched a cockatrice
    Cheese crumbles and not many mites repair
There is a Nature about this
    The spring and rawness tantalise the air

Most proud of being most at ease
    The sea is the most solid ground
Where comfort is on hands and knees
    The nations perch about around

Red hills bleed naked into screes—
    The classics are a single school
—The few large trees are holy trees
    They teach the nations how to rule

They will not teach the Japanese—
    They rule by music and by rites
—They are as like them as two peas
    All nations are untidy sights

The serious music strains to squeeze—
    The angel coolies sing like us
—Duties, and literature, and fees
    To lift an under-roaded bus[2]

---

[1] 'Perhaps the most familiar Japanese poem is that which says, approximately, "The morning-glory has taken hold of the well-bucket; I'll borrow some water elsewhere"' (E.B.).

[2] '. . . when the road gives way under [the bus] and you spend hours digging in the mud and spreading branches' (W.E.).

The paddy fields are wings of bees[1]
　　The great Wall as a dragon crawls
To one who flies or one who sees
　　The twisted contour of their walls

A liver fluke of sheep agrees
　　Most rightly proud of her complacencies
With snail so well they make one piece
　　Most wrecked and longest of all histories.

WILFRED NOYCE

1917–1962

228 　　　　　*Breathless*

(Written at 21,000 ft. on 23 May 1953)

Heart aches,
lungs pant
dry air
sorry, scant.
Legs lift—
why at all?
Loose drift,
heavy fall.
Prod the snow
easiest way;
a flat step
is holiday.
Look up,
far stone
many miles
far, alone.
Grind breath
once more then on;
don't look up
till journey's done.
Must look up,
glasses dim.
Wrench of hand,
faltering limb

---

[1] 'The paddy fields in hill country, arranged of course to make level patches to hold water, are extremely beautiful, look like microscopic photographs of bees' wings...' (W.E.).

Pause one step,
breath swings back;
swallow once,
throat gone slack.
Go on
to far stone;
don't look up,
count steps done.
One step,
one heart-beat,
stone no nearer
dragging feet.
Heart aches,
lungs pant
dry air
sorry, scant.

D. J. ENRIGHT

1920–

229   *Dreaming in the Shanghai Restaurant*

I would like to be that elderly Chinese gentleman.
He wears a gold watch with a gold bracelet,
But a shirt without sleeves or tie.
He has good luck moles on his face, but is not disfigured with fortune.
His wife resembles him, but is still a handsome woman,
She has never bound her feet or her belly.
Some of the party are his children, it seems,
And some his grandchildren;
No generation appears to intimidate another.
He is interested in people, without wanting to convert them or pervert
   them.
He eats with gusto, but not with lust;
And he drinks, but is not drunk.
He is content with his age, which has always suited him.
When he discusses a dish with the pretty waitress,
It is the dish he discusses, not the waitress.
The table-cloth is not so clean as to show indifference,
Not so dirty as to signify a lack of manners.
He proposes to pay the bill but knows he will not be allowed to.
He walks to the door like a man who doesn't fret about being
   respected, since he is;

A daughter or granddaughter opens the door for him,
And he thanks her.
It has been a satisfying evening. Tomorrow
Will be a satisfying morning. In between he will sleep satisfactorily.
I guess that for him it is peace in his time.
It would be agreeable to be this Chinese gentleman.

JAMES KIRKUP

1923–

230   *Sumo Wrestlers*

If looks could kill,
These two hunks
Of sullen meat would long ago
Have eyed each other dead.

Bestowing on the fan-flocked air
Brief cascades of salt,
They stump slowly,
With studied boredom,
Into the ring of sand,
Huge flesh slopping,
Rumps and hams pocked and scarred
In black breechclouts.

Adjusting their bland bellies,
They arrange dainty hands
On the ground before them,
Crouch like grumpy toads.
But something tells them this
Is not the moment to engage.

They stretch up,
Tall in lacquered topknots,
And give each other long looks.
Contempt? No.
Intimidation? Perhaps.

Slowly lumber away
And leisurely return,
Spraying parabolas of tired salt
To purify the ring,
Propitiate the gods.

Crouched again, calm thighs
Spread, clash
Suddenly together
Push slap shove hook grunt heave
Buttressed against each other

Bare backsides cruppered
Black-belted bellies uddering
Paws groping for a girth-hold
Brute buttocks and bellies grappled
In shuddering embrace.

Till one is toppled,
Flopped like an avalanche,
Ten tons of rice-balls tumbling
Into a pleased ringside geisha's lap.

JAMES FENTON
1949–

231   *Dead Soldiers*

When His Excellency Prince Norodom Chantaraingsey
Invited me to lunch on the battlefield
I was glad of my white suit for the first time that day.
They lived well, the mad Norodoms, they had style.
The brandy and the soda arrived in crates.
Bricks of ice, tied around with raffia,
Dripped from the orderlies' handlebars.

And I remember the dazzling tablecloth
As the APCs fanned out along the road,
The dishes piled high with frogs' legs,
Pregnant turtles, their eggs boiled in the carapace,
Marsh irises in fish sauce
And inflorescence of a banana salad.

On every bottle, Napoleon Bonaparte
Pleaded for the authenticity of the spirit.
They called the empties Dead Soldiers
And rejoiced to see them pile up at our feet.

Each diner was attended by one of the other ranks
Whirling a table-napkin to keep off the flies.
It was like eating between rows of morris dancers—
Only they didn't kick.

On my left sat the prince;
On my right, his drunken aide.
The frogs' thighs leapt into the sad purple face
Like fish to the sound of a Chinese flute.
I wanted to talk to the prince. I wish now
I had collared his aide, who was Saloth Sar's brother.
We treated him as the club bore. He was always
Boasting of his connections, boasting with a head-shake
Or by pronouncing of some doubtful phrase.
And well might he boast. Saloth Sar, for instance,
Was Pol Pot's real name. The APCs
Fired into the sugar palms but met no resistance.

In a diary, I refer to Pol Pot's brother as the Jockey Cap.
A few weeks later, I find him 'in good form
And very skeptical about Chantaraingsey.'
'But one eats well there,' I remark.
'So one should,' says the Jockey Cap:
'The tiger always eats well,
It eats the raw flesh of the deer,
And Chantaraingsey was born in the year of the tiger.
So, did they show you the things they do
With the young refugee girls?'

And he tells me how he will one day give me the gen.
He will tell me how the prince financed the casino
And how the casino brought Lon Nol to power.
He will tell me this.
He will tell me all these things.
All I must do is drink and listen.

In those days, I thought that when the game was up
The prince would be far, far away—
In a limestone faubourg, on the promenade at Nice,
Reduced in circumstances but well enough provided for.
In Paris, he would hardly require his private army.
The Jockey Cap might suffice for café warfare,
And matchboxes for APCs.

But we were always wrong in these predictions.
It was a family war. Whatever happened,
The principals were obliged to attend its issue.

A few were cajoled into leaving, a few were expelled,
And there were villains enough, but none of them
Slipped away with the swag.

For the prince was fighting Sihanouk, his nephew,
And the Jockey Cap was ranged against his brother
Of whom I remember nothing more
Than an obscure reputation for virtue.
I have been told that the prince is still fighting
Somewhere in the Cardamoms or the Elephant Mountains.
But I doubt that the Jockey Cap would have survived his good
    connections.
I think the lunches would have done for him—
Either the lunches or the dead soldiers.

OCEANIA

ERASMUS DARWIN

1731–1802

232 *Visit of Hope to Sydney Cove, near Botany Bay*

Where Sydney Cove her lucid bosom swells,
And with wide arms the indignant storm repels;
High on a rock amid the troubled air
Hope stood sublime, and waved her golden hair;
Calmed with her rosy smile the tossing deep,
And with sweet accents charmed the winds to sleep;
To each wild plain she stretched her snowy hand,
High-waving wood, and sea-encircled strand.
'Hear me,' she cried, 'ye rising realms! record
Time's opening scenes, and Truth's prophetic word.
There shall broad streets their stately walls extend,
The circus widen, and the crescent bend;
There, rayed from cities o'er the cultured land,
Shall bright canals, and solid roads expand.
There the proud arch, colossus-like, bestride
Yon glittering streams, and bound the chasing tide;
Embellished villas crown the landscape-scene,
Farms wave with gold, and orchards blush between.
There shall tall spires, and dome-capped towers ascend,
And piers and quays their massy structures blend;
While with each breeze approaching vessels glide,
And northern treasures dance on every tide!'
Then ceased the nymph—tumultuous echoes roar,
And Joy's loud voice was heard from shore to shore—
Her graceful steps descending pressed the plain,
And Peace, and Art, and Labour, joined her train.

THOMAS PERRY

fl. 1772–1775

233   *The Antarctic Muse*

It is now my brave boys we are clear of the sea
And keep a good heart if you'll take my advice
We are out of the cold my brave boys do not fear
For the Cape of Good Hope with good hearts we do steer

Thank God we have ranged the globe all around
And we have likewise the South Continent found
But it being too late in the year as they say
We could stay there no longer the land to survey

So we leave it alone for we give a good reason
For the next ship that comes to survey in right season
The great fields of ice among them we were bothered
We were forced to alter our course to the northward

So we have done our utmost as any men born
To discover a land so far south of Cape Horn
So now my brave boys we no longer will stay
For we leave it alone for the next ship to survey

It was when we got into the cold frosty air
We was obliged our mittens and Magdalen caps to wear
We are out of the cold my brave boys and perhaps
We will pull off our mittens and Magdalen caps

We are hearty and well and of good constitution
And have ranged the globe round in the brave *Resolution*
Brave Captain Cook he was our commander
Has conducted the ship from all eminent danger

We were all hearty seamen no cold did we fear
And we have from all sickness entirely kept clear
Thanks be to the captain he has proved so good
Amongst all the islands to give us fresh food

And when to old England my brave boys we arrive
We will tip off a bottle to make us alive
We will toast Captain Cook with a loud song all round
Because that he has the South Continent found

Blessed be to his wife and his family too
God prosper them all and well for to do
Blessed be unto them so long as they shall live
And that is the wish to them I do give.

ANONYMOUS

late 18th–early 19th century

234   *Van Dieman's Land*

Come all you gallant poachers, that ramble free from care,
That walk out on moonlight nights, with your dog, gun and snare,
The jolly hares and pheasants, you have at your command,
Not thinking that your last career is to Van Dieman's Land.

Poor Tom Brown from Nottingham, Jack Williams and poor Joe,
We are three daring poachers, the country does well know,
At night we are trepanned, by the keepers hid in sand,
Who for fourteen years transported us unto Van Dieman's Land.

The first day that we landed upon this fatal shore,
The planters they came round us, full twenty score or more,
They ranked us up like horses, and sold us out of hand,
And yoked us up to ploughs, my boys, to plough Van Dieman's Land.

Our cottages that we live in, are built of brick and clay,
And rotten straw for bedding, and we dare not say nay,
Out cots are fenced with fire, we slumber when we can,
To drive away wolves and tigers upon Van Dieman's Land.

It's often when in slumber I have a pleasant dream,
With my sweet girl a-sitting down, all by a purling stream,
Through England I've been roaming, with her at command,
Now I awake broken hearted upon Van Dieman's Land.

God bless our wives and families, likewise that happy shore,
That isle of great contentment, which we shall see no more,
As for our wretched females, see them, we seldom can,
There's twenty, to one woman, upon Van Dieman's land.

234 Van Dieman's Land] Tasmania, discovered by Tasman in 1642, was first named after
Anton van Diemen, governor of the Dutch East Indies 1636–45   tigers] probably tiger-
cats, which are native to Tasmania

There was a girl from Birmingham, Susan Summers was her name,
For fourteen years transported, we all well know the same,
Our planter bought her freedom, and married her out of hand,
She gave to us good usage upon Van Dieman's Land.

So all you gallant poachers, give ear unto my song,
It is a bit of good advice, although it is not long,
Throw by your dogs and snares, for to you I speak plain,
For if you knew our hardships, you would never poach again.

ANONYMOUS

mid 19th century

235

The warlike of the Isles,
   The men of field and waves,
Are not the rocks their funeral piles,
   The sea and shore their graves?

Go, stranger, track the deep,
   Free, free, the white sail spread;
Wave may not foam nor wild wind sweep
   Where rest not British dead.

ALFRED DOMETT

1811–1887

236

from *Ranolf and Amohia*

It was a wondrous realm beguiled
Our youth amid its charms to roam;
O'er scenes more fair, serenely wild,
Not often summer's glory smiled;
When flecks of cloud, transparent, bright,
No alabaster half so white—
Hung lightly in a luminous dome
Of sapphire—seemed to float and sleep
Far in the front of its blue steep;
And almost awful, none the less
For its liquescent loveliness,

Behind them sunk—just o'er the hill
The deep abyss, profound and still—
The so immediate Infinite;
That yet emerged, the same, it seemed
In hue divine and melting balm
In many a lake whose crystal calm
Uncrisped, unwrinkled, scarcely gleamed;
Where sky above and lake below
Would like one sphere of azure show,
Save for the circling belt alone,
The softly-painted purple zone
Of mountains—bathed where nearer seen
In sunny tints of sober green,
With velvet dark of woods between,
All glossy glooms and shifting sheen;
While here and there, some peak of snow
Would o'er their tenderer violet lean.

And yet within this region, fair
With wealth of waving woods—these glades
And glens and lustre-smitten shades,
Where trees of tropic beauty rare
With graceful spread and ample swell
Uprose—and that strange asphodel
On tufts of stiff green bayonet-blades,
Great bunches of white bloom upbore,
Like blocks of seawashed madrepore,
That steeped the noon in fragrance wide,
Till by the exceeding sweet opprest
The stately tree-fern leaned aside
For languor, with its starry crown
Of radiating fretted fans,
And proudly-springing beauteous crest
Of shoots all brown with glistening down,
Curved like the lyre-bird's tail half-spread,
Or necks opposed of wrangling swans,
Red bill to bill—black breast to breast—
Aye! in this realm of seeming rest,
What sights you met and sounds of dread!
Calcareous caldrons, deep and large
With geysers hissing to their marge;
Sulphureous fumes that spout and blow;
Columns and cones of boiling snow;
And sable lazy-bubbling pools
Of sputtering mud that never cools; .
With jets of steam through narrow vents

Uproaring, maddening to the sky,
Like cannon-mouths that shoot on high
In unremitting loud discharge
Their inexhaustible contents;
While oft beneath the trembling ground
Rumbles a drear persistent sound
Like ponderous engines infinite, working
At some tremendous task below!—
Such are the signs and symptoms—lurking
Or launching forth in dread display—
Of hidden fires, internal strife,
Amid that leafy, lush array
Of rank luxuriant verdurous life:
Glad haunts above where blissful love
Might revel, rove, enraptured dwell;
But through them pierce such tokens fierce
Of rage beneath and frenzies fell;
As if, to quench and stifle it,
Green Paradise were flung o'er Hell—
Flung fresh with all her bowers close-knit,
Her dewy vales and dimpled streams;
Yet could not so its fury quell
But that the old red realm accurst
Would still recalcitrate, rebel,
Still struggle upward and outburst
In scalding fumes, sulphureous steams.
It struck you as you paused to trace
The sunny scenery's strange extremes,
As if in some divinest face,
All heavenly smiles, angelic grace,
Your eye at times discerned, despite
Sweet looks with innocence elate,
Some wan wild spasm of blank affright,
Or demon scowl of pent-up hate;
Or some convulsive writhe confest,
For all that bloom of beauty bright,
An anguish not to be represt.
You look—a moment bask in, bless,
Its laughing light of happiness;
But look again—what startling throes
And fiery pangs of fierce distress
The lovely lineaments disclose—
How o'er the fascinating features flit
The genuine passions of the nether pit!

ROBERT LOUIS STEVENSON
1850–1894

237   *To an Island Princess*

Since long ago, a child at home,
I read and longed to rise and roam,
Where'er I went, whate'er I willed,
One promised land my fancy filled.
Hence the long roads my home I made;
Tossed much in ships; have often laid
Below the uncurtained sky my head,
Rain-deluged and wind-buffeted:
And many a thousand hills I crossed
And corners turned—Love's labour lost,
Till, Lady, to your isle of sun
I came, not hoping; and, like one
Snatched out of blindness, rubbed my eyes,
And hailed my promised land with cries.

Yes, Lady, here I was at last;
Here found I all I had forecast:
The long roll of the sapphire sea
That keeps the land's virginity;
The stalwart giants of the wood
Laden with toys and flowers and food;
The precious forest pouring out
To compass the whole town about;
The town itself with streets of lawn,
Loved of the moon, blessed by the dawn,
Where the brown children all the day
Keep up a ceaseless noise of play,
Play in the sun, play in the rain,
Nor ever quarrel or complain;—
And late at night, in the woods of fruit,
Hark! do you hear the passing flute?

I threw one look to either hand,
And knew I was in Fairyland.
And yet one point of being so
I lacked. For, Lady (as you know),
Whoever by his might of hand,
Won entrance into Fairyland,
Found always with admiring eyes
A Fairy princess kind and wise.

It was not long I waited; soon
Upon my threshold, in broad noon,
Gracious and helpful, wise and good,
The Fairy Princess Moë stood.

238   *Tropic Rain*

As the single pang of the blow, when the metal is mingled well,
Rings and lives and resounds in all the bounds of the bell,
So the thunder above spoke with a single tongue,
So in the heart of the mountain the sound of it rumbled and clung.

Sudden the thunder was drowned—quenched was the levin light—
And the angel-spirit of rain laughed out loud in the night.
Loud as the maddened river raves in the cloven glen,
Angel of rain! you laughed and leaped on the roofs of men;

And the sleepers sprang in their beds, and joyed and feared as you fell.
You struck, and my cabin quailed; the roof of it roared like a bell.
You spoke, and at once the mountain shouted and shook with brooks.
You ceased, and the day returned, rosy, with virgin looks.

And methought that beauty and terror are only one, not two;
And the world has room for love, and death, and thunder, and dew;
And all the sinews of hell slumber in summer air;
And the face of God is a rock, but the face of the rock is fair.
Beneficent streams of tears flow at the finger of pain;
And out of the cloud that smites, beneficent rivers of rain.

D. H. LAWRENCE
1885–1930

239   *Kangaroo*

In the northern hemisphere
Life seems to leap at the air, or skim under the wind
Like stags on rocky ground, or pawing horses, or springy scut-tailed
    rabbits.

Or else rush horizontal to charge at the sky's horizon,
Like bulls or bisons or wild pigs.

Or slip like water slippery towards its ends,
As foxes, stoats, and wolves, and prairie dogs.

Only mice, and moles, and rats, and badgers, and beavers, and perhaps
    bears
Seem belly-plumbed to the earth's mid-navel.
Or frogs that when they leap come flop, and flop to the centre of the
    earth.

But the yellow antipodal Kangaroo, when she sits up,
Who can unseat her, like a liquid drop that is heavy, and just touches
    earth.

The downward drip
The down-urge.
So much denser than cold-blooded frogs.

Delicate mother Kangaroo
Sitting up there rabbit-wise, but huge, plump-weighted,
And lifting her beautiful slender face, oh! so much more gently and
    finely lined than a rabbit's, or than a hare's,
Lifting her face to nibble at a round white peppermint drop which she
    loves, sensitive mother Kangaroo.

Her sensitive, long, pure-bred face.
Her full antipodal eyes, so dark,
So big and quiet and remote, having watched so many empty dawns in
    silent Australia.

Her little loose hands, and drooping Victorian shoulders.
And then her great weight below the waist, her vast pale belly
With a thin young yellow little paw hanging out, and straggle of a long
    thin ear, like ribbon,
Like a funny trimming to the middle of her belly, thin little dangle of
    an immature paw, and one thin ear.

Her belly, her big haunches
And, in addition, the great muscular python-stretch of her tail.

There, she shan't have any more peppermint drops.
So she wistfully, sensitively sniffs the air, and then turns, goes off in
    slow sad leaps

On the long flat skis of her legs,
Steered and propelled by that steel-strong snake of a tail.
Stops again, half turns, inquisitive to look back.

While something stirs quickly in her belly, and a lean little face comes
    out, as from a window,
Peaked and a bit dismayed,
Only to disappear again quickly away from the sight of the world, to
    snuggle down in the warmth,
Leaving the trail of a different paw hanging out.

Still she watches with eternal, cocked wistfulness!
How full her eyes are, like the full, fathomless, shining eyes of an
    Australian black-boy
Who has been lost so many centuries on the margins of existence!
She watches with insatiable wistfulness.
Untold centuries of watching for something to come,
For a new signal from life, in that silent lost land of the South.

Where nothing bites but insects and snakes and the sun, small life.
Where no bull roared, no cow ever lowed, no stag cried, no leopard
    screeched, no lion coughed, no dog barked,
But all was silent save for parrots occasionally, in the haunted blue
    bush.

Wistfully watching, with wonderful liquid eyes.
And all her weight, all her blood, dripping sack-wise down towards the
    earth's centre,
And the live little-one taking in its paw at the door of her belly.

Leap then, and come down on the line that draws to the earth's deep,
    heavy centre.

RUPERT BROOKE
1887–1915

240   *Waikiki*

Warm perfumes like a breath from wine and tree
    Drift down the darkness. Plangent, hidden from eyes,
    Somewhere an *eukaleli* thrills and cries
And stabs with pain the night's brown savagery;
And dark scents whisper; and dim waves creep to me,
    Gleam like a woman's hair, stretch out, and rise;
    And new stars burn into the ancient skies,
Over the murmurous soft Hawaian sea.

And I recall, lose, grasp, forget again,
     And still remember, a tale I have heard, or known,
An empty tale, of idleness and pain,
     Of two that loved—or did not love—and one
Whose perplexed heart did evil, foolishly,
A long while since, and by some other sea.

WYNFORD VAUGHAN-THOMAS
1908–

241   *Farewell to New Zealand*

Super-suburbia of the Southern Seas,
Nature's—and Reason's—true Antipodes,
Hail, dauntless pioneers, intrepid souls,
Who cleared the Bush—to make a lawn for bowls,
And smashed the noble Maori to ensure
The second-rate were socially secure!
Saved by the Wowsers from the Devil's Tricks,
Your shops, your pubs, your minds all close at six.
Your battle-cry's a deep, contented snore,
You voted Labour, then you worked no more.
The Wharfies' Heaven, the gourmet's Purgat'ry:
Ice-cream on mutton, swilled around in tea!

A Maori fisherman, the legends say,
Dredged up New Zealand in a single day.
I've seen the catch, and here's my parting crack—
It's under-sized; for God's sake throw it back!

CHARLES CAUSLEY
1917–

242   *H.M.S. Glory at Sydney*
August 1945

Now it seems an old forgotten fable:
The snow-goose descending on the still lagoon,
The trees of summer flowering ice and fire
And the sun coming up on the Blue Mountains.

241 Wowsers] do-gooders   Devil's Tricks] the demon drink, etc.   Wharfies]
dock-workers

But I remember, I remember Sydney,
Our bows scissoring the green cloth of the sea,
Prefaced by plunging dolphins we approached her:
The land of the kookaburra and the eucalyptus tree.

The harbour bridge, suddenly sketched by Whistler,
Appeared gently on a horizon of smudges and pearls,
And the sun came up behind us
With a banging of drums from the Solomons.

O! I shall never forget you on that crystal morning!
Your immense harbour, your smother of deep green trees,
The skyscrapers, waterfront-shacks, parks and radio-towers,
And the tiny pilot-boat, the *Captain Cook*,
Steaming to meet us:
Our gallery deck fringed with the pale curious faces of sailors
Off the morning watch.

O like maidens preparing for the court ball
We pressed our number-one suits,
Borrowing electric irons and starching prim white collars,
And stepped forth into the golden light
With Australian pound-notes in our pockets.

O there is no music
Like the music of the Royal Marine bugler
Sounding off *Liberty Men*.
And there is no thrill
Like stepping ashore in a new country
With a clean shirt and with pound-notes in your pocket.

O Sydney, how can I celebrate you
Sitting here in Cornwall like an old maid
With a bookful of notes and old letters?

I remember the circular bar in Castlereagh Street
And the crowds of friendly Aussies with accents like tin-openers,
Fighting for schooners of onion-beer.
I remember Janie, magnificent, with red hair,
Dressed in black, with violets on her reliable bosom,
Remembering a hundred names and handling the beer engines
With the grace and skill of ten boxers.

O Janie, have the races at Melbourne seen you this year?
And do matelots, blushing, still bring you flowers?
Across three continents: across monsoon, desert, jungle, city,
Across flights of rare birds in burning Africa,

Across crowds of murderous pilgrims struggling grimly to Mecca,
Across silver assaults of flying-fish in the Arabian Sea,
I salute you and your city.

I remember the deep canyons of streets, the great shafts of sunlight
Striking on fruitshop, flowershop, tram and bookstall,
The disappearing cry of the Underground Railway,
The films: *Alexander Nevsky* and *Salome*,
The plays: *Macbeth* and *Noah* in North Sydney,
And travelling there, across the fantastic bridge,
Our ship, the *Glory*, a lighted beetle,
A brilliant sarcophagus far below
On the waterfront at Woolloomoolloo.

O yes, I remember Woolloomoolloo,
The slums with wrought-iron balconies
Upon which one expected to find, asleep in a deckchair,
Asleep in the golden sun, fat, grotesque and belching:
Captain Cook.

The Chinese laundries, the yellow children in plum-coloured brocade,
The way they fried the eggs, the oysters and champagne.
I remember Daphne and Lily, and the black-market gin
And crawling back to the docks as the dawn
Cracked on my head.

O the museum with the gigantic, terrifying kangaroo,
Who lived, as huge as a fairy story,
Only ten thousand years ago.

O the sheepskin coats, the woollen ties,
And our wanderings in David Jones' store
Among the rubble of silk stockings and tins of fruit-salad.
The books I bought at Angus & Robertson's bookshop,
Sir Osbert Sitwell, and Q (to remind me of home).

I remember the ships and ferries at Circular Quay,
And the tram ride to Botany Bay,
So magnificently like the postage stamp
I bought as a child.
I remember the enormous jail at La Perouse,
The warders on the walls with their rifles.
I remember the Zoo at Taronga Park,
The basking shark I gazed down at in terror,
And the shoes I wore out walking, walking.

And so I celebrate this southern city
To which I shall never return.
I celebrate her fondly, as an old lover,
And I celebrate the names and faces of my companions:

George Swayne, Ron Brunt, Joney,
Tug Wilson, Jan Love, Reg Gilmore,
Pony Moore, Derby Kelly, Mac,

Where are they now?

Now it seems an old forgotten fable:
The snow-goose descending on the still lagoon,
The trees of summer flowering ice and fire
And the sun coming up on the Blue Mountains.

ALAN ROSS

1922–

243   *Koala*

for Victoria

How should I describe you—eternal
Image of the cuddly bear, solace
Of your button-nosed familiars of every race,
Who on cold nights or those long cheerless
Afternoons, when to be small
Is to be misunderstood, clasp your toy belly and kiss
Injustice away—whom to possess most surely is to miss.

Drawing your iron-bark claws along my wrist
You narrow two rheumy eyes where indifference
Has laid a deposit of pink mist—
Your hold on life so delicate,
That to lessen those twin and absorbing opiates
You live on—ladles of sleep and of eucalypt,
Storehouses of bored over-intelligence

Into which you continually dip—would be to remove
For ever the Empire's one pure Existentialist.
Fatalist, addict, catalyst
Of early but enduring emotions, you lay like a glove

A clenched fist over mine, twitching a tar
Nose as if it was snuff not gum leaves you sniff—
Crybaby, as passive as a teddy, you simply *are*.

And restoring you to that high fork
In the tree where the juiciest morsels bunch
I watch you pluck with the tiniest tremble a stalk,
Thrusting the gum sap home with a crunch
Like the breaking of celery, passenger to oblivion—
Perfervid muncher, whom tomorrow I shall come upon
Sun-doped and happy, a gnawed twig in your paw like a pen.

FLEUR ADCOCK

1934–

244   *Instead of an Interview*

The hills, I told them; and water, and the clear air
(not yielding to more journalistic probings);
and a river or two, I could say, and certain bays
and ah, those various and incredible hills . . .

And all my family still in the one city
within walking distances of each other
through streets I could follow blind. My school was gone
and half my Thorndon smashed for the motorway
but every corner revealed familiar settings
for the dreams I'd not bothered to remember—
ingrained; ingrown; incestuous: like the country.

And another city offering me a lover
and quite enough friends to be going on with;
bookshops; galleries; gardens; fish in the sea;
lemons and passionfruit growing free as the bush.
Then the bush itself; and the wild grand south;
and wooden houses in occasional special towns.

And not a town or a city I could live in.
Home, as I explained to a weeping niece,
home is London; and England, Ireland, Europe.
I have come home with a suitcase full of stones—
of shells and pebbles, pottery, pieces of bark:
here they lie around the floor of my study
as I telephone a cable 'Safely home'

and moments later, thinking of my dears,
wish the over-resonant word cancelled:
'Arrived safely' would have been clear enough,
neutral, kinder. But another loaded word
creeps up now to interrogate me.
By going back to look, after thirteen years,
have I made myself for the first time an exile?

HUGO WILLIAMS

1941–

245   *Aborigine*

He is only beautiful
In the manner of his country,
For he was burnt by the same enemy,
Was at the same treaty.

And now he lives on a concession
Which shifts with each season,
That he must follow it
As a jackal follows his lion,

Licking at gnawed bones
Till he himself is one,
Hollow and dry as an old tree,
Full of strange, delicate energy.

For he can walk a whole month
Into the desert in the dreamtime,
Can scent water on wind
And make rabbits jump into his hand.

He can hit a snake with a stone,
Birds with a boomerang;
Can play a long, sad note
And paint stories on bark,
Beautiful in the manner of his country.

THE AMERICAS

SOUTH AMERICA AND THE CARIBBEAN

JOSEPH WARTON
1722–1800

246   *The Revenge of America*

When fierce Pizarro's legions flew
O'er ravaged fields of rich Peru,
Struck with his bleeding people's woes,
Old India's awful Genius rose.
He sat on Andes' topmost stone,
And heard a thousand nations groan;
For grief his feathery crown he tore,
To see huge Plata foam with gore;
He broke his arrows, stamped the ground,
To view his cities smoking round.
　'What woes,' he cried, 'hath lust of gold
O'er my poor country widely rolled;
Plunderers proceed! my bowels tear,
But ye shall meet destruction there;
From the deep-vaulted mine shall rise
Th' insatiate fiend, pale Avarice!
Whose steps shall trembling Justice fly,
Peace, Order, Law, and Amity!
I see all Europe's children cursed
With lucre's universal thirst:
The rage that sweeps my sons away,
My baneful gold shall well repay.'

Pizarro] Francisco Pizarro (*c.*1471–1541), discoverer and conqueror of Peru

EDWARD THOMPSON
?1739–1786

247   *The Indian Maid*

Demararie, 27 October 1781

The Indian maid who lightly trips,
   The Dryad of the Guava grove,
The zone of Venus round her hips,
   And graced with youth, and blessed in love!
Gold rings adorn her nose and arms,
And leaves of beads veil naked charms.

Or if she quits the golden wood,
   Pierced by the scorching solar beam,
She plunges in the cooler flood,
   And swims the Naiad of the stream:
Adores the god in ev'ry air,
And smiles the maid without a care.

Or if more distant creeks invite
   To fish, to fowl, or seek her love,
She paddles the canoe upright,
   Where Christian maids would fear to move;
On some fair tree her hammock swings,
Nor envies she the beds of kings.

Like other belles of other shores,
   She daubs her limbs, her face, her hair:
Raucoo and launa stop the pores
   Against mosquitoes and the air.
But these, I trust, nor spoil her skin,
They're to defend—not lure to sin.

A beauteous bronze she stands confessed,
   Venus nor Hebe more complete;
With various feathers tricked and dressed,
   Perfumed with Tonkay flow'rs most sweet!
And when she moves, her mien and grace
Prove her the goddess of the place!

Raucoo and launa] red paint and black paint used by the Indians   Tonkay] the Tonkay
tree bears a sweet flower which smells like newly cut hay

MATTHEW GREGORY LEWIS
1775–1818

248   What triumph moves on the billows so blue?
In his car of pellucid pearl I view,
With glorious pomp, on the dancing tide,
The tropic Genius proudly ride.

The flying fish, who trail his car,
Dazzle the eye, as they shine from afar;
Twinkling their fins in the sun, and show
All the hues which adorn the showery bow.

Of dark sea-blue is the mantle he wears;
For a sceptre a plantain branch he bears;
Pearls his sable arms surround,
And his locks of wool with coral are crowned.

Perpetual sunbeams round him stream;
His bronzed limbs shine with golden gleam;
The spicy spray from his wheels that showers,
Makes the sense ache with its odorous powers.

Myriads of monsters, who people the caves
Of ocean, attendant plough the waves;
Sharks and crocodiles bask in his blaze,
And whales spout the waters which dance in his rays.

And as onward floats that triumph gay,
The light sea-breezes around it play;
While at his royal feet lie bound
The Ouragans, hushed in sleep profound.

Dark Genius, hear a stranger's prayer,
Nor suffer those winds to ravage and tear
Jamaica's savannas, and loose to fly,
Mingling the earth, and the sea, and the sky.

From thy locks on my harvest of sweets diffuse,
To swell my canes, refreshing dews;
And kindly breathe, with cooling powers,
Through my coffee walks and shaddock bowers.

Ouragans] hurricanes

Let not thy strange diseases prey
On my life; but scare from my couch away
The yellow Plague's imps; and safe let me rest
From that dread black demon, who racks the breast:

Nor force my throbbing temples to know
Thy sunbeam's sudden and maddening blow;
Nor bid thy day-flood blaze too bright
On nerves so fragile, and brain so light:

And let me, returning in safety, view
Thy triumph again on the ocean blue;
And in Britain I'll oft with flowers entwine
The Tropic Sovereign's ebony shrine!

Was it but fancy? did He not frown,
And in anger shake his coral crown?
Gorgeous and slow the pomp moves on!
Low sinks the sun—and all is gone!

D. H. LAWRENCE

1885–1930

249   *Mountain Lion*

Climbing through the January snow, into the Lobo canyon
Dark grow the spruce-trees, blue is the balsam, water sounds still
     unfrozen, and the trail is still evident.

Men!
Two men!
Men! the only animal in the world to fear!

They hesitate.
We hesitate.
They have a gun.
We have no gun.

Then we all advance, to meet.

Two Mexicans, strangers, emerging out of the dark and snow and
     inwardness of the Lobo valley.
What are you doing here on this vanishing trail?

What is he carrying?
Something yellow.
A deer?

Qué tiene, amigo?
León—

He smiles, foolishly, as if he were caught doing wrong.
And we smile, foolishly, as if we didn't know.
He is quite gentle and dark-faced.

It is a mountain lion,
A long, long slim cat, yellow like a lioness.
Dead.
He trapped her this morning, he says, smiling foolishly.

Lift up her face,
Her round, bright face, bright as frost.
Her round, fine-fashioned head, with two dead ears;
And stripes in the brilliant frost of her face, sharp, fine dark rays,
Dark, keen, fine eyes in the brilliant frost of her face.
Beautiful dead eyes.

Hermoso es!

They go out towards the open;
We go on into the gloom of Lobo.
And above the trees I found her lair,
A hole in the blood-orange brilliant rocks that stick up, a little cave.
And bones, and twigs, and a perilous ascent.

So, she will never leap up that way again, with the yellow flash of a
    mountain lion's long shoot!
And her bright striped frost-face will never watch any more, out of the
    shadow of the cave in the blood-orange rock,
Above the trees of the Lobo dark valley-mouth!

Instead, I look out.
And out to the dim of the desert, like a dream, never real;

To the snow of the Sangre de Cristo mountains, the ice of the
    mountains of Picoris,
And near across at the opposite steep of snow, green trees motionless
    standing in snow, like a Christmas toy.

And I think in this empty world there was room for me and a mountain
    lion.

Hermoso es!] It is beautiful!

And I think in the world beyond, how easily we might spare a million
      or two of humans
And never miss them.
Yet what a gap in the world, the missing white frost-face of that slim
      yellow mountain lion!

A. S. J. TESSIMOND

1902–1962

250   *Jamaican Bus Ride*

The live fowl squatting on the grapefruit and bananas
in the basket of the copper-coloured lady
is gloomy but resigned.
The four very large baskets on the floor
are in everybody's way,
as the conductor points out
loudly, often, but in vain.

Two quadroon dandies are disputing
who is standing on whose feet.

When we stop,
a boy vanishes through the door marked ENTRANCE;
but those entering through the door marked EXIT
are greatly hindered by the fact that when we started
there were twenty standing,
and another ten have somehow inserted themselves
into invisible crannies
between dark sweating body and body.

With an odour of petrol
both excessive and alarming
we hurtle hell-for-leather
between crimson bougainvillea blossom
and scarlet poinsettia
and miraculously do not run over
three goats, seven hens and a donkey
as we pray
that the driver has not fortified himself
at Daisy's Drinking Saloon
with more than four rums:
or by the gods of Jamaica
this day is our last!

LAWRENCE DURRELL

1912–

251

Green Coconuts: Rio

At insular café tables under awnings
Bemused benighted half-castes pause
To stretch upon a table yawning
Ten yellow claws and
Order green coconuts to drink with straws.

Milk of the green loaf-coconuts
Which soon before them amputated stand,
Broken, you think, from some great tree of breasts,
Or the green skulls of savages trepanned.

Lips that are curved to taste this albumen,
To dredge with some blue spoon among the curds
Which drying on tongue or on moustache are tasteless
As droppings of bats or birds.

Re-enacting here a theory out of Darwin
They cup their yellow mandibles to shape
Their nuts, tilt them in drinking poses,
To drain them slowly from the very nape:
Green coconuts, green
Coconuts, patrimony of the ape.

ALUN LEWIS

1915–1944

252

Port of Call: Brazil

We watch the heavy-odoured beast
Of darkness crouch along the water-front
Under the town exorcised by the priest.
The light entice the paramours to hunt.

Tropical thunder creams the glassy bay,
White sails on bamboo masts disturb the night,
The troopship turns and drags upon her stay,
The portholes cast a soft, subjective light.

And we who crowd in hundreds to the side
Feel the lights prick us with a grey distaste
As though we had some guilty thing to hide—
We, who thought the negroes were debased

This morning when they scrambled on the quay
For what we threw, and from their dugout boats
Haggled cigars and melons raucously
Lifting their bleating faces like old goats.

But now the white-faced tourist must translate
His old unsated longing to adventure
Beyond the European's measured hate
Into the dangerous oceans of past and future

Where trembling intimations will reveal
The illusion of this blue mulatto sleep
And in that chaos like a migrant eel
Will breed a new direction through the deep.

TONY HARRISON

1937–

253   from *Sentences*

Brazil

Even the lone man
in his wattle lean-to,
the half-mad women
in their hive of leaves,
pitched at the roadside
by a low shared fire
so near the shoulder
that their tethered goat
crops only half-circles
of tough, scorched turf,
and occasional tremors
shake ash from the charcoal,
live for something more
than the manioc and curds

they're preparing,
barely attentive to speech
as they strain
through the oppressive mid-day drowse,
or, at night, through the noise
of the insects drilling into them
the lessons of loneliness
or failed pioneering
over miles of savannah,
for the punctual Bahia–Rio
coaches as they come
to the village of Milagres
they are outcasts from
for a quick *cafezinho*,
a quick piss,
edible necklaces
and caged red birds.

NORTH AMERICA

WILLIAM STRACHEY
fl. 1609–1618

254   *Aecclesiae et Reipub.*

Wild as they are, accept them, so were we:
To make them civil, will our honour be:
And if good works be the effects of minds,
Which like good angels be, let our designs,
As we are Angli, make us angels[1] too:
No better work can state- or church-man do.

---

[1] Cf. Bede, *A History of the English Church and People*, II. i.

---

253 Bahia–Rio] a distance of about 750 miles

ROBERT HAYMAN
?1579–?1631

255   from *Quodlibets*

(i) *The four elements in Newfound-land.*
To the worshipful Captain John Mason, who did wisely and
worthily govern there divers years

The air in Newfound-land is wholesome, good;
The fire, as sweet as any made of wood;
The waters, very rich, both salt and fresh;
The earth more rich, you know it is no less.
Where all are good, fire, water, earth, and air,
What man made of these four would not live there?

(ii) *To all those worthy women, who have any desire to live in*
Newfound-land, specially to the modest and discreet
gentlewoman Mistress Mason, wife to
Captain Mason, who lived there divers years

Sweet creatures, did you truly understand
The pleasant life you'd live in Newfound-land,
You would with tears desire to be brought thither.
I wish you, when you go, fair wind, fair weather:
For if you with the passage can dispense,
When you are there, I know you'll ne'er come thence.

(iii) *To my very loving and discreet friend,*
Master Peter Miller of Bristol

You asked me once, what here was our chief dish:
In winter, fowl; in summer, choice of fish.
But we should need good stomachs, you may think,
To eat such kind of things which with you stink,
As ravens, crows, kites, otters, foxes, bears,
Dogs, cats, and soiles, eaglets, hawks, hounds,[1] and hares.
Yet we have partridges, and store of deer,
And that (I think) with you is pretty cheer.

---

[1] 'Dogs and Cats are fishes so call'd, and Hounds a kind of Fowle' (R.H.).

---

soiles] seals

Yet let me tell you, sir, what I love best:
It's a poor-John[1] that's clean and neatly dressed;
There's not a meat found in the land, or seas,
Can stomachs better please, or less displease.
It is a fish of profit, and of pleasure,
I'll write more of it, when I have more leisure.
These and much more are here the ancient store;
Since we came hither, we have added more.

(iv) *To a worthy friend who often objects the coldness of the*
winter in Newfound-land, and may serve for all those
that have the like conceit

You say that you would live in Newfound-land,
Did not this one thing your conceit withstand:
You fear the winter's cold, sharp, piercing air.
They love it best that have once wintered there.
Winter is there short, wholesome, constant, clear,
Not thick, unwholesome, shuffling, as 'tis here.

ANDREW MARVELL
1621–1678

256   *Bermudas*

Where the remote Bermudas ride
In the ocean's bosom unespied,
From a small boat that rowed along
The listening winds received this song.
   'What should we do but sing His praise
That led us through the watery maze
Where He the huge sea-monsters wracks,[2]
That lift the deep upon their backs,
Unto an isle so long unknown,
And yet far kinder than our own?
He lands us on a grassy stage,
Safe from the storms, and prelate's rage:

---

[1] 'Cald in French *Poure Gens*, in English corruptly *Poore John*, being the principall Fish
brought out of this Countrie' (R.H.).
[2] A reference to the 'dreadful fight' between the Bermudans and two stranded whales in
Edmund Waller's *The Battle of the Summer Islands* (as Bermuda was called after the shipwreck
there of Sir George Somers in 1609).

He gave us this eternal spring
Which here enamels everything,
And sends the fowls to us in care
On daily visits through the air.
He hangs in shades the orange bright
Like golden lamps in a green night,
And does in the pomegranates close
Jewels more rich than Ormus shows:
He makes the figs our mouths to meet,
And throws the melons at our feet;
But apples plants of such a price,
No tree could ever bear them twice.
With cedars chosen by His hand
From Lebanon He stores the land;
And makes the hollow seas that roar
Proclaim the ambergris on shore.
He cast (of which we rather boast)
The Gospel's pearl upon our coast;
And in these rocks for us did frame
A temple where to sound His name.
O let our voice His praise exalt
Till it arrive at Heaven's vault,
Which then perhaps rebounding may
Echo beyond the Mexique bay!'
—Thus sung they in the English boat
A holy and a cheerful note:
And all the way, to guide their chime,
With falling oars they kept the time.

GEORGE BERKELEY

1685–1753

257   *Verses on the Prospect of Planting Arts and*
Learning in America

The Muse, disgusted at an age and clime,
    Barren of every glorious theme,
In distant lands now waits a better time,
    Producing subjects worthy fame:

256 Ormus] pearl- and jewel-trading town of Hormuz in the Persian Gulf   apples]
pineapples   Mexique Bay] Gulf of Mexico

In happy climes, where from the genial sun
   And virgin earth such scenes ensue,
The force of art by nature seems outdone,
   And fancied beauties by the true:

In happy climes the seat of innocence,
   Where nature guides and virtue rules,
Where men shall not impose for truth and sense,
   The pedantry of courts and schools:

There shall be sung another golden age,
   The rise of empire and of arts,
The good and great inspiring epic rage,
   The wisest heads and noblest hearts.

Not such as Europe breeds in her decay;
   Such as she bred when fresh and young,
When heav'nly flame did animate her clay,
   By future poets shall be sung.

Westward the course of empire takes its way;
   The four first acts already past,
A fifth shall close the drama with the day;
   Time's noblest offspring is the last.

THOMAS MORRIS

1732–?1806

258   Ease is the pray'r of him who, in a whaleboat
           Crossing Lake Champlain, by a storm's o'ertaken;
           Not struck his blanket, not a friendly island
                      Near to receive him.

           Ease is the wish too of the sly Canadian;
           Ease the delight of bloody Caghnawagas;
           Ease, Richard, ease, not to be bought with wampum,
                      Nor paper money.

   258 blanket] the soldier's blanket used as a sail

Not colonel's pay, nor yet a dapper sergeant,
Orderly waiting with recovered halberd,
Can chase the crowd of troubles still surrounding
        Laced regimentals.

That sub lives best who, with a sash in tatters
Worn by his grandsire at the fight of Blenheim,
To fear a stranger, and to wild ambition,
        Snores on a bearskin.

Why like fine-fellows are we ever scheming,
We short-lived mortals? Why so fond of climates
Warmed by new suns? O who, that runs from home, can
        Run from himself too?

Care climbs radeaux with four-and-twenty pounders,
Not quits our light troops, or our Indian warriors,
Swifter than moose-deer, or the fleeter east wind,
        Pushing the clouds on.

He, whose good humour can enjoy the present,
Scorns to look forward; with a smile of patience
Temp'ring the bitter. Bliss uninterrupted
        None can inherit.

Death instantaneous hurried off Achilles;
Age far-extended wore away Tithonus:
Who will live longer, thou or I, Montgom'ry
        Dicky or Tommy?

Thee twenty messmates, full of noise and laughter,
Cheer with their sallies; thee the merry damsels
Please with their titt'ring; whilst thou sitt'st adorned with
        Boots, sash and gorget.

Me to Fort Hendrick, midst a savage nation,
Dull Connajohry, cruel fate has driven.
O think on Morris, in a lonely chamber,
        Dabbling in Sapphic.

sub] subaltern   radeaux] floating batteries, used on Lake Champlain

THOMAS MOORE
1779–1852

259   *Song of the Evil Spirit of the Woods*

Now the vapour hot and damp,
Shed by day's expiring lamp,
Through the misty ether spreads
Every ill the white man dreads;
Fiery fever's thirsty thrill,
Fitful ague's shivering chill!
Hark! I hear the traveller's song,
As he winds the woods along!
Christian! 'tis the song of fear;
Wolves are round thee, night is near,
And the wild, thou dar'st to roam—
Oh! 'twas once the Indian's home![1]
Hither, sprites, who love to harm,
Wheresoe'er you work your charm,
By the creeks, or by the brakes,
Where the pale witch feeds her snakes,
And the cayman loves to creep,
Torpid, to his wintry sleep:
Where the bird of carrion flits,
And the shuddering murderer sits,
Lone beneath a roof of blood,
While upon his poisoned food,
From the corpse of him he slew
Drops the chill and gory dew!

Hither bend you, turn you hither
Eyes that blast and wings that wither!
Cross the wandering Christian's way,
Lead him, ere the glimpse of day,
Many a mile of mad'ning error
Through the maze of night and terror,
Till the morn behold him lying
O'er the damp earth, pale and dying!
Mock him, when his eager sight
Seeks the cordial cottage-light;

[1] The Five Confederated Nations (of Indians) were settled along the banks of the Susquehanna and the adjacent country until 1779, when General Sullivan drove them out.

cayman] alligator

Gleam then, like the lightning-bug,
Tempt him to the den that's dug
For the foul and famished brood
Of the she-wolf, gaunt for blood!
Or, unto the dangerous pass
O'er the deep and dark morass,
Where the trembling Indian brings
Belts of porcelain, pipes, and rings,
Tributes, to be hung in air,
To the Fiend presiding there!
Then, when night's long labour past,
Wildered, faint, he falls at last,
Sinking where the causeway's edge
Moulders in the slimy sedge,
There let every noxious thing
Trail its filth and fix its sting;
Let the bull-toad taint him over,
Round him let musquitoes hover,
In his ears and eye-balls tingling,
With his blood their poison mingling,
Till, beneath the solar fires,
Rankling all, the wretch expires!

WILLIAM McGONAGALL
1825/1830–1902

260   *Jottings of New York*
               A Descriptive Poem

Oh mighty City of New York! you are wonderful to behold,
Your buildings are magnificent, the truth be it told,
They were the only thing that seemed to arrest my eye,
Because many of them are thirteen storeys high.

And as for Central Park, it is lovely to be seen,
Especially in the summer season when its shrubberies and trees are
    green;
And the Burns' statue is there to be seen,
Surrounded by trees, on the beautiful sward so green;
Also, Shakespeare and Sir Walter Scott,
Which by Englishmen and Scotchmen will ne'er be forgot.

There the people on the Sabbath-day in thousands resort,
All loud in conversation and searching for sport,
Some of them viewing the menagerie of wild beasts there,
And also beautiful black swans, I do declare.

And there's beautiful boats to be seen there,
And the joyous shouts of the children do rend the air,
While the boats sail along with them o'er Lohengrin Lake,
And the fare is five cents for children and adults ten is all they take.

And there's also summer-house shades and merry-go-rounds,
And with the merry laughter of the children the Park resounds
During the livelong Sabbath-day,
Enjoying the merry-go-round play.

Then there's the elevated railroads, about five storeys high,
Which the inhabitants can see and hear night and day passing by,
Oh! such a mass of people daily do throng,
No less than five hundred thousand daily pass along,
And all along the City you can get for five cents,
And, believe me, among the passengers there are few discontent.

And the tops of the houses are all flat,
And in the warm weather the people gather to chat,
Besides on the house-tops they dry their clothes,
And also many people all night on the house-tops repose.

And numerous ships and steamboats are there to be seen
Sailing along the East River Water so green;
'Tis certainly a most beautiful sight
To see them sailing o'er the smooth water day and night.

And Brooklyn Bridge is a very great height,
And fills the stranger's heart with wonder at first sight,
But with all its loftiness, I venture to say,
For beauty it cannot surpass the new Railway Bridge of the Silvery
    Tay.

And there's also ten thousand rumsellers there,
Oh! wonderful to think, I do declare!
To accommodate the people of that city therein,
And to encourage them to commit all sorts of sin.

And on the Sabbath-day, ye will see many a man
Going for beer with a tin can,
And seems proud to be seen carrying home the beer
To treat his neighbours and family dear.

Then at night numbers of the people dance and sing,
Making the walls of their houses to ring
With their songs and dancing on Sabbath night,
Which I witnessed with disgust, and fled from the sight.

And with regard to New York and the sights I did see,
One street in Dundee is more worth to me,
And, believe me, the morning I sailed from New York
For Bonnie Dundee, my heart it felt as light as a cork.

SAMUEL BUTLER

1835–1902

261   *A Psalm of Montreal*

Stowed away in a Montreal lumber room,
The Discobolus standeth, and turneth his face to the wall;
Dusty, cobweb-covered, maimed, and set at naught,
Beauty crieth in an attic, and no man regardeth.
                              O God! O Montreal!

Beautiful by night and day, beautiful in summer and winter,
Whole or maimed, always and alike beautiful—
He preacheth gospel of grace to the skins of owls,
And to one who seasoneth the skins of Canadian owls.
                              O God! O Montreal!

When I saw him, I was wroth, and I said, 'O Discobolus!
Beautiful Discobolus, a Prince both among Gods and men,
What doest thou here, how camest thou here, Discobolus,
Preaching gospel in vain to the skins of owls?'
                              O God! O Montreal!

And I turned to the man of skins, and said unto him, 'O thou man of
    skins,
Wherefore hast thou done thus, to shame the beauty of the
    Discobolus?'
But the Lord had hardened the heart of the man of skins,
And he answered, 'My brother-in-law is haberdasher to Mr Spurgeon.'
                              O God! O Montreal!

'The Discobolus is put here because he is vulgar,—
He has neither vest nor pants with which to cover his limbs;
I, Sir, am a person of most respectable connections,—
My brother-in-law is haberdasher to Mr Spurgeon.'
　　　　　　　　　　　　　　　　　O God! O Montreal!

Then I said, 'O brother-in-law to Mr Spurgeon's haberdasher,
Who seasonest also the skins of Canadian owls,
Who callest "trousers" "pants", whereas I call them "trousers",
Therefore thou art in hell-fire, and may the Lord pity thee!'
　　　　　　　　　　　　　　　　　O God! O Montreal!

'Preferrest thou the gospel of Montreal to the gospel of Hellas,
The gospel of thy connection with Mr Spurgeon's haberdashery to the
　　gospel of the Discobolus?'
Yet none the less blasphemed he beauty, saying 'The Discobolus hath
　　no gospel,—
But my brother-in-law is haberdasher to Mr Spurgeon.'
　　　　　　　　　　　　　　　　　O God! O Montreal!

J. K. STEPHEN
1859–1892

262　　　　　　from *England and America*

On a Rhine Steamer

Republic of the West,
　　Enlightened, free, sublime,
Unquestionably best
　　Production of our time.

The telephone is thine,
　　And thine the Pullman Car,
The caucus, the divine
　　Intense electric star.

To thee we likewise owe
　　The venerable names
Of Edgar Allan Poe,
　　And Mr Henry James.

In short it's due to thee,
    Thou kind of Western star,
That we have come to be
    Precisely what we are.

But every now and then,
    It cannot be denied,
You breed a kind of men
    Who are not dignified,

Or courteous or refined,
    Benevolent or wise,
Or gifted with a mind
    Beyond the common size,

Or notable for tact,
    Agreeable to me,
Or anything, in fact,
    That people ought to be.

RUDYARD KIPLING
1865–1936

263   *Philadelphia*

If you're off to Philadelphia in the morning,
    You mustn't take my stories for a guide.
There's little left, indeed, of the city you will read of,
    And all the folk I write about have died.

Now few will understand if you mention Talleyrand,
    Or remember what his cunning and his skill did;
And the cabmen at the wharf do not know Count Zinzendorf,
    Nor the Church in Philadelphia he builded.

It is gone, gone, gone with lost Atlantis,
    (Never say I didn't give you warning).
In Seventeen Ninety-three 'twas there for all to see,
    But it's not in Philadelphia this morning.

---

263 Talleyrand] Charles Maurice de Talleyrand-Périgord (1754–1838), French statesman,
spent two years in exile in Philadelphia (1794–6)

If you're off to Philadelphia in the morning,
  You mustn't go by anything I've said.
Bob Bicknell's Southern Stages have been laid aside for ages,
  But the Limited will take you there instead.
Toby Hirte can't be seen at One Hundred and Eighteen
  North Second Street—no matter when you call;
And I fear you'll search in vain for the wash-house down the lane
  Where Pharaoh played the fiddle at the ball.

        It is gone, gone, gone with Thebes the Golden,
          (Never say I didn't give you warning).
        In Seventeen Ninety-four 'twas a famous dancing floor—
          But it's not in Philadelphia this morning.

If you're off to Philadelphia in the morning,
  You must telegraph for rooms at some Hotel.
You needn't try your luck at Epply's or 'The Buck',
  Though the Father of his Country liked them well.
It is not the slightest use to inquire for Adam Goos,
  Or to ask where Pastor Meder has removed—so
You must treat as out of date the story I relate
  Of the Church in Philadelphia he loved so.

        He is gone, gone, gone with Martin Luther
          (Never say I didn't give you warning).
        In Seventeen Ninety-five he was (rest his soul!) alive,
          But he's not in Philadelphia this morning.

If you're off to Philadelphia this morning,
  And wish to prove the truth of what I say,
I pledge my word you'll find the pleasant land behind
  Unaltered since Red Jacket rode that way.
Still the pine-woods scent the noon; still the catbird sings his tune;
  Still autumn sets the maple-forest blazing;
Still the grape-vine through the dusk flings her soul-compelling musk;
  Still the fire-flies in the corn make night amazing!

        They are there, there, there with Earth immortal
          (Citizens, I give you friendly warning).
        The things that truly last when men and times have passed,
          They are all in Pennsylvania this morning!

EDWIN MUIR
1887–1959

264   *Salem, Massachusetts*

They walked black Bible streets and piously tilled
The burning fields of the new Apocalypse.
With texts and guns they drove the Indians out,
Ruled young and old with stiff Hebraic rod,
The Puritan English country gentlemen;
And burned young witches.

                       Their sons' grandsons
Throve on Leviathan and the China trade
And built and lived in beautiful wooden houses,
Their Jordan past.

                   You may see the Witches' Trail
Still winding through the streets to a little knoll
That looks across a tideless inland bay
In the clear New England weather. This they saw,
The women, till the fire and smoke consumed
Sight, breath and body while the Elders watched
That all was well and truly consumed by fire.
The House with the Seven Gables is gone, consumed by fire,
And in the evenings businessmen from Boston
Sit in the beautiful houses, mobbed by cars.

LAWRENCE DURRELL
1912–

265   *Owed to America*

I

America   America
I see your giant image stir
O land of milk and bunny
Where the blue Algonquin flows
Where the scrapers scrape the ceiling
With that dizzy topless feeling
And everything that simply *has* to, goes!

II

Land of Doubleday and Dutton
Huge club sandwiches of mutton
More zip-fastener than button
Where the blue Algonquin flows
Home of musical and mayhem
Robert Frost and Billy Graham
Where you drain their brains but pay 'em
Then with dry Martinis slay 'em
Everyone that drinks 'em knows.

III

America   America
Terra un peu hysterica
For me as yet incognita
I see your giant image stir
Here no waffle lacks for honey
Avenues paved with easy money
Land of helpless idealism
Clerical evangelism
Land of prune and sometimes prism
Every kind of crazy ism
Where the blue Algonquin flows.

IV

America   America
So full of esoterica
One day I'll pierce the veils that hide
The spirit of the great divide
The sweet ambition which devours
You, super duper power of powers—
But for the nonce I send you flowers.

V

If there was a cake you'd take it
If I had one heart you'd break it
Where the blue Algonquin flows
Looking forward, looking back
There seems nothing that you lack
America   America
Pray accept this cordial greeting
On a visit far too fleeting
Rest assured I'll soon be back.

JOHN WAIN
1925–

266   *Brooklyn Heights*

This is the gay cliff of the nineteenth century,
Drenched in the hopeful ozone of a new day.

Erect and brown, like retired sea-captains,
The houses gaze vigorously at the ocean.

With the hospitable eyes of retired captains
They preside over the meeting of sea and river.

On Sunday mornings the citizens revisit their beginnings.
Whole families walk in the fresh air of the past.

Their children tricycle down the nineteenth century:
America comes smiling towards them like a neighbour.

While the past on three wheels unrolls beneath them,
They hammer in the blazing forge of the future.

Brooklyn Bridge flies through the air on feathers.
The children do not know the weight of its girders.

It is the citizens carry the bridge on their shoulders:
Its overhead lights crackle in their blood-vessels.

But now it is Sunday morning, and a sky swept clean.
The citizens put down the bridge and stroll at ease.

They jingle the hopeful change in their pockets.
They forget the tripping dance of the profit motive.

The big ships glide in under the high statue,
The towers cluster like spear-grass on the famous island.

And the citizens dream themselves back in a sparkle of morning.
They ride with their children under a sky swept clean.

Dream on, citizens! Dream the true America, the healer,
Drawing the hot blood from throbbing Europe!

Dream the dark-eyed immigrants from the narrow cities:
Dream the iron steamers loaded with prayers and bundles:

Breathe the ozone older than the name of commerce:
Be the citizens of the true survival!

THOM GUNN

1929–

267   *Lights Among Redwood*

Of Muir Woods

And the streams here, ledge to ledge,
take care of light. Only to
the pale green ribs of young ferns
tangling above the creek's edge
it may sometimes escape, though
in quick diffusing patterns.

Elsewhere it has become tone,
pure and rarified; at most
a muted dimness coloured
with moss-green, charred grey, leaf-brown.
Calm shadow! Then we at last
remember to look upward:

constant, to laws of size and
age the thick forms hold, though gashed
through with Indian fires. At once
tone is forgotten: we stand
and stare—mindless, diminished—
at their rosy immanence.

268   *Iron Landscapes*
          (and the Statue of Liberty)

No trellisses, no vines
                    a fire escape
Repeats a bare black Z from tier to tier.
Hard flower, tin scroll embellish this landscape.
Between iron columns I walk toward the pier.

268 the pier] Barrow Street Pier, New York

And stand a long time at the end of it
Gazing at iron on the New Jersey side.
A girdered ferry-building opposite,
Displaying the name LACKAWANNA, seems to ride

The turbulent brown-grey waters that intervene:
Cool seething incompletion that I love.
The zigzags come and go, sheen tracking sheen;
And water wrestles with the air above.

But I'm at peace with the iron landscape too,
Hard because buildings must be hard to last
—Block, cylinder, cube, built with their angles true,
A dream of righteous permanence, from the past.

In Nixon's era, decades after the ferry,
The copper embodiment of the pieties
Seems hard, but hard like a revolutionary
With indignation, constant as she is.

From here you can glimpse her downstream, her far charm,
Liberty, tiny woman in the mist
—You cannot see the torch—raising her arm
Lorn, bold, as if saluting with her fist.

TED WALKER

1934–

269   *The Emigrés*

Visiting from Britain, I take my ease
In a Massachusetts yard. Willows
Have opened overnight along the ridge;
This is the second spring I've seen this year.

I watch as my once-English hostess
Moves across the shadow of the spruces
At her door. She calls her home a cottage
And puts on homeliness like a sweater.

She's tried, over and over, to grow grass
Around the place; grass, and a few roses,
And even, look, a bit of privet hedge
To remind her of home in Warwickshire.

She brings me bourbon in an ice-packed glass
And tinkles on about the neighbours' houses.
Americanisms glint like a badge
Pinned onto her. She much prefers life here,

She protests, remembering what life was
For her in England—the dirt, rising prices,
Always having to live at the edge
Of her nerves. Not to mention the weather.

I stir my drink. 'I'd not mind it either,
For a while,' I say. Martins lodge,
Like my swallows at home, in crevices
Of her roof. 'Oh, purple martins, those

Damn things. I'll have to rake them down from there,'
She says. 'Mind you, it's not that I begrudge
Them somewhere to live. But if you saw the mess
They make, you wouldn't think me heartless.'

Now, in his office near a fall-out shelter
High over downtown Boston, husband Reg
Will be turning his calendar (English Views
In Summertime) into May. The two of us,

Last evening, swept the last of the winter
Cones into a heap. Outside his garage
Afterwards, he told me, watching the flames,
Of all his new, perpetual worries:

There's his job—they daren't have kids. And Russia.
And how he'll never keep up with the mortgage.
Not to mention the droughts, the six-foot snows,
In the yard where nothing English ever grows.

DEREK MAHON

1941–

270   *A Lighthouse in Maine*

It might be anywhere,
That ivory tower
Approached by a dirt road.

Bleached stone against
Bleached sky, it faces
Every way with an air

Of squat omniscience—
A polished Buddha
Hard and bright beyond

Vegetable encroachment.
The north light
That strikes its frame

Houses is not
The light of heaven
But that of this world;

Nor is its task
To throw a punctual
Glow in the dark

To liners wild
With rock music and calm
With navigation.

Though built to shed
Light, it prefers
To shelter it, as it does

Now in the one-bird hour
Of afternoon, a milky
Glare melting the telephone poles.

It works both ways,
Of course, light
Being, like love and the cold,

Something that you
Can give and keep
At the same time.

Night and day it sits
Above the ocean like
A kindly eye, keeping

And giving the rainbow
Of its many colours,
Each of them white.

It might be anywhere—
Hokkaido, Normandy, Maine;
But it is in Maine.

You make a right
Somewhere beyond Rockland,
A left, a right,

You turn a corner and
There it is, shining
In modest glory like

The soul of Adonais.
Out you get and
Walk the rest of the way.

HOME THOUGHTS

ANONYMOUS
early 16th century

271
Westron wind, when will thou blow,
The small rain down can rain?
Christ if my love were in my arms,
And I in my bed again.

SIR THOMAS WYATT
1503–1542

272
Tagus, farewell, that westward with thy streams
Turns up the grains of gold already tried;
With spur and sail for I go seek the Thames,
Gainward the sun that showeth her wealthy pride,
And to the town that Brutus sought by dreams
Like bended moon doth lend her lusty side.
My King, my country, alone for whom I live,
Of mighty love the wings for this me give.

EDWARD THOMPSON
?1739–1786

273
from *An Humble Wish*
Off Porto-Sancto, 29 March 1779

I never yet arraigned the will of Heaven,
Nor asked to turn the dispensation given;
I ne'er implored for any higher boon,
But supped the mess allotted to my spoon.

---

272 Gainward] toward   Brutus] legendary founder of Troynovant or New Troy
(London) and of the British race   bended] crescent

Each man at thirty should his doctor be
Of soul and body, in some small degree;

. . . . . .

I've ne'er had soul and body yet at strife,
But kept them, cheek by jowl, good friends through life.
I've served my country nine and twenty years,
A mere light chip, the sport of all the spheres:
To India I was early sent in youth;
Then bandied to the north, the west, and south;
France, Holland, Prussia, Portugal, and Spain,
America, and all the western main.
Now I'm for Guinea, in an infant war,
Chief of a gallant ship, where ev'ry tar,
Ragged and lousy, hungry is and poor,
Well fitted a rich Frenchman to devour.
As for sea hardships, they create my smiles—
We'll bury them in the Canary Isles,
In the soft lap of beauteous Portuguese,
The olive Sirens of those summer seas.
Now for my wish—and Venus hear the strain!
When I've this bark conducted o'er the main,
And I return with golden laurels bound,
Parcel me out a little fertile ground,
And build thereon a house, by some thick wood,
And at the mountain's foot a rapid flood:
The river stored with trout, the wood with game,
And lovely Emma my propitious dame!
Retired from war, the bustle of the seas,
Let me repose with her in health and ease;
I seek no star or honours of the land;
I'd rather have a kiss of her white hand
Than all the salutations of St James,
Where nobles truck their characters for names.
I only bend my knee to her and heaven,
Nor pray for aught, but thank for what is given.
If ye who rule the clouds, and guide the sun,
Will perfect this before my sand is run,
I bow—if not, your mighty wills be done.

WILLIAM LISLE BOWLES
1762–1850

274   *Sonnet*

At Ostend, 22 July 1787

How sweet the tuneful bells' responsive peal!
  As when, at opening morn, the fragrant breeze
  Breathes on the trembling sense of wan disease,
So piercing to my heart their force I feel!
And hark! with lessening cadence now they fall,
  And now, along the white and level tide,
  They fling their melancholy music wide;
Bidding me many a tender thought recall
Of summer-days, and those delightful years
  When by my native streams, in life's fair prime,
  The mournful magic of their mingling chime
First waked my wond'ring childhood into tears!
But seeming now, when all those days are o'er,
The sounds of joy once heard, and heard no more.

WILLIAM WORDSWORTH
1770–1850

275   I travelled among unknown Men,
    In Lands beyond the Sea;
Nor, England! did I know till then
    What love I bore to thee.

'Tis past, that melancholy dream!
    Nor will I quit thy shore
A second time; for still I seem
    To love thee more and more.

Among thy mountains did I feel
    The joy of my desire;
And She I cherished turned her wheel
    Beside an English fire.

Thy mornings shewed—thy nights concealed
The bowers where Lucy played;
And thine is, too, the last green field
Which Lucy's eyes surveyed.

SAMUEL TAYLOR COLERIDGE

1772–1834

276   *Lines Written in the Album at Elbingerode, in the Hartz Forest*

I stood on Brocken's sovereign height, and saw
Woods crowding upon woods, hills over hills,
A surging scene, and only limited
By the blue distance. Heavily my way
Downward I dragged through fir groves evermore,
Where bright green moss heaves in sepulchral forms
Speckled with sunshine; and, but seldom heard,
The sweet bird's song became a hollow sound;
And the breeze, murmuring indivisibly,
Preserved its solemn murmur most distinct
From many a note of many a waterfall,
And the brook's chatter; 'mid whose islet-stones
The dingy kidling with its tinkling bell
Leaped frolicsome, or old romantic goat
Sat, his white beard slow waving. I moved on
In low and languid mood: for I had found
That outward forms, the loftiest, still receive
Their finer influence from the Life within;—
Fair cyphers else: fair, but of import vague
Or unconcerning, where the heart not finds
History or prophecy of friend, or child,
Or gentle maid, our first and early love,
Or father, or the venerable name
Of our adorèd country! O thou Queen,
Thou delegated Deity of Earth,
O dear, dear England! how my longing eye
Turned westward, shaping in the steady clouds
Thy sands and high white cliffs!

                My native Land!
Filled with the thought of thee this heart was proud,

276 Brocken] the highest peak in the Harz Mountains

Yea, mine eye swam with tears: that all the view
From sovereign Brocken, woods and woody hills,
Floated away, like a departing dream,
Feeble and dim! Stranger, these impulses
Blame thou not lightly; nor will I profane,
With hasty judgment or injurious doubt,
That man's sublimer spirit, who can feel
That God is everywhere! the God who framed
Mankind to be one mighty family,
Himself our Father, and the World our Home.

ROBERT BROWNING
1812–1889

277   *Home-Thoughts, from Abroad*

I

Oh, to be in England
Now that April's there,
And whoever wakes in England
Sees, some morning, unaware,
That the lowest boughs and the brushwood sheaf
Round the elm-tree bole are in tiny leaf,
While the chaffinch sings on the orchard bough
In England—now!

II

And after April, when May follows,
And the whitethroat builds, and all the swallows!
Hark, where my blossomed pear-tree in the hedge
Leans to the field and scatters on the clover
Blossoms and dewdrops—at the bent spray's edge—
That's the wise thrush; he sings each song twice over,
Lest you should think he never could recapture
The first fine careless rapture!
And though the fields look rough with hoary dew,
All will be gay when noontide wakes anew
The buttercups, the little children's dower
—Far brighter than this gaudy melon-flower!

CHRISTINA ROSSETTI
1830–1894

278   *Italia, Io Ti Saluto!*

To come back from the sweet South, to the North
  Where I was born, bred, look to die;
Come back to do my day's work in its day,
      Play out my play—
  Amen, amen, say I.

To see no more the country half my own,
  Nor hear the half familiar speech,
Amen, I say; I turn to that bleak North
      Whence I came forth—
  The South lies out of reach.

But when our swallows fly back to the South,
  To the sweet South, to the sweet South,
The tears may come again into my eyes
      On the old wise,
  And the sweet name to my mouth.

MARY COLERIDGE
1861–1907

279   *Where a Roman Villa Stood, above Freiburg*

On alien ground, breathing an alien air,
  A Roman stood, far from his ancient home,
And gazing, murmured, 'Ah, the hills are fair,
    But not the hills of Rome!'

Descendant of a race to Romans kin,
  Where the old son of Empire stood, I stand.
The self-same rocks fold the same valley in,
    Untouched of human hand.

Over another shines the self-same star,
  Another heart with nameless longing fills,
Crying aloud, 'How beautiful they are,
    But not our English hills!'

JAMES ELROY FLECKER
1884–1915

280   *From Grenoble*

Now have I seen, in Graisivaudan's vale,
The fruits that dangle and the vines that trail,
The poplars standing up in bright blue air,
The silver turmoil of the broad Isère
And sheer pale cliffs that wait through Earth's long noon
Till the round Sun be colder than the Moon.

Mine be the ancient song of Travellers:
I hate this glittering land where nothing stirs:
I would go back, for I would see again
Mountains less vast, a less abundant plain,
The Northern Cliffs clean-swept with driven foam,
And the rose-garden of my gracious home.

RUPERT BROOKE
1887–1915

281   *The Old Vicarage, Grantchester*

(Café des Westens, Berlin, May 1912)

Just now the lilac is in bloom,
All before my little room;
And in my flower-beds, I think,
Smile the carnation and the pink;
And down the borders, well I know,
The poppy and the pansy blow . . .
Oh! there the chestnuts, summer through,
Beside the river make for you
A tunnel of green gloom, and sleep
Deeply above; and green and deep
The stream mysterious glides beneath,
Green as a dream and deep as death.
—Oh, damn! I know it! and I know
How the May fields all golden show,
And when the day is young and sweet,
Gild gloriously the bare feet

That run to bathe . . .
                    Du lieber Gott!

Here am I, sweating, sick, and hot,
And there the shadowed waters fresh
Lean up to embrace the naked flesh.
Temperamentvoll German Jews
Drink beer around;—and *there* the dews
Are soft beneath a morn of gold.
Here tulips bloom as they are told;
Unkempt about those hedges blows
An English unofficial rose;
And there the unregulated sun
Slopes down to rest when day is done,
And wakes a vague unpunctual star,
A slippered Hesper; and there are
Meads towards Haslingfield and Coton
Where *das Betreten*'s not *verboten*.

εἴθε γενοίμην . . . would I were
In Grantchester, in Grantchester!—
Some, it may be, can get in touch
With Nature there, or Earth, or such.
And clever modern men have seen
A Faun a-peeping through the green,
And felt the Classics were not dead,
To glimpse a Naiad's reedy head,
Or hear the Goat-foot piping low: . . .
But these are things I do not know.
I only know that you may lie
Day-long and watch the Cambridge sky,
And, flower-lulled in sleepy grass,
Hear the cool lapse of hours pass,
Until the centuries blend and blur
In Grantchester, in Grantchester. . . .
Still in the dawnlit waters cool
His ghostly Lordship swims his pool,
And tried the strokes, essays the tricks,
Long learnt on Hellespont, or Styx.
Dan Chaucer hears his river still
Chatter beneath a phantom mill.
Tennyson notes, with studious eye,
How Cambridge waters hurry by . . .
And in that garden, black and white,
Creep whispers through the grass all night;

---

das Betreten . . . *verboten*] trespass . . . forbidden   εἴθε γενοίμην . . .] would that
I were . . . (εἴθε σοι τότε συνεγενόμην 'Would that I had been with you' (Xenophon))

And spectral dance, before the dawn,
A hundred Vicars down the lawn;
Curates, long dust, will come and go
On lissom, clerical, printless toe;
And oft between the boughs is seen
The sly shade of a Rural Dean . . .
Till, at a shiver in the skies,
Vanishing with Satanic cries,
The prim ecclesiastic rout
Leaves but a startled sleeper-out,
Grey heavens, the first bird's drowsy calls,
The falling house that never falls.

God! I will pack, and take a train,
And get me to England once again!
For England's the one land, I know,
Where men with Splendid Hearts may go;
And Cambridgeshire, of all England,
The shire for Men who Understand;
And of *that* district I prefer
The lovely hamlet Grantchester.
For Cambridge people rarely smile,
Being urban, squat, and packed with guile;
And Royston men in the far South
Are black and fierce and strange of mouth;
At Over they fling oaths at one,
And worse than oaths at Trumpington,
And Ditton girls are mean and dirty,
And there's none in Harston under thirty,
And folks in Shelford and those parts
Have twisted lips and twisted hearts,
And Barton men make Cockney rhymes,
And Coton's full of nameless crimes,
And things are done you'd not believe
At Madingley, on Christmas Eve.
Strong men have run for miles and miles,
When one from Cherry Hinton smiles;
Strong men have blanched, and shot their wives,
Rather than send them to St Ives;
Strong men have cried like babes, bydam,
To hear what happened at Babraham.
But Grantchester! ah, Grantchester!
There's peace and holy quiet there,
Great clouds along pacific skies,
And men and women with straight eyes,
Lithe children lovelier than a dream,
A bosky wood, a slumbrous stream,

And little kindly winds that creep
Round twilight corners, half asleep.
In Grantchester their skins are white;
They bathe by day, they bathe by night;
The women there do all they ought;
The men observe the Rules of Thought.
They love the Good; they worship Truth;
They laugh uproariously in youth;
(And when they get to feeling old,
They up and shoot themselves, I'm told) . . .

 Ah God! to see the branches stir
Across the moon at Grantchester!
To smell the thrilling-sweet and rotten
Unforgettable, unforgotten
River-smell, and hear the breeze
Sobbing in the little trees.
Say, do the elm-clumps greatly stand
Still guardians of that holy land?
The chestnuts shade, in reverend dream,
The yet unacademic stream?
Is dawn a secret shy and cold
Anadyomene, silver-gold?
And sunset still a golden sea
From Haslingfield to Madingley?
And after, ere the night is born,
Do hares come out about the corn?
Oh, is the water sweet and cool,
Gentle and brown, above the pool?
And laughs the immortal river still
Under the mill, under the mill?
Say, is there Beauty yet to find?
And Certainty? and Quiet kind?
Deep meadows yet, for to forget
The lies, and truths, and pain? . . . oh! yet
Stands the Church clock at ten to three?
And is there honey still for tea?

GEORGE BARKER

1913–

282   *The Oak and the Olive*

Seven years lived in Italy leave me convinced
that the angel guarding us knows only too well
what she is doing. There is a curious sense
in which that place whose floral sophistication
—whose moral sophistication—we all happily acknowledge,
resembles in fact a delicious garden inhabited
by seven-year-old children. I can perceive
this innocence of spirit even in the most cynical
of Italians I have loved, and I think that
this innocence ensues simply from the sun. There
it is perfectly possible to assassinate one's best friend
with a kind of histrionic guiltlessness, because
the sun would continue to shine after the crime,
the gardens to dream in the afternoon, and later
the evening cast a benevolent shadowing over
the corpse of one's cold friend. Furthermore years
of white and gold sunlight tend to deprive one of
the pessimistic faculty. It is harder to indulge there
the natural Anglosaxon melancholy
because I, for instance, found a bough of oranges
growing through the skylight of my lavatory.
And all these mother of pearl evenings and these
serene Venus green skies and Lucullan landscapes
have in the end the effect of depriving one
of precisely that consciousness of shame out
of which the adult Nordic monster
of evil is generated. There are no Grendls here.
And so it is possible often in the Borghese
Gardens to act as though one was, of course,
a criminal cynic but a criminal cynic whom
the sun does not decline to befriend, to whom small
birds still confide, and whom the sylvan
evening landscape is still prepared to sleep with.
Then it seems likely that Providence or Italy or
even the conscience has forgiven us the enormities
that brought us here. When the chilling
rain falls upon me in the North I know
only too well that it does so as

Grendls] Grendel is the male monster in the Anglo-Saxon epic *Beowulf*

a moral punitive. I write this in
a Norfolk August and the rains pour down
daily upon a landscape which derives
its masculine nobility from the simple
fact that it has survived. It has survived
the flood, the winter, the fall and the Black
nor'-easter. The old oak tree hangs out
that great twisted bough from which the corpse
of the criminal cynic has just dropped in decay.
The clouds do not decorate the sky, they entomb it,
and the streams have swollen to cataracts. Weeds
flourish and the summer corn is crushed flat.
What could ever come from all this hopeless
melancholy save a knowledge, as by allegory,
of our culpability? Why, then, should I find
a child's face bright with tears haunting my mind?

LAURIE LEE
1914–

283   *Home from Abroad*

Far-fetched with tales of other worlds and ways,
My skin well-oiled with wines of the Levant,
I set my face into a filial smile
To greet the pale, domestic kiss of Kent.

But shall I never learn? That gawky girl,
Recalled so primly in my foreign thoughts,
Becomes again the green-haired queen of love
Whose wanton form dilates as it delights.

Her rolling tidal landscape floods the eye
And drowns Chianti in a dusky stream;
The flower-flecked grasses swim with simple horses,
The hedges choke with roses fat as cream.

So do I breathe the hayblown airs of home,
And watch the sea-green elms drip birds and shadows,
And as the twilight nets the plunging sun
My heart's keel slides to rest among the meadows.

DAVID HOLBROOK

1923–

284   *Coming Home from Abroad*

The air is high and blue yet, as we drive
Northwards across High Marne: summer
Again, after the stormy cold of June.
Yet there's a ghostliness, a sadness in the wind:
I feel it first, in the little park at Enghein
Where the tall plane trees shivered in the breeze.

Oh, I am so content, sitting beside you,
Driving home over the Northern plains of France,
The sun still strong, everything going well,
The wine and *poulard* good at lunch at Chalons;
Yet, in the sky, there's this tall hustling ghost
Drawing a veil across the face of summer.

On Zeebrugge beach all next day, the sand
Unites me to Suffolk: the cold onshore breeze
Whispers of Cotman, and those severe scenes
Of grey half-muted tones, the figures bent
Against the elements: and so we sail
Steering irrevocably into the Felixstowe fog.

Cotman] John Sell Cotman (1782–1842), landscape water-colourist and etcher belonging to the
Norwich school

NOTES AND REFERENCES

REFERENCES are given below for poems by authors whose collected poems are not easily available and for the sources of passages excerpted from longer works. The sources of poems in copyright appear in the section of Acknowledgements (pp. 411–14).

References are generally to first volume publication, and where the poet's revision of a text has been preferred, this is indicated. When first publication occurred long after a poem's composition, manuscript or (where possible) first magazine publication reference is given.

Spelling has been extensively modernized in poems written before 1800 (except in nos. 44 and 45), but only lightly thereafter; many non-standard spellings remain in the nineteenth-century poems because I have deemed them too recent to be altered. Changes made to punctuation are few and minor, and often only in the interests of presentation. Intrusive initial capitalization and italicization have been reduced to a minimum.

These endnotes also allude briefly to a poet's biography and the background to a poem where this seems pertinent.

EN ROUTE

1. Sir Richard Grenville. British Library, Sloane MS 2497, fol. 47; A. L. Rowse, *Sir Richard Grenville of The Revenge* (1937). British naval commander and cousin of Sir Walter Ralegh, whose father commanded and went down in the *Mary Rose*. In 1585, the year in which he wrote this poem, Grenville led a fleet of seven ships taking colonists to Roanoke Island in North Carolina, and captured a Spanish vessel on the way back. Grenville's fight to the death in 1591 against fifteen Spanish ships is the subject of Tennyson's ballad 'The Revenge'.

2. Anonymous. *Wits Recreations*, sel. G[eorge] H[erbert] (1640). Sir Francis Drake, English admiral and circumnavigator of the globe, lived *c.*1545–1596.

3. Thomas Prys. British Library, Add. MS 14872 (Cywydd i ddangos yr hildring a fu i ŵr pan oedd ar y môr), trans. Gwyn Williams in *Welsh Poems: Sixth Century to 1600* (1973). The italic phrases are in English in the original. 'Thomas Prys, gentleman, of Plas Iolyn, Denbighshire, was reputed to be one of "the two filthy Welshmen who first smoked publicly in the streets". He was also a soldier, sailor, pirate, and poet, and up to his eyes in everything' (Gwyn Jones, *The Oxford Book of Welsh Verse in English*).

4. William Cowper. 'The Progress of Error', ll. 367–414.

5. Sir George Dallas. Miss Emily Brittle, *The India Guide; or, Journal of a Voyage, to the East Indies in the Year MDCCLXXX in a Poetical Epistle to her Mother* (Calcutta, 1785), Letter II, ll. 1–20, 61–134, and 199–248.

7. Thomas Moore. *Rhymes on the Road*, Extract IV.

8. Charles Stuart Calverley. *Verses and Translations* (1861).

9. Robert Louis Stevenson. *Collected Poems*, ed. and intr. Janet Adam Smith (1971). The poem was first printed in the *Scots Observer*, 22 December 1888.

11. John Masefield begain training for the merchant navy at the age of 13 and twice sailed across the Atlantic before he was 17. This poem was included in his first book, *Salt-Water Ballads*, published when he was 24.

12. Dorothy Wellesley, Duchess of Wellington. Written in 1927, when Dorothy Wellesley visited Persia with Vita Sackville-West. 'I ordered the German Post, a little two-seater plane which started at 4 o'clock in the morning ... This was my first flight. I looked down once, but not again, though I was far too interested to be frightened' (Dorothy Wellesley, *Far Have I Travelled*).

13. Noel Coward. This lyric comes from *Words and Music.*

17. Sir Charles Johnston. In his one widely remembered line, representative for many of the mystique of travel, J. W. Burgon (1813–88) imagined Petra as 'A rose-red city—"half as old as time"' ('Petra').

FRANCE

19. Anonymous. Nottingham University Library, Taverham MS, fols. 156–8, c.1600–40; *The Common Muse*, ed. V. de Sola Pinto and A. E. Rodway (1957). It is just possible that the poem was written by Sir John Suckling.

21. Joseph Warton. *The Works of the British Poets*, coll. by Thomas Park, vol. xxxvii, *The Poetical Works of Joseph Warton* (1805).

22. William Beckford. *The Travel-Diaries of William Beckford of Fonthill*, ed. Guy Chapman (1928). Beckford wrote this poem while staying at the Grande Chartreuse, also celebrated by Matthew Arnold; after a wild moonlight excursion in pursuit of St Bruno, who founded the Carthusian Order and established the monastery in 1084, Beckford entered the lines 'immediately on my return, in the Album of the fathers, during the stillest watch of night'.

23, 24. William Wordsworth. 23. This is one of five sonnets composed in the autumn of 1802. It was written on the beach near Calais. 24. *The Prelude*, Bk. X, ll. 1–128.

27. Elizabeth Barrett Browning. *Aurora Leigh*, Sixth Bk., ll. 78–149.

28. William Makepeace Thackeray. *The Works of William Makepeace Thackeray*, vol. xiii, *Ballads and Miscellanies* (1900). Thackeray lived and worked as a journalist in Paris from 1834 until 1837.

29. Matthew Arnold. Written on 6 May 1859 while Arnold was in France studying elementary education for the Newcastle Commission. The poem is in part an elegy for the poet's younger brother, William, who had died in Gibraltar in the previous month while on his way home from India.

30. A. C. Swinburne. See note to no. **72.**

31. Agnes Mary Robinson. *The Collected Poems Lyrical and Narrative of A. Mary F. Robinson (Madame Duclaux)* (1902).

32. Sir Owen Seaman. *A Selection* (1937).

23. Arthur Symons. *Poems* (1924), 'Scènes de la Vie de Bohème', 1.

34. Charlotte Mew. *The Farmer's Bride* (1921).

35. Aubrey Beardsley. *The Savoy* (1896); *An Anthology of Nineties Verse*, ed. A. J. Symons (1928). 'I think Beardsley would rather have been a great writer than a great artist ... his patience over a medium so unfamiliar, and hence so difficult, to him as verse, was infinite. We spent two whole days on the grassy ramparts of the old castle at Arques-la-Bataille, near Dieppe; I working at something or other in one part, he working at "The Three Musicians", in another' (Arthur Symons).

37. Ivor Gurney. *Collected Poems of Ivor Gurney*, chosen by P. J. Kavanagh (1984).

38. Wilfred Owen. *Collected Poems*, ed. C. Day Lewis (1963). This final draft of the poem is dated 8 December 1917.

40. Geoffrey Grigson owned a farmhouse near Trôo in the Loir valley and wrote many poems set in France as well as a distinguished travel book, *Notes from an Odd Country* (1970).

42. David Holbrook. This poem was written at Varangeville in 1977.

43. Gillian Clarke. This is the third section of 'A Journal from France: Poems from Aubas, September 1979', *A Letter from a Far Country* (1982).

IBERIA

44. Anonymous. Samuel Purchas, *Haklytus Posthumus or Purchas His Pilgrimes*, vii (1905; 1st edn., 1625), 'The Way to Jerusalem', ll. 41–92. The poem was written in about 1425 and this section is prefixed with the words, 'Here beginneth the way that is marked, and made wit Mount Joiez from the Lond of Engelond unto Sent Jamez in Galis, and from thennez to Jerusalem: and so againe into Engelond, and the names of all the Citeez be their waie, and the maner of her governanuce [*sic*], and namez of her silver that they use be alle these waie'.

45. Anonymous. Trinity College Library, Cambridge, MS R.3.19; *The Stacions of Rome and the Pilgrims Sea-Voyage*, ed. Frederick J. Furnivall (EETS 25, 1867).

46. Thomas Deloney. *The Garland of Good-Will* (*c.*1650). Deloney was a silk-weaver in Norwich. The poem describes the razing of Cadiz, on 21 June 1596, by forces under the command of Lord Howard and the Earl of Essex.

47, 48. William Mickle. **47.** *The Poetical Works* (1808). **48.** *Almada Hill: An Epistle from Lisbon* (Oxford, 1781), ll. 1–102. Mickle, who translated Portugal's national epic, *Os Lusíadas* (*The Lusiad*, 1775), conceived *Almada Hill* while wandering among the ruins of the castle in December 1779, and wrote the poem in Portugal.

49. Robert Southey. Originally published in *Letters from Spain and Portugal* (1797) under the title 'Retrospective Musings'. This is the revised version that appears in *The Poetical Works of Robert Southey*, ii (1837). Southey stayed in Spain and Portugal in 1795.

50. George Gordon, Lord Byron. *Childe Harold's Pilgrimage*, Canto I, XIV–XIX. Byron visited Portugal in July 1809 and completed Canto I of *Childe Harold* on 30 December 1809.

51, 52. Richard Chenevix Trench. *Poems*, i (1885).

53, 54. George Eliot. **53.** *The Spanish Gypsy* (1868), Bk. I, 'The Plaça Santiago'. **54.** *The Spanish Gypsy* (1868), Bk. III, ll. 1–74.

55. William Cory. Text from Faith Compton Mackenzie, *William Cory: a Biography* (1950). Cory wrote the poem at Funchal in Madeira on 8 August 1878, while waiting for horses to take him and his Madeiran bride, Rosa, to live up in the hill country.

56. Arthur Symons. *Poems* (1924). The poem was written at Málaga on 16 February 1899.

59. Ted Hughes. The poem is addressed to Sylvia Plath.

ITALY

61. Joseph Addison. *Works* (1721), 'A Letter from Italy to the Right Honourable Charles Lord Halifax', ll. 69–140.

62. George Keate. *Ancient and Modern Rome. A Poem Written at Rome in the Year 1755* (1760), ll. 103–87.

63, 64. William Parsons. *A Poetical Tour* (1787). In naming his 'man of taste' Cymon, Parsons probably took a hint from Dryden's 'Cymon and Iphigenia':

> Now scorned of all and grown the public shame,
> The people from Galesus changed his name,
> And Cymon called, which signifies a brute;
> So well his name did with his nature suit.

65. Samuel Rogers. *Italy* (1822–8). Text from 1844 edition.

66. William Wordsworth. *The Prelude*, Bk. VI, ll. 491–657. In his letter to Dorothy Wordsworth, September 1790, Wordsworth wrote of Lake Como: 'It was impossible not to contrast that repose, that complacency of spirit, produced by these lovely scenes, with the sensations I had experienced two or three days before, in passing the Alps. At the lake of Como, my mind ran through a thousand dreams of happiness, which might be enjoyed upon its banks, if heightened by conversation and the exercise of the social affections. Among the more awful scenes of the Alps, I had not thought of man, or a single created being, my whole soul was turned to him who produced the terrible majesty before me.'

67. George Gordon, Lord Byron. *Childe Harold's Pilgrimage*, Canto IV, I–IV. Byron lived in Venice in 1817 and began the fourth and last Canto of *Childe Harold* while visiting Rome during that year.

68. Percy Bysshe Shelley. 'Julian and Maddalo', ll. 1–92. Begun at Este after Shelley's first visit to Venice in autumn 1818, where he stayed in a villa lent to him by Byron, and completed at Leghorn the following summer. In his Preface, Shelley wrote that 'Count Maddalo is a Venetian nobleman of ancient family and of great fortune ... Julian is an Englishman of good family, passionately attached to those philosophical notions which assert the power of man over his own mind ... He is a complete infidel ...'

69. John Henry Newman. *Verses on Various Occasions, 1821–1862* (1868). Newman joined the Church of Rome in 1845.

70. Elizabeth Barrett Browning. *Aurora Leigh*, Seventh Bk., ll. 467–503 and 515–41. The Brownings lived at Casa Guidi in Florence (with extended visits to other Italian cities, Paris, and London) from 1846 until Elizabeth Barrett's death in 1861. *Aurora Leigh* was published in 1857.

71. Richard Monckton Milnes. *Collected Poetical Works* (1876). Scott made his last journey to Italy in 1832. The Stuarts entombed in St Peter's are Prince Charles Edward and his father.

72. Alfred, Lord Tennyson. Either Catullus or a member of his family owned a villa on the Sirmio promontory of Lake Garda. It was there in 56 BC that Catullus wrote his famous salutation to his brother, whose grave near Troy he had visited the previous year.

74. Robert Browning. '"De Gustibus—"', II.

76. Arthur Hugh Clough. 'Amours de Voyage', Canto I, I and II: Claude to Eustace. The poem was first printed in *Atlantic Monthly* in 1858.

77. Thomas Hardy. Fiesole has been much celebrated by English poets, amongst them Thomas Gray, Robert Browning, D. H. Lawrence and Charles Tomlinson. Walter Savage Landor is buried there.

78. Oscar Wilde. Shelley was drowned in August 1822 when he was caught in a sudden storm while sailing back to his beach house on the bay of Lerici from a visit to

Byron and Hunt at Livorno. His ashes were buried in the Protestant cemetery in Rome; his heart was brought back to England.

79, 80. D. H. Lawrence. **79.** Written during September 1921 while Lawrence was staying at 32 Via dei Bardi in Florence. **80.** Written during December 1920 at Fontana Vecchia in Taormina in Sicily.

83. Dylan Thomas. These lines constitute the opening of a verse-and-prose letter written to T. W. Earp on 11 July 1947 from Villa del Beccaro, Mosciano, Scandicci, Florence, where Thomas had been staying for the previous two months. Thomas continued, 'I am awfully sick of it here, on the beautiful hills above Florence, drinking chianti in our marble shanty, sick of vini and contadini and bambini, and sicker still when I go, bumby with mosquito bites, to Florence itself, which is a gruelling museum.'

86. Peter Porter stayed in Campagnatico at the Italian home of David Malouf, Australian poet and novelist, in 1981. An annual British-run opera festival is held near by at Batignano.

GREECE AND THE BALKANS

87. John Milton. *Paradise Regained*, Bk. IV, ll. 236–84.

88. Mark Akenside. *The Pleasures of Imagination*, Bk. I, ll. 567–604.

90, 91. William Haygarth. *Greece, A Poem in Three Parts* (1814), II, ll. 50–139, and I, ll. 594–663. 'It is the object of the following work to describe some of the most remarkable features of Greek scenery, manners, and antiquities. It was designed in the country which it attempts to delineate, and a part of it was written at Athens in the winter of 1811' (W.H.).

92–4. George Gordon, Lord Byron. **92.** 'On the 3rd of May, 1810, while the *Salsette* (Captain Bathurst) was lying in the Dardanelles, Lieutenant Ekenhead, of that frigate, and the writer of these rhymes, swam from the European shore to the Asiatic—by the by, from Abydos to Sestos would have been more correct. The whole distance, from the place whence we started to our landing on the other side, including the length we were carried by the current, was computed by those on board the frigate at upwards of four English miles, though the actual breadth is barely one ... The water was extremely cold, from the melting of the mountain snows' (Byron). Byron wrote this poem six days later. **93.** *Don Juan*, Canto III, LXXXVI, 1–16. **94.** The poem was written on 26 May 1811 and first published in 1832.

95. Richard Monckton Milnes. *Memorials of a Tour in some Parts of Greece* (1834). The Ionian Islands were placed under a British protectorate in 1815 and Corfu became the seat of the British High Commissioner. The islands were ceded to the kingdom of Greece in 1864.

96. Sir Owen Seaman. *A Selection* (1937).

100. Patrick Leigh-Fermor. The author has made several emendations to the version printed in *The Penguin New Writing 37* (1949) for this anthology.

THE LOW COUNTRIES

103. Samuel Butler. *The Poetical Works of Samuel Butler*, iii (Edinburgh, 1777).

104. Andrew Marvell. Written in 1653. Marvell travelled in Holland, France, Italy, and Spain between 1643 and 1647, and returned to Holland, perhaps on espionage, from 1662 until 1663.

105. Matthew Prior. *The Literary Works of Matthew Prior*, ed. H. Bunker Wright and Monroe K. Spears, vol. i (1959). The poem is often called 'The Secretary' but it was not given this name until 1742, and then without authority.

106. Mark Akenside. *The Poetical Works* (1805), 'On Leaving Holland', 1.

107. William Parsons. *A Poetical Tour* (1787).

108. William Wordsworth. Written in 1828. 'Mr. Coleridge, my Daughter, and I made a tour together in Flanders, upon the Rhine, and returned by Holland. Dora and I, while taking a walk along a retired part of the town, heard the voice as here described, and were afterwards informed it was a Convent in which were many English. We were both much touched, I might say affected, and Dora moved as appears in the verses' (Wordsworth).

109. George Canning. Josceline Bagot, *George Canning and His Friends*, ii (1909). On 31 January 1826 Canning wrote to Sir Charles Bagot, Ambassador to Holland, 'I enclose to your Excellency, for your information, copies of two Orders in Council . . . imposing an *additional* duty of 20 per cent. upon Netherlands vessels and merchandise.' On the same day, he sent this verse to Bagot in cipher, as a practical joke. The Ambassador did not hold the appropriate cipher, and, anxious lest Canning's dispatch was an important one, replied, 'I sincerely hope that the circumstance will not be productive of any public inconvenience, but I am concerned to state that I do not possess any cypher by which I am enabled to decypher your despatch . . .'.

110. Samuel Taylor Coleridge. Written in June 1828.

113. Dante Gabriel Rossetti. 'A Trip to Paris and Belgium', v.

114. May Sinclair described her experiences in the Motor Field Ambulance Corps that set out for Flanders on 25 September 1914 in *A Journal of Impressions in Belgium* (1915). She wrote twenty-four novels and was an advocate of women's suffrage.

GERMANY AND AUSTRIA

117. Sir George Etheredge. *The Works of Sir George Etherege: Containing His Plays and Poems* (1704). The second and substantially revised version of this poem is here preferred to the first in *The History of Adolphus, Prince of Russia* (1691). Etheredge was an envoy of James II in Ratisbon (Regensburg) from 1685 to 1689.

118. Matthew Prior. *The Literary Works of Matthew Prior*, ed. H. Bunker Wright and Monroe K. Spears, vol. i (1959). In *Scaligerana ou Bons Mots, Rencontres Agréables, et Remarques Judicieuses & Sçavantes* (1695), J. Scaliger comments, 'Les Allemans ne se soucient pas quel Vin ils boivent pourveu que ce soit Vin, ni quel Latin ils parlent pourveu que soit Latin.'

119. James Boswell. *Journal of a Tour through the Courts of Germany*, ed. Frederick A. Pottle (1953). Boswell's explanation of the word *pumpernickel* follows that in Thomas Nugent's *The Grand Tour* (2nd edn., 1756): 'Westphalia in general is a good country, abounding in all necessaries of life, and yet there is no part of Germany where the peasants live in a more miserable manner. Their bread is of the very coarsest kind, ill baked, and as black as coal, for they never sift their flour. The people of the country call it *Pumpernickel*, which is only a corruption of a French name given to it by a gentleman of that nation who passed through this country. It is reported that when this coarse bread was brought to table, he looked at it and said *qu'il était bon pour Nickel*, that it was good for Nickel, which was the name of his horse.' In fact, the etymology of *pumpernickel* is uncertain.

Boswell was not taken with Mannheim, where he was informed, 'Sir, our Court preserves its grandeur by not having many strangers at its table'. He angrily wrote to John Johnston: 'The Elector ... treats strangers with a distance which makes some of them laugh at him and others curse him ... I have not been asked once. What an inhospitable dog! I have been obliged to dine at an ordinary, among fellows of all sorts and sizes ... O British, take warning from me and shun the dominions of the Elector Palatine.'

120, 121. Samuel Taylor Coleridge. Both written in 1828 and first published in *Friendship's Offering* (1834) with the titles 'Expectoration the Second' and 'An Expectoration, or Splenetic Extempore, on my joyful departure from the City of Cologne'.

124. George Meredith. *The Works of George Meredith*, vol. i, *Poems* (1910).

125. Rupert Brooke. Written in 1912.

126. Bernard Spencer's last British Council posting before his death in 1963 was in Vienna.

SWITZERLAND

129. Lady Mary Wortley Montagu. Bodleian Library, MS Don., c. 56, fol. 67. Text from Robert Halsband, *The Life of Lady Mary Wortley Montagu* (1956). The poem comprises part of a letter written to the object of her pilgrimage, Conte Francesco Algarotti, in September 1739. Believed by her husband and friends to be travelling for her health, Lady Mary settled in Venice to await Algarotti but they did not meet until March 1741 and, then, nothing came of it.

130. Oliver Goldsmith. *The Traveller*, ll. 165–208. After studying medicine in Leiden, Goldsmith set out through Europe on foot, and in 1755 and early 1756 he visited Flanders, France, Germany, Switzerland, and Italy. He wrote *The Traveller* during this time.

131. William Parsons. *A Poetical Tour* (1787).

132. Samuel Rogers. *Italy* (1822–8). Text from 1844 edition.

133. Percy Bysshe Shelley. This poem is dated 23 July 1816. Shelley wrote it during his elopement with Mary Godwin and first published it in *History of a Six Weeks' Tour* (1817). 'It was composed under the immediate impression of the deep and powerful feelings excited by the objects which it attempts to describe; and, as an indisceelible overflowing of the soul, rests its claim to approbation on an attempt to imitate the untamable wilderness and inaccessible solemnity from which those feelings sprang' (Shelley).

135. Arthur Hugh Clough. *Mari Magno*, 'The First Lawyer's Tale', IV, ll. 1–109.

137. Matthew Arnold conceived the poem when he was in Berne in June 1859, nearly ten years after his parting from Marguerite at Thun; he did not write it until 26 April–14 June 1863.

138. Thomas Hardy. Hardy noted that the poem was written on 'The 110th anniversary of the completion of the *Decline and Fall* at the same hour and place'. Gibbon (1737–94) got to know Lausanne as a boy and retired there in 1783.

139. A. D. Godley. *Fifty Poems*, ed. C. L. Graves and C. R. L. Fletcher (1927). The poem was first printed in the *Climbers' Club Journal*, September 1899.

BEYOND THE IRON CURTAIN

141–3. George Turberville. **141, 142.** Richard Hakluyt, *The Principall Navigations Voyages Traffiques and Discoveries*, iii (1903; 1st edn., 1589). Hakluyt introduces these two poems (and a third 'To his especiall friend Master Edward Dancie) as 'Certaine letters in verse, written by Master George Turberville out of Moscovia, which went as Secretarie thither with Master Tho. Randolph, her Majesties Ambassadour to the Emperour 1568, to certaine friends of his in London, describing the maners of the Countrey and people'. **143.** *Epitaphes, Epigrams, Songs and Sonets* (1567).

144, 145. John Taylor. *All the Workes of John Taylor, the Water Poet* (1630). The poems comprise two sections of 'Taylors Travels from the Cittie of London in England, to the Cittie of Prague in Bohemia. With The manner of his abode there three Weekes, his Observations there, and his returne from thence'. Taylor was a humbly born Thames waterman who made several visits to the Continent, once set off for Sheppey in a brown-paper boat, and, patronized by Jonson and others, wrote spirited and entertaining verse and prose.

148. Hugh MacDiarmid. Lenin's tomb is in Red Square in Moscow.

150. Gerda Mayer was born in Karlsbad (Czech Karlovy Vary) in Czechoslovakia and came to England in 1939. Her 'small park' is Tempelgarten in Neuruppin, which was laid out by Frederick the Great. The author has added the date of composition to the original title of the poem.

151. Tony Harrison. This is the fifth of the 'Curtain Sonnets' in *The School of Eloquence* (1978). Harrison taught for a year at Charles University in Prague.

SCANDINAVIA WITH ICELAND

152. Ambrose Philips. *The Tatler*, 5–7 May 1709; *Poetic Miscellanies*, Sixth Pt. ('Pastorals and other Poems'), ed. Jacob Tonson (1709). Ambrose Philips was in Denmark in 1708–9 as Secretary to the British Envoy, Daniel Pulteney.

153. Sir John Carr. *Poems* (1809).

154, 155. William Morris. *Poems by the Way* (1891). Morris went to Iceland in the summers of 1871 and 1873 and visited Lithend on both occasions.

156. *Three in Norway*, by Two of Them (1883). The poem is ascribed to 'John'.

158. Louis MacNeice. This poem was first printed as Chapter III of *Letters from Iceland* (1937), and there entitled 'Letter to Graham and Anne Shepard'. I have followed the title used in *Collected Poems*, ed. E. R. Dodds (1966).

159. W. H. Auden. This poem was first printed as Chapter II of *Letters from Iceland* (1937), and there subtitled 'A letter to Christopher Isherwood, Esq.'

160. Norman Nicholson. The glacier in question is in Norway at Bøyabreen, where the Jostedal glacier breaks away into Fjærland, an offshoot of the Sognefjord.

161. Francis Berry. Herjolf was one of the original Norse settlers in Greenland. He probably chose the place named after him because, near the southernmost tip of Greenland, it was the first natural landfall for ships from Iceland or Scandinavia.

162. Michael Dennis Browne. The poem was written in the summer of 1966 while Browne was visiting friends at Birkerød, near Copenhagen.

IRELAND

163. Aldfrith (attrib.). Ed. Paul Walsh, *Ériu*, 8/i (1915). Translation from Irish by James Mangan (1803–49) in *Poems of James Clarence Mangan*, ed. D. J. O'Donoghue (Dublin and London, 1903). Aldfrith, king of Anglo-Saxon Northumbria from 685 to 705, studied in Ireland and was, notes R. H. Hodgkin in *A History of the Anglo-Saxons*, 'the best educated of all the early English Kings, a writer of verse in Gaelic and a learned correspondent of Aldhelm in Latin'.

164. John Derricke. *The Image of Irelande* (1581), II, ll. 145–224. In his notes added to the 1883 Edinburgh edition, Sir Walter Scott wrote: 'The Second Part of the poem ... contains a singular and highly unfavourable, yet but too just, an account of the Woodkerne or native Irish in the reign of Queen Elizabeth. Not only were they behind all Europe, at least two centuries in civilisation, but the military oppression under which they groaned added degradation to their natural ignorance and barbarism.' Derricke, a friend of Sir Philip Sidney, probably served under the Lord-Deputy of Ireland and may have designed the new Great Seal for Ireland after 1557.

165. William King. *Miscellanies in Prose and Verse* (1709). 'Mully of Mountown', I.

166. Mary Alcock. *Poems* (1799).

167. William Makepeace Thackeray. Mr M. A. Titmarsh, *The Irish Sketch-Book* (1843). Thackeray visited Ireland in 1842. 'Newtown Limavaddy is the third town in the county of Londonderry. It comprises three well-built streets ... but I am bound to say that I was thinking of something else as we drove through the town, having fallen eternally in love during the ten minutes of our stay.'

168. Geoffrey Grigson. Grigson made substantial revisions to this poem when he reprinted it in *The Faber Book of Poems and Places*, ed. Geoffrey Grigson (1980). That version is followed here.

170. Louis MacNeice. *Collected Poems*, ed. E. R. Dodds (1966), 'The Closing Album', I.

THE LEVANT

171. Fynes Moryson. Samuel Purchas, *Haklytus Posthumus or Purchas His Pilgrimes*, viii (1905; 1st edn., 1625). The epitaph was included in a letter from Aleppo written in 1600 by the traveller William Biddulph: 'About eight miles from Scanderone, we came to a towne called Bylan, where there lieth buried an English Gentleman...'. Fynes Moryson spent much of his life travelling. He and his brother set out for Jerusalem in 1595 but Henry, aged 26, fell ill and, writes Bates in *Touring in 1600: A Study of the Development of Travel as a Means of Education* (1911), 'near Iskenderún he died in his brother's arms, while the Turks stood round, jeering and thieving. Fynes buried him there with stones above him to keep off the jackals, and an epitaph...'.

172, 173. William Lithgow. *Rare Adventures and Painfull Peregrinations* (1632). Lithgow wrote of his experiences in Syria that 'the losse whereof and the deceit of my Janizary made my Muse to expresse, what my Prose can not performe'. His verse may be unpolished but his ear for speech rhythms is good and his indignation unmistakable.

174. Lady Mary Wortley Montagu. *The Letters and Works of Mary Wortley Montagu*, ed. Lord Wharncliffe, 3rd ed. rev. by W. Moy Thomas (1861). Lady Mary's husband, Edward, was the English ambassador in Constantinople from 1716 until 1718. She sent these verses to her uncle Fielding on 26 December 1717.

175. Thomas Lisle. *A Collection of Poems in Six Volumes by Several Hands*, printed for R. and J. Dodsley (1763). Thomas Lisle served as English chaplain at Smyrna; he was one of the brothers of the nine sisters for whom Pope wrote 'Inscription on a Grotto of Shells at Crux-Easton'.

176. William Lisle Bowles. *The Poetical Works of William Lisle Bowles* (Edinburgh, 1855).

177. Richard Hengist Horne. *Cosimo De' Medici—an Historical Tragedy and Other Poems* (1875).

179. Richard Monckton Milnes. *The Poetical Works of Lord Houghton*, 2 vols. (1876), 'The Burden of Egypt', XLIII.

180. J. W. Burgon. *Poems* (1885). The poem was written 'on donkey-back, on the way back to the boats', on 30 January 1862.

181. Sir Edward Arnold. *Potiphar's Wife and Other Poems* (1892).

182. Wilfrid Scawen Blunt. *The Love Sonnets of Proteus* (1880). 'The sole support of Blunt and Lady Anne were their camel-drivers, two Arab boys from Sinai who knew almost nothing of the northern country. For several days they ran short of water, being totally ignorant of where the wells lay . . .' Edith Finch, *Wilfrid Scawen Blunt 1840–1922* (1938).

183. G. K. Chesterton. *The Collected Poems* (1927).

184. Dorothy Wellesley, Duchess of Wellington. 'Leaving Kum on the left, we motored on through the long day. Many were the great white ribs of the camels that we passed, picked clean by vultures. A camel goes on until he drops, and they leave him by the wayside' (Dorothy Wellesley, *Far Have I Travelled*).

186. Lawrence Durrell. The poem was written in 1946.

188. Keith Douglas. The poem was written in Cairo and is dated 8 October 1943.

AFRICA

190, 191. Thomas Campbell. *The Complete Poetical Works of Thomas Campbell*, ed. J. Logie Robertson (1907). Both poems were written in 1835. 'On board the vessel from Marseilles to Algiers I met with a fellow passenger whom I supposed to be a physician from his dress and manners, and the attentions which he paid me to alleviate the sufferings of my sea-sickness. He turned out to be a perruquier and barber in Algeria—but his vocation did not lower him in my estimation—for he continued his attentions until he passed my baggage through the customs, and helped me, when half dead with exhaustion, to the best hotel' (T.C.).

192–4. Thomas Pringle. *Poetical Works* (1837). Beset by debts, and eager 'to collect again into one social circle, and establish in rural independence, my father's family', Pringle led a group of twenty-four emigrants (all of them family and friends) to the Cape of Good Hope in February 1820. They settled at Glen-Lynden, which is on River of Baboons, one of the tributaries of the Great Fish River. Pringle was appointed librarian of the Government Library in Cape Town but, increasingly active on behalf of the Hottentots, was hounded by the Governor and his Chief Justice, and returned to England in 1826.

195. Martin Farquhar Tupper. *Ballads for the Times* (1850), 'The African Desert', ll. 199–226.

196. Sir Alfred Lyall. *Verses Written in India* (1889).

200. Anthony Thwaite was assistant professor of English at the University of Libya from 1965 to 1967.

201. David Gill taught at the Senior Secondary School at Nyakasura outside Fort Portal in Uganda from September 1962 to Christmas 1964. 'Byaruhanga was a village boy about 10 when we knew him. He came from a very poor family . . . We did get him into the local primary school but he had no chance of secondary education which was expensive by local standards. Many village people were not on a cash economy, so things were not going to be very different for Byaruhanga than they were for his parents' (D.G. to K.C.-H.).

203. Stewart Brown taught in Nigeria at Bayero University, Kano, from 1979 to 1982.

THE INDIAN SUBCONTINENT

204. Anonymous. Captain Mundy, *The Journals of a Tour in India* (1833). 'They [guides] show a small marble recess, in which the rhyming portion of the visiters [*sic*] of the Tâj record their extempore effusions in praise of the elegance of the building, the gallantry of the builder and the beauty of its fair tenant; while others simply inform the world that they have visited this celebrated mausoleum by scrawling at full length an uncouth name and date on its marble walls and pillars—a characteristic practice of English travellers. Amid the vast preponderance of trash there scribbled, there are, however, some lines of a superior order...'

205. Richard Owen Cambridge. *The Works of Richard Owen Cambridge* (1803).

206. Reginald Heber. *The Poetical Works* (1842).

207. Captain Thomas Skinner. *Excursions in India*, ii (1832). Modest verse but memorable detail.

208. Edward Lear. First published in the *Times of India*, July 1874.

209. H. G. Keene. *Peepul Leaves* (1879).

210. Sir Edwin Arnold. *The Light of Asia* (1879), Book the Third, ll. 375–414. Arnold was principal of the Poona College, Bombay Presidency, 1856–61.

211, 212. Sir Alfred Lyall. *Verses Written in India* (1890). Lyall was Foreign Secretary to the Government of India (1878–81) and Lieutenant-Governor of the North-West Provinces (1881–7).

213. Thomas Frank Bignold. *Leviora; Being the Rhymes of a Successful Competitor* (Calcutta and London, 1888), 'The Holiday. Port Blair', ll. 1–46 and 72–190. Bignold was employed in Her Majesty's Bengal Civil Service.

214, 215. Rudyard Kipling was born in Bombay in 1865 and, after an English education, worked as a journalist in India from 1882 to 1889.

216. George Orwell served with the Indian Imperial Police in Burma, 1922–7. This is one of two poems written (on Burma Government writing paper) at the end of that time or shortly after he left Burma.

218. Alun Lewis, a lieutenant with the South Wales Borderers, wrote this poem early in 1943, not long after his arrival in India, while stationed at Nira, near Poona.

THE FAR EAST

220, 221. John Leyden. Revd James Morton, *The Poetical Remains of the late Dr. John Leyden with Memoirs of his Life* (1819). Philologist, theologian, and surgeon, John Leyden went to India in 1804 as Surgeon and Naturalist to the Commissioners of the province of Mysore. Suffering from fever and recurring liver complaints, he took a recuperative voyage to Penang at the end of September 1804. His boat, a Parsi vessel (he was the only Englishman aboard), was chased by a French privateer: 'Thinking it also probable, that if we were captured ... they would not throw more than ten or twelve men aboard of us, to conduct us to the Isle of France, I proposed concealing myself with five men among the bales of cloth, till it should be night, when the Frenchmen being necessarily divided into two watches, might be easily overpowered. This was agreed to ... Fortunately the sea ran very high, and we escaped ...'. Leyden stayed in Penang until early in 1806.

222. Francis Hastings Doyle. *The Return of the Guards and Other Poems* (1883).

223. Sir Edwin Arnold. *Japonica* (1891).

224. Rudyard Kipling. Written in 1892.

225. Osman Edwards. *Residential Rhymes* (Tokyo, 1900), nos. I, II, III, and VIII.

227. William Empson. 'The grammar is meant to run through alternate lines; I thought this teasing trick gave an effect of completely disparate things going on side by side' (W.E.).

228. Wilfred Noyce was a member of Sir John Hunt's expedition to Mount Everest in 1953. On 23 May he was at Camp IV on Mount Everest and, two days earlier, he had climbed to a point (about 26,000 ft.) above the South Col. Hillary and Tenzing reached the summit on 29 May.

231. James Fenton was a free-lance reporter in Indo-China from 1973 to 1975.

OCEANIA

232. Erasmus Darwin. *European Magazine*, 16 (Dec. 1789). The poem is described as 'on some Medaillons made by Mr. Wedgwood from a Specimen of Clay from Sydney Cove, presented to him by Sir Joseph Banks'.

233. Thomas Perry. Dixson Library of New South Wales, MS FI; *The Journals of Captain James Cook on his Voyages of Discovery*, vol. ii, *The Voyage of the* Resolution *and* Adventure *1772–1775*, ed. J.C. Beaglehole (1961). A note appended to the manuscript by Louisa Jane Mackrell, the great-niece of Admiral Isaac Smith, reads, 'This song composed by Thomas Perry one of the Sea Men that went round the world with Captain Cook and was very much valued by the Captain. Mrs Cook kept it with the Gold Medal [either the Copley medal or the Royal Society medal] till her death.'

234. Anonymous. Nottingham University Library Collection of Original Broadsides, Album 89375, I, 76; *Modern Street Ballads*, ed. John Ashton (1888). The copy in Nottingham University Library was printed by James Catnach of 2 Monmouth Court, Seven Dials; he was registered as a printer at that address from 1813 to 1835.

235. Anonymous. A. Hope Blake, *Sixty Years in New Zealand* (1909). Blake writes, 'In 1844 Hone Heke, in violation of the celebrated Treaty of Waitangi, took up arms against the Queen's authority. At Kororareka (now Russell) to this day, may be seen a melancholy memento of the first Maori war—the little plot where the remains of New Zealand's first defenders are laid, their brave deeds commemorated by some loving hand in the lines inscribed on the stone that marks their last resting-place.'

236. Alfred Domett. *Ranolf and Amohia: A South-Sea Day-Dream* (1872), Canto I, III. Domett was Browning's friend 'Waring'. He stayed in New Zealand for twenty-nine years, and was briefly Prime Minister. *Ranolf and Amohia* is a very long and lyrical poem about Maori life.

237, 238. Robert Louis Stevenson. *Songs of Travel and Other Verses* (1920). He wrote 'To an Island Princess' at Tantira, Tahiti, on 5 November 1888, shortly after reaching the South Seas. 'Tropic Rain' was written at Vailima in Samoa where Stevenson settled and died.

239. D. H. Lawrence. Written in Sydney and first published in 1923.

240. Rupert Brooke. After a breakdown, Brooke travelled in the United States, Canada, and the Pacific in 1913.

242. Charles Causley. Despite his supposition that he would 'never return', Causley has in fact revisited Australia several times in recent years and written fine poems about it.

244. Fleur Adcock. 'Thorndon is the oldest suburb of Wellington. Katherine Mansfield lived there ... I went to school there, and later lived there during my first marriage' (F.A. to K.C.-H.). Fleur Adcock has lived in England since 1963.

SOUTH AMERICA AND THE CARIBBEAN

246. Joseph Warton. *The Works of the British Poets*, coll. by Thomas Park, vol. xxxvii, *The Poetical Works of Joseph Warton* (1805).

247. Edward Thompson. *Nauticks; or, Sailor's Verses*, 2 vols. (1783). Thompson was a naval officer who made two journeys to the West Indies, the second in 1780–1 to help set up and protect the colonies of Demerara and Essequibo.

248. Matthew Gregory Lewis. *Journal of a West India Proprietor* (1834). Lewis (author of *The Monk*) kept a journal of two residencies in Jamaica in 1815–16 and 1817. The poem printed here is his entry for 10 December 1815.

251. Lawrence Durrell. Written in 1948.

252. Alun Lewis. Lewis's troopship, *Athlone Castle*, called at Belia *en route* for India in December 1942.

253. Tony Harrison. *Palladas* (1975), 'Sentences', 1.

NORTH AMERICA

254. William Strachey. *The History of Travaile into Virginia Britannia*, ed. R. H. Major (1849). William Strachey (*fl.* 1609–18) was the first Secretary of the Colony of Virginia, which was the first permanent English settlement in North America.

255. Robert Hayman. *Quodlibets, Lately Come Over from New Britaniola, Old Newfoundland* (1628), 79, 80, 103, and 81. Robert Hayman, described by a fellow planter as a man 'who with Pen and Person prepares more roome for Christians in the Newfound-World', was Governor of the Plantation of Newfoundland. Newfoundland was annexed for England in 1583 and several attempts were made to colonize the island.

256. Andrew Marvell never travelled to the Bermudas but wrote this poem in 1653 while living at Eton in the house of John Oxenbridge, a Puritan divine, who had been persecuted by Archbishop Laud (cf. l. 12) in 1634 and made two voyages to the islands.

257. George Berkeley. *A Miscellany, Containing Several Tracts on Various Subjects* (Dublin, 1752). The poem was written in 1726, shortly after Berkeley had proposed the building of a missionary college in Bermuda. Berkeley went to America in 1728 in connection with this scheme but the college never materialized.

258. Thomas Morris. *Monthly Magazine*, 1 (Feb. 1796). Morris served in America with the 17th Foot under General Bradshaw. Lonsdale (*The New Oxford Book of Eighteenth-Century Verse*) identifies the poem as an imitation of Horace, *Odes*, II. xvi.

261. Samuel Butler. *The Spectator*, May 1878; *Seven Sonnets and a Psalm of Montreal* (Cambridge, 1904). Butler went to Canada in 1874–5. 'The City of Montreal is one of the most rising and, in many respects, most agreeable on the American continent, but its inhabitants are as yet too busy with commerce to care greatly about the masterpieces of old Greek Art. A cast of one of these masterpieces—the finest of several statues of Discoboli, or Quoit-throwers—was found by the present writer in the Montreal Museum of Natural History; it was, however, banished from public view, to a room where were all manner of skins, plants, snakes, insects, &c., and in the middle of these, an old man, stuffing an owl. The dialogue—perhaps true, perhaps imaginary, perhaps a little of the one and a little of the other—between the writer and this old man gave rise to the lines that follow' (S.B.).

262. J. K. Stephen. *Lapsus Calami* (Cambridge, 1891). 'England and America', 1. The poem did not appear in the first edition of *Lapsus Calami* but in the 'New edition with considerable omissions and additions' published later the same year.

265. Lawrence Durrell. Written in 1968.

267, 268. Thom Gunn has lived in San Francisco since 1960. **268.** Written in May 1973.

HOME THOUGHTS

271. Anonymous. British Library, MS Royal Appendix 58, fol. 5*a*; *Medieval English Lyrics*, ed. R. T. Davies (1963).

272. Sir Thomas Wyatt was ambassador to Charles V's court from 1537 to 1539 and wrote this poem in June 1539.

273. Edward Thompson. *Nauticks; or, Sailor's Verses*, 2 vols. (1783), 'An Humble Wish. Off Porto-Sancto, 29 March 1779', ll. 1–6 and 23–57. Thompson was a naval officer and in 1778–9 commanded the *Hyaena*, a small frigate which he sailed out to the West Indies to escort a convoy home.

274. William Lisle Bowles. *Fourteen Sonnets, Elegiac and Descriptive, Written during a Tour* (Bath, 1789).

275. William Wordsworth. One of the 'Lucy Poems', written in Germany, perhaps in 1799, sent in a letter to Mary Hutchinson in 1801, and first published in 1807. The identity of Lucy remains uncertain.

276. Samuel Taylor Coleridge. First published in the *Morning Post*, 17 September 1799. The poem was included in a letter from Coleridge to his wife dated 17 May 1799.

278. Christina Rossetti and her two elder brothers, Dante Gabriel (b. 1828) and William Michael (b. 1829) were born in England where their father, an Italian patriot, had settled in 1824.

279. Mary Coleridge. *The Collected Poems*, ed. Theresa Whistler (1954). Great-great-niece of Samuel Taylor Coleridge.

280. James Elroy Flecker lived in Cheltenham.

281. Rupert Brooke bought The Old Vicarage at Grantchester in 1909.

ACKNOWLEDGEMENTS

The editor and publishers wish to acknowledge permission to reprint copyright material in this book as follows:

Fleur Adcock: 'Instead of an Interview', © Fleur Adcock 1979, reprinted from *Selected Poems* (1983) by permission of Oxford University Press.

W. H. Auden: 'Brussels in Winter', copyright 1940 and renewed 1968 by W. H. Auden; 'Journey to Iceland', copyright 1937 and renewed 1965 by W. H. Auden, reprinted from *W. H. Auden: Collected Poems*, ed. Edward Mendelson, by permission of Faber & Faber Ltd., and Random House, Inc.

George Barker: 'The Oak and the Olive', reprinted from *Dialogues*, by permission of Faber & Faber Ltd.

Francis Berry: 'Gudveg', reprinted from *Ghosts of Greenland* (1966), by permission of Routledge & Kegan Paul PLC.

Sir John Betjeman: 'The Small Towns of Ireland' reprinted from *Collected Poems*, by permission of John Murray (Publishers) Ltd.

Edmund Blunden: 'The Cottage at Chigasaki', reprinted from *Choice or Chance* (Cobden-Sanderson, 1934), by permission of A. D. Peters & Co., Ltd.

Stewart Brown: 'Anthropology: Cricket at Kano', reprinted from *Zinder* (1986) by permission of Poetry Wales Press.

Michael Dennis Browne: 'The Visitor', reprinted from *The Wife of Winter* (London: Rapp & Whiting/New York: Scribners, 1970), by permission of the author.

Roy Campbell: 'Horses of the Camargue', reprinted from *Collected Poems* (1959) by permission of Francisco Custodío Campbell and Ad. Donker (Pty.) Ltd.

Charles Causley: 'H.M.S. Glory at Sydney', reprinted from *Farewell, Aggie Weston* (Hand & Flower Press, 1951), by permission of David Higham Associates Ltd.

Gillian Clarke: 'Seamstress at St. Léon', © Gillian Clarke, reprinted from *A Letter from a Far Country* (Carcanet, 1982), by permission of the publisher.

David Constantine: 'Watching for Dolphins', reprinted by permission of Bloodaxe Books Ltd., from *Watching for Dolphins* (1983).

Noel Coward: 'Mad Dogs and Englishmen', copyright © the Estate of Noel Coward. Used by permission.

Kevin Crossley-Holland: 'Postcards from Kodai', reprinted from *Time's Oriel* (Hutchinson, 1983), copyright © 1983 by Kevin Crossley-Holland, by permission of Deborah Rogers Ltd., Literary Agency.

Donald Davie: 'A Meeting of Cultures' reprinted by permission of Carcanet Press Ltd.

C. Day-Lewis: 'The Tourists' reprinted from *Pegasus and Other Poems* (1957) by permission of Jonathan Cape Ltd., on behalf of the Executors of the Estate of C. Day-Lewis, and A. D. Peters & Co., Ltd.

Keith Douglas: 'Behaviour of Fish in an Egyptian Tea Garden', © Marie J. Douglas 1978, reprinted from *The Complete Poems of Keith Douglas*, ed. Desmond Graham (1978), by permission of Oxford University Press.

Laurence Durrell: 'At Epidaurus', 'Green Coconuts: Rio', 'Levant', 'Sarajevo' and 'Owed to America' all reprinted from *Collected Poems 1931–1974*, copyright © 1980 by Lawrence Durrell, by permission of Faber & Faber Ltd., and Viking Penguin, Inc.

William Empson: 'China', first published in *The Gathering Storm* (1940) and reprinted in *Complete Poems*, copyright 1949, 1977 by William Empson. Reprinted by permission of Harcourt, Brace Jovanovich Inc., and Chatto & Windus on behalf of the author's estate.

D. J. Enright: 'Deir El Bahari: Temple of Hatsheput' and 'Dreaming in the Shanghai Restaurant', reprinted from *Collected Poems* (OUP, 1981), by permission of Watson, Little Ltd., Authors' Agents.

Gavin Ewart: 'On First Looking into Michael Grant's *Cities of Vesuvius*', reprinted from *The New Ewart* (1982) by permission of Century Hutchinson Ltd.

James Fenton: 'Dead Soldiers', copyright © 1981, reprinted from *The Memory of War* (1982), by permission of The Salamander Press, Edinburgh.

Roy Fuller: 'The Green Hills of Africa', reprinted from *New and Collected Poems 1934–84* by permission of the author and Secker & Warburg Ltd.

David Gill: 'The Kaleidoscope', reprinted from *Men Without Evenings* (1966), by permission of Chatto & Windus Ltd., for the author.

James Russell Grant: 'Africa', reprinted from *Myths of my Age* (1985), by permission of the author.

Robert Graves: 'The Oleaster', reprinted from *Collected Poems 1975* (Cassell), by permission of A. P. Watt Ltd., on behalf of the Estate of Robert Graves.

Geoffrey Grigson: 'Discoveries of Bones and Stones', reprinted from *Discoveries of Bones and Stones* (Macmillan, 1971); 'And Forgetful of Europe', reprinted from *Collected Poems 1924–62* (Phoenix House, 1963); 'Glen Loch', reprinted from *The Faber Book of Poems and Places* (Faber, 1980), all by permission of David Higham Associates Ltd.

Thom Gunn: 'Iron Landscapes', reprinted from *Jack Straw's Castle*, copyright © 1971, 1973, 1974, 1975, 1976 by Thom Gunn; 'Lights Among Redwood', reprinted from *My Sad Captains*, copyright © 1961, 1971, 1973 by Thom Gunn, all by permission of Faber & Faber Ltd., and Farrar, Straus & Giroux, Inc.

Ivor Gurney: 'Tobacco Plant', © Robin Haines, Sole Trustee of the Gurney Estate 1982, reprinted from *Collected Poems of Ivor Gurney*, ed. P. J. Kavanagh, by permission of Oxford University Press.

Tony Harrison: 'Brazil', first appeared in *The Loiners* (London Magazine Editions, 1970) and is reprinted by permission of the author; 'Prague Spring' is reprinted from *The School of Eloquence* (Rex Collings, 1978) by permission of the publisher.

John Heath-Stubbs: 'The Parthenon', reprinted from *Selected Poems* (OUP, 1965) by permission of David Higham Associates Ltd.

David Holbrook: 'A Day in France' and 'Coming Home from Abroad', reprinted from *Selected Poems 1961–78* (1980) by permission of Anvil Press Poetry Ltd.

Ted Hughes: 'You Hated Spain' from *New Selected Poems* (Harper & Row), copyright © 1971 by Ted Hughes. Published in the UK in *Selected Poems 1957–81* (Faber, 1982) and reprinted by permission of Harper & Row, Publishers, Inc., and Faber & Faber Ltd.

Elizabeth Jennings: 'Men Fishing in the Arno', reprinted from *Collected Poems* (Macmillan, 1967), by permission of David Higham Associates Ltd.

Sir Charles Johnston: 'Air Travel in Arabia' reprinted by permission of the author.

James Kirkup: 'Sumo Wrestlers', reprinted from *Paper Windows* (J. M. Dent, 1968) by permission of the author.

Laurie Lee: 'Home from Abroad', reprinted from *Selected Poems* (1983) by permission of André Deutsch.

Patrick Leigh-Fermor: 'Greek Archipelagoes', first published in the UK in *Penguin New Writing* 37, (1949). Used by permission.

Alun Lewis: 'The Mahratta Ghats' and 'Port of Call: Brazil', reprinted from *Ha Ha Among the Trumpets*, by permission of Allen & Unwin.

Hugh MacDiarmid: 'The Skeleton of the Future', reprinted from *The Complete Poems of Hugh MacDiarmid 1920–1976*, by permission of Martin Brian & O'Keeffe and Mrs Valda Grieve.

Louis MacNeice: 'Solitary Travel', 'Ravenna', 'Letter to Graham and Anna', 'Mahabalipuram' and 'Dublin' (one section of 'The Closing Album') all reprinted from *Collected Poems*, ed. E. R. Dodds (Faber) by permission of David Higham Associates Ltd.

Derek Mahon: 'A Lighthouse in Maine', © Derek Mahon 1982, reprinted from *The Hunt by Night* (1982), by permission of Oxford University Press.

John Masefield: 'Sea-Fever', reprinted from *Poems* (New York: Macmillan, 1953) by permission of Macmillan Publishing Company and The Society of Authors as the literary representative of the Estate of John Masefield.

Gerda Mayer: 'Small Park in East Germany: 1969' from *Monkey on the Analyst's Couch* (Ceolfrith Press, 1980). Reprinted by permission of the author and publisher.

Edwin Muir: 'The Cloud' and 'Salem, Massachusetts' reprinted from *Collected Poems of Edwin Muir 1921–1958*, copyright © 1960 by Willa Muir, by permission of Faber & Faber Ltd., and Oxford University Press, New York.

Norman Nicholson: 'Glacier', reprinted from *Selected Poems 1940–1982* (Faber, 1982) by permission of David Higham Associates Ltd.

Wilfrid Noyce: 'Breathless', reprinted from *Poems* (Heinemann, 1960), © by Wilfrid Noyce 1960, by permission of William Heinemann Ltd., and John Johnson (Author's Agents) Ltd.

Frank Ormsby: 'The School Hockey Team in Amsterdam', reprinted from *A Store of Candles* (OUP, 1977), by permission of the author.

George Orwell: 'The Lesser Evil', reprinted from *George Orwell: a Life* (Secker & Warburg, 1980), by permission of A. M. Heath & Co., Ltd., on behalf of the estate of the late Sonia Brownell Orwell.

Sylvia Plath: 'The Goring', reprinted from *The Collected Poems of Sylvia Plath*, ed. Ted Hughes, copyright © 1959, 1981 by Ted Hughes, by permission of Olwyn Hughes Literary Agency, and Harper & Row, Publishers, Inc.

Peter Porter: 'Vienna', reprinted from *Collected Poems*, © Peter Porter 1983, and 'The Cats of Campagnatico', © Peter Porter 1984, reprinted from *Fast Forward*, by permission of Oxford University Press.

Agnes Mary Robinson: 'An Orchard at Avignon' from *The Collected Poems Lyrical and Narrative* (T. Fisher Unwin, 1902).

W. R. Rodgers: 'Summer Journey', reprinted from *Europa and the Bull* (1952), by permission of Secker & Warburg Ltd.

Alan Ross: 'Koala', reprinted from *To Whom It May Concern* (Hamish Hamilton, 1958) by permission of the author.

Siegfried Sassoon: 'Villa d'Este Gardens', reprinted from *Collected Poems 1908–1956*. Copyright 1918, 1920 by E. P. Dutton & Co. Copyright 1936, 1946, 1947, 1948 by Siegfried Sassoon, by permission of George Sassoon and Viking Penguin, Inc.

May Sinclair: 'Field Ambulance in Retreat', copyright May Sinclair 1914. First published in *King Albert's Book: Tribute to the Belgian King and People*, ed. Hall Caine and reprinted by permission of Curtis Brown on behalf of the Estate of May Sinclair.

C. H. Sisson: 'Over the Wall: Berlin, May 1975', © C. H. Sisson, reprinted from *Collected Poems* (Carcanet, 1984) by permission of the publisher.

Bernard Spencer: 'The Empire Clock', © Mrs Anne Humphreys 1981, reprinted from *Collected Poems*, ed. Roger Bowen, by permission of Oxford University Press.

Stephen Spender: 'Port Bou', copyright 1942 by Stephen Spender, reprinted from

Collected Poems 1928–1953 by permission of Faber & Faber Ltd., and Random House, Inc.

Arthur Symons: 'Episode of a Night of May' and 'Spain: To Josefa' reprinted from *Collected Poems* (Secker, 1924), by permission of Mr B. Read.

A. S. J. Tessimond: 'Where?', reprinted from *Voices in a Giant City* (Heinemann, 1947), and 'Jamaican Bus Ride' from *Selection* (Putnam, 1958), by permission of Hubert Nicholson, Literary Executor.

Donald Thomas: 'Tangier: Hotel Rif' reprinted from *Points of Contact* (Routledge & Kegan Paul, 1963) by permission of A. M. Heath & Co. on behalf of the author.

Dylan Thomas: 'In a shuttered room I roast', reprinted from *Selected Letters* (Dent, 1965) by permission of David Higham Associates Ltd.

Wynford Vaughan Thomas: 'Farewell to New Zealand', first published in *The Oxford Book of Light Verse* (ed. Kingsley Amis) and reprinted by permission of David Higham Associates Ltd.

Anthony Thwaite: 'Switzerland' and 'Arabic Script', reprinted from *Poems, 1953–1983* (1984) by permission of Secker & Warburg Ltd.

Terence Tiller: 'Egyptian Dancer', reprinted from *The Inward Animal* (Hogarth, 1943) by permission of Chatto & Windus for the author.

John Wain: 'Brooklyn Heights', reprinted from *Weep Before God* (Macmillan, 1961), copyright © John Wain 1961, by permission of Curtis Brown Ltd.

Ted Walker: 'The Emigrés', reprinted from *Gloves to the Hangman* (Cape) by permission of David Higham Associates Ltd.

Rex Warner: 'Palm Trees', reprinted from *Poems* (1937) by permission of The Bodley Head.

Dorothy Wellesley: 'First Flight' and 'Camels in Persia', reprinted from *Poems of 10 Years 1924–34* (1934). Reprinted by permission of the Executors of the Estate of Dorothy Wellesley.

Gwyn Williams: 'A Poem to show the Trouble that befell him when he was at Sea', reprinted from *Welsh Poems: Sixth Century to 1600*, trs. Gwyn Williams (Faber, 1973) by permission of Faber & Faber Ltd.

Hugo Williams: 'Aborigine', © Oxford University Press 1965, reprinted from *Symptoms of Loss* (1965) by permission of Oxford University Press. ('Aborigines' is also Part 6 of the six-part sequence 'Aborigine Sketches' published later in *Sugar Daddy* by Hugo Williams, OUP, 1970).

Humbert Wolfe: 'Denmark', reprinted from *The Unknown Goddess* (Methuen, 1925) by permission of Associated Book Publishers (UK) Ltd.

While every effort has been made to secure permission, we may have failed in a few cases to trace the copyright holder. We apologize for any apparent negligence.

INDEX OF FIRST LINES

The references are to the numbers of the poems

Spain frightened you. Spain 59
'Still this, still that I would! all I surmise 173
Stowed away in a Montreal lumber room, 261
Such soft ideas all my pains beguile, 129
Super-suburbia of the Southern Seas, 241
Sweet creatures, did you truly understand 255 (ii)

Tagus, farewell, that westward with thy streams 272
Tanagra! think not I forget 89
Tarn, how delightful wind thy willowed waves, 21
Ten years! and to my waking eye 137
That well you drew from is the coldest drink 226
The air in Newfound-land is wholesome, good; 255 (i)
The air is high and blue yet, as we drive 284
The coloured lanterns lit the trees, the grass, 33
The dragon hatched a cockatrice 227
The evening sun-beams threw their golden light, 207
The everlasting universe of things 133
The General 'eard the firin' on the flank, 197
The green, humped, wrinkled hills: with such a look 198
The hero who to Smyrna bay 175
The hills are white, but not with snow: 31
The hills, I told them; and water, and the clear air 244
The Indian maid who lightly trips, 247
The islands which whisper to the ambitious, 99
The Isles of Greece, the Isles of Greece! 93
The live fowl squatting on the grapefruit and bananas 250
The Muse, disgusted at an age and clime, 257
The Musmee has brown-velvet eyes, 223
The painted streets alive with hum of noon, 210
The sheets were frozen hard, and they cut the naked hand; 9
The small towns of Ireland by bards are neglected, 169
The spirit of Romance dies not to those 124
The strong hot breath of the land is lashing 196
The talk of knifed bodies in the canals 116
The traveller has regrets 18
The valleys crack and burn, the exhausted plains 218
The warlike of the Isles, 235
Then Petra flashed by in a wink. 17
These bottle-washer trees that give no shade, 185
They walked black Bible streets and piously tilled 264
Think now about all the things which made up 97
This Imperial city 128
This is the gay cliff of the nineteenth century, 266
This region, surely, is not of the earth. 65
Thou pleasant island, whose rich garden-shores 95
Thy bread, Westphalia, thy brown bread I sing, 119
Tiny slippers of gold and green, 181
'Tis daylight still, but now the golden cross 53
To come back from the sweet South, to the North 278
To Graham and Anna: from the Arctic Gate 158
To orisons, the midnight bell 22
To the fishers of Gjendin the bold Skipper spoke: 156
To thee, dear Henry Morison, 171

INDEX OF POETS AND TRANSLATORS

The references are to the numbers of the poems